Chief Justice Hughs said
"We live under a constitution, but the
constitution is what the justices
say it is."

THE LIVING JEFFERSON

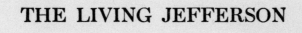

THE LIVING JEFFERSON

The Living Jefferson

The immortality of Thomas Jefferson does not lie in any one of his achievements, but in his attitude toward mankind.

WOODROW WILSON.

By

James Truslow Adams

CHARLES SCRIBNER'S SONS · NEW YORK
CHARLES SCRIBNER'S SONS · LTD · LONDON
1936

PREFACE

THE present mood and questionings of the world are such as scarcely the most pessimistic could have dreamed of a half century ago. The American and French revolutions and the later struggles for liberty in Germany, Italy, and elsewhere had seemed to open the way to a vast extension of human liberty. The advance in science, pure and applied, seemed likewise to open the way to an indefinite expansion of man's powers and standard of life. The newly accepted Darwinian theory of evolution which appeared to indicate that change was improvement, and that men and institutions would advance to greater perfection, increased the buoyant mood of optimism, as did other factors also, not least the promised boundless development of the riches of our own yet almost virgin continent. The fact that in a generation or so more men would be seriously asking whether civilization might be destined to enter upon a new Dark Age would have seemed incredible.

Yet today in some of the nations, formerly leaders in carrying forward the torch of enlightenment, we find such complete suppression of personal liberty, including that of thought and expression, that wise men ask seriously whether the advance of science, on which our complex modern civilization is based, can continue if freedom of thought in all other fields is suppressed. Others ask, again, whether the centralization of control over the economic lives of peoples, which appears to be the tendency in most nations, is possible without such loss of individual liberty. Among the questions suddenly confronting us are whether peoples can govern themselves or must be governed by a dictator or a group? Whether there is any possible place in this modern world of science and machines for the freedom of the individual? What, if this freedom is lost, will be the worth of

v

human life as we have known it, and can civilization itself survive? What price will a promised, but not assured, "economic security" cost the human spirit? Such questions are the most fundamental we can ask in these days.

They are far from being wholly new but they come upon us with a shock because, for a century or so, we have assumed the worth and continued existence of those liberties now threatened. Yet we have always faced these problems to some extent. The question whether man could govern himself or had to be governed was threshed out by opposing parties in the early days of the colony of Massachusetts three centuries ago, in the then almost empty land of America. The problem has remained. The great intellectual and political duel between Jefferson and Hamilton centered chiefly around it. Great political parties still invoke the names of these antagonists to fortify their positions. The fight between these two great leaders has never been settled.

In the difficulties of the present day it is of some importance to know what has been said and done in this quarrel in our own past. In this book, which is neither simply a biography of Jefferson nor a history of Liberal thought in America, we notice the beginning of the fight in early Massachusetts. The major part of it is taken up with the life of Jefferson, and in contrast, his great antagonist. Jefferson was at once the greatest Liberal America has produced and the most intensely "American" of all the great figures of his time. Because of this and of the fact that we are still in the fight in which he fought so valiantly and sanely, he remains a living figure. From him we pass to the present and the phase which the problem and struggle have now assumed. After three centuries, however, Jefferson and Hamilton remain the chief founts from which antagonists draw their examples, philosophies and inspiration. No one knows what the America of the not distant future may become. There need be no apology for illustrating at some length in the course of the struggle what two of the greatest leaders on opposing sides believed and thought it should become. The names of Jefferson and Hamilton are constantly on the lips of politicians. Yet we may ask what did these men really believe? What sort of men were they? What were their dreams for America? Where did they stand in the contest of three centuries? These are some of the questions which this book tries to answer.

For various help the author gladly acknowledges his obligations particularly to Mr. Harold Callender, European representative of the magazine section of *The New York Times;* to Mr. William A. Slade and Mr. Allen R. Boyd, both of the ever helpful staff of the Library of Congress; to Francis W. Hirst, Esq.; and to Mr. Charles Kingsley, of Messrs. Charles Scribner's Sons, London, among many others. It is needless to say they have no responsibility for the opinions expressed or the errors to be found in the book.

J. T. A.

Washington, D. C.,
January 24, 1926.

CONTENTS

CONTENTS

THE LIVING JEFFERSON

CHAPTER I

INTRODUCTORY

In a sense no man ever wholly dies. Just as the elements of what we call his physical body are reabsorbed and transmuted into other forms, so his thoughts, acts and emotions as they have influenced others, continue to mold the world. In the case of the vast majority of human beings, however, these streams of influence can be traced only a very short way and usually not at all. They are like tiny rivulets emptying into a desert where they disappear in the sands immediately. Even when the influence has been great and can be clearly traced upon an art, an institution or a people, the life of the man himself usually takes on, after a time, a certain completeness and finality. No biography, it is true, is ever "final." New ones pour from the presses of the world daily of persons already many times written about. Nevertheless, no matter how important or interesting these persons may have been in their own day, no matter how well their lives may be written, there is a remoteness from our own daily lives about almost all of them. They are figures from the past, museum pieces, stuffed animals in glass cases. They may have deep interest or fascination for us. We may wish to know all we can about them. But they are remote, aloof, finished, complete in themselves.

There is a much smaller company, a very small one, indeed, in whom our interest takes on the warmth of contemporaneity. The difference in interest is shown by the fact that although a biographer may write impartially about any in the first group it is apparently almost impossible for him to do so about any in the second group. It is extremely difficult to be wholly dispassionate about a contemporary, such as Roosevelt or Hoover. It is comparatively easy to be so about President Polk. It is not, however, a question of mere lapse of time. It is rather one of the vitality of the ideas for which the man stood and fought. Contemporary issues move us emotionally. Some men in the past stood for issues which are now so settled as to affect us scarcely, if at all. We can think and write dispassionately about these. There are others who dealt with issues which are still living. Such men, no matter when they lived and died, are still our contemporaries. They gather about them affection or hostility. Writing just a century ago, and a few years after Jefferson's death, one of his earliest biographers said that it had been that statesman's fate "to be at once more loved and praised by his friends, and more hated and reviled by his adversaries than any of his compatriots."[1] The fact that much the same could be said of the writing about him today merely shows that the man is still alive in so far as his influence is both felt and feared.

So is his great antagonist Hamilton. These two exponents of contrasted philosophies of government, though dead, yet live, and are in the thick of the fight today. The issues for which they fought with all their strength are not yet settled. Indeed these issues have broadened and deepened until one in especial has become perhaps the most burning of all in a bewildered and angry world, the question whether the people can govern themselves or must be governed.

The ideas of the two men will, it is hoped, emerge in the following pages, and here there is need for only brief comment. Both men vastly influenced and are influencing the course of their nation. Among the greatest the country has produced, they took opposite sides on issues among the most fundamental and continuing in our history. Those issues have lasted from

[1] George Tucker, *Life of Thomas Jefferson*, London, 1837, Vol. I, p. vii.

the first days of settlement to the present, but for a brief period they became, as it were, embodied in the living forms of Hamilton and Jefferson. In olden days armies sometimes retired from fighting each other while a champion from each side stood forth. So, for a while, the struggle in America seems to be less one of intellectual or social forces backed by multitudes than a personal combat between these two leaders.

We shall be chiefly concerned with the side which Jefferson took, because it seems to us that the question of the survival of what we may call Jeffersonianism is the most important one before us as a people today, for reasons I shall try to give later.

Although a political philosopher, Jefferson never set forth his views in any formal treatise, as did John Adams in his voluminous works or Hamilton in *The Federalist*. Probably the most widely read man of his time in America, Jefferson had a far broader range of interests—political, religious, economic, agricultural, æsthetic, and scientific—than did any other of the leaders. His curiosity was insatiable, but in spite of what has so frequently been asserted, usually by his enemies although sometimes by his friends, he was not a mere theorist. He kept his feet on the ground. It was the practical application of ideas and their practical effects which appealed most to him and not the ideas in themselves as viewed by a philosopher. In his old age he wrote to John Adams that "I am not fond of reading what is merely abstract, and unapplied immediately to some useful science." [2]

Even when he could not use the touchstone of experiment in such matters as his belief in the common man or religious freedom he was never a doctrinaire. He not only believed but said over and over that government and institutions had to be suited to a people of any given time and place, and could not

[2] *Memorial Edition, Writings of Thomas Jefferson*, Washington, 1907, Vol. XV, p. 75. Although this later edition contains material not in that edited by P. L. Ford, New York, 1892, the editing of the Ford edition is so much better that it is referred to when possible.

be true or good everywhere and always. Indeed, it may be affirmed that his opponents were far more doctrinaire than he in their beliefs in the unchanging forces to be found in any human society. They may have been right or not, but at least theirs, and not Jefferson's, was the attitude of the doctrinaire and theorist.

As we have said, Jefferson did not write an ordered treatise on political economy. His ideas have mostly to be patched together from scattered remarks in public and private papers, each written for an occasion. For that reason many of them have assumed a form at once somewhat exaggerated and confused. His nature was markedly sanguine and affectionate. Particularly in his private letters he often expressed himself with heavy over-emphasis. It is quite unfair to treat many of these statements as though they had been deeply pondered and carefully worded for those who, unlike his friends, did not know the background of his mind and understand his mode of expression.

We do not look to Jefferson for a theory of government or of the state. To a great extent the things he had to say about government, and the things for which he strove in his active political life, were based on the America of his day and the slowly developing agricultural one which he envisaged in the future, writing, as he did, before the machine age. What gave Jefferson his profound importance in his own day, as it does now, was his view of human life. He was, and still is, the greatest and most influential American exponent of both Liberalism and Americanism.

Liberalism is rather an attitude than a program. It is less a solution of governmental problems than it is a way of looking at them. It is based on the doctrine of live and let live. A Liberal is bound to insist upon freedom—freedom as far as possible for the individual to manage his own affairs, freedom of thought, speech and of the press, toleration of both the possession and expression of other points of view in religion, politics and modes of life. These the Liberal considers to be values without which a full and humane life cannot be achieved. All freedom involves responsibility, and responsibility involves risks. For the sake of enjoying the above rights the Liberal is willing to take risks feared by both Conservatives and Socialists. Not being a fool, he realizes, as do the others, that society must have a structure; but he is more concerned with the freedom and fullness of the life of the citizen within that structure than with the structure itself.

On the other hand, both the other groups tend to lay stress upon the structure and upon the good of "society." They each, in their several ways, mistrust the individual even when they do not wholly ignore him. Liberalism emphasizes the rights of the individual whereas both Conservatism and Socialism emphasize the coherence of society and the duties of the individual toward it, as do also the new forms of modern dictatorships.

In time, within the framework of any strongly governed society, there grow up all sorts of vested interests and barriers to the freedom of the individual. The belief that most individuals are incapable of governing and must be governed, leads those who govern to build up privileges for themselves. Their private interest, and their view that history is only the record "of the crimes, follies and misfortunes of mankind," cause them to care far more about maintaining strong institutions than risking any change by an increase in the freedom of the individual.

Europe, in the early days of our own country, was filled with restraints and barriers. Its history, moreover, all too well bore out the remark of Gibbon just quoted. Barriers were also present in America, as we shall note in the next chapter, but they existed here in so much slighter degree as to make the American scene, as contrasted with the European, appear idyllic. With all his scepticism, even as to the common man under ordinary conditions of civilization, Jefferson felt that the America of his day offered a unique opportunity in the annals of mankind to try out the great experiment of self-government on an unprecedented scale. His Americanism, written in part into the Declaration of Independence, which he preached throughout life by word and act, grew out of his personal experience of America itself. In so far as those qualities of the American people which we group under the word "Americanism" have been fostered by any one man, in addition to the natural forces of the American environment, Jefferson is beyond question that man.

Although Hamilton had never been out of the western hemisphere, Talleyrand once said that he had "divined" Europe. If he did so it was in part because he not only had an extraordinarily brilliant mind, but a European one. Hamilton could have played a leading part in the public life of either France or England with a success Jefferson could not have achieved. On the other hand, although Hamilton's patriotic loyalty is so far above question as to make even its mention unnecessary, and he spent much of his life in the service of America, it may be questioned if he ever really understood it. He knew practically nothing of the molding influences of the frontier, which was largely making America. His maturer years were spent almost wholly in the gay little cities of New York and Philadelphia among the rich and governing classes. He could even speak of American farmers near New York as "peasants." In a fit of depression toward the end of his life, then soon to be cut short by Burr's bullet, he wrote to Gouverneur Morris that "every day proves to me more and more that this American world was not made for me," and suggests that like Morris he is "by genius an exotic." [3]

But if Hamilton by intuition had "divined" Europe, Jeffer-

---

[3] *Works of Alexander Hamilton,* ed. by H. C. Lodge, New York, 1886, Vol. VIII, p. 591.

son, who knew his Europe by years of residence there as Hamilton did not, had even more deeply "divined" America. It was precisely those qualities and possibilities in our life, which I have summed up elsewhere as the "American Dream," and which have made America unique, that Jefferson recognized and tried to foster. Hamilton also recognized that America and Europe were different but the attitude taken by each of the two statesmen toward that difference is of profound interest, as the results have been of profound importance. Jefferson, who, as I have said, deeply distrusted the common man under European conditions, felt that here in America the world at last had a chance to try out the possibility of such a liberal government as had never yet been attempted, because of the absence in America of certain conditions present in the Old World. Carrying out his belief that a government must be made to fit a people, he fought for the sort of government he thought would suit America, and which at the same time would mark an enormous advance in the happiness of mankind.

On the other hand, Hamilton believed that a government must be strong, as the English Government was. In order to be so, he further believed that elementary selfishness in certain classes had to be played upon. Having decided that there was a more or less fixed type of successful government, and finding that certain classes, particularly a rich financial one, were necessary to it, and that these were lacking in America, he set out to build them up. His policy had other purposes as well, but that this was a leading one is evident from his writings. In other words, Jefferson wanted to make an advance by fitting a government to a people which he believed to be in a peculiarly happy situation. Hamilton wanted to fit a people to a preconceived form of government.

Each believed, with all the depth of religious emotion, that he was right. Hamilton felt he had to save the American nation. Jefferson felt that he had to save the American citizen.

It was inevitable that two such men should clash, especially as parties grew around them, and each leader struggled to form the new nation to his views. Moreover, owing to the peculiar bitterness which our American politics have always bred, so that even Washington was outrageously slandered in his lifetime, it was also inevitable that Hamilton and Jefferson should be assailed by both contemporary and later writers and that, unhappily, they should assail one another.

Both in his lifetime and since, Jefferson suffered in this respect in a much higher degree than Hamilton. It is only fair to the former that some explanation of this should be given. In reading the literature on the two men one is struck by several points. For one thing, no one has written a life of Hamilton, so far as I know, sufficiently notable to command public attention, which has not been in praise of him. The most restrained is perhaps that of W. G. Sumner. On the other hand, a number of lives of Jefferson have been written which seem to have as their object the explaining why he is not worth writing about. As the English economist and Liberal, Mr. Francis W. Hirst, who has written an excellent volume on him, says in his preface, "I am led to believe that when a dyspeptic author has a grudge against Jefferson, he relieves his feelings by writing a Life." Another point is that whereas a considerable number of the lives of Jefferson are fair to the claims of Hamilton, it seems difficult for almost any biographer of Hamilton to refrain from trying to prove that Jefferson was either a fool or a knave or both. Moreover, many of the general histories, particularly the earlier ones, are distinctly more favorable to Hamilton than to his antagonist.

All this might weigh heavily against the claims of Jefferson if we did not recall certain facts. Jefferson left no son whereas Hamilton's son John published a chaotic and absurdly swollen life of his father in five volumes in which he assailed not only Jefferson but John Adams and many other of the leaders of the time with the mistaken notion that by covering others with mud he would make his father shine resplendent. Not only did the writer make false statements about his father but he also even garbled the text of his father's letters. The book, however, as a storehouse of material, long antedating properly edited editions of Hamilton's works, exerted a considerable influence which is still felt. F. S. Oliver, for example, in his extremely biased biography of Hamilton, in which Hamilton appears as a god and Jefferson as a devil, seems to have limited his researches into the lives and work of both men almost wholly to the five volumes by Hamilton's son published almost eighty years ago. Of Oliver's references cited in footnotes, 168 refer to this single unfair and unscholarly work whereas there are only twenty-five to all the other sources and secondary material made available since!

• We may also recall that for a long period most of the historical writing in America came from New England, and that for many reasons Jefferson was peculiarly anathema to the New Englanders. Massachusetts was the home of the most reactionary and venomous of the Federalist Party—the famous Essex Junto—and that party went down to lasting defeat at the hands of the one organized by Jefferson. For the first thirty-six years of our history only one President came from New England. He was also the only one not to be elected to a second term, and he was defeated by Jefferson. Again, although Jefferson was a sincerely ethical and religious man, his belief in religious freedom, and particularly his efforts to disestablish the State church in Virginia, brought down on his head the now almost incredible wrath of the influential New England clergy. Moreover, his economic policies when President seemed to the New Englanders to have been aimed directly at accomplishing their personal destruction. Finally, his vast extension of the national domain in the West was a blow to the influence of the small and comparatively unexpanding New England section in the Union. No wonder that section came to hate him. Unfortunately for him, most of the history, in books if not in life, was produced there in our early republican period.

It may also be noted that even in his native Virginia Jefferson antagonized many of the most important interests and families by what was considered his undermining of an established social order. His struggle to break down entail and primogeniture, to free religion from the fetters of a State church, and his well-known opposition to slavery, have not even yet been forgiven by many Virginians who feel that the downfall of the, in many ways, charming and delightful society of the eighteenth century was due to one whom they consider a renegade from his own order. As we shall see later, when Jefferson was involved in financial difficulties in his old age, the citizens of his own state, unlike many elsewhere, did not offer him the slightest aid.

In considering the historical treatment of him, we may also recall that the party founded by him was essentially the party of the small man, whereas the opposing party was largely that of the "rich, the wise and the good," in the old Federalist phrase, or of the rich and privileged in newer phrasing. Jefferson and his ideas were considered generally, and quite honestly, by his opponents throughout America to be dangers to them and to the nation, with which latter they identified their own private interests. These interests, largely of big business and stemming from the Hamilton philosophy of government, finance and protective tariffs, came to be of vast extent. Jefferson died but his ideas did not. Jefferson dead had to be fought because of his living influence. One does not throw stones at a dead dog.

Lastly it may be suggested that the effect of the philosophies of the two men upon their followers has had more than a little to do with the varying tone of much of the literature about each. The philosophy which calls for a highly concentrated authority, for powerful and privileged groups, tends to create an illiberal and intolerant point of view, especially toward its opponents. On the other hand, the very essence of Liberalism is tolerance and freedom of opinion. There is nothing in the Hamiltonian philosophy which demands tolerance for the views of an opposition. In fact, the contrary is rather the truth. But the philosophy of Jefferson, whether always put into practice or not, calls for a toleration so far as possible of all viewpoints and opponents.

Both men, it seems to me, were necessary for the development of the United States, and I cannot see why that fact should not be frankly and freely admitted. We are all of us as individuals inclined to be either conservative or liberal, depending on temperament, environment, unconscious interest and bias, age, health, energy, and other causes. We are naturally drawn toward one philosophy or the other, into one party or the other. Nevertheless, however strongly we may feel as to our own party and philosophy, the world has always required both for orderly advance. We may think of the past in terms of an incessant conflict between those who would keep society static and those who would change it, between those insisting upon control and those demanding freedom. Between individuals or parties there has been and is this conflict, but taking a larger view, trying to fit the facts into a larger synthesis of both history and society, it would appear that the opposing ideas have operated less in conflict than in harmony. Like motion and gravitation they have worked together to permit advance but to keep it orderly.

A reasonable balance between the two must be maintained to get the best results from each. When there is much too large a dose of one or the other, the body of society moves erratically, in danger of possible disaster. If America had built itself wholly upon the philosophy of Hamilton, without any mitigation, we should have been in a much worse state than we have been. On the other hand, had we attempted to follow Jefferson completely, the nation might not only not have continued but not have survived its first decade.

The contributions made by each of these men to the national life may be exemplified in a broad way by those made by man and woman respectively in the home or the nation. In the past, at any rate, and speaking in general terms, the man has spent his days dealing with affairs, political or economic, and his mind has been largely concentrated upon these on an impersonal basis, that is, on a basis of efficient gaining of results rather than of the happiness of all the individuals involved. The woman has lived in a sphere where the smaller units have counted more and in which she has developed sympathetic understanding of the individual and of personal opportunities, conditions and relationships. To make the illustration clearer we need only think of the effects on either sex due to the isolation of considerable groups of one or the other for a long period. Both deteriorate and lose some of those qualities which seem to be developed only when each exerts, in different ways, its effect upon the other. Had we been all Hamiltonians from the start we might have become even harder-boiled; had we been all Jeffersonians, we might have become too spineless.

The world is entering upon a new phase. We are facing a crisis not wholly unlike that of the two decades following the adoption of our Constitution in 1787. There is to be a new conflict between Jefferson and Hamilton, and for the moment there is a marked tendency toward Hamiltonianism and away from Jeffersonianism. We are thinking to an increasing extent in terms of economics, of "states," of "societies," and not of the individual. There is developing an almost complete forgetfulness of those freedoms and tolerations slowly won through many generations and which have given to life, directly and indirectly, its most civilized values. These were what Jefferson fought for as he saw the tide of Hamilton's philosophy threatening to overwhelm the unique opportunity which Jefferson believed then existent in America.

Today that tide again threatens. It is not the work of any one individual, any more than the tides of the sea are caused by any single drop. We are all caught in a movement which is as vast as it is impersonal. Society, however, differs from the sea in that its individual drops are beings capable of thinking, and of influencing one another. Each may not accomplish much but it is nevertheless incumbent upon each to think and act and take his stand. One of the first things to do is to understand terms which may give a false impression of direction. Many of the great political movements of the day which are carried out in the name of "national regeneration," "economic security," and so on, should be known rather as movements for the political, moral and intellectual slavery of the individual.

We too often forget history in these tumultuous days. New nations in new lands, as contrasted with old nations in old lands, tend to live in the present plus the future instead of the present plus the past. Throughout the entire world, moreover, the marvelous development of applied science in the last few decades has appeared, and to some extent rightly, to set off our own and coming generations completely from the past and all its lessons. Again, the wide and deep swathe cut across civilization by the World War and its effects, seems to have divided us from all that went before. For the time being it is, to recur to a previous simile, as though gravity had ceased to operate and motion alone remained, whirling us off to an unknown destination and fate. The old values and goods of civilized life for the moment have shrunk in relation to new needs and dangers.

It may well prove, however, after the tumult and the shouting die, after the vertigo of speed in a new social direction shall have given place to the returning consciousness of stability in a new and unhappy situation, that we shall too late come to realize that our natures did not change as rapidly as our tools and environment, and that we again crave those values which we have lost. We are largely what a long past has made us, and that past must be taken into consideration if we are to plan wisely for the future. It is time to re-examine and clarify our political philosophy, and we can do this better by paying some attention to how we have become what we are than by thinking only of a future unrelated to the past. Wishful thinking is no substitute for realistic thinking, and a policy of political drift is likely to land us on the rock of spiritual destruction.

The struggle going on almost everywhere today, in our own country no less than in some of those others which have already lost their liberties, is the struggle between the conception of a strong, centralized state, controlling the lives of the citizens for the sake of economics and national power, and the conception of personal liberty affording the greatest possible scope for the individual to live his life as he wills. The old questions which Jefferson and Hamilton fought over were who is to rule, why are they to rule, what is the object of their rule? These are now being fought out again, as they always have been, but with increasing bitterness and among vast masses of populations. This is why both men are living today, and why it is worth while to consider again the life particularly of the one who laid more stress upon freedom and toleration for the individual than on the strength of national power. It is evident that we cannot envisage an American Government with the simplicity of Jefferson's political outlook. On the other hand, how far can we proceed toward erecting a centralized, authoritarian, economic state with any satisfaction to its citizens if we cannot somehow save Jefferson's liberalism and Americanism? That is the problem on which the following pages may serve to some extent as commentary.

· · · · · · · · · · · · · ·

It is as impossible as it is unnecessary to trace for the preceding century and a half the conflict of ideas which Hamilton and Jefferson were to wage so brilliantly after they entered upon the national stage at the beginning of the Revolution. A very brief account, however, is called for so that we may better understand the situation as it appeared in their day.

The attempted solutions of the problem of government in the first two permanent settlements happened to be in striking contrast to one another. That was due partly to accident. The English who planted themselves in Virginia in 1607 did so under a charter from the King. This provided that they should be governed despotically by a self-perpetuating council and without voice in their own affairs. On the other hand, when the so-called Pilgrims settled at Plymouth they had no charter. Finding themselves unexpectedly dumped on the coast far outside the limits of Virginia, and with a considerable element of undesirable and unruly persons in their number, they all signed an agreement before landing that they would abide by the rules made by all. As the easiest way, in their opinion, out of a disagreeable situation they established, by chance and not design, a pure democracy. In time, the Plymouth Government became less democratic and the Virginian more so, but these developments need not detain us. The Virginians had for the moment to accept the government imposed upon them from above and the Pilgrims were merely meeting what they thought would be a temporary problem and were not reasoning out a philosophy of self-government.

The controversy in Massachusetts a few years later is more to our purpose because there the adherents of the theory that the people had to be ruled and those of the theory that the people themselves could and should rule came first in America into open and conscious opposition. The founders of Massachusetts Bay evidently had more decided views as to government than other earlier and later founders of colonies in America. This is evidenced in part by the fact that they alone brought the charter of their colony over to it. The inner group of leaders manipulated what, when granted, had been intended only as the charter of a trading company, into a sort of constitution, although they themselves continually violated its provisions. We cannot go into the details of the struggle which ensued in the colony of a few thousand souls. In brief, what we may call the "inner ring" tried their best, and for a while with much success, to control the citizens. They tried to exclude them from a voice in the making of laws, to tax them without consent, and, quite in the fashion of a modern authoritarian state, even to impress the manual labor of all, except clergymen and political officers. A sedition law, of a type we shall meet later in our story several times, was also passed to the effect that any one who should "defame" any member of the "Court" (which meant the little legislature of the colony) should be fined, imprisoned, disfranchised, or banished.

We are left in no doubt as to the political theories of the small group of leaders. For the most part in New England that group was composed everywhere of a few laymen and the clergy. It is not easy always to determine which influenced the other most. They united in policies, and in a day when there were no newspapers, the clergy in their sermons were the propaganda agents for such policies when agreed upon. The leading layman of the Bay was John Winthrop, one of the ablest, gentlest and best of the colonists. Nevertheless he also engaged in trying to keep political control in the hands of his own small group. "Democracy," he wrote, "is among civil nations accounted the meanest and worst of all forms of government."[4] The opinion of the Reverend John Cotton, clerical leader, was the same. "Democracy," he wrote to Lord Say and Sele, "I do not conceive that ever God did ordeyne as a fit government

[4] R. C. Winthrop, *John Winthrop*, Boston, 1869, Vol. II, p. 430.

eyther for church or commonwealth. If the people be governors, who shall be governed?"[5] The charter had provided for
what we would call a president, a board of directors, and stockholders. These were called Governor, Assistants (later known
as Magistrates), and freemen. The government was run by
the Governor, the small and very influential body of Magistrates (practically never more than nine and often less), and
those among the freemen who were church members. Given the
mistrust of the people on the part of the leaders as noted above,
it is not surprising that the latter tried to increase the powers
of the inner group and were quite willing to violate the terms
of the charter in order to do so. The church test for the franchise, even among the freemen, was one of these violations. Cotton wished to have the Magistrates hold office for life, instead
of standing for re-election. Winthrop also wished to make
them independent of any popular or constitutional control.
"Whatsoever sentence the magistrate gives," he wrote, "the
judgment is the Lord's, though he do it not by any rule pre-
scribed by civil authority."[6] How far toward modern dictatorships this theory could carry the colony was exemplified in the
celebrated trial of Ann Hutchinson. When, after sentence of
banishment had been passed upon her, she asked why she had
been banished, she was answered by the Governor, "Say no
more. The Court knows wherefore and is satisfied."[7] Hitler
or Stalin could not have done a more efficient job.

There were, however, besides Mrs. Hutchinson, Roger Williams, and others, many who objected to the theory of government as preached and practised in Massachusetts. "I should
choose neither to live nor leave my posterity under such a government," wrote the Reverend Thomas Hooker of Newtown to
Winthrop. "That in the matter which is referred to the judge

[5] T. Hutchinson, *History of Massachusetts*, Salem, 1795, Vol. I, p. 437.
[6] *Connecticut Historical Society Collections*, Vol. I, p. 17.
[7] C. F. Adams, *Antinomianism in the Colony of Massachusetts Bay*, Boston, 1894, p. 237.

the sentence should lie in his breast, or be left to his discretion, according to which he should go, I am afraid it is a course which wants both safety and warrant. I must confess, I ever looked at it as a way which leads directly to tyranny, and so to confusion."[8]

Discontent of one sort and another had been particularly rife in the three towns of Watertown, Newtown, and Dorchester. By 1636 the larger part of the inhabitants of these, Hooker among them, had moved westward and settled the towns of Hartford, Windsor, and Wethersfield in Connecticut. The explosive force of Americanism had begun to leave the settled "east" for the frontier.

In 1638 there was a general meeting of men from the three new wilderness towns to consider a frame of government and the defense of the "priviledges and freedoms we now enjoy," as Roger Ludlow wrote. As usual the clergy was called upon to "broadcast" to the people, and, two days after Ludlow wrote to Winthrop, Hooker preached his famous sermon in which he laid down the doctrines that "the foundation of authority is laid, firstly, in the free consent of the people"; that "the choice of public magistrates belongs unto the people by God's own allowance"; and that "they who have the power to appoint officers and magistrates, it is in their power, also, to set bounds and limitations of the power and place unto which they call them."[9]

The late Professor Channing wrote that why Hooker and his companions left Massachusetts is "one of the unsolved problems of New England history." It seems to me that Hooker's letter to Winthrop gives as clear an explanation as we have for almost any movement in all history. Within a half dozen years from the "great migration" which settled the most populous colony of the time in America, the two rival doctrines—

[8] *Conn. Hist. Soc. Coll.,* Vol. I, p. 17.

[9] The notes on this sermon, not itself preserved in full, are in G. L. Walker's *Thomas Hooker,* New York, 1891, p. 125.

the one that the people could and should rule, the other that they were incapable of it and must *be* ruled—had come into sharp conflict. As always in our past until the close of the frontier, those who held to the first doctrine had gone West, and that doctrine was to build up in frontier after frontier, across 3000 miles and for nearly three centuries, what we have always considered as one of the chief elements in Americanism.

During the next century and a quarter, other colonies were founded and population in America rapidly increased. By 1750 all up and down the Atlantic seaboard there were small towns and farms or large plantations. This seaboard civilization was already fairly well "set" in the mold of English provincial society. In New England and the Middle Colonies, the busy little towns were in appearance and life much like provincial towns in England, except that life was freer, more fluid, and the opportunities for gaining wealth greater, while in a number of them the presence of a Royal Governor created a petty court atmosphere and society which were lacking in old world Bristol or Boston. In the South, life was modelled not on that of the English merchant and town dweller, but on that of the English country gentleman and county family.

Ninety per cent of all Americans lived upon the soil, but as far as the wealthier classes were concerned there was already a marked difference between South and North. Those of the former were almost purely agrarian whereas those of the latter were becoming more and more interested in shipping, commerce, merchandising, and other forms of what, on the small stage of the period, was getting to be "big" business. In both sections much mercantile shrewdness had been shown by those who had founded families, but they had been usually greatly assisted in the process by the venality of Royal Governors and even of New England and other legislatures. With a governor in his satin sipping port at your table, and with millions of acres of wilderness lands in the background, the holdings of those who could also wear satin somehow grew. But whereas the Southerner stuck to the land, the Northerner, as we have just said, was extending in all quarters of the business field and making money in all sorts of ways not followed by those in the South. As I pointed out in *America's Tragedy*, city magnates and landed gentlemen develop into quite different and antipathetic types. To the dislike, social and other, of each for each, there is added, on the part of the agrarian, a mistrust of the economic methods and ideas of the commercial class or group, partly because he does not understand them, partly because he feels himself exploited by them, and partly because he does not like the social type evolved by them.

By the mid-eighteenth century there was not only this cleavage beginning between North and South but there had also developed another sectionalism, the conflict in all the colonies between seaboard and frontier. The process which we have just noted as beginning in the settlement of the Connecticut River towns had been steadily going on for many reasons, and for more than a century. As population and wealth increased, people had to push ever farther to the west in every colony, from Maine down to Georgia. It was not wholly, however, a question of land. Along the seaboard, society had become more and more fixed. Money and privilege counted ever more heavily. An "old" society had been formed. Everywhere along the coast the "wise, the rich, and the good," in the Federalist phrase to be used in another half century, felt that they should govern, and that the less rich would be also less wise and good, and could not be trusted. The Massachusetts Bay idea had spread. On the other hand, with the greater equality of condition on the frontier, with the resentment against the pretensions—political and social—of the seaboard, with the greater simplicity of life, the Connecticut idea was everywhere the prevalent one in the "back counties."

Along the seaboard there were poor as well as rich—the

clerks, servants, laborers, artisans and so on in the towns, the poorer farmers, North and South, with their few acres and often inferior soil. Many of these objected to wealth and privilege, and to being governed by the American "upper class," quite as much as by the English Parliament. They could, and did later, join with the forces of democracy along the frontier, but it was on the latter that what we call Americanism was then found, as it largely has been since. The difference between the society folk of New York or Philadelphia and the sturdy farmers on every frontier in 1750 was not simply that of clothes, wealth, or habits, but also psychological. The seaboard was steadily becoming "*Old* World" while the frontier was ever pushing into and extending the "*New* World."

CHAPTER II

THE YOUNG JEFFERSON

IT was in one of the finest parts of the frontier, now one of the loveliest counties in Virginia, that Thomas Jefferson was born on April 2, 1743 (Old Style). His father, Peter Jefferson, a surveyor, had patented a thousand acres of land in what was at the time called Goochland, on the extreme western fringe of white settlement adjoining the wilderness. It is said that there were only three or four white families living there when the Jefferson family settled in 1737, but population increased, and in 1745 Albemarle became a separate county, Peter Jefferson's lands lying in the portion so set off. A man of superb physique and of almost mythical physical strength, he had been a magistrate and sheriff of Goochland County, and now became one of the magistrates and lieutenant-colonel of the militia in the new one.

The Jeffersons, probably originally emigrants from Wales, perhaps as tradition alleged from near Snowdon, were one of the oldest, although not socially great, families in Virginia. Peter's education had been neglected and he was chiefly self-taught, but he had a powerful mind, formed, as Lincoln's was to be, by constant reading of the Bible and of Shakespeare, though other books, such as Swift and the *Spectator*, also bore some share. His influence in the frontier community was great, as it was also, I believe, over his young son. Certainly one of the father's cardinal maxims, "Never ask another to do for you what you can do for yourself," perfectly expresses the theory of the relation of the citizen to government later to be formulated by the younger man. The father was always interested in public affairs, and from 1755, probably until his death two years later, he sat for his county in the House of Burgesses.

The elder Jefferson had been a friend of the Randolphs, perhaps the most distinguished of all Virginia families, and his marriage in 1739 to Jane Randolph ensured to the children to be born of the union high social position throughout the colony but, what was more important, also gave them the best possible inheritance in mingling the vigorous blood of the frontier sheriff and law-maker with that of his gentle and aristocratic wife. Before his death, in his fiftieth year, Jefferson had added largely to his land-holdings, one of the earliest additions, before his marriage, having been a 400-acre tract, bought from his most intimate friend, Colonel William Randolph, the only consideration mentioned being "Henry Weatherbourne's biggest bowl of arrack punch." On this new tract he built the home, "Shadwell," to which he brought his nineteen-year-old bride, and it was there that his son Thomas, the third of ten children, was born.

It speaks highly for both the ability and character of young Jefferson's father that Colonel Randolph, when dying, requested that he should act as guardian for his son, Thomas Mann Randolph, and also manage the Randolph estate. As that estate "Tuckahoe," was located on the James River, a few miles above Richmond, compliance with the colonel's last request was impossible from so far away as Shadwell. For the next seven years the Jeffersons therefore lived at Tuckahoe, Peter carrying out with scrupulous fidelity the trusts bequeathed to him. It was thus at nine years of age, on the return of the family to Shadwell, that the young Thomas began that permanent connection with the neighborhood which was to make it, and especially the little mountain, "Monticello," one of the famous places of pilgrimage in the world.

Meanwhile there had been schooling at Tuckahoe, and on the return to Shadwell the boy was sent to board with the Reverend William Douglass to study French, Latin, and Greek.

Then came the unexpected death, in the prime of life, of
Peter Jefferson, and the little schoolboy found himself, at the
age of fourteen, the head of the family, with a widowed mother,
one younger brother and six sisters. He also found himself
comparatively wealthy. A plantation which the father had
owned on the James River went to the younger son, but
Thomas inherited Shadwell, the slaves of the estate there, and
about 2750 acres of land. With money, position, well-known
throughout the county and socially well-connected throughout
the colony, the boy could look forward to living the life of a
country gentleman of that day or striving for almost any career he might choose. Meanwhile, his father had left instructions that he should be given a good classical education, and in
pursuance of the plan the lad spent the next two years studying under the Reverend James Maury, whom he later described
as "a correct classical scholar."

There is nothing to indicate that Jefferson was anything
but a manly, healthy, normal boy, a little serious perhaps, a
quality likely to be increased by his father's death and his own
new responsibilities, but in no way precocious or peculiar. We
may, however, take brief stock of the influences upon him.
Either from instinct or from the Randolph blood and connection, the boy was to develop into a genuine aristocrat of
the highest type. On the other hand there was no strain
of the snob in him and neither mere wealth nor social standing appears to have counted in his opinion of others. His own
position was so secure that these things never took on disproportionate importance. Moreover, his father whom he had admired, and whom he had seen honored and respected by all,
had belonged to that important social class which, for want of
a better name, we may call the yeomanry, lying socially below
the aristocrats and above the poorer sort. Thomas Jefferson's
boyhood was also happy in its place and time. Albemarle
County by 1757 had passed beyond the crudities of the first

frontier stage and had a population of perhaps seven to eight thousand. It was, however, "West" and not seaboard. There were in it lazy and idle, as everywhere, but on the whole it was, perhaps, as good a spot as any in the world, as it was then, in which to gain a high opinion of the ordinary man. Those who had moved westward to the slopes of the Blue Ridge had been to a great extent of the best stock in Virginia and not without a sprinkling of its bluest blood. There were both freedom and simplicity in the life, and a district in which in less than a hundred miles from one another such boys as Thomas Jefferson, Patrick Henry, James Madison, and John Marshall were growing up simultaneously was evidently no ordinary "frontier" or new country. By an odd chance, Marshall's father, like Jefferson's, was of Welsh descent and had also married into the remarkable Randolph clan. The men and women of this western Virginia country, establishing themselves on small or large farms, were quite capable of looking after themselves and the affairs of government, and in considering Jefferson's career and philosophy it is well to bear in mind the sort of society in which his most impressionable years were spent.

It cannot be said that the western counties of the colonies were radical in any sense subversive of property rights or of a sound foundation of society, any more than the great agricultural West of the national period has been. Those, however, who have lived on the successive fringes of our civilization have naturally been more insistent upon human rights than upon those claimed for property or privilege, and more willing to risk change for the sake of betterment than those remaining in the older settlements where they have built up or inherited comfortable positions which seem endangered by even mere threat of change.

The older section has always feared the newer, not merely for what the older one has considered the radicalism of the new sections but because of their very existence and growth. Those, for example, in control of the political life of the seaboard watched with the deepest anxiety the shift of population into newer counties which, if not checked in some way, might take their power away from them. Various means were used. In New England to a considerable extent, the proprietors who had secured grants of land and planted towns upon them kept the voting rights in their own hands, disfranchising the settlers. In Pennsylvania when Lancaster County was laid off in 1729 it was allowed only *four* votes in the Assembly instead of the eight which all the older counties had. When, in 1749 and 1750, two new counties were erected farther west, after twenty years' delay, they were allowed but *two* votes each; and, two years after, two more frontier counties were allowed only *one* vote each.

This fear on the part of the East was the greater, perhaps, because although privileged classes and groups had developed, they had behind them no long history as in Europe. For that reason they seemed to lie more open to attack in a new and fluid society. The men of the western sections, who by their own efforts and courage were building up a new country, were as anxious to defend fundamental property rights, as they saw them, as was any one else, but they did not want their own personal and property rights infringed upon by the mere privileged position of others. On the other hand capital and privilege are always timorous. Those merchants and others of the rich classes on the seaboard who could not possibly have hewn out a home in a wilderness saw ruin for themselves, and (by an easy transference of identity) ruin to the government, if they themselves and their kind could not retain political control. So at the time of Jefferson's youth, as always, they were bringing every device into play in order that they might not have to share their power, either with the new counties to the west or with the artisans and others of the poorer classes in the East. This was natural, as was also the more independent attitude of those living in the simpler air of the newer settlements where as yet privilege was an enemy to be fought and not a protector to be sought.

Of the two years spent at Mr. Maury's school we know practically nothing, but at seventeen we find Jefferson writing to his then guardian, Mr. John Hervey, that "I was at colo. Peter Randolph's about a fortnight ago, and my Schooling falling into Discourse, he said he thought it would be to my Advantage to go to the College, and was desirous I should go, as indeed I am myself for several Reasons. In the first place as long as I stay at the Mountain, the loss of one fourth of my Time is inevitable, by Company's coming here and detaining me from School. And likewise my absence will in great measure, put a Stop to so much Company, and by that Means lessen the Expenses of the Estate in House-keeping. And on the other Hand by going to the College, I shall get a more universal Acquaintance, which may hereafter be serviceable to me; and I suppose I can pursue my Studies in the Greek and Latin as well there as here, and likewise learn something of the Mathematics. I shall be glad of your opinion, and remain, Sir, your most humble servant."[1]

"The College" was, of course, that of William and Mary at Williamsburg, then the capital of the colony, residence of the governor, and center of social life. Jefferson had never seen it, though Shadwell lay on the road thither from the West, and in those days of abundant hospitality such a house in such a location was almost an inn, with the important difference that the host, and not the guest, paid for the hospitality enjoyed. Such local hospitality could waste time as well as money in old Virginia, and Jefferson wrote that his father "had a devoted friend, to whose house he would go, dine, spend the night, dine with him again on the second day, and return to Shadwell in

---

[1] S. N. Randolph, *The Domestic Life of Thomas Jefferson*, New York, 1871, p. 26.

the evening." His friend in a day or so would do the same with Peter Jefferson, and they thus spent four days out of every week together. Jefferson wrote that often Indians, particularly the Chief Ontassete, would stop on their way to see the governor, and undoubtedly visitors of a different type came also from the East. The road passing near his house, which led to the glamorous center, tiny as it was, of the colony's life, must have held a fascination for the boy. Whatever may have been his real reasons for wanting to go there, his wish was complied with, and in the spring of 1760 he arrived in Williamsburg and enrolled in the college, meeting for the first time, on the way at a house where he stopped for the night, another young man, Patrick Henry.

Virginian boys of good family and means had to a much greater extent than in the North been sent to England for their education and social training. At this time, perhaps owing to the hazards of the sea during the French and Indian War, they were beginning to go to Princeton, King's College (Columbia), and other Northern institutions. While Jefferson's choice of William and Mary College may have been due to financial reasons I think it more likely that it was owing to the slow and normal development of the boy's mind in his surroundings. Neither his guardian nor friends appear to have been active in suggesting any course to him, and he was making his own plans. He still needed the new contacts with men who had seen the world, which he made at Williamsburg, to induce in him a desire to travel. Virginia was the largest, most populous and important of all the colonies. Indeed, the "Old Dominion," then far larger than the present Virginia, was almost an empire in itself, and to the boy from Albemarle County, a few years at the colonial capital might well seem to fulfill the needs of his youthful and inexperienced outlook.

There was in 1760 nothing to indicate that the colonies would ever be independent of England or joined to one another; and the only career open was colonial unless one deserted America and went to the Mother Country. Jefferson, like practically all Americans of that time, was loyal to the British connection but had no wish to leave his own loved country to settle as a stranger in the home one, which his family had not seen for five generations. The natural career for a rich young Virginian was that of country gentleman with, perhaps, politics and law added. Not only was the political stage in Virginia larger and more important than that in any other colony, but, as time was to show, it was also the best one on which to have become known when the future nation was to offer a wider one. We need only note here, therefore, that Jefferson's intense love for his native colony and state was probably fostered by his not having left it for his college training. Both this love and his belief, on account of the leading position of Virginia, in the importance of the character of its own local institutions, played their parts later in actions at critical points in his career and also in the formation of his political philosophy.

Williamsburg, between which and his own loved acres, Jefferson was now to divide his time for many years, has been described so often that it is not needful to go into detail. It contained slightly over 200 houses which faced on its unpaved streets. Its small population constantly varied in size, as many who owned houses occupied them only, as an early observer said, "at Publick times," that is when a sitting of the legislature or some other attraction lured them from their plantations. Contrasted with the bustling cities of the North—Boston or New York with their approximately 15,000 inhabitants each, or Philadelphia with 20,000, and their business interests —Williamsburg was but a village with the air of a small English market town. But certainly no market town, nor probably any village in the world of equal population, has ever seen such a group of distinguished men as Williamsburg was to know between Jefferson's arrival and the change of the capital to Rich-

mond in 1779. Jefferson himself, Patrick Henry, R. H. Lee,
F. L. Lee, George Wythe, George Washington, John Marshall,
George Mason, James Madison, and Peyton Randolph are only
a few of those who were to be met with on the alternate dust or
mud of its streets, or in its delightful homes.

The young Jefferson was fortunate in the friends he soon
made, and from whom he derived far more than the college
alone could ever have given him. None of the colonial colleges
anywhere in America offered the advantages of the European
universities, and William and Mary had suffered from the custom just noted of sending many of the boys of the upper class
to England. An observer writing in 1724, lamenting the low
estate to which the college had fallen, added that it was "hoped,
that in a few Years it will, like the Palm Tree, grow to the
greater Perfection, under the weighty obstacles that load it."[2]
This pious hope was not fulfilled. Jefferson complained, as so
many have of our public school system since, that the standards
of scholarship were so low as to make it "disagreeable and
degrading" for those who were more properly equipped, and
that so much was spent on the incompetent as to leave insufficient funds to take care of the needs of those who required a
higher standard.

Luckily, on the boy's arrival, there was an able Scotch professor, Doctor Small, who remained two years, and deeply
influenced him. The general run of the students, who were
less mentally mature than Jefferson, did not, apparently, interest the new student. He was fond of society, horses, and
racing, and of a good time in general. Eighteenth-century
social life had its ample temptations everywhere and was an
odd mixture of refinement and coarseness. The little provincial
capital was no exception, and although such wild oats as
Jefferson sowed were of the mildest description, the boy, living

[2] Hugh Jones, *The Present State of Virginia,* London, 1724, reprinted New
York, 1865, p. 27.

"on his own" for the first time, had not found himself when Doctor Small found him. Jefferson, in his old age, reviewing his life, wrote that "it was my great good fortune, and what probably fixed the destinies of my life that Dr. Wm. Small of Scotland was then Professor of Mathematics, a man profound in most of the useful branches of science, with a happy talent of communication, correct and gentlemanly manners, and an enlarged and liberal mind. He, most happily for me, became soon attached to me & made me his daily companion when not engaged in the school; and from his conversation I got my first views of the expansion of science and of the system of things in which we are placed. Fortunately the Philosophical chair became vacant soon after my arrival at college, and he was appointed to fill it per interim: and he was the first who ever gave in that college regular lectures in Ethics, Rhetoric & Belles Lettres. He returned to Europe in 1762, having previously filled up the measure of his goodness to me, by procuring for me, from his most intimate friend G. Wythe, a reception as a student of law, under his direction, and introduced me to the acquaintance and familiar table of Governor Fauquier, the ablest man who had ever filled that office. With him, and at his table, Dr. Small & Mr Wythe, his *amici omnium horarum*, & myself, formed a *partie quarrée*, & to the habitual conversation on these occasions I owed much instruction." [3]

Lieutenant-governor Fauquier, who acted as governor for ten years, was much liked by the colonists and an able man. He was well-connected, widely travelled, and accustomed to the best English social circles. His father was a director of the Bank of England, while he himself had been a director of the South Sea Company, and was a member of the Royal Society. A volume by him on public finance went through three editions but unhappily he did not apply its principles to his private affairs and had ruined himself by his fondness for gambling.

[3] *Writings,* Ford, Vol. I, p. 4.

In breeding, manners, knowledge, and conversation he was essentially a cultivated man of the world.

George Wythe was then about thirty-five, the best Greek and Latin scholar in the colony, and was to become, as Jefferson wrote after his death, the leading member of the Virginian bar. "No man," he added, "ever left behind him a character more venerated than George Wythe. His virtue was of the purest tint; his integrity inflexible, and his justice exact; of warm patriotism, and, devoted as he was to liberty, and the natural and equal rights of man, he might truly be called the Cato of his country, without the avarice of the Roman." After speaking of his disinterestedness, modesty, sound judgment, and urbanity, Jefferson added that he did not trouble or perhaps "trust anyone with his religious creed" but left "the world to the conclusion that that religion must be good which could produce a life of such exemplary virtue." [4] Jefferson remained his devoted friend until the death of the elder man, forty years later, and we may here note, as a characteristic, the length and depth of Jefferson's friendships. Among others, that with Lafayette, for example, lasted for a half century, as did that with John Adams, resumed in late life after its unhappy break, which Jefferson had always deplored. Of an affectionate and loyal nature, Jefferson never willingly gave up a friend, of whom he had many, to whom he had once become warmly attached.

It is difficult to over-rate the influence of the intimate association of the young student with the three older men just described, and it also speaks much for him that they should have made him their constant companion. They assuredly would not have bothered with the sort of youth—or man— whom so many writers on Jefferson have apparently delighted to picture him. They did not comprise, however, all of Jefferson's intimate society in Williamsburg. Colonel Archibald

[4] *Memorial Edition,* Vol. I, pp. 169 f.

Cary, who had married a Randolph cousin of Jefferson's mother, looked up the boy when he arrived and made him welcome among his family and social circle. There was also Peyton Randolph, one of the most prominent and popular of Virginians, later to become the first president of the Continental Congress. Every now and then, young Patrick Henry, who had been admitted to the bar, would come to town, and when he did so he stayed with Jefferson.

Of his general society Jefferson was to write long after to his young grandson that "When I recollect that at fourteen years of age, the whole care and direction of myself was thrown on myself entirely, without a relation or friend qualified to advise or guide me, and recollect the various sorts of bad company with which I associated from time to time, I am astonished I did not turn off with some of them, & become as worthless to society as they were. I had the good fortune to become acquainted very early with some characters of very high standing, and to feel the incessant wish that I could ever become what they were. Under temptations & difficulties, I would ask myself what would Doctor Small, Mr. Wythe, Peyton Randolph do in this situation? What course in it will insure me their approbation? I am certain that this mode of deciding on my conduct, tended more to its correctness than any reasoning powers I possessed. Knowing the even & dignified line they pursued, I could never doubt for a moment which of two courses would be in character for them." [5]

Of his younger friends the two most intimate and loved were Dabney Carr, a schoolmate, and John Page, the son of a marriage which had united two of the foremost families of the Tide-water, and whom Jefferson first met at college. Carr later married Jefferson's fourth sister, Martha, and died suddenly in 1773 leaving six children, whom Jefferson, with his usual generosity, took into his own home with their mother and

[5] *Writings,* Ford, Vol. IX, p. 231.

became like a father to them all. Page, after a brilliant career in politics and the Revolutionary army, was thrice Governor of Virginia, and the devoted friend of Jefferson for fifty years, this being another of what we may call his "golden" friendships.

The social influences to which Jefferson was thus subjected in the formation of his manners, mind, and character were not only those of perhaps the best English frontier of the time but also those of the ablest and most distinguished men of the entire colony among his own and the older generation. Both frontier and higher society were different in Virginia from what they would have been in almost any other colony. In New England the severity of the climate and the poverty of the soil, although they bred a hardy race, did not attract the same sort of settlers as had pushed out to the foothills of the Blue Ridge. In the Middle Colonies, and from their frontier pushing down into the Shenandoah Valley, the pioneers were largely of recent foreign stocks, energetic but poor Germans, Celtic Irish, and Scotch Irish, mostly newcomers to America within a decade or two.

The leading men whom Jefferson met at Williamsburg were also of a different type, as we have already noted, from those he would have met in northern towns. There were agrarians, not business men; deeply versed in law and government, which were their chief occupations other than the running of their plantations; steeped in classical literature; most of them disliking and mistrusting an industrial and commercial society. Although it is a mistake to think that there was no white laboring and artisan class in the South, the bulk of such work as was done by them elsewhere was performed in the South by negro slaves whom people did not think of as composing an active voting part in political society any more than they did of enfranchising women. There was no difficult political problem of city populations or a proletariat. As Jefferson studied

the people among whom he moved, whether at home in Shadwell in Albemarle County or at the capital at Williamsburg,
he found a society peculiarly fitted not only for self-government among all classes, except the lowest (slave), but an
agrarian civilization in which government could be reduced to
a minimum. As a colony Virginia had no foreign relations,
unless those with the Mother Country could be so considered.
Her commerce with the world was negligible except for the
tobacco shipped to England. At home that government would
be best which should maintain order, enforce justice, keep taxes
low, and enact as few laws restricting the freedom of the
individual citizen or of the local political unit as might be.

The influence of women is an important one in any man's
education and the development of his character and outlook.
At college Jefferson had the usual and normal attack of calf
love, though it seems to have been of a mild sort. In the earliest
preserved group of his letters, those to his friend Page, we have
the general account of the affair—infatuation is much too
strong a word—with Miss Rebecca Burwell. The letters, mere
boyish effusions, are neither very interesting, nor, it must be
confessed, are they very convincing. He proclaims, according
to custom, that if she will not have him he shall never marry
another, and in time he does make a proposal to her which she
must at once have realized was scarcely in the style of an
ardent lover. In the same letter in which he discusses with
Page whether he should settle his fate by asking the question
of Rebecca, he also suggests a trip of several years to "England, Holland, France, Spain, Italy (where I would buy me a
good fiddle), and Egypt, and return through the British provinces Northward, home." [6] The following year, the spring of
1764, Rebecca settled the matter for the young man, who she
had probably discovered was rather in love with love than
with her, by marrying another young man, who put the crown-

[6] *Writings,* Ford, Vol. I, p. 347.

ing touch to the comedy by asking Jefferson to act as his best man, not having known of his friend's relation to the bride.

I am inclined to think that Professor Chinard, in his excellent life of Jefferson, lays too great stress on this whole affair. He speaks of the young man as "madly in love," indeed, "as madly in love as a young man could be," and suggests that the episode marked a turning point in his life and helped to form his philosophy. It is true that he did not marry for another eight years, but I think this view attributes too much to a mere first affair which did not go very deep. Nor is it quite just to say, at least in the usual meaning of the word, that Miss Burwell "jilted" him. She never accepted the two offers he made her, and Jefferson himself wrote to Page that "she never gave me reason to hope." [7]

During this period of young manhood there appears to have been another affair, somewhat inexplicable as it has come down to us, but which also seems to have left little if any permanent mark, though later brought up in an unfair and indecent way by enemies who wished to discredit him.

That these episodes helped to mature him, as all such things do, is probably true, but the deepening of his thought and the growth of his opinions appear to have pursued a steady and natural course under other influences. There had been the social and mental contacts of all sorts of which we have already spoken, especially the constant dining with Fauquier, Small, and Wythe. Jefferson was always an omnivorous reader, and at Williamsburg he had access, in one way or another, to many books hitherto unknown to him. At the bookshop, he had begun to collect the beginnings of his own library, and there were also the libraries of his friends. In his second and final year at college, 1761–62, he worked far harder than in the first, though this was long before the end of the Burwell affair.

[7] Chinard, *Life*, pp. 18 f.; C. Chinard, *The Literary Bible of Thomas Jefferson*, Johns Hopkins Press, 1928, p. 22; *Works*, Ford, Vol. I, p. 349.

To a great extent he gave up society, riding, and even his beloved violin, though devoted to music. He later said that at this time he was working over his studies fifteen hours a day, taking almost no exercise except at dusk. He was evidently becoming a serious minded young man when he graduated in 1762, and began the study of law in Wythe's office. The cynical extracts about women which he entered in his *Commonplace Book* do not warrant much emphasis. It was a mood which, as the French say, belonged to his age, and these vapors were to disappear in a happy marriage in a few years, if not before. The Burwell affair was probably more the signal than the cause of the arrival at this normal and temporary phase.

Nor is it likely that the little drama, more comic than tragic, was the cause of the change in his religious belief from that in which he had been piously brought up to the deism or Unitarianism toward which he now turned and which he gradually developed through life in his own inner consciousness hidden from the world. It is almost as unlikely that Fauquier had any part, certainly any deliberate part, in the change. We have already noted that Wythe, one of the constant party of four, was extremely reticent about speaking of religion, and it is not probable that Fauquier, who was no corrupter of youth, would in the presence of Wythe and that of Small and a young student discuss at any length views subversive of the established religion of the colony of which he was governor, whatever his personal opinions may have been.

Fauquier was well versed in English literature and philosophy, and was an admirer of Bolingbroke. He may or may not have introduced Jefferson to that author whose *Works* frequently appear in the libraries of the time in Virginia. In any case it would have been difficult for a student, who was reading fifteen hours a day all the deeper literature he could lay his hands on, to have long gone without making the acquaintance of so influential and popular a writer of the time.

Jefferson was throughout life greatly interested in religious, and, more especially, ethical speculation. He was also devoted to the classics. It was natural that a young intellectual of the eighteenth century should question the Christian dogmas, and equally so that an ardent classicist should build for himself a philosophy of life and conduct in which the Stoicism of the Greek and Roman philosophers should form a large element. For a man of ethical nature, of refinement and culture, of deep but suppressed feeling, and who has given up the dogmas of the church, Stoicism has through the ages always formed a refuge. We are here speaking chiefly of the influences on Jefferson at this time, and we may leave a discussion of his beliefs until a more mature period of his life, and need only note in ending this topic for the moment, that one of the great teachers in life is death. Jefferson had been at the impressionable age of fourteen when his father died, and he was now, in 1765, to lose his elder and best loved sister, at the age of twenty-five. Like himself, she had been devoted to music, was apparently charming and accomplished, and had a mind which could fully respond to Jefferson's own. When he was at Shadwell she was his constant companion, and the blow was an unusually heavy one. It is said that fifty years later he would speak of her as though she had died but recently and had been constantly in his thoughts. Her companionship and death were probably of far more influence upon his mind than were Rebecca Burwell's rejections of his offers of marriage.

Meanwhile other influences had also been at work. Jefferson was assiduously studying law with Mr. Wythe, reading widely, making long extracts in his *Commonplace Book* of what appealed to him as especially important, and thinking deeply. Admission to the bar was not difficult in those days, and it has been said that Patrick Henry studied for only three months. No such preparation suited Jefferson who spent five years, certainly from no lack of intellectual ability, in Wythe's office before applying for the examination. From the point of view of legal knowledge he was probably one of the best equipped lawyers of his time. Jefferson's interests were always wider than those of any other noted American of that day, with probably John Adams second, and he was reading not only in the law but in history, the classics, poetry, architecture, science, husbandry, and other topics. A year after entering Wythe's office, however, his attention was to be sharply focussed on political problems, by his friend Patrick Henry.

That able but volatile young man, who was never of the inner circle of Jefferson's friendship, after an unsuccessful attempt at running a store, had been admitted to the bar in 1760 and had been living at Hanover Court House. In the next three years he won most of the 1185 lawsuits which had been placed in his hands. As is well known, the currency of Virginia was tobacco, which, as a commodity and thus also as currency, fluctuated widely in value. The clergy of the colony received their tithes in general in that commodity. Apparently, although left to take care of themselves when tobacco was low, they were treated the same as other creditors when it was high, as in 1755 and 1757, when the legislature decreed that creditors should receive payments for debts at the rate of two pence for a pound of tobacco. The clergy complained to London, and the law was eventually disallowed. Whether the rate was fair or not, the currency was unsatisfactory because of its wide fluctuations. Some such arrangement in general had to be made when it rose suddenly and rapidly in value or debtors would be ruined. Such laws had been passed occasionally for a century. Moreover, nothing annoyed the colonists more than having the laws they passed with understanding of local needs disallowed in England, after long delay. There was much excitement in the colony, which grew when the clergy of the increasingly unpopular established church began to sue for back salaries. In 1763 the Hanover County Court upheld

England and declared the law unconstitutional in the case brought by the Reverend John Maury. It seemed to remain only for the jury to assess the amount due him.

The defense then engaged Patrick Henry. He happened to be the son of the judge who had rendered the decision, a Scotch Presbyterian who had come to America a generation earlier. Young Henry did not argue the law at length but with all the eloquence for which he was famed, he denounced the clergy of the established church for demanding tithes for preaching the Gospel; the idea itself of an established church; and lastly the encroachment of the Crown on the rights of the colonists. He so stirred the audience that the clergy who had come to witness their triumph fled the courtroom, and the jury awarded damages of one penny. The interest of the whole colony in the case had been intense, an interest which was the greater for Jefferson owing to the fact that it was one of his own young acquaintances who had suddenly leaped into fame. Jefferson at once made researches into the law and history of the relations between church and State, carrying them back to the days of the Saxons. He came to the conclusion that there was no warrant in either law or justice for an establishment, and we may trace to this case the origin of those opinions and efforts which were at last to eventuate in his bill for religious freedom in Virginia. There were two other points in the case which dealt with problems to which he was later to devote himself, and which he may have now considered with deeper interest than before. These were the nature and dangers of a fluctuating currency; and the relations between the colonies and England. The first was to be brought to his attention again in 1765 when Henry, then a member of the House of Burgesses, fought the State Treasurer in connection with a proposed plan to avoid certain personal difficulties of that official, originating in connection with the paper money of the State which had been issued for expenses in the French and

Indian War. We need not go into the details, but the fight waged by Henry resulted in a strong cleavage of feeling between the frontier and tide-water sections, and must have brought once more to Jefferson, as he talked it over with his friend, the dangers and disadvantages of a fluctuating medium. That the Treasurer had caused a loss of £100,000 Virginia money to the colony may have been the beginning of Jefferson's fear of paper money and of the juggling of high finance.

Life in Williamsburg was becoming more exciting, and the quiet student of law was witnessing the beginning of great affairs. The Stamp Act had been passed by the British Parliament, and on May 29, 1765, was the subject of debate in the House of Burgesses, Jefferson being among the audience. Henry offered a set of six Resolutions declaring in part that the colonists had brought with them all the rights of British subjects and that among these was the right to tax themselves and to be taxed by no one else. At the end of a fiery speech, in a scene of confusion, he uttered his famous words: "Cæsar had his Brutus—Charles the First his Cromwell—and George the Third" . . . There was a pause and a cry of "Treason!", when Henry added "may profit by their example. If *this* be treason, make the most of it." The mere passage of the Act by Parliament did not at first greatly rouse opinion in the colonies, and the more conservative elements in the Virginia House were much averse to the adoption of the Henry Resolutions, partly because of the way in which they raised issue with England and partly because of the fear lest frontier counties, with their young leader, might be growing too fast in influence. The next day, however, several of the Resolutions, (it is uncertain just how many) were adopted, and all six were printed in the newspapers up and down the whole of the colonies. The torch to the imperial structure had been set by Henry.

Narrating the events long afterward to William Wirt for

his life of Henry, Jefferson is reported to have said that the debate on the last of the Resolutions was "most bloody," and that when carried by one vote only, Peyton Randolph, the Attorney General, broke out to Jefferson as he passed, "By God! I would have given five hundred guineas for a single vote!" Although even Wythe opposed Henry, Jefferson appears to have been on his side, although not a member of the House, and later wrote that the older leaders, such as Randolph, Blair, Pendelton, Wythe, and others, "were honest and able men, [and] had begun the opposition on the same grounds, but with a moderation more adapted to their age and experience. Subsequent events favored the bolder spirits of Henry, the Lees, Pages, Mason, etc., with whom I went on all points." [8]

Jefferson never had the respect or affection for Henry that he had for other friends, if that word indeed can be used in this connection. He greatly admired his eloquence but felt the lack of intellectual training and background. There was more rhetoric than substance in his speeches. Like Samuel Adams, Henry was a born revolutionist, but not at all a constructive statesman. Each became governor of his own state but their great services were rendered as agitators, and after the Revolution, they both became reactionary and not liberal. Speaking of Henry in 1824 Jefferson paid tribute to his extraordinary ability as an orator, comparing him to Homer, and to the manner in which in the beginning he had kept the group of the more radical thinkers together. Of his eloquence he said, "I never heard anything that deserved to be called by the same name with what flowed from him; and where he got that torrent of language is inconceivable," but added, "I have frequently shut my eyes while he spoke, and when he was done asked myself what he had said, without being able to recollect a word of it. He was no logician. He was a truly great man, however, one of enlarged views." [9]

[8] Randall, *Life*, Vol. I, pp. 38 ff.   [9] *Ibid.*, p. 40.

Jefferson was not only at the seat of disaffection but he also had ample opportunity to ponder, for he divided his time between Williamsburg and Shadwell. Admitted to the bar and beginning to practise in the capital in 1767 he was made County Lieutenant of Albemarle three years later. At Shadwell, where in his early twenties he had already collected a valuable library, he read and studied, studying even how to develop his plantation to better advantage. Always in search of facts which could be turned to practical use he was also through life a devoted agriculturist, and a large part of the notes he made, whether here or abroad, were on agricultural matters. His lands at this time were bringing him an income of about $2000 a year, to which he added from his profession about $3000 more. This was a fairly handsome income for the period, and he had for some years been planning a new home of his own on the top of his little mountain. The house itself, "Monticello," was not built until 1770 but long before that the young planter had been paddling himself in his canoe across the Rivanna to climb the height and superintend the levelling of the hilltop.

There were no professional architects in the colony, and both by necessity and desire Jefferson was his own. In his "Notes on Virginia," written some years later, he said that the private buildings were rarely of stone or brick, and that it was "impossible to devise things more ugly, uncomfortable, and happily more perishable." "The genius of architecture seems to have shed its maledictions over this land," he added.[10] He himself had not yet seen Europe, and his travels had taken him only so far, in 1766, as Annapolis, Philadelphia, and New York. His knowledge of architecture from books must have been slight, although apparently he was the only man in the colony to own a copy of Palladio. He had, however, a natural instinct for what was good and appropriate,—both aristocratic

10 *Writings,* Ford, Vol. III, p. 258.

qualities. At twenty-seven he built a home which displayed the three chief elements in architectural ability—design, construction, and ornament. The choice of the site itself throws an interesting light on his nature. His was to be no home in a sheltered spot by the side of river or road, or near a neighbor. With all his political democracy there was nothing of either social democracy or the bourgeois spirit about him, and his essential aloofness was evidenced in his choosing a mountain top for his dwelling. From it he could survey not only his own lands but miles of rolling country lying below him, stretching westward to the ever-changing panorama of the Blue Ridge, and eastward over more level land which seemed in its indefinite expanse almost like the sea. At times mist would hide the landscape and then he literally dwelt in sunshine above the clouds. The spot is a noble one, and Jefferson decided to build a noble home upon it.

His fastidious taste was to be seen not only in the design of the house, which has falsely been called Georgian and which was in fact classical Roman, but also in the arrangement of the entire place. Even in the "great" places of the Virginian rich of his day there was a combination of luxury and slovenliness. Conditions were not so bad, indeed, as Beveridge suggests in his *Life of John Marshall* with that unrestrained prejudice which did so much to mar that author's otherwise great book and to reflect upon his intellectual integrity. But, as we have noted before, the combination was characteristic of the eighteenth century in England, and was accented in Virginia by the climate, life in a comparatively new country, and slave labor. Many of the best houses were jostled by the various offices and shops needed for the work of a plantation, the most familiar example to most Americans today being Mount Vernon.

Jefferson determined to have none of this to spoil the dignity and peace of his mountain top and view. By intelligent plan-

ning all these necessary offices were hidden, while the inside of
the house itself was so arranged with concealed passages and
stairs, as to make it appear as though life went on magically
with no menial work. It was not that Jefferson disliked or
despised those who performed such tasks. The deep affection
in which he was held by all his slaves proves that, if proof were
necessary. He planned thus because deeply imbued with the
spirit of the classics he felt life should not be huddled but
lived with a serene dignity. Of the life in his new home we
have many descriptions by distinguished foreigners and others
who came to visit him in later years, and we may defer further
comment for the present, except to note that it was a peculiarly
patriarchal life that Jefferson, like other large land-owners,
could lead on his domain. He did not have to buy motor-cars
but raised his own horses. His sheep provided him with wool,
which was made into clothes on the estate. Bricks, nails, and
other building materials were also its products. Smiths, carpenters, even fine cabinet-makers, and others, as well as field
hands, were all on the place. His own grain was made into
flour. The life which he planned in his political philosophy as
the happiest for the nation as a whole was the independent
agricultural life he himself led. Except that he believed in
free labor instead of slavery, the nation that he envisaged was
a vast aggregate of free individuals all living like himself a
Monticello life on a large or small scale. With peace, dignity,
and security, with steady and healthful pursuits, with a minimum of dependence on other communities and on buying or
selling, he dreamed his dream. Just as today Monticello would
be ruined by a creeping up its hillsides of factories, banks, and
a town, so he considered that the American life as a whole would
be ruined by commerce, finance, and manufacturing which
would corrupt the people by extravagance, business chicanery,
and a homeless city proletariat. As one stands at the door of
his house today and looks out to the Blue Ridge shrouded in

violet mist, one can understand both his philosophy and fears, and wonders whether even with slavery abolished and vast riches won, the Americans are now either as safe or as contented as they were in his day.

It was fortunate that he had begun his building in 1769 (the year in which he was elected to the House of Burgesses), for on February 1, 1770, Shadwell, where he had been born and where his mother and sisters were living, was burned to the ground. Three weeks later he wrote to his friend John Page that he had lost every paper he had in the world, including those for a number of law cases then pending, and also his entire library with the exception of one volume which he had loaned and which was not in the house. "On a reasonable estimate," he added, "I calculate the *cost* of the books burned to have been £200 sterling. Would to God it had been the money, *then* had it never cost me a sigh." [11] Although he was not to learn the fact, some papers had been saved and were found in 1851 in an old trunk. Included among them were his *Commonplace Book* and other manuscripts now in the Library of Congress. His favorite violin also escaped. A portion of Monticello had been completed, and into that the family moved at once.

Two years later he married, January 1, 1772, Martha Skelton, a widow and a woman of some property, daughter of John Wayles, a well-known lawyer with a good practice. The latter died in another two years, and the legacy left to Mrs. Jefferson doubled Jefferson's property and, as he said, "the ease of our circumstances." At the time of his marriage Jefferson was only twenty-nine, and whether or not, as has been alleged, the connection was one of "convenience," it is certain that, as happily often occurs in such cases, a deep and abiding love followed, even if it had not preceded, the union. Mrs. Jefferson was attractive and accomplished. She was a musician and well

[11] *Writings*, Ford, Vol. I, p. 370.

read, a capable manager of slaves and household. By 1772 her husband was thus married to a delightful wife; he had an ample income and estate, soon to be doubled as we have noted; was County Lieutenant, also about to be made surveyor of the county by his college; a member of the legislature; had an excellent law practice; and lived in one of the finest houses in Virginia. Having thus followed him from childhood to successful manhood, we may pause to note briefly some other boys who had been growing up at the same time.

Eleven years before the birth of Jefferson, George Washington had been born in Westmoreland County, and by the death of his brother had inherited Mount Vernon. A thorough woodsman, due to his long surveying trips, already noted as a soldier on account of his campaign with Braddock, he had married a rich widow, and had for some years been living the life he loved best, that of a planter on his estate on the Potomac. He had been elected to the legislature two years before Jefferson had gone to college but whether they met at Williamsburg is unknown.

Another boy, eight years younger than Jefferson, was James Madison, who was brought up in Orange County, next to Albemarle. He was one of the Southern boys who went North for college, graduating from Princeton in 1771. He remained another year, however, and while Jefferson was enjoying the first months of married life, young Madison was studying Hebrew and ethics in New Jersey. The religious freedom of the neighboring colony of Pennsylvania greatly impressed him, and he contrasted it in a letter with "that diabolical, hell-conceived principle of persecution" which he said raged among some in Virginia.

Yet another boy, four years younger than Madison, was the cousin of Jefferson who has already been mentioned. John Marshall had spent his young life "moving west" with his father, having shifted three times before the boy was nineteen, and until he was twenty he had never been, as he recorded, "out of the simple, crude environment of the near frontier" for more than a year. His education was mostly derived from his father, who promptly bought the first American edition of Blackstone, published in the year of Jefferson's marriage. Young Marshall's only institutional instruction of any sort was a month's study of law. Considering the future enmity between Jefferson and Marshall it is odd that the latter was to get even this slight training from George Wythe, whom Jefferson, when governor, was to appoint to a chair of law at William and Mary founded on funds originally destined for theology and which Jefferson characteristically transferred to law. There was simple comfort but no ease in Marshall's young life, and this may in part account for the great stress he later laid on the rights of property when he acquired some of his own and moved among those who had it. The rights and value of property are often more lightly considered by those who have always had ample economic security than by those who gain it after hardships.

Besides these young Virginians, there were also growing up in distant lands two boys, each fourteen years younger than Jefferson, and whose future lives were to be closely entwined with his own, utterly unlikely as it could then have seemed. On September 6, 1757, in France, there was born to the Marquis and Marquise de Lafayette a son whom they named Marie Joseph Paul Yves Roch Gilbert du Motier, who was to become Marquis when less than two owing to the death of his father in the battle of Minden. The boy went into the army as soon as age permitted, and burned to avenge both his father's death and his country's humiliation at the hands of the English. Time was to give him his opportunity, and to link his life with Jefferson's for an entire half century.

In the same year in which the young Lafayette came into the world, there was also born in the island of Nevis, British West

Indies, a son to a Scotchman, James Hamilton, and a French woman, wife of a Jew, John M. Levine. Owing to her husband's treatment of her, the marriage had been a most unhappy one, and she had left him, unable, however, on account of the law of that time and place to obtain a divorce. She and Hamilton lived together in irreproachable union and were accepted, under the circumstances, as man and wife. Hamilton had come of good family, but was apparently a poor business man, and after his affairs "went to wreck," as the son, Alexander, later said, Mrs. Levine, or Mrs. Hamilton as she was known, had to go to relations at St. Croix because Hamilton was unable to support her. The boy was thus largely left to his own resources from the age of eleven, but displayed almost incredible precocity in affairs. He had intense ambition, and after spending some time in the office of a merchant he was able, through the generosity of some aunts, to leave Nevis for New York when fifteen. His wish was a college education, and very likely he may also have desired to get away from Nevis and make a fresh start entire in some other place. The year of Jefferson's marriage, the boy landed in Boston and proceeded at once to a grammar school at Elizabethtown, New Jersey, entering King's College (Columbia University) in New York in the fall of 1773. His brilliant career in America was, except for a few years' soldiering in the Revolution, to be almost wholly spent in the higher society of that city and Philadelphia, both because of the position he carved out for himself and of his marriage into the wealthy and prominent Schuyler family. There seemed as little likelihood in 1772 when he was starting his career, alone and almost penniless in New York, that he and Jefferson, then settling down to the tasks and pleasures of a rich and well-known Virginia gentleman, would ever become deadly enemies on the wide stage of a nation yet unborn.

CHAPTER III

JEFFERSON ENTERS PUBLIC LIFE

JEFFERSON had been a Justice of the Peace for his county almost since his coming of age, and, as we have already seen, had been elected to the House of Burgesses in 1769, remaining a member until 1775. During this period, or at least until the latter part of 1774, when he gave up the law, his practice had become increasingly successful. He was, in fact, one of the leading lawyers of the colony, associated in many cases with the greatest lights of the bar, such as Wythe, Pendleton and Peyton Randolph, while among his clients were numbered some of the richest and most important families, such as the Blands, Burwells, Byrds, Carters, Careys, Harrisons, Lees, Nelsons, Pages, and Randolphs. By 1771 he had attained a position which allowed him to decline to accept the business of such a noted lawyer as Robert Carter Nicholas when the latter retired from practice. The offer and declination both prove the rank which the young Jefferson had reached when only twenty-eight years of age. He was essentially a thinker and writer, not an orator. Moreover, owing perhaps to some defect in the vocal cords, his voice became weak and husky after a few moments of strain in public speaking. It is nothing against him to admit quite frankly that he possessed neither forensic, military, nor great executive ability. His talents were of a different sort.

In the state legislature, Jefferson aligned himself with the patriotic and liberal group. It was the custom for the House of Burgesses to pass Resolutions as heads of the address in reply to the Governor's speech at the opening of a session. In

Jefferson's first session, 1769, several resolutions were passed which asserted the right of self-taxation, the right of petition for the redress of grievances, and the right of the colonies to unite in such petitions. Complaints were also included as to the recent English parliamentary recommendation to transport colonials, accused of treason, to England for trial under an obsolete statute of Henry VIII. Obviously these resolutions were passed with an eye to recent happenings in Massachusetts, and Governor Botetourt at once dissolved the Assembly. The next day, however, it met at the Apollo Tavern where the members pledged themselves, during the continuance of the recent fiscal measures of the British Parliament, not to import certain articles in a specified list. Among the signers of the agreement Jefferson's name appears with those of Washington, Patrick Henry, R. H. Lee, Nicholas, Archibald Cary, Peyton Randolph and others. It is noteworthy that Jefferson also introduced a bill giving to owners of slaves the power to free them, except under very limited circumstances not then allowed by British law. It failed to pass but it shows that at the very beginning of his public career Jefferson gave expression to those anti-slavery views which he held all his life and which, over and over again, he tried to get embodied in law. For the next two or three years, the feeling against England subsided, and the business of the legislature was largely of a routine nature. In the year of his marriage, 1772, Jefferson did not attend the sessions at all.

We may here note with regard to his personal affairs that he had inherited perhaps thirty slaves from his father, and his wife had received, when her father died, one hundred and thirty-five more with about 40,000 acres of land, though not of the same value as Jefferson's own. With Mrs. Jefferson's inheritance there went also her share of her father's debts, about £3750 Virginian currency. Jefferson at once sold property to pay this, and deposited the proceeds in the Loan Office, receiving the deposit back after the Revolution in paper worth only one in forty of that which he had deposited. Owing to the fluctuations in the currency he had later again to sell land in 1787 and 1792, these successive sales and depreciations eating up about one-half of his wife's entire property. The debt was owing to British merchants, and its story not only emphasizes Jefferson's sensitive personal integrity but also helps to explain his inveterate fear and hatred of paper money and all forms of currency except those based on gold or silver.

The lull in the dispute with England was to come to a sudden end in 1772. On June 9 of that year, the British revenue schooner, *Gaspée*, ran ashore on the coast of Rhode Island, and during the night was burned by persons unknown. As usual, the colonial courts took the side of the colonists against the Crown, and in spite of investigations by a Royal Commission, held in the spring of 1773, nothing could be discovered. Meanwhile there had been talk by the British authorities of transporting those who might be accused of complicity in the affair to England to stand trial for treason.

This brought Jefferson and some of the other younger or more zealous members of the Virginia Assembly to consider once more the question of relations between the colonies and the mother country. In Jefferson's words, "Not thinking our old & leading members up to the point of forwardness & zeal which the times required, Mr Henry, R. H. Lee, Francis L. Lee, Mr Carr [Jefferson's brother-in-law] & myself agreed to meet in the evening in a private room of the Raleigh to consult on the state of things," [1] There may, he added, have been one or two others. They concluded that the most important step to take was to organize in every colony committees of correspondence which should communicate with each other in order that all could unite and present a common front. Samuel Adams had already organized local committees in Massachusetts, and his system

---

[1] *Writings*, Ford, Vol. I, p. 8.

of local committees combined with Jefferson's intercolonial system would evidently produce an efficient and formidable engine of revolution. It has been claimed that the whole system originated in Massachusetts, but it would seem clear that the nationalizing of the system was first proposed in Virginia, though the somewhat antiquarian dispute is of local rather than of national interest.

The group in the tavern drew up a series of resolutions, and next morning these were offered in the Assembly, where they were accepted without dissent. As before, the governor at once dissolved the House, but the members met at the tavern again and before separating despatched letters to the speakers of the legislatures of the other colonies.

Events were henceforth to move more rapidly, and while the House was in session the following spring, 1774, news was received of the closing of the port of Boston as a result of the "Tea Party." There is no need for going into details of the events of these few years, as we are concerned with them only as they were to affect later history and our political ideas and philosophy. When the news was received in Virginia, the leadership had already passed from the older and more conservative element, and, as in the preceding year, it was taken by Jefferson, Henry, the Lees, and a few others. These immediately decided, as Jefferson later wrote, that they "must boldly take an unequivocal stand in the line with Massachusetts," and should take measures to arouse "the lethargy into which they had fallen as to passing events." For this purpose it was decided, the legislature approving, that a general day of fasting and prayer should be appointed for June 1, the day on which the Port Bill was to go into effect. Once more the Governor dissolved the Assembly, whose members then met as usual in the Raleigh Tavern. There they agreed to an Association, and appointed a committee to arrange with the other colonies for a Congress which should meet annually to consider matters and

unite on common policies. It was further recommended to
the several counties to hold meetings and elect representatives
to attend a general meeting at Williamsburg to be held for
the purpose of electing representatives to the inter-colonial
Congress which it was suggested should be held at Philadelphia in September.

It is impossible to over-rate the importance of this action
on the part of the greatest and most populous of the colonies.
Coming thus immediately to the assistance of Massachusetts,
a remote colony (as means of travel and communication then
were), and one so different in social life, ideas and economic
structure from itself, Virginia by this action indicated the existence of a unity among all the colonies which no one could
have predicted a few years previously.

As the most prominent citizen of Albemarle County, and as
one of the most advanced thinkers in all America at that moment on the nature of the imperial ties, Jefferson naturally
took an important part at his county meeting. In one respect
his view was almost precisely that now taken by England of
the British Commonwealth of Nations. The only tenable theory, he wrote, was that "the relation between Gr. Br. and these
colonies was exactly the same as that of England & Scotland
after the accession of James and until the Union, and the same
as her present relations with Hanover, having the same Executive chief but no other necessary political connection." [2] That
is to say, Jefferson envisaged the theory that the colonies
should be self-governing dominions with the Crown as the only
link. He was too far in advance of his time to allow his idea
to be effective in the sphere of practical politics, but if the
British Government and people could have accepted that view
then as they have come to do since, the entire history not only
of America but of the world would have been different, and
probably more peaceful. Jefferson stated that he could find

[2] *Writings*, Ford, Vol. I, p. 12.

no one to agree with him on this point or on his theory of expatriation, which we shall note presently, except Wythe. Nevertheless, the same view had been advocated even earlier, by one or two newspaper writers in New England.

"The true plan of government," wrote one in 1772, "which reason and the experience of nations points out for the British Empire is to let the several parliaments in Britain and America be (as they naturally are) free and independent of each other. . . . And as the King is the center of union . . . the various parts of the great body politic will be united in him." [3] Another writer in the same year had suggested the same idea. "The government thus united in one Sovereign, though divided into distant Parliaments, will be actuated by one Soul. It will have all the advantages of a powerful Republic, and a grand extensive Monarchy. . . . If the supreme Legislature is considered as only in the Majesty of the King as the common Head of all his Parliaments, and exercising his authority with their [several] consents, while no one of them encroaches upon the rights of the rest, harmony will reign through the whole Empire; every part will enjoy freedom and happiness; it may be extended farther and farther to the utmost ends of the earth and yet continue firmly compacted until all the kingdoms of the World shall be dissolved." [4] That Jefferson, devoting himself largely to developing a theory of imperial relations, should have remained ignorant for two years of such suggestions published in so important a paper as *The Boston Gazette*, shows the inadequacy of inter-colonial communication, and the importance of the committees of correspondence when organized.

Jefferson's wide reading, evidenced by the extracts in his *Commonplace Book*, had led him to other conclusions also. Both in government and law he had come to lay great and

[3] "American Solon" in *The Boston Gazette*, Jan. 27, 1772.
[4] Article in *The New Hampshire Gazette*, reprinted in *The Boston Gazette*, Feb. 17, 1772.

somewhat fantastic stress upon the Saxon period. This had already appeared in his opinion upon the question of the rights of an established church which he found to have no foundation in the common law but to have been based on usurpations after Saxon times. He now also, somewhat illogically, came to the conclusion that the home country of England had no more rights over the colonists, who had expatriated themselves, than had the home countries of the Danes and Saxons possessed over their subjects when they had emigrated to England. This would seem to prove rather too much for Jefferson's theory as a whole, for if the mother country had no rights over expatriated subjects it is difficult to see why the Crown should serve as a link except by voluntary acceptance of it by the colonists. But Jefferson did not discuss it from that point of view, nor did he suggest that if the link were based upon a mere voluntary acceptance by the colonists, then that acceptance might be withdrawn at any moment.

Nor according to Jefferson's theory of relations could the position of the Crown derive from the fact that the title to the land was vested in the King, for this Jefferson expressly denied. Going back again to the Saxons he pointed out that when they had conquered in England each man had obtained his own land by his own strength and had held it in fee simple without the over-landlordship of the Crown, which was not asserted until after the Norman conquest. He claimed that the colonists had gone to the wilds of America as had the Saxons to the former wilds of Britain. The Crown, he claimed, had given them no aid, and therefore that they should own the land they had conquered without overlordship.

The original settlers, he said, had been farmers and not lawyers, and had been easily deceived as to the rights of the King over the soil. As Professor Chinard has correctly pointed out, Jefferson roundly asserted what was the American pioneer view of land when he wrote: "It is time, therefore, for us to lay this matter before his majesty, and to declare that he has no right to grant lands of himself. From the nature and purpose of civil institutions, all the lands within the limits which any particular society has circumscribed around itself are assumed by that society, and subject to their allotment only. This may be done by themselves assembled collectively, or by their legislature, to whom they have delegated sovereign authority; and if they are allotted in either of these ways, each individual may appropriate to himself such lands as he finds vacant, and occupancy will give him a title." [5]

Here speaks the genuine voice of pioneer America. The American spirit was to become more and more the spirit of the ever-advancing West, and if any one is in doubt as to why the essentially and spiritually aristocratic Jefferson could become the leader of a great democratic party, he has only to study that statesman's utterances and opinions on all matters of special interest to the westerner and to the laboring classes. We may in this connection make two more quotations from his writing at this time. As we have seen, one of the grievances of the frontier Americans of his day was that of lack of representation as population extended beyond old settled limits. Another appeal Jefferson wished to make to the King was with special regard to this. "But in what terms," he writes, "reconcileable to majesty, and at the same time to truth, shall we speak of a late instruction to his majesty's governor of the colony of Virginia, by which he is forbidden to assent to any law for the division of a county, unless the new county will consent to have no representative in the assembly? . . . Does his majesty seriously wish, and publish it to the world, that his subjects shall give up the glorious right of representation, with all the benefits derived from that, and submit themselves the absolute slaves of his sovereign will? Or is it rather meant to confine the legislative body to their present numbers, that

[5] *Writings*, Ford, Vol. I, p. 444.

they may be the cheaper bargain whenever they shall become worth a purchase?" [6]

Again he writes, "The abolition of domestic slavery is the great object of desire in those colonies, where it was unhappily introduced in their infant state. But previous to the enfranchisement of the slaves we have, it is necessary to exclude all further importations from Africa; yet our repeated efforts to effect this by prohibitions, and by imposing duties which might amount to a prohibition, have been hitherto defeated by his majesty's negative: Thus preferring the immediate advantages of a few African corsairs to the lasting interests of the American states, and to the rights of human nature." [7]

Returning to Jefferson's theory of the Saxons and leaving aside the authenticity of his interpretation of Saxon law, it is quite evident that in the centuries intervening between the Saxon conquests and 1774, the world had completely altered, and that any social system would be resolved into chaos if political and economic relations were suddenly to be changed to conform to questionable precedents of twelve centuries earlier. How questionable such precedents might prove to be has been shown by the alteration within the past two generations in the theories of Saxon law and government since the days of Stubbs and Freeman. Jefferson had studied widely in the origins of English law in the works of Temple, Dalrymple, Pelloutier, Molesworth, and others, but granted that they were correct in their surmises, Jefferson would have been twelve centuries behind the times, in appealing to Saxon precedents, as he was a century or more in advance of the times in his theory of an empire with the Crown as sole link.

At the meeting in Albemarle County, 1774, he drew up the set of Resolves to be forwarded to the meeting of the whole colony at Williamsburg. In writing these he advanced a notable step beyond most of his fellow patriots at this stage, as

[6] *Ibid.*, p. 441.   [7] *Ibid.*, p. 441.

is shown, for example, by the Resolves of Fairfax County adopted a day before those of Albemarle. In these, Washington, George Mason, and others admitted that the colonists were connected with the mother country and owed certain duties to it. While in some cases admitting and in others not, the *constitutionality* of laws passed by the British Parliament for the regulation of such matters as trade, they did admit the *expediency* of such laws, and considered that there was such a thing as a sort of *imperial constitution*. They based the rights of Americans on their having brought with them, when emigrating, all the rights they enjoyed under the British constitution.

On the other hand, Jefferson claimed in the Albemarle Resolves that the colonists could be bound by no laws whatever without their own consent; that their rights to complete freedom did not stem from those derived as Englishmen from the Constitution but that they were held "as the common rights of mankind," confirmed in sundry ways. Proceeding to narrate briefly some of the infractions of these rights by Great Britain, the Resolves suggested discontinuance of trade with her until certain named Acts had been repealed, after which "it will be reasonable to grant to our brethren of Great Britain such privileges in commerce as may amply compensate their fraternal assistance, past and future." [8]

Jefferson himself was elected by the county to attend the larger meeting at Williamsburg, which was to elect delegates to the Congress at Philadelphia and prepare instructions for them. A little before the date of meeting, August 1, Jefferson set out but was taken ill on the way and could not be present. He had, however, drafted a long set of Resolves which might serve as a guide for the Congressional delegates. When prevented from proceeding farther on his journey he despatched two copies of these, one to Patrick Henry and the other to

[8] *Ibid.,* pp. 420 f.

Peyton Randolph. Nothing was heard of the copy sent to Henry but Randolph read his copy to a large company assembled at his house, and Edmund Randolph, who was present, wrote that most of them were received with loud applause. They were, however, considered as too radical for the general state of opinion and were not adopted by the convention. Nevertheless, some of the members had them printed in a small pamphlet of twenty-three pages under the title of *A Summary View of the Rights of British America,* from which the quotations on the preceding paragraph have been taken.

It was in this production that Jefferson set forth at much greater length than was possible in the Albemarle Resolves, his views of the relations of the colonies to Great Britain, the wrongs they had suffered, and also his theories of expatriation, land tenure, and so on, as derived from the Saxon polity. It is interesting to note that Jefferson's advanced views and his Saxon hobby were leading him to consider a complete separation of America from the empire. In his almanac for that year are a number of notes, all of which would seem to be contemporary. One of these is a proposed emblem for "the American States." The discarding of the term colonies and the grouping of them all as American would appear to indicate that he was contemplating a possible radical change of status with reference to Great Britain. Two years later John Adams wrote that Mr. Jefferson proposed for the national arms "the children of Israel in the wilderness, led by a cloud by day and a pillar of fire by night; and on the other side, Hengist and Horsa, the Saxon chiefs from whom we claim the honor of being descended, and whose political principles and forms of government we have assumed." [9] It is not unamusing to note that some eighty years later some of the Southern racial journalists were to be claiming that the base New Englanders were descended from the churlish Saxons whereas the aristocratic

[9] *Ibid.,* p. 420.

Southerners were descended from the ruling race of Normans.

Throughout the colonies, counties were now busily engaged in forming committees of safety with undefined but almost unlimited powers, from the exercise of which there was no appeal. They could examine, fine, disarm, and imprison individuals, raise armed forces, and were distinctly revolutionary organizations. It was indicative both of his position in the movement and in his county that Jefferson received the highest number of votes of any of those elected to the Albemarle Committee.

Jefferson had not been elected to the first Continental Congress in 1774, of which his kinsman, Peyton Randolph, was president. When, however, the second Virginia convention met and it was realized that Randolph might not be able to continue at the next session of Congress because of his duties in the Virginia legislature, Jefferson was appointed to take his place at Philadelphia. Meanwhile the governor, Lord Dunmore, had called the Assembly to meet late in November, 1774, but soon prorogued that body, finding that its members were in favor of enforcing the restrictions on trade, and were in general on the revolutionary side. The same body, however, met at Richmond on March 20, 1775, Jefferson being one of the two members for Albemarle. It was at this meeting, in the debate on whether Virginia should at once arm itself for the impending struggle, that Patrick Henry is said to have ended an impassioned speech in favor of force with the words, "Give me liberty or give me death." There are various versions of the speech and it cannot now be stated with certainty just what he did say, but the Assembly was won over to the side of active preparation for war if it should prove necessary. The vote was 65 to 60 and would seem to indicate that the conservative and radical members, Jefferson being numbered among the latter, were still fairly evenly balanced.

Events, however, were beginning to move with ever faster

speed regardless of any one individual. In Massachusetts the battle of Lexington and the defeat of the British on the return from Concord took place on April 19. The following day, in Virginia, under orders from Lord Dunmore, the powder in the magazine at Williamsburg was seized and placed on board a British vessel. Meanwhile, that governor had intimated to the House of Burgesses that he was expecting conciliatory messages from England and on arrival of these he would convene the legislature. The meeting was called for June 1 and on that day they did meet again at Williamsburg. Peyton Randolph had realized that the work of the first session of the Continental Congress might be undone, and that as he was familiar with the aims and temper of that body it might be well for him to remain on hand in Virginia in case his presence there should prove to be more useful than at Philadelphia. For that reason, at the Richmond meeting, Jefferson had been elected, as we have seen, to Congress as an alternate for his kinsman.

Both, however, attended the June meeting of the Burgesses, and Jefferson drew up the answer of that body to the so-called Conciliatory Propositions as received from Lord North. The reply was moderate in tone, but on account of the fall of Lord Chatham and the situation as it had by then developed on both sides of the water, it was held that the terms suggested by the British Government could not possibly be accepted by Virginia. The matter was therefore referred to the Congress at Philadelphia for united decision by all the colonies. Dunmore soon took refuge on board a British vessel, and Jefferson departed to take his place in Congress, where he heard the news of the battle of Bunker Hill, and was to witness the departure of Washington for the seat of war as Commander of all the American forces.

Before following Jefferson onto the wider stage of what was now rapidly becoming that of a united nation, a word or two must be said of the two aspects of the struggle going on in these momentous years in order to understand his course, which may otherwise appear inconsistent.

There was, first, the struggle for political independence of England which assumed different forms in the minds of different men. There were a few, a very few up to this time, who, with Samuel Adams at their head, desired a complete severance of all ties with the mother country, regardless of redress of grievances. At the other end of the scale was a larger group, who later became the "Loyalists," and which included many of the wealthy and socially prominent people from Philadelphia to Boston and some in the Carolinas, who wished to retain the English connection at any cost to local liberty. In between these groups was the bulk of the nation, or at least such of the nation as took an interest in public matters. These cared little about fine-spun constitutional or legal theory but had been used to a larger degree of local freedom and to a more active part in managing their own affairs than any other people in the world at that period. They were, indeed, loyal to the Crown, and if they had been allowed to go their own way in America, with a minimum of interference by King or Parliament, would have been well content to remain within the empire. Among them was an almost infinite gradation among the shades of opinion as to just how much interference would be allowable or bearable, and as to what the nature of the imperial tie was or should be. In this group, Jefferson was one of the most advanced in his views. Apart from specific grievances and from legal theory, what appealed subconsciously to most Americans was probably the question posed by Jefferson in his *Summary View* when he asked in the course of his argument, "Can any reason be assigned why 160,000 electors in the island of Great Britain should give law to four millions in the states of America, every individual of whom is equal to every individual of them in virtue, in understanding, and in bodily strength?" [10] Or the questions soon to be posed by Tom Paine, such as "To know whether it be the interest of this continent to be Independent, we need only ask this easy, simple question: Is it the interest of a man to be a boy all his life?" Echoing Jefferson he said it was absurd to think of a continent as being ruled by an island, and of its inhabitants as having constantly to be running three thousand miles with a tale or a petition, and waiting months or years for a decision.[11]

Had the "boy" been taken into partnership, as the Dominions of today have been, and as Jefferson and some other Americans then suggested doing, the imperial household and family might not have been broken up. It required, however, nearly another century and a half for Great Britain to advance to that stage of imperial and political wisdom. She insisted on keeping America in leading strings, much as in the next century, Queen Victoria insisted upon keeping her son, the Prince of Wales, who might well have echoed Paine's question as to whether it is the interest of a man to remain a boy all his life.

In spite of all the shades of opinion and of the insuperable difficulties in the then prevailing political psychology on both sides of the Atlantic, this aspect of the Revolution was clear-cut and publicly discussed.

There was a second aspect which was no less important, which was as fully realized, but which was kept as much behind closed doors as possible. That was, who should rule in America itself? In this chapter we have spoken of Jefferson's ideas as to the imperial relation. Interested and decisive as he was on gaining the point that America should rule herself and not be ruled by another people meeting in a legislature 3000 miles away, he was then and always remained far more deeply concerned with the second problem of who should rule America if

---

[10] *Writings*, Ford, Vol. I, p. 436.
[11] *Cf.* J. T. Adams, *Revolutionary New England*, Boston, 1923, pp. 439 f.

she did achieve the possibility of ruling herself. We can never understand his policies and the shifts he made if we do not fully understand that for him the supreme concern of the statesman was the good of the individual citizen rather than abstract theory or forms of government.

Meanwhile, probably quite unknown to Jefferson, Hamilton, the young immigrant from the British West Indies, was pursuing his ambition and career in New York. While in St. Croix, and only twelve years old, the marvellously precocious boy had already written to a friend that his ambition was "prevalent" and that he condemned "the grovelling condition of a clerk or the like, to which my fortune, etc.," condemned him there. Unlike most precocious youngsters Hamilton was to show as a man both power of mind and strength of will, but in his first few years after his arrival in America he was still the boy with much of the enthusiasm of youth. In 1774 he was only seventeen years old, yet we find him already making a speech at a "meeting in the fields" in New York, called to discuss the measures to be taken in connection with the Boston Port Bill, and, soon after, writing pamphlets in defense of the revolutionary movement.

These were naturally immature, though remarkable for a boy. Their chief interest lies in his enunciation of doctrines which he himself was to oppose strongly on many occasions later. He approved, for example, of waging war by commercial means, such as the non-importation agreement. Such agreements as these, neither to import nor to export, contained the germs of Jefferson's later Embargo Acts. Picking up a popular idea of the discussions of the day he also, with youthful enthusiasm, upheld the doctrine of natural rights, which he would have denounced a few years later. At this time, however, he asserted that "Men may betake themselves to the law of nature; and, if they but conform their actions to that standard, all cavils against them betray either ignorance or dishonesty. There are some events in society to which human laws cannot extend, but when applied to them lose all their force and efficacy. In short, when human laws contradict or discountenance the means which are necessary to preserve the essential rights of any society, they defeat the proper end of all laws, and so become null and void." [12]

In view of his later opinions it would be interesting to know just what people Hamilton had in mind when he wrote that they were to decide when, and what, laws might contradict the means necessary to preserve the essential rights of society, and how. In other words, we again come back to the question of who is to rule. Hamilton was already making friends among the rich and socially distinguished in New York and northern New Jersey, such as the Livingstons, Schuylers, and others, who had their own ideas on this question, as well as on the relations to Great Britain. Many of the people of privilege and position had already become greatly alarmed at the spirit shown by mobs, and by the demands of the "common people" for an increasing voice in the government. "The heads of the mobility grow dangerous to the gentry," wrote Gouverneur Morris from New York to Penn, "and how to keep them down is the question." He added that they were beginning to count their chickens before their eggs were hatched, and even before the eggs were half laid, and were disputing as to whether the future government should be "founded upon aristocratic or democratic principles." In other words the old dispute between Winthrop and Hooker in Massachusetts and Connecticut was again becoming a critical issue on a larger stage. "I see," Morris continued, "and I see it with fear and trembling that if the disputes with Great Britain continue, we shall be under the worst of all possible dominions, we shall be under the domination of a riotous mob." [13]

[12] *Hamilton's Works,* Lodge, Vol. I, p. 129.
[13] Force, *American Archives,* Ser. IV, Vol. I, pp. 347 ff.

New York society was split on the point of submission to England, but there was little difference of opinion among its members as to submission to what they called "the mob." Although Hamilton was to join the revolutionary cause, he finally accepted only that aspect of it which demanded the general right of the colonies to manage their own affairs. The boy of seventeen was to grow up among those who firmly believed that *they* were the ones who should govern for all the colonists, and that the safety of the state would be endangered if their personal privileges were in the least curtailed. Jefferson, on the other hand, though neither a demagogue nor a "mobocrat," was never to waver in his belief that in the unique America of his day the people should constitute at least the final fount of power.

CHAPTER IV

CONGRESS

UNLIKE the young Hamilton, Jefferson did not possess ambition in the sense of looking forward to making a "career" for himself which would bring him power, prestige, or fortune. Such an ambition is wholly legitimate, but many years' familiarity with Jefferson's writings has convinced me that such an attitude toward the world and himself was quite alien to his nature. It is an advantage of agriculture that in addition to being a means of livelihood it is in itself a satisfying way of life to those who love it, and the Virginians of that day did love it. Washington, with his intense interest in Mount Vernon, in his crops and everything concerning farming; Jefferson with his affection for Monticello and his careful noting of the first appearance of this or that in the spring and of all that might increase the efficiency of farm work, were but examples of the best planter class of their time. Wherever either travelled, he had his mind constantly on the soil and how to make it productive; and each, in spite of public spirit and a sense of obligation to perform public duty, was always longing to be back in his own home living the life of a planter and not of a statesman. Neither in his military nor his political period did Washington care anything about a notable career. He performed painstakingly the duties to which his country unmistakably called him, but his heart was always at Mount Vernon, and his great desire was to return to his life of farmer and country gentleman.

Although Jefferson's range of intellectual and æsthetic interest was far wider than Washington's, his attitude toward life was much the same. He would have much preferred to have lived on his estate with his family, books, ideas, and music than to have been forced upon the stage of public life. As a boy he had started with all that Hamilton had lacked—moderate wealth, social standing, high connections, an assured future position in his native "country," as he called Virginia, and with his life rooted in ancestral acres. Using the word in no invidious sense Hamilton perforce had to be an adventurer. He had to transfer himself to a country where he was not known, dependent upon the charity of relations, and there carve out a career for himself among strangers in a mercantile community. Ambition and egoism, both of which he possessed in full measure, had to be, under the conditions, his very shield and buckler if he was to rise above an obscure and humble position in the new land to which he had come.

The answer which Jefferson had drawn up to the conciliatory propositions of Lord North, after being moderated somewhat in committee, was reported to the House on June 10, and the following day Jefferson set out on his journey to Philadelphia. The roads were bad, and ten days were consumed in travelling from the capital of Virginia to that of Pennsylvania. Congress, of which the newcomer was the youngest member but one, had already been in session for five weeks when he took his seat. Perhaps no other representative had been awaited with equal eagerness. His *Summary View of the Rights of British North America* had been reprinted in the city where Congress was sitting, and had probably been read by every member. Virginia was the leading colony in wealth and population, and her lead in the matter of Lord North's offer was being awaited with keen anxiety. Not only was Jefferson bringing the document with him, but his arrival had been delayed because the former President of Congress had insisted that the bearer remain at Williamsburg to draft it himself.

The importance of Virginia as a pivotal state was well understood and had been one of the compelling reasons for the appointment of Washington as Commander-in-Chief. Jefferson was also well known, though not in person, to many of the members. As John Adams wrote many years later, "Mr Jefferson had the reputation of a masterly pen: he had been chosen a delegate in Virginia in consequence of a very handsome public paper which he had written for the House of Burgesses," and again, "Mr Jefferson came into Congress in June 1775, and brought with him a reputation for literature, science, and a happy talent of composition. Writings of his were handed about remarkable for the peculiar felicity of expression." [1]

Jefferson's power and influence as a statesman were to owe no more to his tongue than had his career as a lawyer. Although he was eventually to weld together a great political party out of heterogeneous materials, and twice to serve as leader of it in the office of President of the United States, he was well aware of his own shortcomings as an orator. Shy, modest, and reserved, he did his best work by his pen and in conversation among a small group. In the same letter from John Adams to Timothy Pickering in 1822, from which we have just quoted, Adams wrote of Jefferson that "although a silent member in Congress, he was so prompt frank, explicit, and decisive upon committees and in conversation—not even Samuel Adams was more so—that he soon seized upon my heart." [2]

Speech-making in the present day of mass meetings and the radio has come to be considered an indispensable factor in the success of a statesman or certainly of a politician. It is hard to say, for example, what might happen not only to their personal fortunes but to their governments if Mussolini and

---

[1] *Works of John Adams*, C. F. Adams, Boston, 1850, Vol. II, pp. 511, 513.
[2] *Ibid.*, p. 514.

Hitler were suddenly stricken dumb. Jefferson was practically
unknown as a speaker. In his service in Congress he probably
did not rise to say even a word or two more than half a dozen
times. Adams says he never heard him but three. He almost
never spoke in a public meeting. If it is difficult to understand how such a man could become the creator and leader of
a democratic party made up for the most part of scattered,
disunited, and leaderless groups and individuals among the
ordinary people, we may recall what Adams said of the matter
in his *Autobiography*. Commenting on Jefferson's lack of ability in speaking, Adams wrote that "From all I have read of
the history of Greece and Rome, England and France, and all
I have observed at home and abroad, eloquence in public assem-
blies is not the surest road to fame or preferment, at least, unless it be used with caution, very rarely, and with great reserve.
The examples of Washington, Franklin, and Jefferson, are
enough to show that silence and reserve in public, are more effi-
cacious than argumentation or oratory. A public speaker who
inserts himself, or is urged by others, into the conduct of affairs, by daily exertions to justify his measures, and answer
the objections of opponents, makes himself too familiar with
the public, and unavoidably makes enemies. . . . In a course
of years, a nation becomes full of a man's enemies, or at least,
of such as have been galled in some controversy, and take a
secret pleasure in assisting to humble or mortify him." [3]

As Jefferson's organization of his party lies almost a quarter of a century beyond the period of which we are now writing, we need not here discuss his marvellous organizing genius
or methods, but we may note that under the conditions of the
time Adams was probably right. Whether it might be possible
today to become, not a hidden power behind the throne, but
a great popular leader, a tribune of the people, without ha-
ranguing them, may be questioned. But as we shall have many

[3] *Ibid.*, p. 511.

opportunities of noting, Jefferson's mind went, as did no other American's of that era, in the direction in which went also those of ordinary plain men. He did not force it to do so, nor was he hypocritical about it. What he had evolved by thinking, reading, and observing, both in America and Europe, led him to an outlook, a *weltanschauung*, which coincided in fundamental points with that of the ordinary unprivileged American who merely reacted to his environment, and developed emotionally and instinctively that *Americanism* which Jefferson attained to intellectually. Meanwhile he was to become known to every American as the exponent and defender of that Americanism in a succession of pronouncements from time to time without creating those enemies everywhere which a constant appearance in public life and controversy would have brought upon him, as Adams pointed out.

He had been in Congress but five days when he was placed on a committee to draft a "Declaration of the Causes and Necessity of Taking up Arms" by the Americans. It was properly felt that the creation of a Continental Army and the appointment by Congress of Washington to command it, required explanation. Before Jefferson had arrived at Philadelphia, a committee had been appointed to draft the document, but Congress had disapproved of it as drawn, and Jefferson and John Dickinson were added to the committee to draw up a new one.

There were at that time few Americans of any class who genuinely desired independence and a complete rupture with the empire. Short of that there were innumerable opinions as to how far or how fast to go in attempting to influence the British Government in its course. In every step that was taken in every colony the greatest care had to be exercised to go fast enough for the radicals and not too fast for the conservatives. Dickinson, much liked in Congress, belonged to the latter group, and Jefferson to the former. This, apart from Jefferson's reputation for writing, is probably the reason why they both were added to the committee. Jefferson and Adams, in their old age, wrote many statements from memory of the happenings of their early days, often apparently without checking them up, and which therefore are often in error. When seventy-seven years old, Jefferson stated that he prepared a draft of the Declaration, but that it was too strong for Dickinson in its wording, and that Dickinson then prepared one retaining the last four and a half paragraphs of Jefferson's, this being approved by Congress. This statement seems oddly to have been accepted by almost every biographer and most editors in spite of the fact pointed out by P. L. Ford that an examination of Jefferson's draft with Dickinson's and the final form does not bear it out.[4] Dickinson, throughout, retained many of the ideas and expressions of Jefferson, but an examination of the first and revised drafts made by Jefferson himself indicates that on this occasion his "peculiar felicity of phrase" rather failed him, and that the final form as modified by Dickinson was far better than Jefferson's own draft. In a document discussed in committee it is always difficult to attribute a particular idea or phrase to any one, but it is certain that some of the most famous passages of this document, which was read before the army and in almost every home, and which stirred America to its depths, either did not appear in Jefferson's drafts or were much altered for the better. We look in vain, for example, in the Jefferson drafts for the passage which has been so often declaimed by school boys beginning "Our cause is just. Our union is perfect—our internal resources are great," and so on. Comparing Jefferson's slow and cumbrous wording which is changed in the final version into "We fight not for glory or conquest," it can be seen how much he had still to learn before writing the Declaration of Independence. On the other hand, the ringing words do not seem to fit either the mood or style of Dickinson who was cautious, hesitating,

[4] *Works,* Ford, Vol. I, p. 474 n.

rather timorous and working for complete reconciliation with England.[5]

Whatever may be the solution of a rather difficult problem, Jefferson was promptly put on another committee, consisting of Franklin, John Adams, R. H. Lee, and himself, to draft a reply to Lord North's motion. As Jefferson had prepared the reply for Virginia, which had been approved by Congress, the committee members asked him to draft the Congressional one. He did so, but here again we are faced by a considerable difference in phrasing between the Jefferson draft as preserved and the final one submitted. The reply was adopted by Congress on July 31, and that body adjourned next day. Jefferson at once returned to Monticello.

He had now plenty to think about before the re-convening of Congress the following year, to which body he was again elected. As to the first aspect of the Revolution, that of the problem of relations with Great Britain, his mind was made up. His reasoning on the subject, based largely on his historical approach from the Saxons, may have been rather peculiar to himself, but the position to which it led was that of most of the patriot leaders, excluding a few very extreme radicals like Samuel Adams or extreme conservatives like Galloway. Jefferson insisted upon a British respect for American rights and liberties, but greatly desired some settlement of the dispute which might permit America to remain within the empire.

In the draft he prepared for the "Declaration on the Causes of Taking Up Arms," he had written that in order that "this declaration may not disquiet the minds of our good fellow subjects in any parts of the empire, we do further assure them that we mean not in any wise to affect that union with them in which we have so long & happily lived and which we wish so much to see again restored." [6]

[5] See G. H. Moore, *John Dickinson, The Author of the Declaration on Taking Up Arms*, N. Y. Hist. Soc. Pubs., 1890.

[6] *Writings*, Ford, Vol. I, p. 474.

Jefferson's kinsman, John Randolph, brother of Peyton, had finally decided to remain loyal to the king, and had fled to England with his two daughters, his son remaining in Virginia to join the patriots. It is episodes like this which help us to appreciate the difficult situation of so many, particularly of the upper classes. Both John and Peyton Randolph had been sent to England for their education and both had been admitted to the Inner Temple in London. They were torn between their loyalty to the king and empire and that to their own native Virginia. Intellectually honest and highly cultured, they found themselves at last on opposite sides. In such cases, however, the ties of blood and friendship as a rule held firm and prevented those who chose different public loyalties from becoming private enemies.

During the summer at Monticello, Jefferson wrote to Randolph, then in England, that "I am sorry the situation of our country should render it not eligible for you to remain longer in it. I hope the returning wisdom of Great Britain will, ere long, put an end to this unnatural contest. There may be people to whose tempers and dispositions contention is pleasing, and who, therefore, wish a continuance of confusion, but to me it is of all states but one, the most horrid. My first wish is a restoration of our just rights; my second, a return of the happy period when, consistently with duty, I may withdraw myself totally from the public stage, and pass the rest of my days in domestic ease and tranquillity, banishing every desire of ever hearing what passes in the world. . . . I am sincerely one of those [who wish reunion with their mother country] and would rather be in dependence on Great Britain, properly limited, than on any other nation on earth, or than on no nation."[7] Jefferson was hoping that the British Government might agree to a compromise which would secure both American liberty and a continuance of the imperial connection, but,

[7] *Ibid.,* Vol. I, pp. 482 ff.

if not, then he would stand by America in the dispute. This decision taken, there was nothing to do but wait on events from across the water. It was, as we have said, the position taken by the great central body of Americans, including the young Hamilton, who were neither extreme Loyalists nor extreme separatists.

But there was the second aspect of the Revolution which Jefferson like others had to consider that summer. If the quarrel with England should be pushed to an extremity, and if America should become independent of the empire, who would govern the new nation? There had been a good deal of violence during the past few years. Even among the patriots many had condemned and looked with fear on such unlawful acts as, among others, the destruction of the tea at Boston. Especially in the larger cities in the North, where groups of the working classes could be easily led into mob action, the well-to-do had been growing very anxious about the safety of both life and property. The eighteenth century was essentially one of privilege. It was part of the air which every one breathed. The governing class felt not only that it had the right, but that, for the preservation of property and society, it was its duty, to govern the whole community. The doctrine that each individual should have an equal voice in affairs, and that all should be enfranchised, seemed then as wild and dangerous as that of the enfranchisement of women or of slaves.

Conditions in America, where groups of men found themselves by necessity managing their own local affairs, and who had, over and over again, in thousands of advances from old settlements to wilderness, found themselves responsible for their own government, safety, and liberty, had bred a doctrine which cut counter to the prevailing one both in England and among the non-pioneering upper class in seaboard America. It was, however, with great dread that the American governing class regarded this encroachment by the "mob," and the new ideas seething in the developing American democracy.

In New England the governing class was made up of a comparatively few rich families in alliance with the clergy, an alliance that was to have great influence on Jefferson's career and reputation. Southward the clergy counted less, but whether, as in New York, the combination was of a few great landed families, rich merchants and lawyers, or as in the South one of the great planters, everywhere the fabric of society and the safety of property were conceived by the governing groups to depend wholly upon the retaining of control by themselves. Among them, the fears quoted in the previous chapter as expressed by Morris were well-nigh universal.

Although the necessities of the first aspect of the Revolution, that of protecting American liberties from Great Britain, raised difficulties enough, yet among the leaders there always appeared the menace of the second aspect, that of the problem of who should govern if America became independent. There were two reasons why this aspect should be alarming. First, in the ten years of discussion with the mother country the colonists had been driven from one legalistic interpretation of the imperial constitution to another until finally forced to take stand upon the ancient doctrine of certain "natural rights" as inherent in all men. Second, if American freedom was to be gained it could not be by the governing class alone. All Americans would have to fight or take some part in the struggle. If victory was won, what would be the attitude of the American democracy toward their own exercise of those "natural rights" which the leaders had had so emphatically to invoke? It was on this point that Jefferson was eventually to take a stand opposed to that of almost all the other revolutionary leaders and those who established the new American Government.

There was nothing new in the doctrine of a law of nature

and of natural rights. To go no farther back, the Romans had laid considerable stress on the law of nature which did away in certain cases with the distinctions of the Civil Law between persons of different classes, such as citizen and foreigner, slave and free. One of the legal maxims of the Antonine period was "omnes homines natura aequales sunt," *i.e.*, literally, "all men are by nature equal." This, however, was intended to be merely a legal and not a political maxim, and it was only gradually through the centuries that, as Maine says, the words began "to express the sense of a great standing wrong suffered by mankind" from governments and rulers.[8]

It is not necessary here to trace the development of the doctrine in general nor the sources from which Jefferson derived it for his own eclectic philosophy. We may say, however, that these were almost wholly English and not French, as was asserted for political reasons during his lifetime and has often been repeated from ignorance since. As we shall note later, it was to the political interest of the Federalists, whose stronghold was in New England, and especially of the New England clergy, to try to link Jefferson, who declined to discuss his religion, as closely as possible with the infidelism of the French Revolution. Some years ago the French historian, Bernard Faÿ, stated that not only Jefferson but Madison, Monroe, and "all the group of liberal politicians and patriots from Virginia" found certain inspirations in the French philosophers. Professor Faÿ, not seldom mistaken in his understanding of American psychology and intellectual life, is quite wrong in claiming that the political philosophy of Jefferson stemmed from the French *philosophes*. Indeed, another and abler French professor, Gilbert Chinard, who has spent nearly twenty years in studying Jefferson and who is the leading authority on him, has denied that the French influence on Jefferson's thought was of importance.

[8] H. S. Maine, *Ancient Law*, London, 1878, pp. 92 ff. *Cf.* also A. S. Ritchie, *Natural Rights*, London, 1895, and Carl Becker, *The Declaration of Independence*, New York, 1922, Chap. II.

Jefferson had read and noted some of Montesquieu and also of Voltaire, but as Chinard says "he used both books as repertories of facts rather than as founts of ideas." [9] For some years before 1776, "natural rights" and all theories of government were matters of common conversation. Years later, in writing to Henry Lee, Jr., of the Declaration of Independence Jefferson said that "all its authority rests on the harmonizing sentiments of the day, whether expressed in conversation, in letters, printed essays, on the elementary books of public right, as Aristotle, Cicero, Locke, Sidney, etc." [10] Almost entirely, Jefferson's mind had followed the main stream of classical and English thought, though he should have added to the above names that of a Scotchman, Lord Kames, who appears to have influenced him considerably.

Jefferson, however, accepted no ready-made philosophy of others. Using their thoughts as a basis he developed his own. Although, as we have said, the doctrine of natural rights had become a common one before 1776 in America for the reasons stated above, Jefferson's position with regard to it was almost unique in two particulars. First, the natural rights he believed in, he believed in quite as much with reference to any future government to be established in America as with reference to British overlordship. He believed that if the doctrine of natural rights offered a sound basis on which to assert the right of Americans against the British government, it was also a sound basis for insisting upon a wide sphere of individual and local freedom as against any future American government. This was essentially that difference between his own philosophy and that of others which forced him later to break with Hamilton and the rest of the Federalists.

He had also, however, developed for himself a distinction between what were natural rights and what were mere civil rights. In an important memorandum made by him and first

[9] *Life,* Chinard, p. vii.   [10] *Writings,* Ford, Vol. X, p. 343.

found among his papers and published by Professor Chinard, Jefferson sought to clarify his own mind as to this distinction.[11] As this document is of the greatest importance not only for his doctrine of *personal* rights, but also for that of States' rights, it must be quoted at some length.

Jefferson began by assuming that twenty individuals, strangers to each other, meet in a country not before inhabited, and wish to live together, that is, to form a society. He considered that each when alone was a "sovereign in his own natural right." But when they lived in contact with one another, each would be subjected to encroachment on his sovereignty by the others. Each would thus not be able to maintain some of the "rights" he had possessed in his solitary state unless the others, that is, society at large, agreed to protect him in them. Those rights which required social protection and agreement for their preservation would become *civil* rights.

Jefferson then continued: "As all their rights, in the first case are natural rights, and the exercise of those rights supported only by their own natural individual power, they would begin by distinguishing between those rights they could individually exercise fully and perfectly and those they could not. Of the first kind are the rights of thinking, speaking, forming and giving opinions, and perhaps all those which can be fully exercised by the individual without the aid of exterior assistance. Of the second kind are those of personal protection, of the acquiring and possessing property, in the exercise of which the individual natural power is less than the natural right. Having drawn this line they agree to retain individually the first Class of Rights or those of personal Competency; and to detach from their personal possession the second Class, or those of defective power and to accept in lieu thereof a right to the whole power produced by a condensation of all the parts. These I conceive to be civil rights or rights of Compact, and are

[11] Printed in *Life*, Chinard, pp. 80 ff.

distinguishable from Natural rights, *because in the one we act wholly in our own person, in the other we agree not to do so, but act under the guarantee of society.* [Italics mine.]" At the end of the document Jefferson made the application to a confederation of states, which we shall consider later.

In the theory of the hypothetical formation of a society Jefferson followed Hobbes and Locke, but his theory of liberty was wholly different from that of Rousseau, and of the French Declaration of the Rights of Man of 1793. In the formation of a society Jefferson considered that the individual members retained one whole group of rights, those they could exercise without the help of other members of society, and gave up others for the sake of enhanced security. "Liberty," in Jefferson's opinion, as Chinard comments, "except liberty of speech and thought, cannot be unlimited and unrestricted in any society; it is a matter of bargain and exchange." The importance to Jefferson of a Bill of Rights at the formation of a society would clearly be fundamental in stating which rights were retained and which modified or given up.

We cannot enter at length upon a disquisition on rights, natural or other, but as in this volume we are considering the controversy between Jefferson and Hamilton as an episode not so much in itself but as forming part of a continuing controversy in our history, a few words may be allowed. As we have seen, in Roman law the "law of nature" had a purely juridical meaning, and served to mitigate to a certain extent the injustices in a social sense of the civil law. I think it may be questioned, however, whether in the political sense, which natural rights later came to assume, they were not based upon not only a false but a dangerous meaning.

In a pre-social state, a solitary man would seem to possess no "rights." He is, indeed, in a genuine "state of nature," but would not a tiger or a crocodile have as much "right" to kill the man as the man would have to kill them, and so on? In a

pure state of nature the only right is that of might. It is true
that a state of nature is not always as Hobbes and others considered it a state of war. There are innumerable instances of
animal communities which indulge in mutual help. In a highly
differentiated one of that sort, as among the ants, one group,
such as the warriors, who give up seeking for food in order to
protect the other groups, might claim a right to their share
of the food which could not be raised safely unless they fought
instead of raising food for themselves. But even such "rights"
can be only the resultant of co-operative and social life. An
isolated individual, human or animal, may have the freedom to
do as he will and can in the face of a universe full of hostile
forces, but it is impossible to conceive of his having a right to
do any of these things in the modern sense of right, that is as
something to which he is entitled regardless of the rest of the
universe. He has no "right" to ample food, to a mate, to his
cave or other "home," to killing, to protection, to self-expression, to anything, any more than he has a "right" to fine
weather or not to be wet by rain, unless he can gain these
things which he claims by his own powers.

As social life develops, rights do come into being, which
vary in different types of society and at different stages of the
same society. But these are civil and not natural rights. They
are not abstract or logical but develop because society best
develops by allowing and protecting them. We may compare
what the late Justice Holmes said of the common law. Its life,
he wrote, "has not been logic; it has been experience. . . . The
very considerations which judges most rarely mention, and always with an apology, are the secret root from which the law
draws all the juices of its life. I mean, of course, the consideration of what is expedient for the community concerned." [12]

It is hard to see how Jefferson's definition of natural rights

[12] Cited by C. E. Merriam, *American Political Ideas, 1865–1917*, New York,
1929, p. 173.

can stand when he calls them "those which can be exercised individually and fully as contrasted with those which need for their exercise the help of the society." I can, for example, steal or murder without the help of any one, but it cannot be claimed that that is a natural right, except in the sense that I could do such things in a pre-social state in which the victim would have received no help from society and I no punishment. If it be claimed that these things are not natural rights because of their "immorality," then the idea of morality again brings in society. If, once more, it be said that they are not natural rights because they cannot be indulged in without the consent of society, then what becomes of the "natural" quality of *any* right? Aside from the long struggle, lasting for centuries and with thousands of victims, which was required for even a small part of mankind to obtain relative freedom of thought and speech, it is all too sadly evident today, in such countries as Italy, Germany, and Russia, to mention the worst in this respect, that such freedom cannot be exercised by "individual power" but only with the consent or aid of society as a whole. This would seem, therefore, to put such rights in the category of civil rights, and indeed wholly clear the board, as I think it has to be cleared, of any natural rights at all in the modern sense.

The doctrine of natural rights, however, has played an enormous part in the gaining of freedom for the modern world. What these "rights" have really represented, however, in my opinion, have been the "ideals" of the minimum of freedoms required by the most advanced part of a society when itself advancing. By the use of freedom of thought, speech, and the press, society had already advanced and was advancing very rapidly by the end of the eighteenth century. The "natural rights" claimed were useful tools, and enjoyable in themselves, as I believe they must ever be in a free and rising society. Had they, nevertheless, been considered as ideals, partly achieved, which must at all hazards be preserved and enlarged and not allowed to be abridged by law, instead of as "rights," it would perhaps have saved much disillusionment and strife in the centuries to follow.

We have noted that as natural rights passed from the status of useful legal fictions to that of political demands they altered their character. The very name, "rights," seemed to give them an eternal and universal validity as demands regardless of society. Because certain things were deemed highly desirable and essential they ceased to be ideals to be striven for, and were called "rights" in the modern sense, valid claims to be demanded whether or not society could provide them. As society is passing in its preoccupations from the political to the economic stage, and as the meaning of natural rights has already been warped, there is now a growing tendency to consider any *general desire* for an economic good as a *"natural right."* Just as there is danger, in a legal system, of certain purely legal or traditional concepts coming to be regarded as everlasting concepts of the science of law, thus producing what Roscoe Pound has called a "mechanical jurisprudence," so there is the same danger of such social concepts as "natural rights" becoming everlasting concepts in the science of society, and thus similarly producing a "mechanical sociology." This may result in the demanding of more from a given society than it can yield, causing a break-down of its particular type of civilization without another to take its place except after a long period of chaos and suffering. A distinction must be retained between those aims which make for the rise of civilization, and those which tend to break it down, though both may be desired at a given time. If certain desirable aims become considered as "natural rights," then all desirable aims tend to become so considered indiscriminately. The distinction between ideals and claims becomes lost and society first staggers and then falls under a load of demands against it which it cannot meet.

As Jefferson pondered that summer at Monticello, however, he could not escape basing his political philosophy on the natural right theory. It was the universal language of the advanced thinkers of his time. Nor could he foresee the entirely changed world of a century and a half later. It is interesting to note that just as the Romans had considered and used the concept of natural law only to mitigate the cruelties of law itself, so the eighteenth-century men used the concept only in the political field as then understood. Indeed, one of the not least interesting features of Jefferson's theory as to the distinction between natural and civil rights was that it ruled economics out of the field of natural law. He deliberately excluded property from being a natural right because it could be maintained only by the help of society, and it was therefore, according to him, a civil right only. He did so not because he was a communist or even a parlor socialist, but because he believed that the logic of his theory demanded it. He would have equally excluded many of the modern demands in the name of natural rights, such as "the right to work," the right to support from the state, and so on. If we accept the theory of natural rights, Jefferson's distinction between them and civil rights would appear to be just; and the natural rights doctrine was held by practically every leader of the time among the patriots, Hamilton included.

The summer of 1775 was an anxious one, though Jefferson went ahead with the development of Monticello. He was now thirty-two years old and his domestic responsibilities were very considerable. His "family" in Albemarle consisted of thirty-four free persons and eighty-three slaves, or one hundred and seventeen people for whom he was wholly or partly responsible. He was to have in all six children, of whom only three grew beyond infancy, and he was deeply devoted to them with all the depth of his sensitive and affectionate nature. During this summer there was added to the ordinary anxieties of his "family" not only the quarrel with England but the illness of his second child, then about one and a half years old. Although Congress convened on September 5, Jefferson was waiting at Monticello for the death of his daughter, which occurred soon after. On the 25th he set out for Philadelphia where he arrived after a fast journey of six days on October 1, full of anxiety for his wife and also for his mother whom he had had to leave dangerously ill. Moreover, Lord Dunmore had been threatening military operations in Virginia, and there was talk of his trying to stir the slaves to revolt. Although Jefferson's slaves were always devoted to him, they outnumbered the whites of his family, mostly women and children, nearly three for one, and the dread of a servile insurrection always overhung the South. The day after he left Monticello he was also appointed Commander-in-Chief of the Militia of Albemarle County, and from these circumstances it was with a sad and much divided mind that he set to work on his Congressional duties.

Although he had hoped against hope that an accommodation of the imperial dispute could be reached, it was fast becoming evident that the king and his ministers were determined to crush the revolt in the colonies by force, and that not only could no peaceful settlement be won but that no guarantee could be secured for the future liberties of the colonists. Authentic news reached Congress of the despatch of troops, and of plans for an active campaign in the following spring, with the employment by England of foreign mercenary soldiers against her own citizens. The petition which had been sent by Congress to the King in its previous session had been contemptuously refused.

The change now coming over the feelings of even the most loyal of the colonial patriots is evident in a second letter which Jefferson wrote in November to John Randolph, then in England, acquainting him with the death of his brother, Peyton. Speaking of the King and of his rejection of the petition,

Jefferson continued, "To undo his empire, he has but one truth more to learn; that, after colonies have drawn the sword, there is but one step more they can take. That step is now pressed upon us by the measures adopted, as if they were afraid we would not take it. Believe me, dear Sir, there is not in the British empire a man who more cordially loves a union with Great Britain than I do. But by the God that made me, I will cease to exist before I yield to a connection on such terms as the British Parliament propose; and in this I think I speak the sentiments of America. We want neither inducement nor power, to declare and assert a separation. It is will, alone, which is wanting, and that is growing apace under the fostering hand of our King. One bloody campaign will probably decide, everlastingly, our future course; and I am sorry to find a bloody campaign is decided on." [13] Well had Horace Walpole in England written months earlier of the American affair that "We are at our wit's end—which was no great journey. . . . The Americans at least have acted like men, gone to the bottom at once, and set upon the whole. Our conduct has been that of pert children: we have thrown a pebble at a mastiff, and are surprised it was not frightened." [14]

Jefferson was again placed on important committees but suddenly left Congress and departed hastily for home on December 28. Much has been made of this by his enemies, but I think unjustly. To mention only a few other instances, John Adams had left the same Congress on December 9, and did not return until February; later he was to remain for long periods at his home in Massachusetts while President; and during the Civil War his grandson, Charles Francis Adams, tarried six weeks to attend the wedding of his son after being appointed Minister to England in a crisis. We have already pointed out

[13] *Writings,* Ford, Vol. I, p. 493.
[14] *Letters of Horace Walpole,* ed. Mrs. Paget Toynbee, Oxford, 1904, Vol. IX, p. 107.

the anxieties with which Jefferson left Virginia immediately after the death of his daughter in September. Since then, for some reason, he had been unable to receive any word from home, although he himself had written regularly every week. He could learn nothing of the health of either his wife or his mother. Lord Dunmore was threatening Norfolk with British ships, and did bombard and burn the city four days after Jefferson left Philadelphia on his way to Virginia. His anxiety had been steadily increasing. On October 31 he had written John Page that he had never, since starting from Monticello, "received the scrip of a pen from any mortal breathing." [15]   In November he repeated the complaint to his brother-in-law, Francis Eppes, saying he had been unable to find out anything about his family even by inquiries directed to others. "I had hoped that when Mrs. Byrd came I could have heard something of them; but she could tell me nothing . . . The suspense under which I am is too terrible to be endured. If anything has happened, for God's sake let me know it." [16]   No explanation has ever been found for this lack of news, though the statement made usually is that no explanation has been found for Jefferson's sudden departure from Philadelphia. All the above facts, combined with his own nature, would seem to be sufficient. He was one of the very youngest members of Congress. He was always modest as to his abilities and importance. He was the last man to believe that his presence in Philadelphia was essential to the safety of the country. Moreover, besides his personal anxieties, he was the head of the militia in the county from which he could get no information. He stood the strain for more than three months and then went home to investigate for himself. Nothing could be more natural, and the fact that he has incurred heavy blame from many writers for doing what he did merely shows that any stone is good enough to shy at a dog you do not like. When attending

[15] *Writings*, Ford, Vol. I, p. 489.   [16] *Ibid.*, p. 490.

the Congressional session of 1783 he was to stick to his post when almost every one else left. Now, however, he remained at Monticello for some months. His mother's health had evidently grown worse though she lingered until the last day of March. Within six weeks following her funeral Jefferson was once more in Philadelphia.

Meanwhile, the movement of events had been gaining momentum. The very day Jefferson reached the capitol, Congress passed a resolution instructing the various colonies to frame new constitutions for themselves. This at once drew Jefferson's attention back to Virginia. Here was a chance, in drafting the new constitution, to put his Liberal ideas into practice and perhaps enormously to advance the social welfare of the continent. It may again be emphasized that Virginia was then, even before her vast extension northwestward by Clark's expedition in the war, by far the largest and most important colony, being two-thirds the size of Great Britain. It was also the most populous, and the ideas introduced into her new government might well be expected to be of corresponding influence upon the America of the future. It may also be recalled that Jefferson believed local State governments would be of more direct importance to humanity than any Federal one to be formed. The latter would have to do only with certain general matters of importance to all, such as the conduct of foreign relations, whereas the former would impinge at all points upon the daily life of their citizens.

In spite, however, of the fact that he was keen to return and to take part in the framing of the new Constitution, he remained in his place in Congress, drawing up, nevertheless, a model of a possible form of government for his State. The suggestions he made are interesting as showing that he was not then, if ever, ready to go full length along the democratic road. He provided for complete separation of the three governmental branches, executive, judiciary, and legislative, the last to consist of two houses, a House of Representatives and a Senate. Representatives were to be elected by all male citizens of sound mind, twenty-one years of age, and who had either a quarter of an acre in a town, twenty-five acres in the country, or who paid a parish assessment. The proposed Governor, whom he called the "Administrator," the Senators, the Attorney-General, and a "Privy Council," were all to be appointed by the House of Representatives and not elected by the people. We need not enter upon the remainder of the political details, as the more social aspects of his plan are of more importance for an understanding of his outlook.

Among other great advances, he proposed that there should be a complete toleration of religious opinions, and that the church should be disestablished; that there should be no standing army except in time of war; that the press should be wholly free "except so far as by commission of private injury cause may be given of private action"; that the introduction of slaves into the state should be thereafter prohibited; that primogeniture should be abolished and that estates should be equally divided not only among sons but among all the children including the daughters. Except for military offenses and for murder he advocated the abolition of the death penalty, and that of torture in every case whatsoever.

This extraordinarily liberal document, far in advance of the age and indeed in some respects of our own, did not reach the Virginia Convention until too late to be used to any extent in the debates. It may be considered doubtful, however, whether Jefferson could have had most of his reforms embodied in the new fundamental law even if he had been present at the discussion. They struck too early and too hard at long-established property rights and privileges. Moreover he was about to be set a task in Philadelphia, the accomplishment of which he chose at the end of life to list on his gravestone as one of the three by which he wished most to be remembered by posterity.

Jefferson had not been a member of the Virginia Convention, because he was a member of Congress, but during the months he had spent at home he had not been politically idle. We have already noted the importance he attached to local affairs and to actions taken in Virginia, and his feeling that in helping to guide these he was doing the most useful work of which he was himself capable. The situation was fast approaching the crisis at which the great decision of declaring independence would have to be taken, and the decision of Virginia would be of vast influence upon all the other colonies. Not being a public speaker, Jefferson's political technique was that of working through committees, and, above all, of personal conversation and correspondence. The western counties were in motion, as the representation to the convention from Augusta County, next to Albemarle, is evidence. Jefferson's acquaintance both in the West and in Tidewater was extensive and important. He left Monticello May 7 and arrived at Philadelphia the 14th. On the 10th, Augusta County made its representations, and on the 15th the convention resolved unanimously that the Virginia delegates in Congress should declare "the United Colonies, free and independent States, absolved from all allegiance to, or dependence upon, the Crown or Parliament of Great Britain." [17] It is a fair inference from the combination of these dates that Jefferson had not wished to leave Virginia until assured of her stand, and that, by his own methods, he had been exerting his influence toward the desired end. Indeed, we get more than a hint of what he had been doing in a letter written to him long after by James Madison who, speaking of the instruction to the delegates as passed by the convention, wrote that "you probably can best tell where the instruction had its origin & by whose pen it was prepared. The impression at the time was, that it was communicated in

[17] *Writings of James Madison,* ed. Gaillard Hunt, New York, 1900, Vol. I, p. 32.

a letter from you to (Mr Wythe) a member of the Convention." [18]

Three weeks after Jefferson's arrival in Philadelphia, Richard Henry Lee, speaking for the Virginia delegation, submitted three resolutions to Congress, the first declaring that "these United Colonies are, and of right ought to be, free and independent States, that they are absolved from all allegiance to the British Crown, and that all political connection between them and the State of Great Britain is, and ought to be, totally dissolved." The second stated that it would be expedient to make foreign alliances, and the third that a plan for a confederated government should be drawn up and submitted to the respective colonies. The first of these resolutions was passed by Congress on July 2, and as Professor Becker has pointed out, "if we were a nation of antiquaries" we should celebrate the anniversary of our independence on the third and not on the fourth of July.[19]

Meanwhile, however, on June 10, Congress had appointed a committee to "prepare a declaration to the effect of the said first resolution," and appointed as members of the committee Thomas Jefferson, John Adams, Benjamin Franklin, Roger Sherman, and Robert R. Livingston; Jefferson, as first named, being chairman. Evidently his temporary absence from Congress had made no such impression on his fellow members as it seems to have done on his later critics.

Modern research into the Declaration of Independence has been exhaustive in trying to trace the exact wording of every phrase, and the changes made, to the various members of the committee and to alterations made by Congress sitting in secret and unrecorded session as a committee of the whole. Also the sources of the ideas and phrases in previous writings have been analyzed with almost meticulous scholarship. All of this cannot

[18] *Ibid.*, Vol. IX, p. 156.
[19] Carl Becker, *The Declaration of Independence,* New York, 1922, p. 3.

be recounted briefly, and in any case there is no need to recite again what has been so admirably set forth by others in works easily attainable. We may merely say that, with few exceptions, the text is practically that which Jefferson drew up for submission to the other members of the committee.

As to his sources, Jefferson wrote long after to Henry Lee, Jr., in a letter already quoted, that his object in writing the Declaration was "Not to find out new principles, or new arguments, never before thought of, not merely to say things which had never been said before; but to place before mankind the common sense of the subject, in terms so plain and firm as to command their assent, and to justify ourselves in the independent stand we are compelled to take. Neither aiming at originality of principle or sentiment, nor yet copied from any particular and previous writing, it was intended to be an expression of the American mind . . . All its authority rests then on the harmonizing sentiments of the day," whether expressed in the terms of old books and documents or in the conversation of the very hour.[20]

Two points stand out both in this statement and in his original draft of the document. One is his insistence on expressing the "common sense" of the situation, which is essentially characteristic of the man. As I have noted before, he was no doctrinaire. He had his general ideas, but in the application of them he always tried to conform not to rigidity of theory but to the "common sense" of whatever the situation might be, as he saw it. Every statesman must do the same, or he is a fanatic and not a leader of men, but it was this very trait which has drawn upon Jefferson some of the bitterest of the jibes from his enemies.

The other point is his modesty. One of the youngest members of Congress, chosen to make their Declaration to the world at large, with a reputation for felicitous phrasing, he might well

[20] *Writings,* Ford, Vol. X, p. 343.

have been led into trying to make the document wholly his own. Instead of that he not only took phrases and ideas from the wide reading he had noted in his *Commonplace Book,* and from Locke and others who had become almost as familiar to members of Congress as the Bible, but also from current documents which were even then passing from hand to hand.

One of these latter was the Virginia Bill of Rights, written by George Mason and adopted only two days after Jefferson was appointed to draft the Declaration. Although others might easily be cited we shall quote only from this, as most pertinent to the main thread of this book. The Virginia Convention had asserted, while Jefferson was at work on his own Declaration, that

"All men are by nature equally free and independent, and have certain inherent rights, . . . namely, the enjoyment of life and liberty, with the means of acquiring and possessing property, and pursuing and obtaining happiness and safety.

"That all power is vested in, and consequently derived from the people; that Magistrates are their trustees and servants, and at all times amenable to them.

"That government is or ought to be, instituted for the common protection and security of the people, nation, or community; of all the various modes and forms of government, that is best, which is capable of producing the greatest degree of happiness and safety, and is most effectually secured against the danger of mal-administration; and that when any government shall be found inadequate or contrary to these purposes, a majority of the community hath an indubitable, unalienable, and indefeasible right, to reform, alter, or abolish it, in such manner as shall be judged most conducive to the public weal." [21]

This document is itself full of echoes. We have seen that the phrase "all men are by nature free and equal" goes back

[21] K. M. Rowland, *Life Geo. Mason,* New York, 1892, Vol. I, pp. 483 ff.

at least to the Rome of the Antonines. The second paragraph is almost a paraphrase of Hooker's sermon in early Connecticut when he said that "the choice of public magistrates belongs unto the people" and "that they who have the power to appoint officers and magistrates, it is within their power, also, to set the bounds and limitations of the power and place unto which they call them." [22]

We need not, however, take time to trace all the sources of Jefferson's immortal Declaration. He perfectly succeeded in making it, as he said "it was intended to be, an expression of the American mind." That is the important thing about it, and also that "the American mind" has developed along the lines of thought and emotion laid down by Hooker in Connecticut and not by Winthrop in Massachusetts, by Jefferson of Virginia and not by Hamilton of New York. In the great crisis which had now come upon the colonies, the "American mind" was set on popular control of government, on freedom, independence, and equality; not on submission to dictatorial authority, on an obedient submission to a central power, nor on privilege. The ringing phrases of the Declaration appealed to Americanism in the depth of the people's souls. We need not consider the long indictment of George the Third nor other matters contained in the document. The core of the Americanism to which Jefferson gave lasting impetus is found in eleven lines:

"We hold these truths to be self-evident: that all men are created equal; that they are endowed by their Creator with certain unalienable rights; that among these are life, liberty, and the pursuit of happiness. That, to secure these rights, governments are instituted among men, deriving their just powers from the consent of the governed; that, whenever any form of government becomes destructive of these ends, it is the right of the people to alter or abolish it, and to institute a new

[22] *Vide supra.*

government, laying its foundation on such principles, and organizing its powers in such form, as to them shall seem most likely to effect their safety and happiness."

This paragraph, and Lincoln's Gettysburg speech, are the two literary springs from which Americans have drunk most deeply. There is no use in analyzing them in a spirit of carping criticism. They inevitably stir in the American heart the passion of Americanism in its most profound form. One point only need be noted. We have already seen why Jefferson could not list, according to his doctrine, property as a natural right. For the phrase "life, liberty, and property," used by the First Continental Congress, he substituted "life, liberty, and the pursuit of happiness." Property is not sacred according to Jefferson's idea, and neither is any government unless it conduces to both the "safety and happiness" of the people, although he went on to say that "governments long established, should not be changed for light and transient causes." Nevertheless, he believed in the ownership of private property, and in the due process of law.

On June 28, the committee reported the Declaration to Congress. On July 2, that body adopted the Lee resolution declaring the colonies independent, and on the 4th it adopted the Declaration as presented by Jefferson's committee, with some slight modifications. On the 19th it was voted that the Declaration should be "fairly engrossed," and on August 2, this engrossed copy was signed by such members as were then present, others signing later, so that neither was independence first declared on the fourth of July nor was the Declaration fully signed until nearly a month later. Except for the extremely meticulous, however, this now makes little difference.

The Declaration so solemnly passed by Congress was more than a political manifesto declaring bonds severed with the mother country. It was the affirmation by the representatives of the American people of a new social and political philosophy, an affirmation taken by the people themselves to mean that a new era was opening in which they should wield the power, and that nothing should stand in the way of their rights to freedom and at least their individual pursuit of happiness and well-being. The Declaration in its breaking of ties with Great Britain signified rebellion. In announcing a new relation between rulers and ruled, between privilege and the happiness of the citizen, it signified revolution.

Independence had now been declared, although the new States were still politically unconnected with one another. By July 12, a committee which had been appointed to draw up "articles of confederation and perpetual union" had completed its task, but the proposed new form of government was not adopted even by Congress until the fall of 1777, and not put into operation until 1781. Although Congresses continued to sit and administer general control, Jefferson's interest now shifted again to his own state, and he left Philadelphia in September of 1776, his great task done.

Meanwhile, in New York, the brilliant young Hamilton, then only twenty, had raised a military company, had fought in the army of Washington in the battle of Long Island, and had shared in the retreat to New Jersey and the attacks on Trenton and Princeton. Washington had been so impressed by the young man's ability with his pen that he had made him a secretary, and on March 1, 1777, he became one of the general's aides with the rank of lieutenant-colonel.

CHAPTER V

HOME AGAIN

JEFFERSON had been worrying about his family during his last weeks in Philadelphia. He had been re-elected for the next session of Congress but had declined. Writing in July to Edmund Pendleton he had said, "I am sorry the situation of my domestic affairs renders it indispensably necessary that I should solicit the substitution of some other person here in my room. The delicacy of the House will not require me to enter minutely into the private causes which render this necessary. I trust they will be satisfied. I would not urge it again, were it not unavoidable." [1]

His term was up August 11, but as at that time he was the only representative present from Virginia he remained at his post until September 2, though six weeks earlier he had had news from home which, as he wrote, had caused him great anxiety. He was deeply attached to his wife, who had become apparently a semi-invalid and was now expecting a child, which was born the following May. The transmission of news from Monticello was not only slow but infrequent, and Jefferson had to work in Philadelphia in a constant state of worry and even dread as to the condition of Mrs. Jefferson. He had scarcely reached home in September when on the 30th, Congress appointed him as one of the Commissioners to France, with Benjamin Franklin and Silas Deane, to negotiate a treaty of commerce and alliance. He had long wished to travel and here was a brilliant opportunity not only to do so but to perform at the same time a signal and historic service. Moreover, although all the evidence throughout his life points clearly to

[1] *Writings*, Ford, Vol. II, p. 61.

his genuine lack of desire for public office, and his preference for a quiet life in his own beautiful home, he did answer the call of duty again and again, and never shirked his public obligations. The best answer to his critics on this point, both contemporary and ever since, is the fact that his services were constantly demanded through nearly forty years by the people of his own county and state, by the Virginia Assembly, by President Washington, by Congress, and by the nation at large. Such a record is not that of one who is considered, by those best able to judge, either a shirker or a slack and inefficient public servant.

Like many other men, however, he had to take his wife's health into consideration. If the week to ten days which was required for the journey from his home to Philadelphia made it difficult not only to see but even to hear from the invalid and expectant mother, the six weeks or more and the war hazards on the sea of the trip to Paris made the foreign post impossible. Even so, Jefferson considered the matter with care and found it hard to decline. He finally, however, felt it imperative to do so, and wrote to John Hancock, then President of the Congress, that "it would argue great insensibility in me could I receive with indifference so confidential an appointment from your body. My thanks are a poor return for the partiality they have been pleased to entertain for me. No cares for my own person, nor yet for my private affairs would have induced one moment's hesitation to accept the charge. But circumstances very peculiar in the situation of my family, such as neither permit me to leave nor to carry it, compel me to ask leave to decline a service so honorable and at the same time so important to the American cause. The necessity under which I labour and the conflict I have undergone for three days, during which I could not determine to dismiss your messenger, will I hope plead my pardon with Congress, and I am sure there are too many of that body, to whom they may with better hopes con-fide this charge, to leave them under a moment's difficulty in making a new choice." [2]

Franklin could remain contentedly in Europe for years, leaving his ill-tempered, capable, and buxom spouse to take care of his house and children, legitimate and illegitimate, without anxiety. John Adams was of a different type, but the letters of his wife, during his stay in Paris, a few years later, testify to what a wife could suffer when completely cut off from even communication with her husband. She wrote in one that she had not heard from him or her son, John Quincy, for six months; and again that she had not received from the latter a single word in a year and a half. In one letter to her husband she wrote that "in the very few lines I have received from you not the least mention is made that you have ever received a line from me." [3] Abigail Adams was a strong woman, mentally and physically, but the remainder of the last letter quoted indicates the terrible strain under which she labored. With Jefferson it was different. His wife was ill. At the times of the births of her children, and usually for months afterwards, she was dangerously so. His home was neither a smug little town house like Franklin's nor a small New England farm with a few New Englanders as "help," like Adams's, but a large mansion on a lonely hilltop, 10,000 acres of land to care for, and nearly a hundred slaves. He himself was not only a solicitous husband but an extremely sensitive and considerate man. There could at present, under the circumstances, be no foreign mission for him, and throughout this earlier period of his public life, consideration must always be given to the conditions under which he had to serve.

Meanwhile he had been elected again to represent his county in the Virginia House of Delegates, and took his seat four days before he declined the Paris mission. Young James Madison

2 *Writings*, Ford, Vol. II, pp. 91 ff.
3 J. T. Adams, *The Adams Family*, Boston, 1930, p. 82.

was likewise there, for his first term. One reason for Jefferson's preferring service in the state legislature to that in Congress was his desire to revise the laws of the greatest State in the new union. With his ideas of the importance not only of the state governments but of what he considered would be their permanent place in the future, he was keen to begin the work of abolishing privilege in many of the feudal forms which were yet retained, and to start the State on its new career unhampered by class rights and distinctions. For the next two or three years his work was to lie almost wholly in this field, and his contribution was to be a notable one.

He was far from losing interest, however, in what we may call, even so early, "national" affairs, and his letters to John Adams and others show that he was deeply interested in the form to be taken by the government for the Confederacy. In a letter to Adams, May 16, 1777, he shot extraordinarily close to what has since become known as the "great compromise" in the later Federal constitution of 1787. "I learn from our delegates," he wrote, "that the confederation is again on the carpet, a great and a necessary work, but I fear almost desperate. The point of representation is what most alarms me, as I fear the great and small colonies are bitterly determined not to cede. Will you be so good as to collect the proposition I formerly made to you in private, and try if you can work it into some good to save the union? It was, that any proposition might be negatived by the representatives of a majority of the people of America, or of a majority of the colonies of America. The former secures the larger, the latter, the smaller colonies. I have mentioned it to many here." [4] This is almost precisely the compromise adopted by the Constitutional Convention in 1787 when a House of Representatives was provided for, representing the people of America by numbers, and a Senate representing it by States with equal votes, each House to have a

[4] *Writings,* Ford, Vol. II, p. 130.

negative vote on the action of the other in practically all cases but treaties with foreign powers. This suggestion by Jefferson, antedating the final solution by ten years, appears to have been almost wholly overlooked.

Immediately on taking his seat in the State legislature in 1776, Jefferson was at once placed on a considerable number of committees. Although attending to his duties on these, his chief interest was in an immediate assault on the privileges which he wished to sweep away. Five days after he appeared in the session he obtained leave to bring in two bills, one for the abolition of entail on estates and the other for a revision of the whole body of laws.

The ruling class in Virginia had been largely built up by primogeniture, which kept the large landed properties in the hands of the eldest son, and thus maintained leading families in their position. By intermarriage and in other ways, these families had become established as practically a ruling class. Jefferson himself was a large landowner and allied to this group by birth, but in his love for freedom he was opposed to an American ruling class quite as much as to a British monarch. His ideal appears to have been a State and nation,—and he usually thought of the nation in terms of what he wished for his own State,—made up of small landowners all of whom in time might become capable of taking part in government. He was far from believing that a man, simply because he belonged to the human species, was *ipso facto* entitled to a vote. We have already seen in his notes for a new constitution for Virginia that he had provided for the election by the people at large of representatives to a lower house only, and that the upper house and the chief officials were to be appointed by a sifting process which would far remove them from the local elections. Also we have noted that he established a property qualification, though a small one, for the franchise. He believed, moreover, that education was a requirement essential to make any voter worthy of exercising the privilege of voting, and that the form of occupation in which a citizen was engaged had also a distinct influence on character. His ideas are well brought out in a letter to John Adams which although written many years later may be quoted here:

"I agree with you," he wrote, "that there is a natural aristocracy among men. The grounds of this are virtue and talents." He then speaks of the aristocracy which had been based on bodily strength and power before gun-powder destroyed them. These were followed by an aristocracy of wealth and birth without, necessarily, virtue or talents. But, he continues, "the natural aristocracy I consider as the most precious gift of nature, for the instruction, the trusts, and the government of society. . . . May we not even say, that that form of government is the best, which provides the most effectually for a pure selection of these natural aristoi into the offices of government?" [5] Jefferson made it clear over and over again that he did not believe in government merely by the "mob."

He believed in America then, and later, because of its peculiar situation and opportunity. "I think," he wrote to Madison in 1787, "our governments will remain virtuous for many centuries; as long as they are chiefly agricultural; and this will be as long as there shall be vacant lands in any part of America. When they get piled upon one another in large cities, as in Europe, they will become corrupt as in Europe. Above all things I hope the education of the common people will be attended to; convinced that on their good sense we may rely with the most security for the preservation of a due degree of liberty." [6]

Jefferson never trusted the vast populations of cities as conservators of democracy. Indeed the combination of a self-governing people with the landless and usually property-less proletariat seemed insoluble to him. Without property of their

[5] *Writings,* Ford, Vol. IX, p. 425.   [6] *Ibid.,* Vol. IV, p. 480.

own, sometimes without means of subsistence, and, above all, without that self-reliant character which he considered as peculiarly the resultant of the life of the small farmer tilling his own soil as owner and not as tenant, Jefferson feared that a proletariat would exert its power in government to loot society and not to defend it. But to develop a nation of small landed proprietors there was needed a constant supply of land which could be obtained easily in fee simple and at not too great cost. This could not be the case if a comparatively few families should be allowed to engross huge tracts for themselves, and then preserve them by primogeniture and entail.

Jefferson's attack was thus launched not in a spirit of hostility to property but with the object of building up a sound and conservative electorate which because of education, substance, and character would make government stable and property safe. He felt that the wider the base of government, the firmer would be the structure, but he never believed in widening the base merely by extending the franchise. Unless the human material of the base were itself sound, there could be no strength or durability in any structure built upon it. So much for the political aspect of Jefferson's belief.

He also believed that the effect of his proposed reform would be beneficial from both the social and economic standpoints. In his view, to state the case with the simplicity of exaggeration, a system in which there were a few great magnates, living and tilling rather wastefully, surrounded by poor relations, poor families, and a great number of people without land, could never be satisfactory from the standpoint either of the social happiness of all or of the efficient use of the soil. His aim was a society in which landed property would be much more equally distributed among the people generally, who would thus feel the satisfaction and responsibility of ownership and who, because their properties were smaller, would farm them more intensively and carefully.

By taking this view, however, and by forcing the political issue, Jefferson naturally aligned against himself some of the most rich and powerful families in Virginia. As we have already noted, these never forgave him, but many considered him as a wild and dangerous radical, and ever after pursued him politically. In the debates on the bill, the leader of the opposition to the measure was Edmund Pendleton, of whom Jefferson wrote, long after, that "taken all in all, [he] was the ablest man in debate I have ever met with," adding that he "was one of the most virtuous and benevolent of men, the kindest friend, the most amiable and pleasant of companions." [7] Patrick Henry was another opponent of the bill. Nevertheless it was passed, and for better or worse, as one may consider it, a deadly blow had been struck at what we may call the hereditary landed aristocracy of the Old Dominion.

We need not detail the various committees upon which Jefferson served, nor the measures he introduced, save in so far as the latter gave expression to his leading doctrines and his position as a Liberal. The abolition of entail was merely the first step in the remodelling of the State, and he at once proceeded to further measures. As a member of the committee on religion he only partially succeeded, against a hostile majority, in beginning the work which eventually was carried to triumphant success some years later in his Statute of Virginia for Religious Freedom, the second of the three achievements he desired to have noted on his tombstone.

The Church of England had been the established church in the colony, and although its members had become outnumbered by those of the dissenting churches, the latter were still required to pay taxes for the maintenance of the established church while at the same time maintaining their own by voluntary subscriptions. Jefferson wrote that the legislature was flooded in 1776 with appeals for the abolition of this abuse,

[7] *Writings,* Ford, Vol. I, p. 50.

and that the argument brought on "the severest contests" in which he ever had been or was to be engaged. However, disestablishment and complete religious freedom, which were Jefferson's goals, could not be attained at that time. Both the clergy of the established church, and the laymen who were members of it, clung desperately to their privileged and wholly unjust position. "We prevailed," wrote Jefferson, "so far only as to repeal the laws which rendered criminal the maintenance of any religious opinions, the forbearance of repairing to church, or the exercise of any mode of worship; and further, to exempt dissenters from contributions to the support of the established church; and to suspend, only until the next session, levies on the members of that church for the salaries of their own incumbents." [8]

We have already noted the injustices caused by the inequalities in representation, more particularly as between eastern and western counties. It was not the least of these abuses that although a majority of the population of the entire state were dissenters, a majority of the legislature were members of the established church. Nevertheless, the progress made, though far from being what Jefferson desired, or was just, was by no means negligible. By the two measures spoken of, Jefferson had made enemies of much of the aristocracy of Virginia, and of the clergy and members of the established church. In fact, in his constant efforts, then and later, to achieve religious freedom, he was to make enemies not only of the clergy in his own state but of those in other states, notably New England, where there were also established churches.

We may pause a moment here to make two comments on Jefferson's devotion to Liberalism and his leadership of the movement in America in his lifetime. The first is, that other leaders who appealed to radical ideas and to the people at large before and during the revolution, mostly, like Patrick Henry and

[8] *Writings,* Ford, Vol. I, p. 53.

Samuel Adams, became conservative and even severely reactionary afterward. Jefferson was never to waver. Liberalism and love of liberty were not phases of his youth. They were of the very fibre of his being. Secondly, even his enemies have always admitted that he was a consummate "politician." Yet until a liberal party came into power in 1800 with Jefferson at its head, office and power were to be almost wholly the prerogatives of the conservatives. If he possessed all the political ability ascribed to him, and if he were the office-seeker painted by many, he would not, at thirty-three and with wide experience of public life, have deliberately and consciously made enemies of some of the most powerful forces in society, to wait a quarter of a century for the pendulum to swing in his favor. What he did, he did from nature and from deep conviction.

After securing the abolition of entails and what was then possible for religious freedom, Jefferson next desired a complete revision of all the laws of the state. A bill for this purpose was passed by both houses, October 26, 1776, and within a fortnight a committee of five was appointed for the purpose with Jefferson as chairman, the others being Edmund Pendleton, George Wythe, George Mason, and T. L. Lee. It was soon reduced to three by the death of Lee and the resignation of Mason, who although an extremely able man was not a lawyer, and who felt himself to be out of place.

At a preliminary meeting of the committee it was decided by three to two, Jefferson, Wythe, and Mason in the affirmative, that the procedure should be to preserve the general existing system, merely adapting it to new conditions and to the advance of thought, and not to draw up an entirely new one. Had Jefferson been the ardent theorist and doctrinaire claimed by some, instead of going about the matter in a common-sense way, and voting as chairman with Wythe and Mason, he would have welcomed the opportunity to become the head of an early "Brain Trust" and to make all things anew. The work of revision as parcelled out among the three members was slow and difficult, occupying much of their time until they reported the completed draft in the form of 126 bills to the legislature in February, 1779.

Meanwhile, Jefferson had been attending the sessions, to which he was regularly elected, and serving on a great variety of committees. In 1777 he had to be absent for a period owing to the birth, and, within scarcely more than a fortnight, the death, of his third child.

If Jefferson did not wish to make all things new, he did, however, desire to alter institutions in the direction of greater liberty and personal freedom, and without involving ourselves in references even to all the statutes which he revised we may confine ourselves to several which most clearly show his objective.

By act of the legislature he had already succeeded in breaking the entail of estates. The next step to which he proceeded was the abolition of primogeniture. "I proposed," he wrote, "to abolish the law of primogeniture, and to make real estate descendible in parcenary equal shares to the next of kin, as personal property is by the statute of distribution. Mr. Pendleton wished to preserve the right of primogeniture, but seeing at once that that could not prevail, he proposed we should adopt the Hebrew principle, and give a double portion to the elder son. I observed that if the eldest son could eat twice as much, or do double work, it might be a natural evidence of his right to a double portion; but being on a par in his powers and wants, with his brothers and sisters, he should be on a par also in the partition of the patrimony, and such was the decision of the other members." [9]

An artificial aristocracy, as contrasted with Jefferson's natural aristocracy, can only be built up and continue if sustained by hereditary possessions, so that a family may remain secure

[9] *Writings,* Ford, Vol. I, p. 60.

in power, wealth, and position even if the "virtue and talents" of Jefferson's natural aristocracy are lacking for a number of generations until they may appear again. We usually speak of an aristocracy as based on land and of a plutocracy as based on money. Both are artificial in the sense that in any given generation the power and influence of the temporary possessor may bear no relation to his own personal abilities. There is nothing much to be said for a plutocracy. There is a good deal to be said both for and against an aristocracy. Jefferson considered that the balance was on the negative side, and in doing away with the right of an owner to decide through whose hands his property shall forever descend, and also in forcing the equal division of it among all the children of the owner in each generation, he destroyed the possibility of the continuance of an aristocracy based on land. We shall see in later chapters how bitterly he opposed Hamilton's theories which he believed led direct to a permanent plutocracy based on money.

But he did not believe that a man would necessarily be a good citizen merely because he had a small property; or that, even with the abolition of entail and primogeniture, it would necessarily follow, because monopoly had been destroyed and real property made easier to acquire, that all men would be able to acquire it. These acts merely closed the door over which was written "aristocracy and privilege," and opened somewhat wider that over which was written "opportunity for all." Another door had to be opened marked "education."

The three bills dealing with education are of unusual interest. First there was the one entitled the "Bill for the more General Diffusion of Knowledge," which is worthy of the most careful consideration even today. Indeed, perhaps even more consideration than in Jefferson's own day. In the introduction to the bill, Jefferson indulged in some general reflections.

"Experience has shewn," he wrote, "that even under the best forms, those entrusted with power have, in time, and by slow operations, perverted it into tyranny; and it is believed that the most effectual means of preventing this would be, to illuminate, as far as practicable, the minds of the people at large, and more especially to give them knowledge of those facts, which history exhibiteth, . . . and whereas it is generally true that people will be happiest whose laws are best, and are best administered, and that laws will be wisely formed, and honestly administered, in proportion as those who form and administer them are wise and honest; whence it becomes expedient for promoting the publick happiness that those persons, whom nature hath endowed with genius and virtue, should be rendered by liberal education worthy to receive, and able to guard the sacred deposits of the rights and liberties of their fellow citizens, and that they should be called to that charge without regard to wealth, birth, or other accidental condition or circumstance; but the indigence of the greater number disabling them from so educating, at their own expense, those of their children whom nature hath fitly formed and disposed to become useful instruments for the public, it is better that such should be sought for and educated at the common expense of all, than that the happiness of all should be confined to the weak and wicked." [10]

In organizing this system Jefferson believed in a rigorous selection of those students who were to be educated at the public cost at every stage above the lowest. The system was to rest upon the common schools, of which there was to be one located in every school district into which the State was to be divided. In these the children were to be taught the "three R's," and, although they were not to learn the classical languages, the reading books were to contain such material as should give the pupils some knowledge of Greek, Roman, English, and American history. Scholars were to be taught in these schools at public expense for three years, girls as well as boys sharing

[10] *Writings*, Ford, Vol. II, pp. 220 f.

the advantages. Next above the common schools were to be a lesser number of grammar schools, receiving boarders. In these, boys were to be taught geography, grammar, Greek, and Latin, and the higher mathematics. The common school overseers, each of whom was to have ten schools in his charge, were to be given the duty of choosing from among the pupils who were too poor to continue with the grammar schools at their own expense, those who showed "the best and most promising genius and dispositions." These were to go to the boarding grammar schools at the cost of the public for two years more. At the end of that time, the best of them were again to be culled out and allowed to remain for another two years. Finally, in each school the best of these four years pupils was to be selected and sent to college for four years.

In another bill Jefferson provided for a thorough reorganization of the college of William and Mary, abolishing the school of theology, and establishing six professorships in moral law, history, anatomy, and medicine, natural philosophy and natural history, ancient languages, and modern languages. Finally, a free public library was to be erected at Richmond with an income of £2000 a year for the acquisition of books and maps.

As Professor Chinard well points out, "no system so complete, so logically constructed and so well articulated had ever been proposed in any country in the world."[11] It is moreover not unlikely, as he says, that Jefferson's plan, as published in his *Notes on Virginia* in the French edition of 1786, was the origin and source of the modern French educational system.

In this plan Jefferson added another stone to the edifice of his reorganized society. In the abolition of primogeniture and entail he had gone far in abolishing economic privilege and social class distinction. He had to that extent opened equality of opportunity to all. In his educational system he

[11] Chinard, *Life.*

would have opened another door looking toward the equality of intellectual opportunity. But no man knew better than he that all men are not equal in either ability or character. When he wrote that "all men are created equal" he never meant that they were all equally intelligent, strong-willed, honest, well-meaning, capable, disinterested or loyal, any more than he meant that they were all of the same height, bodily strength, health, or appearance.

Recognizing these distinctions he planned his social laws accordingly. He believed that self-government could not endure unless the citizens were educated, and also that the state, for its own sake, should develop the latent talent and intellectual possibilities of its people to the utmost. But Jefferson, who kept carefully detailed records of his crops at Monticello and of the development of various seeds, well knew that in a commonwealth all citizens are not capable of benefiting equally from opportunities nor of rendering precisely the same service to society. As a careful and efficient planter, Jefferson would not spend as much in fertilizing and cultivating one crop as another if the returns would not warrant it.

He believed that any sound-minded boy or girl was capable of benefiting from the rudiments of education, and would make a better citizen from acquiring them. From that point on, however, he believed in keeping open the door of equal opportunity only to the extent that a poor boy with a mind equal to that of a rich boy should not be debarred from continuing his education merely because of his poverty. In that way also the state might ensure the maximum benefit from the minds of its people. On the other hand, Jefferson did not believe that the money of the people, taken from them by taxation, should be spent in keeping boys in school and college for years whether they showed an aptitude and desire to benefit from such an enforced social expenditure or not. To have gone farther and made a higher education compulsory on all would have seemed as absurd to him as to have decreed that every crop on his farm, whether tobacco, potatoes, rye, corn, or what-not, must be treated and cultivated in precisely the same way as every other. His theory of government is admirably represented in the educational laws as drawn by him. In terms of the citizen, he believed in the maximum of equality of opportunity. In terms of the state, he believed in the minimum of compulsion and interference compatible with the training of all its citizens as citizens to the maximum of the capacity of each.

There was still one more step for him to take to secure liberty and opportunity for the individual, and he again returned to the attack on the established church in his "Bill for Establishing Religious Freedom." In some rough notes he made, perhaps while debating the earlier bill in the Assembly, we may see some of the aspects in which he regarded the subject. "The care of every man's soul belongs to himself," he wrote. "But what if he neglect the care of it? Well, what if he neglect the care of his health or estate, which more nearly relate to the state? Will the magistrate make a law that he shall not be poor or sick? Laws provide against injury from others; but not from ourselves. God himself will not save men against their wills. . . . No man has *power* to let another prescribe his faith. Faith is not faith without believing. No man can conform his faith to the dictates of another. The life and essence of religion consist in the internal persuasion or belief of the mind. . . . Compulsion in religion is distinguished peculiarly from compulsion in every other thing. I may grow rich by an art I am compelled to follow, I may recover health by medicines I am compelled to take . . . but I cannot be saved by a worship I disbelieve." [12]

In the bill itself he wrote that we are "Well aware that the opinions or belief of men depend not on their own will, but follow involuntarily the evidence proposed to their minds; that

[12] *Writings,* Ford, Vol. II, pp. 99 ff.

Almighty God hath created the mind free, and manifested his supreme will that free it shall remain by making it altogether insusceptible of restraint; that all attempts to influence it by temporal punishments, or burthens, or by civil incapacitations, tend only to beget habits of hypocrisy and meanness . . . to compel a man to furnish contributions of money for the propagation of opinions which he disbelieves and abhors, is sinful and tyrannical; . . . that our civil rights have no dependence on our religious opinions, any more than our opinions in physics or geometry; . . . that the opinions of men are not the object of civil government." Again he says, "that it is time enough for the rightful purposes of civil government for its officers to interfere when principles break out into overt acts against peace and good order; and finally, that truth is great and will prevail if left to herself; that she is the proper and sufficient antagonist to error, and has nothing to fear from the conflict unless by human interposition disarmed of her natural weapons, free argument and debate; errors ceasing to be dangerous when it is permitted freely to contradict them." [13]

Although Jefferson's labors in the revision of the laws extended to a great number of bills, one or two of which we shall mention, beyond the four named above, it was on these that he particularly based his hope for the reorganization of Virginia society. In his autobiography written late in life, referring to this task, he wrote that "I considered 4 of these bills, passed or reported, as forming a system by which every fibre would be eradicated of antient or future aristocracy; and a foundation laid for a government truly republican. The repeal of the laws of entail would prevent the accumulation and perpetuation of wealth, in select families, and preserve the soil of the country from being daily more and more absorbed in Mortmain. The abolition of primogeniture, and equal partition of inheritances, removed the feudal and unnatural dis-

[13] *Writings*, Ford, Vol. II, pp. 237 ff.

tinctions which made one member of every family rich, and all the rest poor, substituting equal partition, the best of all Agrarian laws. The restoration of rights of conscience relieved the people from taxation for the support of a religion not theirs; for the establishment was truly of the religion of the rich, the dissenting sects being entirely composed of the less wealthy people; and these, by the bill for a general education, would be qualified to understand their rights, to maintain them, and to exercise with intelligence their parts in self-government; and all this would be effected, without the violation of a single natural right of any individual citizen." [14]

The broad outlines of Jefferson's political philosophy have, I trust, already become clear. They were as remote as possible from the rapidly developing ideas of Washington's brilliant young aide Hamilton, who, during the years that Jefferson was at work revising both Virginian laws and Virginian society, was building up his logical system of a highly centralized nation with the strongest possible powers, knit together by finance. The boy, scarcely yet more than twenty, was turning out a series of reports, and letters that were almost reports, on military, political, and financial organization, and, although interested in few other subjects, he showed unusual command over at least the latter two of those. One other interest, indeed, he was soon to have, that in Miss Elizabeth Schuyler, a daughter of one of the richest and most influential families in New York, whom he married in 1780 when he was twenty-three. The unknown little boy, who had arrived in New York, practically orphaned and penniless, eight years before, had already had an amazing career, and his mind had attained to intense concentration.

On the other hand, the master of Monticello, as always, enjoyed allowing his intelligence to range over wide and varied fields. If one point has become clear, it is that Jefferson's

14 *Ibid.*, Vol. I, p. 68.

primary concern with the art or theory of government was its effect on the daily life and happiness of the individuals governed, as individuals. Not for him did the mere abstractions of "the state" or of "society" become real entities in themselves. The only reality behind these terms for him was the reality of individual human beings, individual men, women, and children.

In several of the revised laws Jefferson showed his humanity and his interest in those at the bottom of society, the criminal and the slave. The laws on crime and punishment were barbarous, and he tried to have them made more humane. Although the committee agreed with many of his suggestions, he noted that "the general idea of our country [Virginia] had not yet advanced to that point," and he could do little but abolish the death sentence in some cases. Witchcraft and sorcery still remained crimes, and rape, sodomy, and polygamy were to be punished by castration for a man, and for a woman by the boring of a hole at least a half inch in diameter through the cartilage of the nose. The principle of retaliation was also retained, so that a poisoner suffered death by the same poison he had administered; and a person who maimed another was to be similarly maimed himself. The criminal law and at that time punishments were less severe than those in England, but Jefferson was not able materially to hasten reform in this direction.

Nor could he do much more for the slaves. He was himself a slave-owner, though a most kindly one. So long as the slave economy held generally throughout the State there was no way to force an individual to break away from it. Aside from the impossibility of securing any other form of labor with which to run a large plantation, the lot of the negroes themselves as slaves was better than it would have been had they been freed. Jefferson, however, had constantly given expression to his hostility to slavery, and was to continue to do so throughout life, attempting to do all in his power for the amelioration, limitation, and eventual abolition of the institution. In view of public sentiment, the committee felt it to be best in revising the laws as to slavery merely to digest those already existing, and then when up for debate to bring in amendments. What Jefferson had in mind as to these was to propose that all slaves born after the passage of the Act should be declared free. These free negro children, according to his plan, were then to be brought up by their parents to a certain age, after which they should be supported by the State while being taught "tillage, arts or sciences according to their geniuses" until attaining the respective legal ages of eighteen and twenty-one for females and males, when they should be sent to some colony established for them, with ample implements and supplies.

It was, perhaps, a crude solution of the problem, although similar ones were to gain many devoted adherents in the next century. In spite of the Civil War, the problem has never really been solved yet. Commenting later on the reception of the solution he then proposed, Jefferson wrote that "it was found the public mind would not yet bear the proposition, nor will it bear it even at this day. Yet the day is not far distant when it must bear and adopt it, or worse will follow. Nothing is more certainly written in the book of fate than that these people are to be free. Nor is it less certain that the two races, equally free, cannot live in the same government. Nature, habit, opinion has drawn indelible lines of distinction between them. It is still in our power to direct the process of emancipation and deportation peaceably and in such slow degree as that the evil will wear off insensibly, and their place be *pari passu* filled up by free white laborers. If on the contrary it is left to force itself on, human nature must shudder at the prospect held up." [15] Unfortunately, colonization was never to prove practical, nor, naturally, acceptable to the negro himself, who

[15] *Writings,* Ford, Vol. I, p. 68.

knew only his surroundings in America and has never had the pioneer spirit.

We need not consider other laws as revised, or attempted to be revised, by Jefferson in his alloted share of the general task. In so far as their subject matter might allow, all would show the same spirit of liberalism and fit into his general social plan. The committee, which had prepared in all 126 bills, made its report on June 18, 1778, and in the course of time the legislature passed about 100 of them. The "Bill Establishing Religious Freedom" was not passed until 1786, and then only after a most bitter fight, which Madison carried through to success while Jefferson was in France. The latter's elaborate educational program was never put into operation. The plan for a public library was dropped completely, and his efforts to remodel the half-moribund college of William and Mary also failed. In spite of these failures it is quite fair to speak of Jefferson in these years as "the architect of Virginia government." [16]

Although Jefferson, who later kept his papers with extreme care, and was always particular about detailed accounts and memoranda, did not preserve his personal letters until 1779, we get occasional glimpses at this time of his activities other than those dealing with legislation. His love of music, which had indeed been a passion with him, is shown in a letter to an unknown correspondent, apparently in Italy, in June, 1778. After saying that "tho' much of my time is occupied in the councils of America I have yet a little leisure to indulge my fondness for philosophical studies," and suggesting topics for correspondence, he takes up the possibility of importing a private orchestra in an ingenious way.

In 1773 an Italian, Philip Mazzei, had arrived in Virginia and had settled a few miles from Charlottesville to experiment in the raising of grapes and olives. He was an extraordinary

---

[16] Dumas Malone, in *Dict. of Am. Biog.*, Vol. X, p. 20, col. 2.

man, with an extraordinary career ahead of him in which he
was to become first a naturalized citizen of Virginia, then of
Poland, and to live, first and last, in twenty-odd different cities
of the new and old worlds. Jefferson, always intensely interested in new ideas, and living at Monticello near Charlottesville, naturally came to know Mazzei, and it was probably
through him that Jefferson had been approached by the correspondent noted above. To this now unknown person he wrote:
"If there is a gratification which I envy any people in this
world, it is to your country its music. This is the favourite
passion of my soul, and fortune has cast my lot in a country
where it is in a state of deplorable barbarism. From the line
of life in which we conjecture you to be, I have for some time
lost the hope of seeing you here. Should the event prove so, I
shall ask your assistance in procuring a substitute, who may
be a proficient in singing, & on the Harpsichord. I should be
contented to receive such an one two or three years hence,
when it is hoped he may come more safely and find a greater
plenty of those useful things which commerce alone can furnish.
The bounds of an American fortune will not admit the indulgence of a domestic band of musicians, yet I have thought
that a passion for music might be reconciled with that economy
which we are obliged to observe. I retain for instance among
my domestic servants a gardener (Ortolans), a weaver (Tessi-
tore di lino e lin), a cabinet maker (Stipeltaio) and a stone
cutter (Scalpellino laborante in piano) to which I would add a
vigneron [one who looks after grape vines]. In a country
where like yours music is cultivated and practised by every
class of men I suppose there might be found persons of those
trades who could perform on the French horn, clarinet or haut-
boy & bassoon, so that one might have a band of two French
horns, two clarinets, & hautboys & a bassoon without enlarging
their domestic expenses." [17]

[17] *Writings*, Ford, Vol. II, pp. 158 ff.

We have already noted Jefferson's interest and taste in architecture, his talent for which was now employed by friends in the absence of professionals in the colony. The month after he had turned in his work on the revised laws to the legislature, we find him displaying a new facet of his indefatigable activity and curiosity in a letter to David Rittenhouse of Philadelphia, whose scientific attainments were to make him president of the American Philosophical Society and a Fellow of the Royal Society of London. Jefferson regretted that he had not been able to observe the eclipse of the sun (the first to be carefully observed in America), because his instruments, especially his timepieces, were not sufficiently accurate, and he asked Rittenhouse to make more accurate ones for him. It is this wide range of Jefferson's mind and the variety of his interests, which adds so much to our own interest in the man. Hamilton's mind, powerful as it was in the fields of government and finance, is singularly lacking in interest once we abandon those two fields. This statement has nothing to do with the question of the ability or influence of the two men. It is a simple statement of fact as to one aspect of each of them.

Another passage in the same letter to Rittenhouse leads us to another phase of Jefferson's thought—that of his attitude toward war. Mentioning the fact that he had heard that the scientist had been devoting much of his time to government and public affairs, he acknowledges the value of such services but adds "yet I am also satisfied there is an order of geniuses above that obligation, and therefore exempted from it, nobody can conceive that nature ever intended to throw away a Newton upon the occupations of a crown. . . . Cooperating with nature in her ordinary economy we should dispose of and employ the geniuses of men according to their several orders and degrees." [18]

This same belief that war, which is temporary, should not

[18] *Writings*, Ford, Vol. II, p. 163.

be allowed to destroy the humanities, was shown by him in another way about the same time. Four thousand prisoners who had been taken with Burgoyne at Saratoga had been sent to Virginia and encamped near Charlottesville. There they had settled down for the duration of the war, the officers renting houses as they could in the neighborhood, and the men living in barracks which had been built for them, and cultivating gardens. Many of the officers were cultured men, both British and German, and were received by the Virginians socially, especially by Jefferson. The private soldiers were orderly and well behaved, and all went well until a sudden alarm seized upon many of the native farmers lest the presence of so large an extra population might create a famine in the county. The demand was made that a considerable part of the men be sent elsewhere, which would separate them from their own officers and work hardship in many ways. There was a rumor that Patrick Henry, then governor, was about to accede to the popular clamor.

Jefferson at once wrote a long letter of protest as to what he considered a breach of public faith, explaining the situation. "As an American," he wrote, "I cannot help feeling a thorough mortification that our Congress should have permitted an infraction of our public honour," and as a Virginian he hoped that the Governor would not permit the separation of men and officers contrary to the terms of surrender. He explained at length that the food supplies were ample, and that there was no danger of shortage. He mentioned that the barracks had been built at great expense, and the gardens had been started for the soldiers. "Their health is also of importance," he wrote, adding, "I would not endeavour to show that their lives are valuable to us, because it would suppose a possibility, that humanity was kicked out of doors in America, and interest only attended to." Continuing, he pointed out that the officers had had to take their houses on lease at high rents, and that many had had to spend much to make them habitable. "Is any enemy so execrable that, though in captivity, his wishes and comforts are to be disregarded and even crossed? I think not. It is for the benefit of mankind to mitigate the horrors of war as much as possible. The practice, therefore, of modern nations, of treating captive enemies with politeness and generosity, is not only delightful in contemplation, but really interesting to all the world, friends, foes and neutrals." [19]

As a result of Jefferson's interposition no removals were made, and the British and German officers were profuse in acknowledging their indebtedness to him. Among them were Major General Phillips, the Baron de Riedesel, Brigadier General Specht, Baron de Giesmar, De Unger, and others. Unhappily, Jefferson's views as to humanity in war were not to be shared by those British officers who before long were to arrive from the east on a marauding expedition and to plunder his estate.

[19] *Works,* Ford, Vol. II, pp. 169 ff.

CHAPTER VI

THE GOVERNORSHIP

By the spring of 1779 the war with Great Britain had been going on for three years. There was no strong central government in America, indeed scarcely any real central government at all, except for a loose voluntary cooperation of the states. The states themselves were being governed under new constitutions, framed in the midst of war, without the prestige of the old colonial forms, and with no representatives of a superior power such as had been afforded by the royal governors. The political power of Congress and the military power of the army had both declined. The year 1777 had turned out 20,000 less militia and regulars than 1776. By the end of 1778 there were 17,000 less than even in 1777. Almost on the last day of the year Washington wrote that he then felt more distress and uncertainty than at any previous time. He complained bitterly of the lack of public spirit, and begged that better men be sent to Congress, asking where were Mason, Wythe, Jefferson, Nicholas, and others?

Washington, in his vain endeavors to get supplies, food, money, everything needed for his small army from Congress, was learning the value of a strong government. His young secretary, Hamilton, was learning the same lesson also, and discussion must often have waxed warm in the general's official "family" as its members talked over the troubles with Congress. The army had to function through Congress, and that body was almost ceasing to function itself because it could for the most part only politely ask the states to contribute what it tried to collect. When on one occasion in answer to Washington's passionate plea for food for his starving troops Congress replied by suggesting that he subsist his army on the country, it did so because it could not itself get its requisitions honored by the states. It was natural that the officers of the army should keep their thoughts largely on Congress and on the problems of how to make it more efficient. Washington's call for better men to represent the states was natural, but one may question, in view of the lack of power over the states by Congress, whether the strategic points at which to place the best men were not, after all, in the state legislatures rather than in Congress. Nothing could be accomplished unless the states voluntarily gave the greatest aid possible to the general cause. The ablest leaders in each state would be more likely to secure that result working in the state itself rather than in distant Philadelphia. For a man trying to decide where he would be most useful there was much to be said on both sides.

Moreover, even yet, it was difficult to think nationally. Men never had done so in the sense of deep loyalty to a common union. The citzens of the several colonies were jealous and not too fond of one another. They felt themselves as closely iden-tified with their own colony as does a Canadian, Australian, or South African with his own Dominion today. The one uniting bond—the Crown—had been broken, and it would take time for new ones to be re-knit. Moreover, each colony feared for its own safety. They were all on the coast, and England ruled the sea. If troops were embarked from any of the British forces in America no one could tell their intended destination until a marauding expedition appeared suddenly at some point where troops could be landed. On the other hand, the American forces could move only slowly, owing to bad roads and trans-port difficulties. If Congress steadily deteriorated in quality, the reason is to be found, I think, in the fact that the two important stages of action were the army and the individual states. The position of a member of Congress was becoming by 1779 or 1780 almost intolerable. To a great extent that body had to receive agonized appeals from the army and to pass them on to thirteen legislatures. Financially, it was fast headed for bankruptcy. The paper money of its own, which it had conjured from the printing presses to help finance its needs, was approaching extinction,—the ultimate end of every form of paper money, for which the demand is ever for more. In March, 1777, it took $109.00 of Continental money to buy a normal $100.00 worth of goods; in March, 1778, $370.00; in 1779, $1,000.00; in 1780, $3,736.00; in 1781 a wagon load of paper "Dollars" would not buy a potato.

The country owes much to those men who sat in Congress and struggled with their thankless and almost impossible task. It is not strange, however, that a steadily larger proportion of the abler men of the states, who were not already in the army, preferred service in their own states rather than in Congress, nor that the experience of those years should in many cases have affected them differently. The army, in reality, was as yet the only "nation." The men in the army had to think nationally if for no other reason than that the army was dependent on the one national legislative body, the Congress. On the other hand, those responsible for state action tended to think in terms of their states. They had the constant dread that the war might shift to their own coasts with no help afforded by the national government or national army. They were constantly being requisitioned for men, supplies, and money; and the point was constantly being raised whether these requisitions were fairly apportioned among them all. There was already much economic suffering, and the fear grew of a central government strong enough to force the several states to contribute whether each believed it was being treated fairly as compared with the others or not. To put it in the simplest terms, the men in the army wanted money and supplies to ensure success. Watching the weakness of Congress, they saw the need of a stronger government at the center. On the other hand, the men in the states were the ones who had to pay. As many of them watched the constant demands from Congress, demands which could not be enforced, they wondered what would happen if a government might be set up which could enforce such demands and take without asking.

It was in a way a phase of the debtor-creditor relationship, and an experience that undoubtedly did much to fix the opinions of many on the problem of a national government. The depreciated currencies, Continental and state, brought out different reactions. No one suffered more heavily from this cause than did Jefferson, who never got over his fear and hatred of paper money. As we have noted, at the beginning of the war he had sold land to the amount of £4,200 in order to pay off some of his father-in-law's debts in England which had been a burden on his wife's estate. The war prevented the payment, and the whole £4,200 was lost by depreciation of the currency. Both Hamilton and Jefferson were sound money men, but whereas Hamilton's experience led him later to favor a central bank, a funded debt, and other elements of the modern financial systems, Jefferson's led him to mistrust all of these.

In spite of Washington's question as to where Jefferson and other leading Virginians were instead of being in Congress, I think it may fairly be said, of Jefferson at least, that he was where his particular talents would prove most useful. As he had written to Rittenhouse, we have to "employ the geniuses of men according to their several orders and degrees." Jefferson had no military genius and little or no military capacity. For him to have gone into the army would have been sheer waste. Nor, as he was to find by an experience which was to prove bitter to him, was he first-class as an executive. The recollections of the governorship and the presidency were both to become so distasteful to him that he put neither in his epitaph. He was not a speaker, and as we have seen had been a silent member when in Congress, though extremely capable on com-

mittees. Congress at this time was not interested in questions
of government or of society or drawing up state papers, in
all of which Jefferson made his greatest contributions. It was
a multi-headed executive struggling daily, for the most part,
with problems of administration. No one can tell whether
Jefferson would have been more useful to America in the long
run working on Congressional committees than engaged in the
work in Virginia which we have described in the preceding
chapter, but it would appear to be extremely doubtful, to say
the least. The work he had done in helping to draft the new
constitution of the state, in the revision of the laws, in the
drafting of the Bill for Religious Freedom, and so on, would
seem to outweigh what he could have done on military or other
committees in Philadelphia.

Moreover, a man of great talents may well be allowed to use
them as he himself thinks most meet. Other men, many of them,
could do some things in public life quite as well or better than
Jefferson, but no other man in all our history has so contributed to the forming of the American spirit as Jefferson
did by his life-long devotion to the principles of freedom,
equality of opportunity, and of Liberalism. He himself felt
that the time to strike for these was during the war, not after.
Others might ask why bother about a revision of laws while
victory still hung in the balance, but Jefferson had his own
reason, expressed in a passage, striking from every point of
view, in his "Notes on Virginia." In it, speaking particularly
of the laws as to religion, he says:

"Let us, too, give this experiment of religious freedom fair
play, and get rid, while we may, of those tyrannical laws. It
is true we are as yet secured against them by the spirit of the
times. I doubt whether the people of this country would suffer
an execution for heresy, or a three years' imprisonment for
not comprehending the mysteries of the Trinity. But is the
spirit of the people an infallible, a permanent reliance? Is it

government? Is this the kind of protection we receive in return for the rights we give up? Besides, the spirit of the times may alter, will alter. Our rulers will become corrupt, our people careless. A single zealot may commence persecution, and better men be his victims. It can never be too often repeated, that the time for fixing every essential right on a legal basis is while our rulers are honest, and ourselves united. From the conclusion of this war we shall be going downhill. It will not then be necessary to resort every moment to the people for support. They will be forgotten, therefore, and their rights disregarded. They will forget themselves, but in the sole faculty of making money, and will never think of uniting to effect a due respect for their rights. The shackles, therefore, which shall not be knocked off at the conclusion of this war, will remain on us long, will be made heavier and heavier, till our rights shall revive or expire in a convulsion." [1]

This passage must be kept clearly in mind, not only to explain why Jefferson preferred in these years to work in Virginia rather than in Congress but also to enable us to understand his attitude after his return from France, ten years or so later, when he found the reaction in full swing, and even such "radicals" as Patrick Henry and Samuel Adams transformed into strong reactionaries. The people, he felt, had no time to lose if they wanted the concession of greater rights and liberties. If they waited until their help was no longer considered necessary, they would then have waited too long. Not only that, but their own better selves would have to be protected against their lower selves, and this is merely another example of what Jefferson was always preaching, but what has largely been lost to sight in the Jefferson legend, namely that he did not believe in *every* people at *all* times, but only in a people who made themselves worthy of being entrusted with the custody of their own liberty and that of others.

[1] *Writings,* Ford, Vol. III, pp. 265 f.

On June 1, 1779, Jefferson, then thirty-six years old, was elected Governor of Virginia, to succeed Patrick Henry who, having served three annual terms, was ineligible for re-election. Jefferson was to be in a more real sense than usual a "War Governor," for he was not only governor during a war, but even before he could take office, the war had invaded his own state. Henry's term had expired at a most opportune moment for that gentleman's peace of mind and perhaps reputation. The Virginia treasury was practically empty. Washington had written to a Virginian six months before that Virginia money was depreciating at the rate of five per cent a day and would soon be refused at any price. Washington had also insisted, and properly had insisted in view of the larger strategy of the war (although Virginia was his own state, and his loved Mount Vernon was exposed to possible raids), that Henry should not attempt to prepare the state for defense but should forward all possible men and material to the Continental Army.

It was thus a defenseless and practically bankrupt state which Jefferson was called upon to govern in June. But there was worse. In May, the British had begun the southern operations they had long had in mind, and had landed troops from ships in Hampton Roads, and sent marauding parties inland, destroying a larger amount of ammunition at Suffolk.

Jefferson's problems may well be said to have been more difficult than those of the governor of any other state at that time. All suffered more or less alike from the evils of paper money, the disinclination of men to serve in the army for long terms, and other difficulties felt in common. But Virginia had her special troubles. She was the largest state in area, which made transport over her bad roads, and also rapid communication of news, more difficult than in other states. Moreover, her long coast line, with the many waterways, such as the Potomac, James, and other rivers, penetrating far inland, made her peculiarly liable to unexpected attack from the sea. This topography also prevented rapid movements of troops up and down the coast across the succession of the parallel waterways running inland from it.

There was another point. As the war progressed during Jefferson's term, two major military campaigns were developed, one in the North and one in the South. Washington with the northern army lay well beyond Virginia northward, and Gates, succeeded later by Greene, lay with the Southern army outside Virginia to the southward. Both these armies called upon Jefferson for all possible aid, and it was with the advice and consent of Washington, indeed by his request, that Jefferson threw the weight of Virginia into the national rather than into the local scales. This meant that his own state must of necessity lie more or less open to attack. As in the course of the campaign the British army was to be pushed northward from Carolina into Virginia, and toward the coast, almost the whole of the state east of the Blue Ridge became open to attack. It would have been utterly impossible to have raised and maintained forces sufficient to repel attacks from the Southern border in the interior and raids from the sea along a wide range of landing places in the choice of the British; and at the same time to have complied with the requisitions for men, arms, ammunition, food, and transport made by the main Northern and Southern armies on whose success the fate of the war would turn.

Naturally, however, the policy of leaving parts of a country open to attack in order to concentrate resources at some other part is never popular with those who feel themselves left defenseless locally. In the subsequent wars in which we have been opposed by naval powers, such as that of 1812, and the Spanish and World Wars, various parts of the coast have suffered from panic and called loudly for defense regardless of the general campaign plans. In the Revolution, when people were still thinking mainly in terms of their particular states rather than in those of a nation yet in process of creation, this feeling that their state must be protected first was especially strong.

Jefferson, both living and dead, has been criticized by many for his policy and conduct as war governor. Most of the critics have been either Virginians taking the local view or enemies who wished to fasten something on him, whatever it might be. His position was one in which he would be damned whichever course he took. If he failed to meet as far as possible the calls made upon him by Gates, Greene, and Washington, he would be condemned by those taking the national view. If he largely stripped the state to do this, he would be condemned by those taking the provincial view. If he straddled too much, he would neither have defended the state nor helped the generals engaged in the larger and more important campaigns. Whatever he did he could not escape criticism which some well-meaning persons would think merited. The main decision he had to make was whether he would co-operate to the greatest extent with the main two Continental armies or build up what in any case would be an inadequate system of local defense all over Virginia. He decided, and wisely, in favor of the former. Just as Washington exposed his Mount Vernon by suggesting this policy, so Jefferson exposed his equally loved Monticello by accepting it.

The three years following his election to the governorship were the most unhappy of his life, but they are not important for the purpose of this volume, and we need touch on the details only briefly. Nor is there need to defend him at length as to the military aspect of his work. It cannot be justly claimed, I think, that he was either a great soldier or administrator, though in the latter rôle he appears to have been painstaking, active, and as successful as the circumstances allowed. A careful examination of the correspondence from and to him, including that of Washington, Gates, Lafayette, and other high officers, reveals practically complete understanding on both sides of the situation and its difficulties for all, and the satisfaction of the officers with the actions of the governor.

Jefferson was generous in the comprehension of the difficulties of others, realizing them as well as he did his own. On one occasion he wrote to Madison in Congress that he had sent reinforcements to the southern army because more than a fourth or fifth of all the British forces were in South Carolina and it could not be expected that North Carolina, which contained but a tenth of the American militia, could be left to support the southern war alone. Again, writing to General Stevens of Virginia, he said, "You wish to know how far the property of this State, in your hands, is meant to be subject to the orders of the Commander-in-chief. Arms and military stores, we mean to be perfectly subject to him. The provisions going from this country will be for the whole army." [2]

Jefferson was hampered in many ways. There was a tremendous shortage of firearms and no factories to produce them. Empty-handed recruits forwarded to the Continental armies might perhaps there receive arms but were useless for local defense without them. No tents could be had because there was no cotton duck to make them of. As everywhere, there was a shortage of wagons for transport. There had been enough before the war only for the agricultural purposes of the state, and agriculture had to go on simultaneously with war if people and soldiers were to be fed. There was also great shortage of leather, and if cattle were slaughtered too rapidly, for sake of their skins, then the supply of meat would be imperilled. When on one occasion Gates asked Jefferson to forward no more men without shoes, Jefferson replied courteously, pointing out that this would mean simply forwarding no men as there were no shoes to be had.

Another difficulty was the lack of money. The Continental

2 *Memorial Edition*, Vol. IV, p. 91. Not in Ford.

currency was soon to become worthless, and Virginia's was also approaching the same point. Jefferson rightly claimed that there could be only one end to printing-press money, and that the way to finance the war was by taxation, loans, and keeping to a sound currency. He wished to sell state lands, redeem the paper and raise taxes, but the evil had progressed too far. It had to go on to the bitter end. Virginia had a very bad year for its staple crop, tobacco, during his first term. That made taxes harder to raise, but he also saw that taxes would soon be negligible as, owing to the constant and rapid depreciation of money and rising prices, the deficits would grow faster than taxes could be paid in. The only way in which supplies of all sorts could be obtained was by "impressment," which in view of the growing worthlessness of government obligations was understood to be a polite word for confiscation. This method was naturally resented, especially by the farmers with small resources.

There was also a growing party in the legislature which was opposed to the conduct of the war. Many not only objected to sending resources out of the state, but also, after the war to the south of Virginia had taken on alarming proportions, these critics insisted that Washington's policy of remaining in the north instead of taking the field in person in Carolina was a fatal one. It proved to have been a wise one, but Washington himself was hampered by those who opposed it, and Jefferson found himself between two fires. His own letters to Washington were always respectful, and he properly allowed himself to be guided by the supreme commander, although by no means without ideas of his own, which he occasionally suggested. For example, one of the brilliant feats of Virginia arms was the successful expedition under Colonel George Rogers Clark which captured the fort of Vincennes from the British and opened the way to the subjugation of the whole Northwest. Jefferson asked Washington for aid for this purpose, the results of which would be so vast as contrasted with the means employed, but acquiesced when Washington could not see his way to granting the request.

Jefferson's office was political. He was in no way under the command of Washington. The histories of wars are filled with the difficulties created for commanders at the front by politicians at the rear. That Jefferson, himself one of the most noted of Americans and governor of the largest and most important colony, should have subordinated his own wishes and plans, made political enemies of many, and given himself wholeheartedly to the forwarding of the plans of Washington and Greene speaks volumes for both his sense and his self-denying loyalty to the general cause.

But if he could do this on the one hand, and, on the other, treat captured enemies with consideration, kindness, and social courtesy, he was no sentimental milk-sop. The British governor, Hamilton, and his aides in the Northwest had been guilty of the utmost brutality and cruelty. Hamilton had not only employed Indians to fight the Americans, with the savages' massacre and torture of men, women, and children, but had offered rewards for scalps though none for prisoners. The captured officers, British and German, interned near Charlottesville, and who were welcomed as guests at Monticello, had been gentlemen and fair foes. But Hamilton was of a different breed. When, after capture by Clark, he came into Jefferson's hands, Jefferson at once placed him in the common jail in irons, and refused him permission to communicate with any one. On being remonstrated with by Washington, Jefferson very reluctantly treated Hamilton as an ordinary prisoner of war, though great cruelties had been proved against him personally. Jefferson made no change in his relations with those officers who had behaved like soldiers, but he had been deeply angered by the turn given to war by some of the British. Writing to Colonel George Mathews at this time he declared that "iron will be retaliated by iron . . . prison ships by prison ships, and like for like in general. . . . I would use any powers I have for the punishment of any officer of our own who should be guilty of excesses unjustifiable under the usages of civilized nations." [3]

At the end of 1780, there began those British raids from the coast, which had long been foreseen as possibilities. During the summer Jefferson had exerted himself to the utmost and had sent 7000 stand of arms to Gates, about to be superseded by Greene, and some thousands of additional troops. Virginia had no soldiers to oppose the British except such untrained militia as Jefferson could raise, and of whom he wrote to Washington that not a single one had ever seen the face of the enemy. Henry Lee, who disliked Jefferson, criticized him severely for not doing all sorts of impossible things, which Lee, in his place, could not himself have done. It must be recalled, however, that the governor was acting closely with Washington as Commander-in-Chief, carrying out his plans, and that during the hard months following the first raid there were three generals in Virginia, Steuben and Mühlenberg of the line and Nelson of the Virginia militia, who were primarily responsible for the military situation. Jefferson was not a dictator—a point we shall note later—but the civil governor of a state. Nearly a century later, the Southern Confederacy at war was to suffer heavily from the insistence of the governor of more than one state upon carrying out a policy he thought best for his own state or his own prestige instead of co-operating with and subordinating himself to the general policy. It is certainly a matter for praise and not for blame if Jefferson avoided that easy political pit-fall, and there would seem no avoidance for Jefferson's critics on this score of the dilemma clearly put to them by Francis W. Hirst. "If," says Mr. Hirst, "the military policy was wrong, the responsibility was Washing-

[3] *Writings,* Ford, Vol. II, pp. 263 f.

ton's; if its execution was wrong, the chief responsibility lay upon Steuben, Mühlenberg, and Nelson." [4]

There was no wavering in Washington's own policy or attitude. Even after the much more serious raid by Benedict Arnold in January, 1781, when that traitor burned a number of buildings in Richmond and inflicted other damage, Washington wrote to Jefferson that while it was mortifying that so much havoc could be done on a raid, it must be expected, and he himself anticipated that perhaps the British might even establish a permanent post in Virginia. Nevertheless, he pressed Jefferson to stick to the plan he had been pursuing in accordance with Washington's former requests.

"As the evils," he wrote, "you have to apprehend from these predatory incursions are not to be compared to the injury of the common cause, and with the danger to your State in particular, from the conquest of the States to the southward of you, I am persuaded the attention to your immediate safety will not divert you from the measures intended to reinforce the southern army and put it in a condition to stop the progress of the enemy in that quarter. The late accession of force makes them very formidable in Carolina, too powerful to be resisted without powerful succors from Virginia; and it is certainly her policy, as well as the interest of America, to keep the weight of the war at a distance from her. There is no doubt that a principal object of Arnold's operations is to make a diversion in favor of Cornwallis, and to remove this motive by disappointing the intention will be one of the surest ways of removing the enemy." [5]

In June, 1781, Cornwallis and the British were rapidly following the retreating American forces into Virginia from the south. The legislature, threatened earlier by the enemy in Richmond, had retired to Charlottesville and was in session

---

[4] *Life and Letters,* p. 156.
[5] *Writings of George Washington,* edited by W. C. Ford, Vol. IX, pp. 135 f.

there when a British force under General Tarleton approached the neighborhood. On the 7th, the legislature adjourned to Staunton, over the mountains, and barely escaped before the British entered the town. Two members had been breakfasting at Monticello with Jefferson, who had sent his wife and children to a friend's house fourteen miles away. After breakfast the two legislators followed the rest westward, Jefferson remaining somewhat longer until through his telescope he saw the British troops swarming into Charlottesville. Meanwhile, he had had a horse in readiness some distance from the house, and barely managed to make his escape before a detachment of troops, who had been unobserved, reached Monticello itself. According to family tradition, two slaves had been hiding the silver and other valuables under the flooring of the front porch, one being down below to place the things handed down to him. So suddenly did the troops appear that the upper negro had just time to drop the planks, imprisoning the slave Cæsar beneath them, where he remained in darkness and without food for eighteen hours guarding the treasure and fearing to make a sound. The detachment of troops, under a Captain Mc-Cleod, were shown over the house by the other slave, Martin, but did practically no damage, and McCleod himself, after looking into Jefferson's study, where his papers were, locked the room and gave Martin the key. Tarleton had given orders that there should be no destruction or looting and McCleod carried out his task not only as a soldier but as a gentleman.

Lord Cornwallis, however, behaved very differently at another plantation of Jefferson's, Elk Hill, on the James. Writting to Doctor William Gordon in 1788, Jefferson recounted his losses. Cornwallis, who had made a shocking reputation for infliction of wanton cruelty upon American civilians and destruction of their property wherever he went, remained at Elk Hill for ten days, making Jefferson's house his headquarters. "I had had time," Jefferson wrote, "to remove most of the effects out of the house. He destroyed all my growing crops of corn & tobacco, he burned all my barns containing the same articles of the last year, having first taken what he wanted, he used, as was to be expected, all my stocks of cattle, sheep & hogs for the sustenance of his army, and carried off all the horses capable of service: of those too young for service he cut the throats, and he burned all the fences on the plantation, so as to leave it an absolute waste. He carried off also about thirty slaves. Had this been to give them freedom he would have done right, but it was to consign them to inevitable death from the smallpox & putrid fever then raging in his camp. This I knew afterwards to have been the fate of 27 of them. I never had news of the remaining three, but presume they shared the same fate. . . . He treated the rest of the neighborhood somewhat in the same stile but not with that spirit of total extermination with which he seemed to rage over my possessions." [6] Jefferson estimated that in the Virginia campaign Cornwallis took over 30,000 slaves, of whom 27,000 were allowed to die of fever and smallpox and the rest were sold into the British West Indies.

This was only part of the damage directly inflicted upon the state which, following desultory but destructive raids from the coast, had now become a principal theatre of the war. Coming at the end of five years' sacrifices for the conflict, the taxes, requisitions, disturbance to normal life, and the ruin of worthless paper money, there was naturally loud and angry murmuring from many. In June, 1780, Jefferson had been re-appointed governor, as he deserved, but he declined to serve again. He knew the criticism of his administration, naturally fanned by some of the politicians and of those others of whom he made enemies in the redrafting of the laws. Virginia was in rather a panic, and Jefferson felt that if a governor was to be considered a military officer he might as well in truth be one.

[6] *Writings,* Ford, Vol. V, p. 39.

Through his support, General Nelson was appointed for the ensuing year, though in fact the worst was over, and Washington's policy, so loyally supported by Jefferson, was to be vindicated in a few months by the surrender of Cornwallis at Yorktown, and the end of military operations, as far as America was concerned.

By the magnanimity of Washington, the young Alexander Hamilton was able to make a brilliant play during the last week of the struggle. In February the Commander had had to administer a just rebuke to his young aide for keeping him waiting without cause when sent for. The egoistic and impetuous boy had then promptly resigned in a fit of temper, and his resignation had been accepted. His refusal to accept friendly advances toward reconciliation from Washington and the slurs which the lad, whose career was being fostered by the greatest man in the country, cast upon his benefactor in private letters and conversation could be taken less seriously if they were not premonitory of similar episodes in his later and more mature life. Washington was personally fond of him and properly rated his abilities high. When Hamilton refused to do anything but sulk, the general gave him his head, and appointed him to command an infantry company in Lafayette's corps, and so, by luck, the boy of twenty-four was able to lead a successful attack upon one of the British redoubts, and finish in a little blaze of glory a war career which might otherwise have ended rather ignobly.

On Jefferson's retirement, Washington had written to him an appreciative letter, ending with "allow me, before I take leave of Your Excellency in your public capacity, to express the obligations I am under for the readiness and zeal with which you have always forwarded and supported every measure which I have had occasion to recommend to you, and to assure you that I shall esteem myself honored by a continuation of your friendship and correspondence, should your country permit you to remain in a private walk of life." [7] Washington was not a superior officer of Jefferson. He was a busy man with heavy responsibilities and anxieties, and there would seem to have been no need for him to write as he did unless he sincerely meant what he wrote. General Greene had been equally appreciative of what Jefferson had done for him in the South, and a fair appraisal of the facts seems to indicate that Jefferson had in truth exerted himself to the utmost. Not only that, but he had also, states' rights man as he was, risen above the conception of the state in the national crisis, and also, as he had done in the revision of the laws, deliberately antagonized some of the most powerful forces in his own state to achieve what he believed larger purposes. Had he been either a demagogue or a mere politician his course would have been a most unwise one.

There were, however, plenty of politicians in Virginia, as elsewhere. In addition there was something going on under the surface which has never been fully or satisfactorily explained. Jefferson once stated that in the crisis of 1776 it had been suggested in the Assembly that a dictator be appointed. Apparently this scheme was now revived, and either this or pure politics had much to do with Jefferson's retirement from public life at this time. Whether or not Patrick Henry had anything to do with the plot for a dictatorship is highly controversial, and has been denied. The episode, however, brought out Jefferson's own ideas so clearly that it deserves treatment at some length as illuminating the main theme of this book.

Obviously, with his belief that the America of his day offered a unique opportunity for the trial of self-government by the people, nothing could be more abhorrent to him than placing them under the rule of one man. In 1818, after Wirt, Henry's biographer, had denied the story that Henry had been impli-

[7] *Works, Washington,* Ford, ed., Vol. IX, p. 276.

cated, Jefferson wrote to a number of men still living and who had been in the legislature at the time. From Archibald Stuart he received the following reply:

"There are many now living who witnessed the part Mr Henry took on that subject. After the Assembly was dispersed to Charlottesville in the year 1781, it met in Staunton where Mr George Nicholas a member of that body proposed that a Dictator be established in this Commonwealth who should have the power of disposing of the lives and fortunes of the Citizens thereof without being subject to account. . . . That although the powers proposed to be conferred were very great the character he proposed to fill the office would remove all apprehensions arising from the abuse of them. That this character was Genl. Washington. That he was our fellow citizen that we had a right to command his services and that he had no doubt but that on such an Occasion he would obey the call of his country. In the course of his speech he referred to the practice of the Romans on similar occasions." Stuart then added that Henry had seconded the motion, saying he did not care whether the officer proposed should be called a Dictator or a governor so long as he had those dictatorial powers now rendered necessary for somebody to wield owing to the confusion of the state in the face of a "licentious enemy." The motion was opposed by Mann Page and others, and easily defeated. [8]

The same George Nicholas, a young man of no experience and then serving his first term in the legislature, next proposed that the legislature conduct an enquiry into Jefferson's official actions as governor, a move which he much regretted later and for which he apologized to Jefferson. It seems evident that he was being used as a cat's paw by other members of the legislature who were of greater importance and more experience. Through an arrangement, a member from Albemarle County resigned his seat, and Jefferson was elected so as to defend him-

[8] *Writings,* Ford, Vol. III, pp. 231 f., note.

self on the floor. The rest of this incident may be told briefly in Jefferson's own words. "Thro' the intervention of a friend," he wrote, "I obtained from Mr Nicholas a written note of the charges he proposed to bring forward & I furnished him in return with the heads of the answers I should make. On the day appointed for hearing the charges he withdrew from the house; & no other undertaking to bring them forward, I did it myself in my place, from his paper, answering them verbatim to the house. The members had been witnesses themselves to all the material facts, and passed an unanimous vote of approbation which may be seen on their journals." [9]

This rather sordid little political dodge, engineered apparently by some of Jefferson's enemies, has been magnified by some later biographers, who should know better, into an "impeachment," and the quite genuine vote approving his conduct in office, coinciding with the opinions of Washington, Greene, and others, into a "whitewashing." Although Jefferson never forgave Patrick Henry, he harbored no grudge against the young Nicholas who made a "candid acknowledgment" that he had been misled in the whole dirty business. The affair did, however, have a profound, and much too great, influence upon Jefferson, of which we shall speak presently. We must here, for the moment, return to the proposition made to create a dictator, and to Jefferson's opinion of it. The mere suggestion had stirred him to the depths, and he put down his feelings in his *Notes on Virginia*, which volume was to be the fruit of his temporary retirement from public life. Speaking of the Revolution, he wrote:

"One who entered into this contest from a pure love of liberty, and a sense of injured rights, who determined to make every sacrifice, and to meet every danger, for the re-establishment of those rights on a firm basis, who did not mean to expend his blood and substance for the wretched purpose of

[9] Chinard, *Life*, p. 114. *Cf.* also *Memorial Edition*, Vol. XVII, pp. 5 ff., 20 f.

changing this master for that, but to place the powers of governing him in a plurality of his own choice . . . must stand confounded and dismayed when he is told, that a considerable portion of that plurality had meditated the surrender of them into a single hand, and, in lieu of a limited monarch, to deliver him over to a despotic one! . . . In God's name, from whence have they derived this power? Is it from our ancient laws? None such can be produced. Is it from any principle in our new constitution expressed or implied? . . . Its fundamental principle is, that the state shall be governed as a commonwealth. It provides a republican organization, proscribes under the name of *prerogative* the exercise of all powers undefined by the laws; places on this basis the whole system of our laws; and by consolidating them together, chooses that they shall be left to stand or fall together, never providing for any circumstances, not admitting that such could arise, wherein either should be suspended; no, not for a moment. Our antient laws expressly declare, that those who are but delegates themselves shall not delegate to others powers which require judgment and integrity in their exercise. . . . Or was this proposition moved on a supposed right in the movers, of abandoning their posts in a moment of distress? The same laws forbid the abandonment of that post, even on ordinary occasions; and how much more a transfer of their powers into other hands and other forms, without consulting the people. . . . Was it from the necessity of the case? Necessities which dissolve a government, do not convert its authority to an oligarchy or a monarchy. They throw back, into the hands of the people, the powers they had delegated, and leave them as individuals to shift for themselves. A leader may offer, but not impose himself, nor be imposed on them. Much less can their necks be submitted to his sword, their breath be held at his will or caprice. The necessity which should operate these tremendous effects should at least be palpable and irresistible. . . . The very thought [of a dictator] alone was treason against the people; was treason against mankind in general; as rivetting forever the chains which bow down their necks, by giving to their oppressors a proof, which they would have trumpeted through the universe of the imbecility of republican government, in times of pressing danger, to shield them from harm. Those who assume the right of giving away the reins of government in any case, must be sure that the herd, whom they hand on to the rods and hatchets of the dictator, will lay their necks on the block when he shall nod to them. . . . Those who meant well, of the advocates of this measure (and most of them meant well, for I knew them personally, had been their fellow-labourer in the common cause, and had often proved the purity of their principles), had been seduced in their judgment by the example . . . of Rome, where alone it was to be found, and where at length, too, it had proved fatal." [10]

Whatever may be the truth as to this dark and tangled little plot which now appears in history as rather a shadow play of vague figures, it has two points of interest for us. Patrick Henry may or may not have been involved. It was at any rate believed that he was, and the fact, or supposition, was used against him in the political debates of 1788. In any case, in company with many others, Jefferson not only believed in the plot, and apparently with justification, but had been a victim of it. His later fears that Hamilton and others preferred a monarchy thus had root in his own personal experience in his own state, where he had seen even those who had been his "fellow-labourers in the common cause," and whose purity of principle he did not question, suggest an overthrow of constitutional government and the transfer of power to a single "savior of society."

The second point of interest is that Jefferson's stand was not only soundly based in law and history, but one hundred

[10] *Writings*, Ford, Vol. III, pp. 231 ff.

and fifty-three years later had to be upheld in a crisis by the Supreme Court of the United States. It is one of the most ancient maxims of the English common law that *delegatus non potest delegare, i.e.,* that a delegate cannot himself delegate the powers delegated to him, which was what those delegates to the Virginia legislature who were in the plot had tried to do. In our own day, no one will accuse President Roosevelt of attempting to become a dictator in the ordinary sense, but in gathering to himself the vast and unprecedented powers which he had asked from Congress and which they had given to him, he had set himself up legally as a dictator to an extent unknown to the Constitution. In the now famous decision handed down by the Supreme Court on May 27, 1935, that body, by a vote which was unusual in that it was unanimous, broke those powers, and laid it down that "Congress cannot delegate legislative power to the President to exercise an unfettered discretion to make whatever laws he thinks may be needed or advisable for the rehabilitation and expansion of trade and industry." They affirmed again in the twentieth century what Jefferson had affirmed in the eighteenth, indeed, what any one with a knowledge of common and constitutional law would have to affirm.

Jefferson, as we have noted before, was of an extremely sensitive nature, much too "thin-skinned" for the rough and tumble of political life. He realized this himself. Writing to Mrs. Adams from Paris four years after the unpleasant episode noted above, he said, speaking of the position of John Adams as Minister in London and the slanders he had to encounter, "It would have illy suited me. I do not love difficulties. I am fond of quiet, willing to do my duty, but irritable by slander & apt to be forced by it to abandon my post. These are weaknesses from which reason & your counsels will preserve Mr Adams." [11]

[11] *Writings,* Ford, Vol. IV, p. 100.

He had worked hard as governor, and not spared himself in any way. Although a civilian, and not by temperament a soldier, he had kept at the front during Arnold's raid, assisting General Steuben in various ways, spending the greater part of four days in the saddle, one horse dying under him of fatigue. His enemies claimed that he "ran away" when the British came to Monticello. The legislature had already properly moved to Staunton. Jefferson, although head of the state, was undefended, and it can hardly be claimed that rather than escape it would have been more heroic for the governor to sit on his piazza and allow himself to be captured and turned over by subordinates to Cornwallis, who, judging from his record, would promptly and gladly have hung the author of the Declaration of Independence to one of his own trees.

Combining his sense of what he had both tried to do and had done, the commendation he had received from Washington and Greene, the personal property losses he had suffered in the cause, and the slur which some of the legislature of his own state had tried to cast on his record, Jefferson refused, in a fit of peevishness or nerves, to remain for the present in public life. He had been under heavy strain for two years in a sort of work for which he was not fitted by nature. In his own family there had been both birth and death, which in view of his wife's health had meant deep anxiety as well as sorrow. He himself had had a bad fall from a horse which had much shaken him and from which recovery was slow. Whatever the causes may have been, he retired to Monticello and devoted himself for the next year or so to the writing of his *Notes on Virginia*, a storehouse of information about the state and also about his own views on affairs. His friends remonstrated, and his letter to Mrs. Adams, quoted above, indicates that he himself later came to feel that it had perhaps been weakness to retire. In order to answer his opponents in the legislature in person he had even declined the appointment by Congress to go to Paris to join the four plenipotentiaries already assembled there to negotiate peace.

At any rate, the war was over, and we owe to his temporary retreat an invaluable book, which was later to be printed in France, England, and Germany, and to go through many editions in America. Professor Bernard Faÿ dismisses it as "ponderous and without literary value," and adds that it was not until 1788 that a book, naturally in French, was to appear that gave a clear idea of the United States! On the other hand, Professor Chinard, French like Professor Faÿ but with far better knowledge of the United States, says that Jefferson's book "probably did more than any other publication to propagate the doctrine of Americanism . . . and gave final expression to the hopes, aspirations, and feelings that were to govern the country for several generations." [12]

The book of some 367 pages, with a long appendix containing documents, is a compendium of all sorts of information on the geography, scenery, natural history, social and economic conditions, and almost every other aspect of Jefferson's native state. Imbedded in the informative material are rich veins of his own philosophy as to government and society. It was written as an answer to enquiries addressed to him by Barbé-Marbois, the secretary of the French legation, which accounts for the particular form in which it was written, a form which would probably have been quite different had Jefferson been writing merely a book on Virginia for the general reader. One of the chief marks of the work is its intense Americanism. It was the custom then, as it has since remained, for many Europeans to indulge in a vast amount of supercilious and ignorant criticism of matters American, and Jefferson answered a number of these in the spirit of a sensible and devoted if not a modern "hundred per cent" American. It was in respect to devel-

[12] Bernard Faÿ, *The Revolutionary Spirit in America*, New York, 1927, p. 202; Chinard, *Life*, p. 120.

oping the feeling of Americanism, rather than in the information given as to a particular state, that the book exerted its greatest influence. Jefferson's wide reading and knowledge made some of the Europeans easy prey, and Americans naturally enjoyed seeing European slanders answered by one who stood on a level with the best minds of the Old World.

The French naturalist, Buffon, for example, had asserted that animals in America were smaller than in Europe and that there was something in the American physical environment which caused them to degenerate. The Abbé de Raynal carried this a step further and declared the same true of the human species. Jefferson's knowledge of natural history enabled him to refute these unfounded assertions without difficulty by giving physical descriptions of the Indians and a considerable list of the American fauna. Jefferson himself was six feet two and a half inches, whereas the Abbé has been described as a "shrimp." Some years later in Paris they were both dining with Franklin and a group of Americans and French, on which occasion the Abbé repeated his assertion. Characteristically Franklin suggested they all rise. The American guests towered above the French. In the next edition of the Abbé's book, his argument as to physical degeneration in America disappeared. In his own volume, Jefferson also answered the jibe of Europe that America had not as yet produced a great poet, or a man of genius in science or art. Considering the circumstances, most of the European contentions were either untrue or silly, though always ill-natured, and Jefferson's answers are not so important in themselves as in the remarkably tonic effect they had in creating a sort of proud and hopeful American over-soul in place of a number of local provincial egotisms.

We have already mentioned some of the political ideas in the book, and will here note those on suffrage and its relation to education on the one hand and immigration on the other, as further clarifying Jefferson's outlook.

In criticizing the Virginia constitution as then in operation, he noted that "the majority of the men in the state, who pay and fight for its support, are unrepresented in the legislature" and that "among those who share the representation, the shares are very unequal," pointing to the fact that 19,000 men living in the coastal region were enabled to give the law to 30,000 living in the western uplands.[13] In another part of his work he wrote that "In every government on earth is some trace of human weakness, some germ of corruption and degeneracy, which cunning will discover, and wickedness insensibly open, cultivate and improve. Every government degenerates when trusted to the rulers of the people alone. The people themselves therefore are its only safe depositaries. And to render even them safe, their minds must be improved to a certain degree. This indeed is not all that is necessary, though it be essentially necessary. . . . The influence over government must be shared among all the people. If every individual which composes their mass participates of the ultimate authority, the government will be safe; because the corrupting the whole mass will exceed any private resources of wealth; and public ones cannot be provided but by levies on the people. In this case every man would have to pay his own price. The government of Great Britain has been corrupted, because but one man in ten has a right to vote for members of parliament. The sellers of the government, therefore, get nine-tenths of their price clear. It has been thought that corruption is restrained by confining the right of suffrage to a few of the wealthier of the people; but it would be more effectually restrained by an extension of that right to such numbers as would bid defiance to the means of corruption." [14]

Although, as Jefferson noted above, he never regarded education as the means of making every citizen a wise voter, he

---

[13] *Writings*, Ford, Vol. III, pp. 222 f.
[14] *Writings*, Ford, Vol. III, pp. 254 f.

did believe that it was necessary to the voter. He describes at considerable length the plan already mentioned which he had devised for the educational system of the state. He never believed, as we have tried to emphasize, that every man by virtue of simply being human was necessarily wise, good, or to be entrusted with the liberties of the state. He uses a significant expression in describing how children shall be selected from the common schools to advance to the grammar schools at public expense when he says that "by this means twenty of the best geniuses will be raked from the rubbish annually." He had claimed that the inalienable rights of every man were those of "life, liberty, and the pursuit of happiness" but he had not included that of the franchise, and the expression just noted does not bear out the legend of Jefferson as believing that every man was as good as every other, and as some have added later, "better too." This note, we may insist again, runs all through Jefferson's writings.

There was also, in his opinion, the danger of lowering the level already attained by the electorate. "The present desire of America," he wrote, "is to produce rapid population by as great importation of foreigners as possible. But is this founded in good policy?" He then pointed out that on the basis of the then rate of immigration and native births it would take fifty-four and one-half years to raise the white population of Virginia from 567,614 to 4,540,912, counting immigrants, or eighty-one and three-fourths years, excluding them.

"It is for the happiness of those united in society," he continues, "to harmonize as much as possible in matters which they must of necessity transact together. Civil government being the sole object of forming societies, its administration must be conducted by common consent. Every species of government has its specific principles. Ours perhaps are more peculiar than those of any other in the universe. It is a composition of the freest part of the English constitution, with others derived from natural right and natural reason. To these nothing can be more opposed than the maxims of absolute monarchies. Yet from such we are to expect the greatest number of immigrants. They will bring with them the principles of the governments they leave, imbibed in their early youth; or, if able to throw them off, it will be in exchange for an unbounded licentiousness, passing, as is usual, from one extreme to another. It would be a miracle were they to stop precisely at the point of temperate liberty. These principles, with their language, they will transmit to their children. In proportion to their numbers, they will share with us the legislation. . . . Is it not safer to wait with patience twenty-seven years and three months longer, for the attainment of any degree of population desired or expected? May not our government be more homogeneous, more peaceable, more durable? . . . I mean not that these doubts should be extended to the importation of useful artificers. . . . Spare no expence in obtaining them. They will after a while go to the plough and the hoe; but, in the mean time they will teach us something we do not know. It is not so in agriculture. The indifferent state of that among us does not proceed from a want of knowledge merely; it is from our having such quantities of land to waste as we please." [15]

We may note from the above extracts and other points already mentioned in Jefferson's philosophy, that his plan for American society was not that of an idle dreamer. It had been carefully thought out, was highly integrated, and rested upon a number of major premises. He wished to keep America preponderantly agricultural, and believed it would long remain so if his ideas should be accepted in practice. He not only wished it to stay agricultural but gradually to become a land of widely distributed small holdings. His belief that a wide base for the suffrage would make for safety of liberty and property did

[15] *Writings*, Ford, Vol. III, pp. 189 f.

not extend to a nation largely urban and proletarian. He wished for a suffrage so wide as to preclude the ability of the rich to buy up its votes, and, on the other hand, to have property so widely distributed as to ensure that the voters would not loot the state because they would then be taxing themselves. This balance, he fully realized, would be destroyed by the creation of great reservoirs of wealth and great masses of propertyless citizens in an industrial state. If citizens could vote themselves money without taxing themselves, Jefferson's whole system could easily fall to the ground. The safeguards he envisaged would be destroyed. Moreover, he foresaw clearly many of the evils which practically unrestricted immigration for a century and more, according to Hamilton's theory, were to bring upon us. There is no use in trying to rebuild history on the basis of an IF but in looking back at some of the results of our huge immigration, such as the rapid growth of cities, the hordes of votes which could be bought, the rise of the boss, the insane rush to exploit our natural resources owing in part to too rapid increase of population, involving also the development of the get-rich-quick mentality with the lowering of moral standards and respect for law, we may agree with Jefferson that the country would have been better off with a slower development attendant upon the natural increase of the stock then in America.

In considering Jefferson's philosophy we must always bear two points in mind. One is his fundamental Liberalism with its insistence upon certain general rights which in his view could alone make life worth living for civilized man—such as the rights to freedom of speech, press, thought, religion, and the "life, liberty, and pursuit of happiness" of the Declaration of Independence. The other point is that of his more specific program of changes which he believed could be made in the America of his day, a program composed of many parts, all of which hung together and on all of which depended the success of the experiment he wished to make in a New World to make men happier and freer. It was because Jefferson felt that the American experiment as he envisioned it, precarious in any case and absolutely new in the world, could not succeed except under the conditions he had predicated for it, that he was later to fight so strenuously against the political and economic views of Hamilton, including the latter's desire for the establishment of finance and manufactures, development of a wealthy class, rapid immigration, and all the rest.

Meanwhile that young man had been serving a term in Congress when that body was at about the nadir of its ability and influence. It had sent the army home unpaid, although Hamilton had wished to use the armed forces to frighten Congress into doing its duty, a suggestion wisely and nobly negatived by Washington. As far as results were concerned, Hamilton, as his fervid biographer Lodge pointed out, had been a complete failure in Congress with regard to every measure proposed by him, and had gone back to private life more firmly convinced than ever that democracy and too popular a government would also prove as complete failures as he himself had as a Congressman.

CHAPTER VII

JEFFERSON RETURNS TO THE NATIONAL STAGE

THE stream of French visitors to America, which was constant for some years after our Revolution, had already set in by 1782. Jefferson was one of the most noted figures in America, and the drain on his hospitality, as also on Washington's, had likewise begun. In the spring of that year he had a visit from the Marquis de Chastellux, who wrote a book from which we may quote a passage displaying his host at this time. After describing Monticello and its distinguished location on the mountain top, he went on to say:

"We may safely aver that Mr Jefferson is the first American who has consulted the fine arts to know how he should shelter himself from the weather. Let me describe to you a man, not yet forty, tall with a mild and pleasing countenance, but whose mind and understanding are ample substitutes for every exterior grace. An American, who, without ever having quitted his own country, is at once a musician, skilled in drawing, a geometrician, an astronomer, a natural philosopher, legislator, and statesman. . . . A philosopher, in voluntary retirement from the world and public business because he loves the world in as much only as he can flatter himself with being useful to mankind, and the minds of his countrymen are not yet in a condition either to bear the light or suffer contradiction. A mild and amiable wife, charming children, of whose education he himself takes charge, a house to embellish, great provisions to improve, and the arts and sciences to cultivate; these are what remain to Mr Jefferson, after having played a principal character on the theatre of the New World, and which he preferred to the honorable commission of Minister Plenipotentiary in Europe." [1]

Chastellux proceeded to describe the variety, charm, and wide intellectual range of Jefferson's conversation, and we may pause here for a moment to describe him in other aspects. His grandson wrote of him long afterward that his hair, when young, was reddish, growing sandy with age. "In addition to his commanding height, he was strong and well formed, his carriage erect; step firm and elastic, which he preserved to his death; his temper, naturally strong, under perfect control; his courage cool and impassive. No one ever knew him exhibit trepidation." [2] Like most Virginians he was an accomplished horseman, always having horses of the finest breed in his stables. Carrying his philosophy into practice, he never was attended in his rides by a slave, and always made his own fire. His manners were polished and of the "old school," and he was noted for his courtesy to those of lower station. The grandson recalled that when, as a boy, he was riding with Jefferson, the latter bowed in return to a greeting from a slave whereas the boy did not, incurring from his grandfather the rebuke: "Do you permit a negro to be more of a gentleman than yourself?" [3]

The pleasant life which Chastellux described in the spring of 1782 was soon to be rudely destroyed. Six months later Jefferson made the bald entry in his prayer book: "Martha Wayles Jefferson died September 6, 1782, at 11 o'clock 45 minutes A.M." His wife had never recovered from the birth of her sixth child on May 8, and Jefferson had for some time realized the doom that hung over his home. His affections for his household were peculiarly strong, and he also had an almost womanly solicitude for all within it. Years later, his daughter, Martha, set down her recollections of these days of her moth-

---

[1] S. N. Randolph, *Domestic Life*, p. 59.   [2] *Ibid.*, p. 338.   [3] *Ibid.*, p. 337.

er's illness, when she herself was just short of ten years of age.
Speaking of her father, she said, "As a nurse, no female ever
had more tenderness nor anxiety. He nursed my poor mother
in turn with Aunt Carr and her own sister—sitting up with
her and administering her medicines and drink to the last. For
four months that she lingered he was never out of calling; when
not at her beside, he was writing in a small room which opened
immediately at the head of her bed. A moment before the
closing scene, he was led from the room in a state of insensibility by his sister, Mrs Carr, who with great difficulty got him
into the library, where he fainted, and remained so long in-
sensible that they feared he would never revive. The scene that
followed I did not witness, but the violence of his emotion, when,
almost by stealth, I entered his room by night, to this day I
dare not describe to myself. He kept his room three weeks, and
I was never a moment from his side. He walked almost incessantly night and day, only lying down occasionally, when
nature was completely exhausted. . . . When at last he left his
room, he rode out, and from that time he was incessantly on
horseback, rambling about the mountain, in the least frequented
roads." [4]

The depth of Jefferson's affection for his wife, and his incessant anxiety over her frail health, have to be taken into
consideration in considering his public life up to the time of
her death. Besides Rebecca Burwell, the object of his calf-
love, in his college days, and the episode in youth already
mentioned, there is not the slightest real evidence, in spite of
gross political slanders, that Jefferson ever cared for any
woman beside the one he had now lost, or that during or after
her life he was ever unfaithful to her. He never married
again, and from the day he interred his wife in the cemetery
in the grounds of Monticello, his affections were concentrated
upon his daughters, one of whom died within two years, and

[4] *Ibid.*, p. 63.

only two of whom, the last of his children, grew to womanhood.

Before continuing with Jefferson's career, now to be greatly altered by the death of his wife, we may look forward for a moment to note the extraordinarily sensible advice which he wrote his daughter, as a young bride of a few months in 1798, as to married life, and which may have had a bearing on his own. "Harmony in the married state," he wrote, "is the very first object to be aimed at. Nothing can preserve affections interrupted but . . . a determination in each to consider the love of the other as of more value than any object whatever on which a wish had been fixed. How light, in fact, is the sacrifice of any other wish when weighed against the affections of one with whom we are to pass our whole life! And though opposition in a single instance will hardly of itself produce alienation, yet every one has their pouch into which all these little oppositions are put; while that is filling the alienation is insensibly going on, and when filled it is complete. It would puzzle either to say why; because no one difference of opinion has been marked enough to produce a serious effect in itself. But he finds his affections wearied out by a constant stream of little checks and obstacles. Other sources of discontent, very common, indeed, are the little cross-purposes of husband and wife, in common conversation, a disposition in either to criticise and question whatever the other says, a desire always to demonstrate and make him feel himself in the wrong, and especially in company. Nothing is so goading. Much better, therefore, if our companion views a thing in a different light from what we do, to leave him in quiet possession of his view. What is the use of rectifying him if the thing is unimportant; and if important, let it pass for the moment, and wait a softer moment and more conciliatory occasion of revising the subject together."

In view of the later and much exaggerated reports of the slovenliness of Jefferson's dress, which so upset a British Minister, the continuation of his advice to his daughter is of interest. "The article of dress," he goes on, "is perhaps that in which economy is the least to be recommended. It is so important to each to continue to please the other, that the happiness of both requires the most pointed attention to whatever may contribute toward it—and the more as time makes inroads on our person." [5]

When Jefferson had felt it necessary to decline the French mission offered him, in order to remain and defend himself in the legislature, he had written to Lafayette that the necessity had given him "more mortification than almost any occurrence of my life," and expressed his regret at not being able to combine with service to his country the European experiences he had so long desired. [6]

Two months after the death of his wife, while nursing his children through the then somewhat serious inoculation for smallpox, he received notice that he had been appointed a Minister Plenipotentiary to Europe to join Adams and Franklin, already in Paris, in negotiating for peace. This time he gladly embraced the opportunity. But again he was to be disappointed. By the time he was able to start, after receiving the appointment in the middle of November, the ship on which he was to sail was frozen fast in Chesapeake Bay, with no probable chance of getting off until March. The negotiations were proceeding and had advanced to such a point in February that Jefferson asked Congress whether they still wished to incur the expense of sending him when opportunity offered. On April 1 he was told that in view of the progress made, it would be unnecessary for him to go, and he returned to Monticello. Two months later he was chosen, with James Monroe and others, a delegate to the Continental Congress and at once accepted. The death of his wife had rendered his presence at home no

[5] *Ibid.*, pp. 246 f.
[6] *Letters of Lafayette and Jefferson*, ed. G. Chinard, Baltimore, 1929, p. 49.

longer necessary. Since the death of his friend and brother-in-law, Dabney Carr, Jefferson's sister, Mrs. Carr, had lived at Monticello with her children whom he had adopted. His own children would thus be looked after, and he was free to go where his career might call.

Jefferson arrived at Philadelphia to take his seat on November 4, 1783, but the next day Congress agreed to adjourn to Annapolis on the 26th. Meanwhile during the summer, Jefferson had drawn up a draft of another constitution for Virginia, as there was general talk of calling a convention to adopt one. No convention, as it turned out, was in fact called but the draft is interesting as showing how far Jefferson was from the ultra-democratic ideas ascribed to him. He did indeed extend the franchise to the point of almost complete male white suffrage, but the powers he gave to these electors were extremely limited. They could not even elect state senators but only the members of the lower house. In electing members of the senate they voted only for electors who, in turn were to choose senators, a system much like that later adopted in the Federal Constitution for the election of the President through an electoral college.[7] Moreover all the higher officers of the state were to be beyond their reach, such as the governor, who was to be elected by the legislature, or the many officials who were to be appointed by him. The document is chiefly interesting as showing that Jefferson then believed that under American, perhaps we might almost say Virginian, conditions, most of the male population should have a voice in electing, directly or indirectly, their representatives but not directly in the higher concerns of the state, which he considered beyond their abilities and cognizance.

Jefferson arrived at Annapolis to attend Congress on November 25 but, to his disgust, sufficient delegates to make a quorum for ordinary business did not arrive until December

[7] Cf. Chinard, *Life,* p. 141, and *Writings,* Ford, Vol. III, p. 323.

13, while the additional number necessary to ratify the treaty with France remained absent until January 13. The business to be handled during the session included ratification of the peace treaty, the authorizing of Ministers to make treaties of alliance and commerce, the establishing of arsenals and ports, settling the problem of the Western territory, making treaties with the Indians, establishing a system of money, and other important matters. Jefferson, as he sat in Annapolis for nearly two months and a half while waiting and unable to get ahead with pressing business, became firmly convinced of the absurd incompetency of a national executive which consisted only of a legislative mob, mostly absent. If he had had any doubts about the safety of a single head, they were resolved for good during those annoying ten weeks or so. He remained in Annapolis waiting or attending the session until May 11, 1784, and during that time was the leading member of the body, of which he was elected chairman on March 30.

According to the Articles of Confederation it was necessary to secure favorable votes of nine states to ratify a treaty, and for a whole month a futile debate went on as to whether the seven states which alone had sent representatives could act for the whole. Jefferson, Monroe and others strongly insisted that they could not, which was clearly the only position legally tenable. Meanwhile time was flying and it began to look as though it would be impossible to secure ratification by the proper number of states in time to get the signed copy of the ratified treaty to Paris before the expiration of the period set. Finally on January 13, delegates appeared from Connecticut, and the next day a single one turned up from South Carolina, so that nine states were represented and the treaty was signed. The absurd situation was thus avoided of the states' having fought a war for eight years and then not caring enough about it to sign the treaty of peace which its Ministers had been sent to Europe to negotiate.

As Congress acted as both legislature and executive, there was no organ of government to carry on affairs when Congress was not in session or when it did not have a quorum. To remedy this impossible situation, which had now become palpable but which could not be constitutionally altered without revising the Articles of Confederation, Jefferson proposed that Congress appoint a committee which could carry on in interim. This plan, although adopted, proved a failure. As he wrote in his autobiography, Congress appointed the committee "who entered on duty on the subsequent adjournment of Congress, quarrelled very soon, split into two parties, abandoned their post, and left the government without any visible head until the next meeting of Congress. We have since seen the same thing take place in the Directory of France; and I believe it will forever take place in any Executive consisting of a plurality." [8]

Meanwhile, financial affairs had had to be considered. Jefferson was made chairman of a committee to report on the arrears of public debt and the expenses of the current year, apportioning the amount due from each state. Hamilton had retired from Congress at the end of the preceding session, and, in view of future events, it is interesting to observe Jefferson taking the lead in the financial discussions. He was also made chairman of the committee to establish a currency and standard coin. Robert Morris, the chief financier of the Revolution, had previously made a report, with notable assistance from Gouverneur Morris, and Jefferson now took this as a basis for his own suggestions. Gouverneur Morris had made the happy choice of a decimal system, and this Jefferson at once accepted.

The standard coin proposed in the Morris report, however, was absurdly small, though serving as a measure of the older coins in circulation in varying amounts without in any case "leaving a fraction." Against the advice of the Morrises, but

8 *Writings*, Ford, Vol. I, pp. 75 f.

with approval by Congress, Jefferson made the standard our present dollar, which was the old "Spanish dollar" familiar in all the colonies. This divided decimally into coins convenient for business, bearing close resemblance to many of the smaller ones already in circulation. Jefferson also recognized Gresham's Law according to which if gold and silver were both in use as coins the one whose precious metal content became least valuable commercially would drive the other out of circulation and into secret hoards. He inclined to favor a ratio of fifteen to one. He did not first suggest the decimal system for the United States but he did establish our present currency. It is perhaps possible to over-rate his report. Francis W. Hirst, the distinguished English financial writer, former editor of *The Economist*, wrote of it that it constituted "an epoch in monetary history, ranking with Sir Isaac Newton's representation to the Lords of the Treasury in 1717 (to which Jefferson refers) or with the Bullion Report, which led to the resumption of cash payments in England a few years after Waterloo." [9] On the other hand, the more bigoted biographers of Hamilton unfairly give little credit or none at all to Jefferson. Indeed, the late Senator Lodge, in writing of Hamilton's report on the mint in 1791, suggests that Hamilton first established the decimal system and our coinage. He does not mention Jefferson at all in this connection, and merely states that Hamilton's views on the currency "have been in the main closely followed ever since." [10] Of the later Hamilton report, although anticipating somewhat, we may here quote the American economist Sumner who wrote that Hamilton's "discussion of this entire subject has a superficial aspect of learning; but he had not mastered any point in the question, and the jealousy between himself and Jefferson cannot be overlooked," [11] a jealousy inherited by almost all Hamilton's biographers.

[9] *Life and Letters,* p. 200.
[10] H. C. Lodge, *Alexander Hamilton,* Boston, 1882, p. 108.
[11] William Graham Sumner, *Alexander Hamilton,* New York, 1890, p. 171.

The greatest paper which Jefferson drew up during the session was that dealing with the government of the new territory acquired by the Confederacy in the Northwest. We need not go into the general history of that acquisition beyond saying that in order to make the Articles of Confederation acceptable to all the states, those which had large claims to unsettled lands in the West had agreed to cede these to the general government instead of retaining them for themselves, Virginia making much the largest sacrifice of any of the states. The Confederacy had thus come into possession of a vast area which was owned by *all* the states in common and not by some in severalty. The cessions agreed to and the Articles of Confederation accepted, the question next arose of government in the new territory.

The cession of the lands of Virginia in the Northwest, a veritable empire in themselves and embracing many of the most prosperous states now in the union, was formally executed by the Virginia delegates, with Jefferson at their head, on March 1, 1784, though the state had made its first tender some years before. A few days later a committee, of which Jefferson was chairman, was appointed to draw up a frame of government.

The plan as prepared by Jefferson provided for the extinction by purchase of Indian titles to any part of the new territory, the lands then to be sold to settlers by the United States, and divided into states whose boundaries and absurd names were suggested. Temporary governments were to be established in each state by agreement of all free males of full age. These were to continue in force only until a state had 20,000 inhabitants, when its citizens were to call a convention and adopt a constitution for themselves with certain provisos. Among these should be that the state should forever remain a part of the United States; that its inhabitants should be subject in all ways to the United States in Congress assembled, and to the Articles of Confederation in all those cases in which the original states shall be so subject; that they should pay their proportion of the federal debts; that they should establish only governments of republican form and admit no one as a citizen who held a hereditary title; and, finally, that after 1800 there should be no slavery, or involuntary servitude except for those convicted of crime. It was also provided that as soon as any of the new states should have as numerous a population as that of the least numerous of the original ones, it should be admitted into the Confederation on equal terms with all the others. The report was adopted by Congress, with certain amendments, among them, unfortunately, the elimination of the anti-slavery clause, although Jefferson with his life-long consistence as to slavery voted for its retention.

When Jefferson drafted this fundamental charter for the West it was with the idea that the time had come for the Confederacy and all the land it owned to assume its "permanent form" so that the ordinance has the highest degree of interest as an expression of his views. As to its value, the eminent scholar and editor of Jefferson's works, wrote that "next to the Declaration of Independence (if indeed standing second to that), this document ranks in historical importance of all those drawn by Jefferson; and, but for its being superseded by the 'Ordinance of 1787,' would rank among all American state papers immediately after the National Constitution." [12] The Ordinance of 1787 was drawn by Northerners while Jefferson was in France, and, as Ford points out, Northern historians who have wished to give the credit to men of their own section have studiously avoided noting that the later ordinance, in its more famous clauses, was all drawn from Jefferson's, but that whereas Jefferson had excluded slavery from the entire new West, the Northern ordinance excluded it only from the Northwest. Moreover, on account of the slavery

[12] *Writings*, Ford. Vol. III, p. 430 note.

clause, Jefferson's ordinance became increasingly unpopular in the South. The idea, however, that the new states to be formed should not be "colonies" but eventually admitted as states on an equal basis, which has been one of the most fruitful ideas in our whole political history, was that of a consummate statesman and was wholly Jefferson's own. Had his clauses declaring that none of the newly acquired territory could ever secede and that slavery could never exist in any of it after 1800 also been adopted, the slavery problem would almost certainly have been solved without a civil war. In any case, Jefferson's fundamental idea of equal union and not of an imperial control over the West, the ordinance which he next drew up for a Land Office, though then defeated, followed many years later by his acquisition of the territory of Louisiana from Napoleon, all make him the father of our westward expansion and of our national as contrasted with a mere imperial growth. Had he had his way, the West would have been white and free from the Gulf to Canada. As he himself pointed out, the anti-slavery clause in 1784 was lost by only one vote, so close sometimes are the chances of history.

Jefferson next proceeded to consider our foreign relations. As we have noted, even so important a treaty as that making peace with Great Britain had almost been allowed to go by default because of the lack of interest in the several states in seeing that they sent the necessary delegates to Congress. It was obvious to Jefferson that it would be impossible to carry on ordinary negotiations for treaties, such as those of commerce, in that way. He proposed, therefore, that Congress send accredited Ministers abroad for the express purpose of negotiating such treaties. This was agreed to on May 7. The plans for the treaties as drawn up by Jefferson are chiefly interesting as indicating his enlightened and liberal, although then not politically practical, views as to the conduct of war. These were in part due to humanitarian motives but they also formed an essential part of Jefferson's whole social and political philosophy which assumes, the more we study it, the shape of an organic doctrine in which each part is carefully integrated with all the rest.

As we cannot point out too often, Jefferson in his thinking was at the opposite pole from the French. They believed that their ideas would be true everywhere and among all peoples. On the other hand, Jefferson took pains over and over again to say and write that the experiment he wished to try would in his opinion be possible only in America, owing to the peculiar circumstances existing there. One of the fundamental and most essential of these was the limitless, as it then appeared to him, amount of free land which might ensure an agricultural civilization for centuries to come. He was a thorough-going agrarian, and his views are nowhere better expressed than in a long and well-known passage in his *Notes on Virginia*.

"The political economists of Europe," he wrote, "have established it as a principle, that every State should endeavour to manufacture for itself; and this principle, like many others, we transfer to America, without calculating the difference of circumstance which should often produce a difference of result. In Europe the lands are either cultivated, or locked up against the cultivator. Manufacture must therefore be resorted to, of necessity, not of choice, to support the surplus of their people. But we have an immensity of land courting the industry of the husbandman. Is it best then that all our citizens should be employed in its improvement, or that one half should be called off from that to exercise manufactures and handicrafts for the other? Those who labour in the earth are the chosen people of God, if ever he had a chosen people, whose breasts he has made his peculiar deposit for substantial and genuine virtue. It is the focus in which he keeps alive that sacred fire, which otherwise might escape from the face of the earth. Corruption of morals in the mass of cultivators is a phænomenon of which no age nor nation has furnished an example. It is the mark set on those, who not looking up to heaven, to their own soil and industry, as does the husbandman, for their subsistence, depend on casualties and caprice of customers. Dependence begets subservience and venality, suffocates the germ of virtue, and prepares fit tools for the designs of ambition. . . . While we have land to labour then, let us never wish to see our citizens occupied at a work-bench or twirling a distaff. Carpenters, masons, smiths, are wanting in husbandry: but for the general operations of manufacture, let our work-shops remain in Europe. It is better to carry provisions and materials to workmen there, than bring them to the provisions and materials, and with them their manners and principles. The loss by the transportation of commodities across the Atlantic will be made up in happiness and permanence of government. The mobs of great cities add just so much to the support of pure government, as sores do to the strength of the human body." [13]

Jefferson constantly said that he based his great experiment on a nation overwhelmingly made up of farmers owning their own lands. Unlike the platforms of most reform third-parties into which are swept together a heterogeneous mass of unrelated ideals, Jefferson's were all bound inextricably together. He was always interested in the development westward as increasing the amount of agricultural land available to settlement. He had fought primogeniture and entail to prevent the tying up of large tracts and to make them open to small ownership. He was in favor of keeping as large a proportion of the people on the land as possible because he considered that a city and industrial proletariat, as such were known in his day, was incapable of carrying on the experiment of self-gov-

[13] *Writings,* Ford, Vol. III, pp. 268 f.

ernment as he saw it. Thus he was opposed to the growth of manufacturing and of "business" which bred up a different type of man with a different outlook on life.

All this being so, it followed naturally that Jefferson required for his system as free and unimpeded foreign markets as possible for the sale of American natural produce, and equally unimpeded imports of manufactured articles from foreign countries which, not having the American choice open to them, had already proceeded beyond recall on the industrial path of development. The co-ordinated structure of his whole system thus called for free trade, or as free as might be; for peace and not for war; and, if war should come, for a minimum of interference with trade during its continuance.

All of this hangs together in perfect logic, and explains why, later, Jefferson should have become more and more bitterly opposed to Hamilton as he saw Hamilton's equally logical system clashing at one point after another with these fundamental bases of his own, without the support of which he believed that self-government must fail.

As part of his system, therefore, Jefferson in drawing up his plans for a series of treaties of commerce with other nations suggested many innovations then far beyond the age. He asked, for example, that after a declaration of war, merchants of either country residing and carrying on business in the other, should have nine months in which to wind up their affairs, and be allowed to depart unmolested with their property; and that for the most part alien fisherman, farmers, artisans, and so on, should be allowed to remain and carry on there peaceably their several employments. He also asked that neither belligerent power should grant letters of marque to private vessels to take or destroy the trading ships of the other; that contraband should not be confiscated without payment; and that no neutral vessel should be stopped without well-grounded cause. In these and other respects, the treaties

which Jefferson hoped for would have embodied a far greater
degree of free trade in peace time in the world than then existed, and also a much enlarged freedom of trade for both neutrals and belligerents in war time.

We may pause over one of the resolutions, namely, "that
these United States be considered in all such treaties . . . as one
nation" [14] to note the steady development of Jefferson's
thought toward nationalism since he had written eight years
earlier that "these United Colonies are, and of right ought to
be, free and independent States." His first period of service in
Congress had been more concerned with gaining independence
from Great Britain for the colonies as separate states than in
thinking of union between them. Next had come his important
services in the Virginia legislature, in which the reorganization
of the social and political structure of that state was his
proper and chief concern. During his governorship in the war
years he had perforce to think in national terms, and, as we
have seen, he had done so, supporting national, at the expense
of local, defense, thereby deliberately incurring the hostility
of many in his own state. Then had come the problem of the
cession of the Western lands in order to bring about the acceptance of the Confederation, and in his plan for the government of the national domain thus acquired we can see the great
step ahead which he had made. Whatever he may have believed
as to the rights of the original thirteen states, he laid it down
that the new states to be erected could never carry states'
rights to the point of secession but that their territory must
forever remain a part of the "United States." The implications of this were very great. In this respect his second period
of Congressional service was of great influence upon him. On
the one hand, he experienced the difficulties, as Hamilton had
just before him, of the loose and inefficient organization which
bound the states together at home and which endeavored to

[14] *Writings,* Ford, Vol. III, p. 490.

function for them in foreign relations. He himself noted the difference between the point of view to be gained by serving in even the weak Congress of the Confederation and that in a state legislature. Writing from Annapolis to his friend, James Madison, he noted that "I see the best effects produced by sending our young statesmen here. They see the affairs of the Confederacy from a high ground; they learn the importance of the Union & befriend federal measures when they return. Those who never come here, see our affairs insulated, pursue a system of jealousy & self interest, and distract the Union as much as they can." [15]

Through the lessons of experience as governor and Congressman, reacting to foreign criticism of "America," and by the processes of thought, Jefferson the American had now clearly emerged from Jefferson the great Virginian.

His contacts with Washington had become both frequent and friendly. We have already seen how closely he had worked with the Commander-in-Chief when governor and endeavored in every way to carry out his policy. We have also noted Washington's appreciation. Correspondence had continued, and invitations came to visit Mount Vernon. When Washington appeared before Congress to resign his commission and retire from public service, Jefferson had charge of the arrangements. When criticism became vehement against the formation of the order of the Cincinnati, which Washington had favored, he wrote to Jefferson for his views and for advice. It had been proposed that the officers who had served in the war should join in an organization to perpetuate their common memories of service, and also that the society should be hereditary. Many people felt that this savored too much of an incipient aristocracy when they had just gone through a war, in part, to do away with privilege and class distinctions. Historians have sometimes laughed at this fear, but fear of a veterans'

[15] *Writings,* Ford, Vol. III, p. 403.

organization was, I think, justified. In reply to Washington's enquiry, Jefferson sent a very sensible answer. The impulse, he said, of men who have gone through identical experiences and hardships, to form an organization which shall enable them to meet and renew old friendships, was a natural one.

Nevertheless, there were difficulties. As to Washington himself, Jefferson said that he had served his country with a remarkable disinterestedness, and hinted that now it would be unwise for him to back an organization which would encounter much public hostility, both in Congress and among the people. As to the organization, Jefferson considered that the danger of a hereditary class might be remote, but that there were more immediate dangers, such as "that a distinction is kept up between the civil & military, which it is for the happiness of both to obliterate; that when the members assemble they will be proposing to do something, & what that something will be will depend on actual circumstances; that being an organized body under habits of subordination, the first obstructions to enterprize will be already surmounted." [16] What that "something" is which organizations of veterans may "try to do" has been all too amply shown by the successive organizations which have exerted a most pernicious influence upon our public life, and which by generations of political pressure upon Congress, and even by threats of force, have looted the public treasury and have taken for themselves as a privileged class many billions of dollars from their fellow citizens, and are ever demanding more. The previsions of Jefferson and many others of the dangers in a democracy of an organization based on military service were fully justified, and had Washington foreseen the pension scandals of a later day and dreamed of "Bonus Marchers" moving on the Capitol to over-awe Congress, demanding not back pay but largess, he also would have realized the danger and would have killed the first veterans' organiza-

16 *Writings,* Ford, Vol. III, p. 467.

tion before its birth, although the Order of the Cincinnati itself has not been involved.

On the very day when Jefferson's "Instructions to Ministers" were reported to Congress, that body elected him to the post of Minister to France to act jointly with John Adams and Benjamin Franklin in negotiating treaties of commerce with foreign nations. This time, Jefferson was free to go, and to indulge in the double pleasure of serving his country in an honorable capacity and of seeing that Europe which he had longed to visit ever since his boyhood days at college. Four days later he left Annapolis on his way to Paris, a nationalist and thorough-going American off to face and study the Old World.

CHAPTER VIII

MINISTER TO FRANCE

JEFFERSON, accompanied by the eldest of his three little girls, set sail from Boston, and arrived in Paris August 6, 1784, after a short stop in England. For the next five years and more he was to remain in Europe, being appointed Minister to France on Franklin's retirement the year after his own arrival. Two things are likely to happen to a good American who remains long abroad. On the one hand he is likely to feel more and more remote from actual happenings at home, which lose in vividness; and, on the other, to have his patriotism take on a livelier hue, becoming, moreover, national rather than local. Both these influences were exerted upon Jefferson. It was fortunate for him perhaps that during Shays's rebellion, the drafting and adoption of the new federal constitution, and the formation of political parties, he was far from the immediate hurly-burly of the scene, and could take a detached view. Also, always intensely American, his European experiences made him even more so.

Later in life, when his political enemies grasped at any weapon with which to strike him, and the French Revolution in its later excesses—which did not occur until after Jefferson had left France—had alarmed all conservatives in state and church, he was accused of having been greatly influenced by French revolutionary ideas and of being a Jacobin. Such accusations may have been good politics but they were certainly far from being the truth. The fact is that it would scarcely be an exaggeration to say that he came back without a single major idea which he had not taken with him when he sailed from Boston. This does not mean that he did not acquire a vast amount of information and also of experience. It means that when in his forty-second year he arrived in France he had already rounded out a complete political philosophy which was thereafter to be modified only in details and not in fundamentals. So far as new ideas were concerned, instead of receiving them, he rather gave them to the leaders of the new movement in Paris which was for the most part in the hands of the moderates during his stay. What France did do for him in the realm of political thought was to deepen and intensify the conclusions he had already reached, particularly on such matters as the burden on a people of monarchy and privilege, the value of self-government, the necessity of preparing the people by education and otherwise for the task, and the belief, from which he never wavered, that so far from democracy and self-government being possible everywhere, they were at that time possible only in America, and even there only under the conditions which he was trying to conserve, foster, and improve.

Thus, both for his personal life and for his impress on our history, the French years were less important than the space usually allotted to them by most biographers would indicate. Consideration of them rather naturally divides itself into his social life, his æsthetic experiences, his fact-gathering, his work as Minister, and his political thought.

Jefferson was not extravagant or careless. During all his years, public and private, he set down most minute accounts of his expenses, and endeavored to keep these within the limits of his income, and to care for his debts with scrupulous honesty. The burden of these latter was due either to others or to war conditions, and not to his own heedlessness. On the other hand, he had the love of the born aristocrat for a spacious, comely, and dignified life. His beloved Monticello was 3000 miles away but, after changing quarters several times, he settled himself in "a very elegant house, even for Paris" with extensive gardens. It belonged to the Comte de Langeac, and stood on the corner of the Champs Elysées and the rue Neuve de Berry. His chef and his cellar enjoyed their own reputations, and both Washington and John Adams depended on Jefferson's taste in wines to secure their supplies.

His background for entertaining was soon complete and ample. Nor was acquaintance lacking in the world of wit and fashion. Of his two colleagues, with both of whom he was on most friendly terms, Adams was not a very social person, but Franklin had long been the idol of French society. Moreover, Lafayette was deeply attached to Jefferson, a feeling which the latter reciprocated during his half century of friendship. The young Marquis, as the saying goes, "knew everybody." Again, Jefferson was an accredited representative, soon to be Minister Plenipotentiary, of a new country which was intensely interesting to many leading Frenchmen. Certainly the door of social opportunity was wide. Jefferson himself, although reported as being a little shy and austere on first meeting, delighted in intelligent conversation, and was a hospitable host.

Apparently, however, he neither greatly enjoyed, indulged in, nor profited by European society. During his stays in England, possessing that American sensitiveness of nature so little comprehended by the English, he found himself rebuffed almost brutally at every point. Perhaps no other people can be so courteous or, when they choose to be, so incredibly rude to foreigners and guests as the British. In the years of Jefferson's foreign duties, it chanced that they deliberately chose to be the latter. There was much more coarseness than good-sportmanship among eighteenth-century Englishmen, and they displayed toward the freed Americans none of either the good sense or the magnanimity which their descendants were to show more than a century later toward the conquered Boers. Jefferson, who truly wished to be friends with the British, had reluctantly to confess that their only feeling for us was a "deep rooted and cordial" hatred, and that the Englishmen he met had to "be kicked into common good manners." For the most part there was neither pleasure nor profit for Jefferson in their society.

On the other hand, though the French of the period were far more civilized socially, and, moreover, liked, instead of detesting, Americans, Jefferson found the constant flow of compliment and the artificiality of Parisian society both irksome and insincere. His own good manners sprang directly from the kindly and considerate instincts of a gentleman, and not from form. I think Professor Chinard lays rather too much stress upon the strain of Puritanism in him as making him reticent in expression, and that it was rather due to that instinctive reserve which is so often found in the best of the British people. Ending a letter to Lafayette, signed, as they thenceforth were all to be for forty years, "Yours affectionately," he writes that "the waters must always be what are the fountains from which they flow. According to this, indeed, I should have intermixed, from beginning to end, warm expressions of friendship to you. But according to the ideas of our country, we do not permit ourselves to speak even truths, when they may have the air of flattery. I content myself, therefore, with saying once for all that I love you, your wife and children. Tell them so, and adieu." [1]

Jefferson never cared for cities, and like Englishmen and Virginians, struck his roots deep only in the country. "I am savage enough," he wrote to Baron de Geismer, "to prefer the woods, the wilds, and the independence of Monticello, to all the brilliant pleasures of this gay Capital." [2] There, too, his wife lay buried, and as we have said, there is nothing to show

[1] Chinard, *Letters of Lafayette and Jefferson*, p. 112.
[2] *Memorial Edition*, Vol. V, p. 128.

that he ever had more than the palest of Platonic friendship
with any woman after her death. He knew, indeed, a brilliant
group—Madame Helvétius, Madame d'Houdetout, Comtesse
de Tessé, the young Madame de Corny, the Comtesse de la
Rochefoucauld, and others—but he appears to have been rather
uneasy in the society of intrigue, and although he tried his
hand at corresponding lightly and gaily with some of his
women friends it must be confessed that such efforts are among
the least genuine and satisfying of all his writings. So also are
his letters to his children, although there can be no doubt of
his deep affection for them. He had taken the eldest with him,
as we have seen, to be placed at school in a convent. Not long
after he sailed, the youngest died in Virginia, and he was not
content until he had been able to have his second one sent over
to join him.

The fact is, I think—and it is not without bearing on his
later political career when he was content, so to say, to go out
in the social wilderness to suffer for his ideas—that Jefferson
in spite of his strong affections and many lasting friendships
was essentially not only a lonely man but a very independent
and self-sufficient one. In his struggles for the reform of Virginian government and society he had knowingly and willingly strewn antagonisms all round him among the members
of his own class. When he built his home, he forsook the val-
leys and established himself on a solitary mountain top—a
significant gesture. In spite of his elegant house in Paris with
its ample rooms for work and quiet, "he also had rooms," so
wrote his daughter later, "in the Carthusian Monastery on
Mount Calvary; the boarders, of whom I think there were
about forty, carried their own servants, and took their break-
fasts in their own rooms. They assembled to dinner only. They
had the privilege of walking in the gardens, but as it was a
hermitage, it was against the rules . . . for any voices to be
heard . . . hence the most profound silence. . . . Whenever he

had a press of business, he was in the habit of taking his papers and going to the hermitage where he sometimes spent a week or more." [3] In a letter on travel he wrote that he preferred to journey alone as doing so gave him more time to ponder over what he was seeing. Naturally, he derived the benefits which any intelligent man does from moving in a cultivated and polished society. Moreover, the kind offices which he performed for his friends were endless, especially in shopping, the range extending from wines for Washington, books for Madison, Wythe, and other men, to corsets for Mrs. John Adams and dresses for the women of his family in Virginia, even down to dolls and toys for the children. But the fact remains that his European years seem to have made him less, rather than more, dependent upon society, and to have strengthened, to some extent at least, the instinct of the "lone wolf" in him.

As to his æsthetic interest in what he saw in Europe, I think there has been a good deal of misunderstanding. For the most part the impossible method of deducing facts from negative evidence has been adopted. The comparative paucity of notes, in his brief diaries or his letters, as to galleries, buildings, paintings, landscape, and other such matters, has led even Professor Chinard, who has done more to interpret his mind for us than any other writer, to say that "it must be confessed that Jefferson remained very narrow and provincial, and almost a Philistine in his outlook." [4]

There are several things to be noted about this. On the one hand, there is, as I just said, the impossibility of judging from negative evidence. A letter deals quite as much with what the recipient is likely to be interested in as with what the writer is. Moreover, apart from that, one may be much interested in certain things without writing about them. The entire series of letters of Henry Adams, for example, during his early European years, have scarcely a mention of scenery or art in any

[3] Randolph, *Domestic Life*, p. 73.   [4] Chinard, *Life*, p. 164.

form, though clearly he was not oblivious to all he saw. If I may be pardoned a personal reference, to emphasize the point, most of my own time for some years has been devoted to books and travel, yet there is little of either books or art in my personal letters. They have been my chief occupations, yet it might be argued from negative evidence that I cared for neither.

Coming to positive evidence, it is of two sorts, for and against Jefferson's lack of interest in the arts during these French years. First we may note that Jefferson was the leading architect of his day in America and the one man responsible for the classical revival not only in the United States but in the world, as America, through Jefferson, led that revival by about twenty years, his work considerably preceding the first example in France, that of the Madeleine in Paris. He had not only built Monticello and planned other houses before going abroad, but while there he drew the designs for the Capitol at Richmond, which Fiske Kimball states was, as originally designed by Jefferson, a landmark of the first importance in the history of our architecture.

As we have already seen, one of his chief passions all his life was music. Moreover, in his book on Virginia he had been the first American author to draw attention to the beauty of American scenery. He happily chose Houdon, as the first sculptor in Europe of the time, to do the bust of Washington. In his home at Monticello all the furnishings and appointments, chosen by himself, indicated a man of cultivated taste. Given all that, it seems incredible that he should not have been interested in the arts while abroad, and wrong to infer that he was not so because he does not descant upon them in his private letters. As a matter of fact he did do so at times.

"Were I to proceed to tell you," he wrote to Mr. Bellini after speaking of the French, "how much I enjoy their architecture, sculpture, painting, music, I should want words. It is in these arts they shine. The last of them, particularly, is an enjoyment, the deprivation of which with us, cannot be calculated. I am almost ready to say, it is the only thing which from my heart I envy them, and which, in spite of all the authority of the Decalogue, I do covet." [5] In an often quoted letter to the Comtesse de Tessé he wrote from Nismes: "Here I am, Madam, gazing whole hours at the Maison Quarrée, like a lover at his mistress. . . . This is the second time I have been in love since I left Paris. The first was with a Diana at the Chateau de Laye-Epinaye in Beaujolais, a delicious morsel of sculpture by M. A. Slodtz. . . . While in Paris I was violently smitten with the Hotel de Salm, and used to go to the Tuileries almost daily to look at it. . . . From Lyons to Nismes I have been nourished with the remains of Roman grandeur." He then speaks of the vandalism of the French in destroying some of the most beautiful of the Roman structures, but gets into a good humor again when he mentions "the sublime triumphal arch" at Orange, and the "Pont du Gard, a sublime antiquity, and well preserved." [6]

In spite of Jefferson's æsthetic tastes, which appear to be evident throughout life, in spite of the fact that two of his most intimate friends in Paris were artists, in spite of such passages as the above, and his designing of the Virginia Capitol (what American ambassador before or since ever designed a masterpiece in architecture?) we are asked to believe that he was not interested in the arts in Europe because his letters rarely mentioned them and are filled with utilitarian and political matters. It is true that he was greatly interested in both the latter. On his travels in France and Italy, he wrote to Lafayette, that in the great cities, "I go to see what travellers think alone worthy of being seen; but I make a job of it, and generally gulp it all down in a day. On the other hand, I am never satisfied with rambling through the fields and farms,

[5] *Memorial Edition,* Vol. V, p. 154.   [6] *Ibid.,* Vol. VI, pp. 102 ff.

examining the culture and cultivators." [7] Writing again to the same friend as to how to travel so as really to learn about the people, he said, "to do it most effectually, you must be absolutely incognito, you must ferret the people out of their hovels as I have done, look into their kettles, eat their bread, loll on their beds under pretence of resting yourself, but, in fact, to find if they are soft." [8]

There are several points to consider as to Jefferson's interests in France. Government for Jefferson was a necessary evil. It was neither a game to be played nor a theoretical problem to be worked out. It was merely a practical arrangement for securing at any time and place the greatest happiness possible for the individual citizen. Therefore, for Jefferson as observer, the place to study the nature of monarchy as seen in France was neither the court of Versailles nor the closet of the paper constitution-maker but the hovel of the peasant. There he could see government in operation. He was in France not as a man of leisure but as the hard-working representative of a new and undeveloped country. Time was precious, and he had never dreamed of remaining five years when he had sailed. His idea of the work of a Minister was not merely to negotiate treaties and attend to office routine but to secure all possible information of every sort which might be of use to the ordinary citizens of his own land.

It was with this last object in mind that he penned what Professor Chinard terms a "most damning document" which "has to be read to be believed." [9] At the risk of setting myself down as a "Philistine" I shall say frankly that I see nothing damning in it. It was a series of notes for Messrs. Rutledge and Shippen on travelling, scribbled, as Jefferson wrote in the covering letter, "hastily and informally." [10] These gentlemen were anxious for information to take to America, and their

[7] Chinard, *Life*, p. 166, quoted from Jeff. Mss., Lib. Cong.
[8] *Letters of Lafayette and Jefferson*, ed. Chinard, p. 111.
[9] *Life*, p. 164.   [10] *Memorial Edition*, Vol. VII, p. 52.

mission had a semi-official character, as they were accompanied by the Minister's private secretary from the Legation. After some very sensible general advice, Jefferson made the special notes which have so scandalized his delightful and cultured biographer. To understand them, we must recall the nature of the tour to be taken, and that they were specially marked "Objects for the attention of an American." They were, "(1) Agriculture. Everything belonging to this art. . . . Useful or agreeable animals which might be transported to America. Species of plants for the farmer's garden, according to the climate of the different states. (2) Mechanical arts, so far as they respect things necessary in America, and inconvenient to be transported thither ready-made. . . . (3) Lighter mechanical arts, and manufactures. . . . (4) Gardens peculiarly worth the attention of an American, because it is the country of all others where the noblest gardens may be made. . . . (5) Architecture worth great attention. [As population doubles every twenty years, he wrote, the number of houses must, and as built of perishable material, half of those built must be rebuilt in the same period] and it is desirable to introduce taste into an art which shows so much. (6) Painting. Statuary. Too expensive for the state of wealth among us. It would be useless, therefore, and preposterous, for us to make ourselves connoisseurs in those arts. They are worth seeing, but not studying. (7) Politics of each country, well worth studying so far as respects their internal affairs. Examine their influence on the happiness of the people. Take every possible occasion for entering into the houses of the laborers, and especially at the moments of their repast; see what they eat, how they are clothed, whether they are obliged to work too hard; whether the government or their landlord takes from them an unjust proportion of their labor; on what footing stands the property they call their own, their personal liberty, etc., etc. (8) Courts. To be seen as you would see the tower of London or menagerie of Versailles with their lions, tigers, and other beasts of prey." [11]

In a later letter, Jefferson urged the trio to make a detour by all means to Nismes "to see the most perfect remains of antiquity which exist on earth." [12] As he had listed the statue of Diana as one of the three things with which he had fallen in love in France we need not take his suggestion to *see* but not to take time to *study* paintings and sculpture as indicating too strongly that he had suddenly become a Philistine. We have quoted the notes—which might almost be called instructions, as his Secretary of Legation was of the party—at length not so much to labor further the point as to Jefferson's æsthetic interests while abroad as because they bring out so clearly his attitude toward what Europe had to offer an American, and his own policy of observation.

We gather more light from various letters which he wrote as to the wisdom of sending young men abroad to study and travel. Many of his objections were moral. The man who could fall in love with a statue of Diana, who loved a good table, fine wines and horses, was no Puritan in the kill-joy sense, but he was a strict moralist. At that period, the manners and morals of both England and France were deeply corrupt. It was the end of an era in both countries. Short, his secretary, used to laugh later over how even when the conversation merely got "broad" Jefferson would blush like a boy. He felt that to send young Americans to Europe under the circumstances would be likely to ruin them. But there was also the feeling, much increased by his foreign years, that America was different from Europe, and must stay so. That had been, and always remained, the corner-stone of his belief that America alone could try a new form of government. If America were to become and to remain a land of widely distributed agricultural free-hold properties of moderate size, a certain type

[11] *Memorial Edition,* Vol. XVII, pp. 290 ff.   [12] *Ibid.,* Vol. VII, p. 153.

of civilization, on which he based his hopes for the happiness of her people, would arise. He wished it to become a beautiful and intelligent civilization. From this came his insistence upon the improvement of our architecture, upon gardens (for which alone he had unqualified praise in England), upon education and public libraries. The America of his dream was to be a land of widely distributed comfort, independence, and wealth, not of concentrated population or large fortunes. There was thus much good sense in his arguments when he claimed that a foreign education, under conditions so alien to what existed in America, would tend to unfit a youth for living in his own country, and being happy there. Every country has its good and bad points. Any one who has lived in several realizes how difficult it is to be wholly content thereafter in any one, as he is always missing the special charms of one or another. As William James wrote after long European experience: "One should not become a cosmopolitan, one's soul becomes 'disintegrated,' as Janet would say. Parts of it remain in different places, and the whole of it nowhere." [13] It was this, rather than crass Philistinism or Puritan repression, I think, which led Jefferson to advise his tourists not to linger to study paintings or sculpture.

But if the America which Jefferson envisaged was to be a land of comfort and beauty and not a land of luxury and the more costly arts, it was still a very new and undeveloped one, needing many things to produce comfort and beauty. As a good American, and one living abroad at the expense of his government, Jefferson felt it his duty, as well as his inclination, to discover as many things useful to America as he could. As a fact gatherer he has surely never been equalled by any other of our diplomats. He tried to do all the work now done by ministers, attachés, consuls, and commercial representatives. He learned about printing presses, wheelbarrows, canals and

[13] *Letters of William James,* ed. by Henry James, Boston, 1926, p. 347, note.

locks, the new steam engine, innumerable mechanical devices, processes of manufacture. He studied minutely soils, crops, and everything connected with agriculture. He even risked his life to smuggle some seed rice out of Italy, a crime punishable by death. It was, however, considered the best, far better than the American of that day, and the American Minister crossed the border with his pockets stuffed! Pages could be filled with a mere enumeration of facts which he gathered and sent to American colleges, societies, friends, or Congress.

Although far from being unimportant, the more normal diplomatic duties which he performed need not be discussed at length. Most of their specific diplomatic interest has faded and they concern us here chiefly as bringing out Jefferson's ideas or influencing his viewpoints.

Jefferson's original appointment had been to join Franklin and Adams in negotiating trade treaties. In this they were unsuccessful, the only nation then willing to treat with the United States for that purpose being Prussia. A treaty with the King was negotiated and signed, embodying Jefferson's liberal ideas as to the treatment of merchants, privateers, and the freedom of the seas as expressed by him before leaving America in the *Instructions to Ministers Plenipotentiary* and accepted by Congress. The doctrines enunciated were far in advance of their time, and as to the freedom of the seas have never yet been accepted by England. It was a triumph, however, for the new young country that it should both advance more humane views as to war and have them embodied in at least one international treaty with an European power.

After Franklin's retirement, when Adams had become Minister to England and Jefferson to France, Adams asked the latter to go over to London to help in making trade treaties with England and Portugal. Nothing could be done with England and the projects fell through. As to England, Jefferson wrote his friend John Page that "the nation hates us, their ministers hate us, and their King more than other men. They have the impudence to avow this, tho' they acknolege [*sic*] our trade important to them. But they say we cannot prevent our countrymen from bringing that into their laps. . . . They say they will pocket our carrying trade as well as their own." He added that the British treated the idea of a trade treaty with derision, and that "their hostility toward us is much more deeply rooted at present than during the war." [14]

It had been with great reluctance that Jefferson, as was the case with most Americans, had felt called upon to sever the ties with the mother country. He would gladly have entered again into amicable relations with Great Britain from which, as he said, America had more to gain as a friend and to lose as an enemy, than from any other. The chief result of his diplomatic efforts in London was to bring home to him the impossibility of working on friendly terms with Great Britain for a long time ahead if ever, and therefore the importance to America of developing the French friendship. On the other hand, the longer he remained abroad, the more he realized the hollowness of any international friendship, and both the necessity and the desirability of America's cutting loose from Europe and depending solely on herself.

One of his diplomatic failures confirmed him in this opinion. For long, the European powers had paid a regular tribute to the Barbary pirates to keep them from preying on the commerce passing through the Mediterranean. It was a humiliating position in which even England acquiesced. Jefferson, although Adams preferred tribute, was strongly in favor of bringing the matter to an end by maintaining a blockade of the pirates' ports by a joint fleet provided by the United States and some of the European powers. In view of the fact that owing to his embargo policy when President he is often painted as a peace-at-any-price man, his insistence, both then and

[14] *Writings*, Ford, Vol. IV, p. 215.

later, on war with the pirates is interesting. He could, however, secure no co-operation in Europe, and eventually young America did the job herself, while the greatest sea power in the world sat still.

In trying to negotiate a trade treaty in England, Jefferson had had to meet and parry the question of debts due from Americans to British merchants. He insisted, with Adams, that although the principal of legitimate debts should be paid as soon as conditions permitted, there could be no allowance for interest during the war years, as Great Britain by her own acts had made commerce between the two countries impossible. He proceeded further, however, and advanced the thesis, of importance today in view of the now reversed debt situation between the Old and New Worlds, that the debts could not be considered apart from the whole question of trade relations, and that some settlement of the latter was necessary "were it only as a means of enabling our country to pay its debts. That they had been contracted while certain modes of remittance had existed here, and had been an inducement to us to contract these debts." [15]

The debts due to France by the United States, and even more the arrears of pay due to French officers who had fought in the American Army, gave Jefferson much trouble in that country. He displayed patience, and considerable skill and tact in the handling of this matter, rendered so embarrassing to him from the inability of Congress to pay. His idea of borrowing sufficient from Dutch bankers to pay off the French Government, and so turn a "political debt" into a commercial one, was sound, but of more interest was his reaffirmation of his stand taken in England, namely that the debts could not be considered and paid unless at the same time arrangements were made for freer trade between the two nations. The United States of that day had no gold or silver mines and so could pay

[15] *Writings*, Ford, Vol. IV, p. 211.

debts owing abroad only by the export of goods of some sort.[16]
Although his long negotiations concerning tobacco, fish, and
other commodities did not bring the results hoped for, France
did remove some of the trade barriers she had erected and went
farther to meet America than had England. During the whole
of his term Jefferson had a valuable ally in Lafayette, whose
views on most matters, from the tobacco monopoly of the
Farmers-general to the proper handling of the Barbary corsairs, usually coincided with his own. French trade interests,
however, were almost as deeply entrenched and opposed to
change as were the English.

During the whole of his five years, whether he was trying
to negotiate loans or treaties, Jefferson was constantly en-
countering the opposition and intrigues of the financiers and
larger business interests. He came to realize the immense
though silent powers exerted by them, against which the political powers came to seem helpless. Always mistrustful of
large-scale finance, he became more so than ever. Here, he felt,
was a monster which might throttle government and extend its
tentacles throughout a nation.

Meanwhile the coming storm of the Revolution was brewing,
though it was not to break in its full intensity until after Jefferson had returned to duties in America. Jefferson watched
its earlier stage with interest and sympathy, taking, however,
a very conservative stand with regard to its possibilities, and
not foreseeing the blood and agony to come.

His observation in Paris and in the homes of the humble
throughout the country, had shown him both sides of contemporary France. "It is a true picture," he wrote to Bellini in
the letter already quoted, "of that country to which they say
we shall pass hereafter, and where we are to see God and his
angels in splendor, and crowds of the damned under their
feet." [17] And again writing to Edward Carrington of the con-

---

[16] *Vide infra,* Chapter X.   [17] *Memorial Edition,* Vol. V, p. 152.

ditions in Europe he said of the rulers that "under the pretence of governing they have divided their nations into two
classes, wolves & sheep. I do not exaggerate. This is a true
picture of Europe. Cherish therefore the spirit of our people,
and keep alive their attention. . . . If once they become in-
attentive to the public affairs, you and I, & Congress & Assem-
blies, judges & governors shall all become wolves. It seems to
be the law of our general nature, in spite of individual exceptions; and experience declares that man is the only animal
which devours his own kind, for I can apply no milder term to
the governments of Europe, and to the general prey of the
rich on the poor." [18] Speaking in a letter to Washington of
monarchy and aristocracy he wrote that "to know the mass of
evil which flows from this fatal source, a person must be in
France, he must see the finest soil, the finest climate, the most
compact state, the most benevolent character of people, &
every earthly advantage combined, insufficient to prevent this
scourge from rendering existence a curse to 24 out of 25 parts
of the inhabitants of this country." [19]

Nevertheless, nothing shows better the balance of Jefferson's
mind, and expresses again his disbelief in a doctrinaire theory
of a government which should be perfect for all times and all
peoples than his attitude in his last two years in France. He
was, as he wrote long after, in close personal touch with all the
leaders of the reform movement, with Lafayette then at their
head. Nevertheless, he continually counselled them to go slowly, and, so far from advocating the American Government as
model, advised the retention of the monarchy and the introduction of a mild imitation of the English constitution. He had
entered the homes of too many peasants to think of them in
the same terms as the free-hold farmers of Albemarle County,
Virginia, and he displayed his unfailing trait of mind of adapting an ideal or a theory to the practical conditions of a specific

[18] *Writings,* Ford, Vol. IV, p. 360.   [19] *Ibid.,* Vol. IV, p. 329.

case. In March, 1787, writing to Madame de Tessé, Lafayette's cousin, in the same letter in which he had descanted on the Maison Quarrée at Nismes, Jefferson continued on the newly called Assembly of the Notables. "Under a good and young King, as the present," he said, "I think good may be made of it." He suggested a division into two houses, and then went on: "Two Houses so elected, would contain a mass of wisdom which would make the people happy, and the King great; would place him in history where no other act can possibly place him. They would thus put themselves in the track of the best guide they can follow; they would soon overtake it, become its guide in turn, and lead to the wholesome modifications wanting in that model, and necessary to constitute a rational government. Should they attempt more than the established habits of the people are ripe for, they may lose all, and retard indefinitely the ultimate object of their aim." [20]

Throughout the remainder of his term of office, until his departure for America in October, 1789, he maintained much the same opinion. On several occasions he rather transgressed the limits of interference, perhaps, in the internal affairs of a nation by a minister accredited to it by another power. In June of his last year, he drew up a suggested constitution for France, which he sent not only to his intimate friend Lafayette but also to Rabaud de Saint Etienne, and about the same time he opened himself to criticism by the French Government, though none was forthcoming, by allowing Lafayette, with eight of his friends, to dine at his house to discuss their plans. Jefferson himself took no part in the discussions, but the impropriety of the American Minister's allowing his house to be used for such a purpose was obvious, though Lafayette had merely told him they were coming, with little notice ahead.

Jefferson was in fact getting himself rather deeply involved but he was far from taking a revolutionary or even a radical

[20] *Memorial Edition*, Vol. VI, p. 105.

stand. As we have pointed out before, it is a mistake to think that he trusted the common man under all circumstances to exercise all the functions of government. He certainly trusted the farmer of Albemarle County more than the peasant of France or a citizen of Paris, but on July 19, 1789, with the Revolution soon to break over society in tumultuous waves, he wrote to the Abbé Arnond [21] that "we think in America that it is necessary to introduce the people into every department of government as far as they are capable of exercising it; and that this is the only way to ensure a long continued & honest administration of its powers. (1) They are not qualified to exercise themselves the Executive department; but they are qualified to name the person who shall exercise it. With us therefore they chuse this officer every four years. (2) They are not qualified to Legislate. With us therefore they only chuse the legislators. (3) They are not qualified to *Judge* questions of *law;* but they are very capable of judging questions of *fact.* In the form of juries therefore they determine all matters of fact, leaving to the permanent judges to decide the law resulting from those facts. But we all know that permanent judges acquire an *Esprit de corps*, that being known they are liable to be tempted by bribery, that they are misled by favor, by relationship, by a spirit of party, by a devotion to an Executive or Legislative; that it is better to leave a cause to the decision of cross & pile, than to that of a judge biased to one side. . . . Were I called upon to decide whether the people had best be omitted in the Legislative or Judiciary department, I would say it is better to leave them out of the Legislature. The execution of the laws is more important than the making them." [22]

That Jefferson was in favor of the Revolution, as he saw it, is true, but he wished it to take a moderate course. He believed

[21] The Ford Edition has *Arnond;* the Memorial Edition *Arnoud.*
[22] *Writings,* Ford, Vol. V, pp. 103 f.

from his observations that the people were not yet prepared to undertake a large measure of direct self-government. "In science," he had written of the French soon after arrival, "the mass of the people are two centuries behind ours; their literati, half a dozen years before us." [23] Meanwhile, as one of the great world dramas was beginning to unfold before him in France, a small revolution which almost equally shared his interest had flared up in New England, and we must turn our attention homeward. The stage was small, the events few, the violence negligible as revolutions or insurrections go, but, as having a profound influence upon the formation of our Federal Constitution, Shays's Rebellion was an event of prime importance in our history.

Massachusetts and Virginia had been the leading states in developing the philosophy of the Revolution of 1776. We have already noted how in rationalizing the case against England, the colonists had been driven from mere interpretation of the British constitution to the broader ground of natural rights, the rights of man, inalienable rights, and such slogans as "no taxation without representation" and so on. As against England, these were useful weapons. They were also good recruiting propaganda, and when spread before ordinary citizens in newspapers, pamphlets, or impassioned speeches, they were believed. They were what the ordinary American was fighting or suffering for. On the other hand, the rich and governing class had always been uneasy lest the common people take such ideas too seriously, once independence was won, and threaten property by taking the government into their own hands. In plain words the Conservative leaders used the philosophy of natural rights against England but were prepared to deny it if turned as a weapon against their own entrenched privileges by the American people. Almost alone of the prominent leaders in the events leading up to independence, Jefferson kept

[23] *Memorial Edition*, Vol. V, p. 152.

faith with the people by upholding the doctrines he had espoused in 1776. It was no accident that he was in 1800 to become the standard bearer of the democracy of the day. It is true that he had consummate ability as a political organizer, but it is also true that the people naturally turned to him as the most prominent man who had consistently and without wavering clung to the doctrines which they believed were the basis of Americanism as contrasted with the then European theories and practice of government. As a leader he was to have to provide the machinery through which the inchoate masses could act, but it was his long record of belief in them that was to make them so readily accept him as their leader.

In the continuous debate in our history as to who shall govern, Shays's Rebellion was one of the most important turning points. Massachusetts had adopted a new constitution in 1780. It was a distinctly reactionary document, and those responsible for drafting and securing its adoption largely rejected the doctrine of the rights of man in favor of that of the rights of property. When New Hampshire was granting the franchise to every male over twenty-one who paid a poll tax, and Vermont had introduced universal suffrage for males over legal age, Massachusetts took away the right to vote from many of her citizens by doubling the required property qualification. The old ruling caste tried to entrench itself more firmly in power than ever. By 1786, although many had lost the right to vote, over forty per cent of the state taxes were levied solely on polls. Thus a considerable step backward had been taken toward the European theory of a ruling class and of a people which was to be taxed but not allowed to vote.

Economic conditions following the peace of 1783 had taken their almost inevitable course after the close of a prolonged war. There had been two years of extravagance, of mal-adjustment, of false prosperity, and of running into debt. Then came the usual primary post-war crash. Most Americans were farmers. Prices for farms and their produce had fallen heavily. The decline in paper money and the final repudiation of the Continental currency had wrought confusion in the economic system. The burden of debt, national, state, and personal, had become unbearably heavy, the more so as there was no proper system of finance or taxation. The Massachusetts legislature levied no taxes one year and then imposed far more than could be borne the next. In Groton in 1784 to 1786 one farmer out of every four or perhaps three was subject to from one to twelve suits for debt. In Worcester County the head of practically every family was being sued. Farms could not be sold at decent prices or even at such as would clear the debts on them. As persons could be imprisoned for debt, a large part of the hard-working, honest population faced not only destitution but jail.

Petitions to the legislature were treated with almost as much contempt as had been those of the colonists to the English King. At last, after all peaceful means had been exhausted, a part of the people, particularly in the western, but also in the eastern, counties rose in revolt, attempting to close the courts and to secure redress of grievances. They were not, as even Samuel Adams, who had now become a rather pitiable reactionary, called them, "a rabble." They were small farmers for the most part, who under ordinary conditions would have been wholly law-abiding. The chief leader, Daniel Shays, had been a captain with a good record in the war, and of those who in 1787, after the revolt had been crushed, were indicted for treason, fifteen out of twenty-one were denominated "gentlemen" and only six "yeomen." These were the leaders of the "twelve or fifteen thousand desperate and unprincipled men," in the phrase of General Knox, whom he claimed were threatening to seize and divide the property of the rich. There was the same propaganda made of the fear of a "red terror" as in America after the World War.

The legislature, which had largely brought the situation about by its own unwillingness to listen to legitimate grievances and its inability to govern with common sense, handled the crisis with equal stupidity. A force of about 4400 troops under General Lincoln, privately paid for by the richer men of Boston, finally crushed the forces under Shays, but only after Congress had authorized the raising of Federal troops under the blind of danger of an Indian war, though actually to be sent against the insurgents.

We are here not concerned with the details of the struggle which I have related at length elsewhere, but with the effect of it on the nation.[24] That effect was profound. Even the level-headed Washington became alarmed at the rumors and garbled news which reached him. In October, 1786, he wrote to David Humphreys, "For God's sake, tell me what is the cause of all these commotions? Do they proceed from licentiousness, British influence disseminated by the Tories, or real grievances, which admit of redress? If the latter, why were they delayed until the public mind had become so agitated?" And again, a few days later he wrote to Henry Lee that "You talk, my good sir, of employing influence to appease the present tumults in Massachusetts. . . . *Influence* is no *government*. Let us have one by which our lives, liberties, and properties will be secured, or let us know the worst at once." [25]

That, in general, was the reaction produced throughout the propertied class of the entire country. Fear gripped it. Most people did not stop to consider, or did not wish to, that the trouble had come about chiefly because of the constitution adopted by what had become perhaps the most reactionary state in the union and which only a few years before had been one in which the demand for liberty had been most loudly voiced; and also because of the unintelligent way in which those

[24] *New England in the Republic,* Boston, 1926, pp. 149 ff.
[25] Washington, *Writings,* Ford ed., Vol. 11, pp. 76 f.

who had come into power under the new state constitution had used it. In the neighboring states, where the farmers were in equally serious plight, and where there was also practically manhood suffrage, there were no disturbances. The governing group in Massachusetts, although they themselves were the real danger to society, used all the devices of propaganda to make the farmers, whose grievances they would not hearken to, appear as desperate enemies of property. In a word, they treated America to its first red terror, and sent the shivers down the spines of all the Conservatives.

The question as to who was to govern had become painfully acute. In a decade, most of those who had led the people in a war ostensibly waged for the rights of man had turned to the consideration of how they could best protect the rights of property. The rebellion was crushed in February, 1787, and in May the convention already arranged for met in Philadelphia to draw up a stronger constitution for the Union, under the influence of the shock which armed revolt in what had been considered one of the most conservative states had given to many of the delegates.

Almost alone, Jefferson, in far-away Paris, had been left unmoved. Writing to Madison he said that the events in Massachusetts caused him no uneasiness, and spoke in much the same terms in a letter to Mrs. John Adams. "Indeed," he wrote, "the spirit of resistance to government is so valuable on certain occasions, that I wish it to be always kept alive. It will often be exercised when wrong but better so than not to be exercised at all. I like a little rebellion now & then. It is like a storm in the atmosphere." [26]   Even more emphatically he wrote some months later to W. S. Smith, saying, "Can history produce an instance of rebellion so honorably conducted? I say nothing of its motives. They were founded in ignorance, not wickedness. God forbid we should ever be 20 years with

[26] *Writings,* Ford, Vol. IV, p. 370.

such [italics mine] a rebellion. The people cannot be all, &
always, well informed. The part which is wrong will be dis-
contented in proportion to the importance of the facts they
misconceive. If they remain quiet under such misconceptions it
is a lethargy, the forerunner of death to the public liberty.
. . . The remedy is to set them right as to facts, pardon & pacify
them. What signify a few lives lost in a century or two? The
tree of liberty must be refreshed from time to time with the
blood of patriots and tyrants. It is its natural manure. Our
Convention has been too much impressed by the insurrection
in Massachusetts: and in the spur of the moment they are setting up a kite to keep the henyard in order." [27]

In writing freely to personal friends, Jefferson often indulged in exaggerated statement, but there is no doubt he did
prefer the occasional threat or use of force to what he called
public lethargy and a too complete submission. Moreover, he
knew the American farmer, and ninety per cent of Americans
were then farmers. He knew he was usually a conservative person and not at all a blood-thirsty or cruel one. By "rebellion"
he intended no such affair as we have learned to connote wholesale revolution and massacre. He was not to be fooled by the
talk of the Massachusetts reactionaries, and he knew that the
farmers of that state, owning their own farms and merely in
temporary difficulties over debts and taxes, were not dangerous anarchists threatening the complete overturn of society.
As to the last point, Jefferson was quite right. We have had
similar farmer revolts against debt collectors and courts in
every period of major depression in our history, but that has
never meant that the farmers have been either anti-property
or anti-society, and Jefferson's view of the affair was much
saner than that taken by the more frightened leaders at home.

The "rebellion," however, played straight into the hands of
those who wished to establish a strong central government **and**

[27] *Ibid.*, p. 467.

facilitated the difficult task of getting the new Constitution accepted by the people when drafted. Jefferson had practically nothing to do with the drawing up of the new instrument. He watched the progress of the convention's work as closely as he could from Paris. He wrote to friends about it, but he was too far away and letters took too long in passing over-seas to enable him to be of influence even had he wished to be. Indeed, although he was naturally interested, he was rather surprisingly less so than one would have expected of such an inveterate constitution maker.

Writing to George Wythe in September, 1787, he passed with unexpected lightness over enquiries on which we should have thought he would have written pages. "You ask me," he writes, "in your letter what ameliorations I think necessary in our federal constitution. It is now too late to answer the question, and it would always have been presumption in me to have done it. Your own ideas & those of the great characters who were to be concerned with you in these discussions will give the law, as they ought to do, to us all. My own general idea was that the states should severally preserve their sovereignty in whatever concerns themselves alone, & that whatever may concern another state, or any foreign nation, should be made a part of the federal sovereignty. That the exercise of the federal sovereignty should be divided among three several bodies, legislative, executive & judiciary, as the state sovereignties are: *and that some peaceable means should be contrived for the federal head to enforce compliance on the part of the states.*" [28] That is all, though the portion I have put in italics is significant.

When the Constitution was finished, Jefferson appears to have been fairly well satisfied with it. His experience in Congress and as Minister to France had led him to believe some strengthening of federal power necessary. To his friend, Ed-

[28] *Writings,* Ford, Vol. IV, p. 445.

ward Carrington, he wrote, "As to the new Constitution I find myself nearly a Neutral. There is a great mass of good in it, in a very desirable form: but there is to me a bitter pill or two," [29] and referred him to a longer letter written to Madison. In that letter Jefferson had given his opinions more at length, and much of it is worth quoting for a clear expression of his views.

"I like much," he wrote, "the general idea of framing a government which should go on of itself peaceably, without needing continual recurrence to the state legislatures. I like the organization of the government into Legislative, Judiciary & Executive. I like the power given the Legislative to levy taxes, and for that reason solely approve of the greater house being chosen by the people directly. For tho' I think a house chosen by them will be very illy qualified to legislate for the Union, for foreign nations &c. yet this evil does not weigh against the good of preserving inviolate the fundamental principles that the people are not to be taxed but by representatives chosen immediately by themselves. I am captivated by the compromise of the opposite claims of the great and little states, of the latter to equal, and the former to proportional influence. . . . I like the negative given to the Executive with a third of either house, though I should have liked it better had the Judiciary been associated for that purpose, or invested with a similar and separate power." [30]

He then goes on to tell what he does not like, which was mainly the omission of a Bill of Rights, and the eligibility of the President for re-election, believing that the latter might result in life tenure of office. However, he wrote at the close, "it is my principle that the will of the majority should always prevail. If they approve the proposed Convention in all its parts, I shall concur in it chearfully, in hopes that they will amend it whenever they shall find it work wrong. I think our

[29] *Ibid.*, p. 481.   [30] *Ibid.*, pp. 475 ff.

governments will remain virtuous for many centuries; as long as they are chiefly agricultural; and this will be as long as there shall be vacant lands in any part of America. When they get piled upon one another in large cities as in Europe, they will become corrupt as in Europe. Above all things I hope the education of the common people will be attended to; convinced that on their good sense we may rely with the most security for the preservation of a due degree of liberty."

Two points are interesting to note in the above as opposed to the traditional views supposed to be held by Jefferson, and in part adopted later. One is his opinion that a national legislature directly elected by the people would be unlikely to be a wise one; and the other is his suggestion that the judiciary should have a negative vote on legislation by Congress. We may mention one more point in Jefferson's views at this time, his belief that even the old Articles of Confederation gave the Federal Government the right to coerce a state. Replying to a list of questions propounded to him by M. de Meusnier, who was writing an article for a French encyclopædia, Jefferson wrote that it was often said that the decisions of Congress had no force because they had no compulsory power. It was unnecessary to have put this power into the Articles, he avowed, because when two or more nations enter into compact it is not usual for them to say what shall be done to the party who infringes it, but "the right of compulsion naturally results to the party injured by the breach. When any one state in the American Union refuses obedience to the Confederation by which they have bound themselves, the rest have a natural right to compel them to obedience." [31] And again in writing to James Monroe the same year of 1786, he says, "there will never be money in the treasury till the confederacy shows its teeth. The states must see the rod; perhaps it must be felt by some one of them. . . . Every rational citizen must wish to see an ef-

[31] *Ibid.*, Vol. IV, p. 147.

fective instrument of coercion, & should fear to see it on any other element but the water." [32]

Such were some of Jefferson's ideas as to a federal form of government when he returned from France. He had also come to hate and fear monarchy and aristocracy, which he had seen at their very worst in that country. To allow privilege the slightest entry into America would, he believed, be the eventual ruin of the nation and of the experiment on which it had embarked. As we shall see in the next chapter, parties had rapidly been forming at home, and efforts had been made to draw the returning Minister into one camp or the other. Wisely he wished to remain aloof until he had been able to study the situation at first hand. Answering carefully and at length a letter from Francis Hopkinson, evidently designed to draw him out, he wrote, "I am not a Federalist because I never submitted the whole system of my opinions to the creed of any party of men whatever in religion, in philosophy, in politics, or in anything else where I was capable of thinking for myself. Such an addiction is the last degradation of a free and moral agent. If I could not go to heaven but with a party, I would not go there at all. Therefore I protest to you I am not of the party of the Federalists. But I am much farther from that of the Antifederalists." He then goes on to explain why, and what he had already told Madison. [33]

The refusal of Jefferson to align himself with either party was both natural and prudent, as well as decently modest, for a man who had been out of the country for five of its most critical years. I doubt, however, as has been said, if he then had the slightest idea of heading a new party on new lines himself. He liked such work as he had done on the revision of the laws of Virginia, or in drafting papers such as the Declaration of Independence or the Virginia constitution in which he could express his political philosophy. He did not, however, care for

---

[32] *Ibid.*, Vol. IV, p. 265.   [33] *Ibid.*, Vol. V, pp. 75 ff.

the rough-and-tumble of politics. He had no itch for publicity. Unlike Hamilton and almost all the leaders of the day, he did not write for the newspapers. He loved quiet, and many times in analyzing himself he admitted that he was thin-skinned. He had applied for leave of absence from his post in Paris to go home temporarily to look after his affairs, but he had no idea when he sailed from France that the remainder of his career was to be a stormy one in America instead of a tranquil one in Paris or at Monticello. I see no reason to doubt his own statement at the time. "My great wish," he wrote in the letter just quoted, "is to go on in a strict but silent performance of my duty; to avoid attracting notice & to keep my name out of newspapers, because I find the pain of a little censure, even when it is unfounded, is more acute than the pleasure of much praise. The attaching circumstances of my present office is that I can do its duties unseen by those for whom they are done."

Thus it was that Jefferson came back to America with his two children and with every expectation of returning to his foreign duties after a brief holiday. He already occupied the highest post in our diplomatic service, and one for which he was well fitted. He had been remote from all the currents which had swept men into one or the other of the new parties, and all the wire-pulling which might lead to possible high offices. He had openly and frankly stated that he considered himself as owing allegiance to neither party. However, when, on November 23, 1789, he landed at Norfolk, he read in the first newspaper he saw that Washington, the new President under the new Constitution, intended to name him as Secretary of State. His career had been cut clean, as with a knife, and for the next twenty years or so he was to ride the whirlwind of political life in the young republic, which thirteen years before he had declared to be free and independent, designed in its liberty to serve a new ideal of human capacity and happiness.

CHAPTER IX

SECRETARY OF STATE

JEFFERSON made his way at once toward Monticello by way of Richmond and Eppington, at the latter of which lived his wife's sister, who had looked after his children after Mrs. Jefferson's death. It was there that the newspaper rumors received confirmation in the form of two letters from Washington in which the President, led as he wrote "as well by motives of private regard, as a conviction of public propriety," offered Jefferson the post of Secretary of State.

The office was far from being alluring to him. He loved Monticello, but if he was to be required to leave it on public service he preferred Paris to New York, the capital of the new government. He was settled abroad, had learned the work he had to do, and felt that he would be more useful there. He also characteristically dreaded the arena of American politics. As he wrote in part of his reply, "I should enter on [the office] with gloomy forebodings from the criticisms and censures of a public, just indeed in their intentions, but sometimes misinformed and misled, and always too respectable to be neglected. I cannot but foresee the possibility that this may end disagreeably for me, who, having no motive to public service but the public satisfaction, would certainly retire the moment that satisfaction should appear to languish." [1] He mentioned his familiarity with the work of his office in Paris, and modestly suggested that his abilities might not be commensurate with the new one offered. He agreed, however, to do whatever Washington might wish, as "it is not for an individual to choose his

[1] *Writings*, Ford, Vol. V, p. 140.

post. You are to marshall us as may be best for the public good."

It may be noted here, with reference to both Jefferson's hesitation and his later relations with Hamilton, that the new government was scarcely more than an embryo, and the work of the departments not yet defined. Jefferson in his letter spoke of the extent of the State Department, "embracing as it does the principal mass of domestic administration, together with the foreign." We have become so accustomed to thinking of the State Department as chiefly concerned with foreign affairs, although it is far from being wholly so, that we cannot understand some of the hostility Jefferson came to feel personally for Hamilton without a realization that the Department was originally conceived of as chiefly domestic. This was not only the opinion of Jefferson but also those of Congress and of Washington. The latter wrote to Jefferson with regard to the point that "it was the opinion of Congress, that, after the division of all the business of a domestic nature between the departments of the treasury, war, and state, those which would be comprehended in the latter might be performed by the same person, who would have the charge of conducting the department of foreign affairs." [2] The whole national government had to be developed from nothing. Domestic affairs were far more important than foreign, and although the latter were clearly made an adjunct to the office of Secretary of State the chief concern of that officer was considered to be domestic.

Jefferson, leaving the decision in Washington's hands, continued his journey homeward. As typical of the Virginia of that period, we may quote his daughter's description of the homecoming in full. "There were no stages in those days," she wrote. "We were indebted to the kindness of friends for horses; and visiting all on the way homeward, and spending more or less time with them all in turn, we reached Monticello

[2] Washington, *Writings*, Ford, Vol. II, p. 468 f.

on the 23d of December. The Negroes discovered the approach of the carriage as soon as it reached Shadwell [about four miles from Monticello], and such a scene I never witnessed in my life. They collected in crowds around it, and almost drew it up the mountain by hand. The shouting, etc., had been sufficiently obstreperous before, but the moment it arrived at the top it reached the climax. When the door of the carriage was opened, they received him in their arms and bore him to the house, crowding around and kissing his hands and feet—some blubbering and crying—others laughing. It seemed impossible to satisfy their anxiety to touch and kiss the very earth which bore him." [3]

Jefferson, as we noted in the previous chapter, had long been out of close touch with the course of affairs in America, but Madison now paid him a visit at Monticello, and from him the returned Minister must have learned much of what had been going on, at which we must ourselves now glance.

We have already noted the gradual breakdown of government under the Confederation, the growing feeling that a stronger organ was needed, and the shock administered by Shays's rebellion, both as it actually was and even more as it was made to appear.

We cannot, of course, say what Jefferson talked over with his younger but much loved and trusted friend Madison. It is not difficult, nevertheless, to surmise what the topics were with a fair degree of accuracy. Jefferson could now get detailed and first-hand information as to the new Constitution, its adoption in the several states, and the views of leading men with regard to it. While in France he had read the *Federalist*, written by Madison, Hamilton, and Jay, but Madison was better able than any other man in America to inform Jefferson as to the entire situation. During the constitutional convention he had kept accurate notes of the debates, and had, of course,

[3] Randolph, *Domestic Life*, p. 152.

personally met and talked with the delegates. If today we have to rely mainly on his written words to learn what went on behind the closed doors of the convention, what men said and what they thought, we can well imagine the mine of information he could open to Jefferson in intimate talk.

As they chatted before the open fire in those January days, Jefferson must have begun to sense the struggle which might lie ahead if the American experiment, as he viewed it, were to succeed based upon the conditions which he had always claimed alone might make success possible. In Paris he had read and studied the Constitution as a completed document, and the able defense made of it even by Hamilton, but as he talked with Madison and learned of the ideas which had been put forth in the convention, of the motives which had actuated some of its members, of the general insistence upon a "strong" central government and defense of property interests, of the practically universal distrust of the people, he must also have realized how he stood almost alone in his own views. He had founded his hope of a new and happier world on an agricultural civilization in which property would be widely distributed among the people in small holdings. That was why he had fought against property rights as conceived of by the privileged classes when he had destroyed entail and primogeniture in his own state. He did not, as we have repeatedly pointed out, believe that the people were capable of direct government. In that sense he was no democrat. But he did deeply believe that the people should be the reservoir of power, and that indirectly they should have the ultimate control of government.

But now a new picture of America was opened to him. At the time of his departure from France his own desire for a moderately strong central government had probably reached its highest point. He did not greatly disapprove of the new Constitution in itself, and his opinion as to new form of government was not wholly irreconcilable with that of Hamilton, as so ably expressed in his written defense of it. Jefferson now understood, however, all that had been going on under the surface. He might agree with Hamilton and the other Federalists, with reservations, to accept the Constitution, but he and they had reached that point of partial agreement by walking far from opposite directions. He believed that the people should govern, whereas the strong Federalists believed that the people had to *be governed*. It was the old dispute over again between Hooker and Winthrop in 1636. Jefferson, at least, believed in placing the ultimate power below in the mass. The Federalists wished to keep it as much as possible at the top in a special class, or, as they designated it, among "the rich, the wise, and the good." He began to see that the Constitution had been drawn to a great extent in favor of the business and mercantile classes as against his own favorite agricultural class, and that its chief popular strength was among the former whereas the latter had largely opposed its adoption.

Moreover, he had been watching the gross misgovernment in France, and his fear and hatred of monarchy had been steadily growing. He had warned Washington and others in his letters that the slightest step toward introducing in America anything whatever that might savor of the monarchical principle would prove fatal to all American hopes and would eventually lead to the downfall of free government and of the unique American experiment. He received, therefore, a tremendous shock when he discovered that some at least of the important Federalist leaders, including Hamilton, had been desirous of establishing monarchy in newly liberated America. They had not been able to do so because the people generally would have been too strongly against it, but it was the opinion, as it was the hope, of a good number that it would come in time, perhaps after a period of chaos.

Washington, of course, was against any such attempt or hope, and Jefferson probably over-rated the numbers of those in favor of either, but it is unquestionable that some of the most important men had been so, and had been restrained only by the impossibility of securing public support. Papers and private correspondence indicate that much. The writings of others had been ambiguous, to say the least. Since the Constitution had been agreed upon in the convention there had been no public demand made for a monarchical government, and even those, such as Hamilton, who felt most strongly that the new government was too weak and inefficient, had come out publicly in favor of it. Indeed it was chiefly owing to Hamilton's zeal and ability that it was finally adopted by the state of New York, a personal success which was probably his greatest contribution to his adopted country. But it is likely that now Jefferson first found out Hamilton's real opinions from Madison.

Hamilton had taken almost no part in the debates during the convention, but he had made one long speech of about five hours, and Madison had made his usual careful report of it at the time. Some extracts from this will probably represent what Jefferson learned from his friend. As reported by Madison, Hamilton said that his "view of the subject almost led him to despair that a Republican Govt. could be established over so great an extent. He was sensible at the same time that it would be unwise to propose one of any other form. In his private opinion he had no scruple in declaring, supported as he was by the opinion of so many of the wise & good, that the British Govt. was the best in the world. . . . Their house of Lords is a most noble institution. Having nothing to hope for by a change, and a sufficient interest by means of their property, in being faithful to a national interest, they form a permanent barrier agst. every pernicious innovation, whether attempted on the part of the Crown or Commons. No temporary Senate will have firmness eno' to answer the purpose. . . . As to the Executive, it seemed to be admitted that no good one could be established on Republican Principles. Was not this giving up the merits of the question; for can there be a good Govt. without a good Executive. The English Model was the only good one on this subject. The Hereditary interest of the King was so interwoven with that of the Nation, and his personal emoluments so great, that he was placed above the danger of being corrupted from abroad—and at the same time was both sufficiently independent and sufficiently controlled to answer the purpose of the institution at home." [4]

Hamilton admitted that we could not have that form of government, but suggested a President for life, though "it will be objected probably, that such an Executive will be an *elective Monarch*, and will give birth to the tumults which characterize that form of Govt. He would reply that *Monarch* is an indefinite term. If this Executive Magistrate would be a monarch for life—the other propd. by the Report from the Committee of the whole, would be a monarch for seven years." [5]

No one could express himself more clearly than Hamilton, who was always lucid though usually diffuse, and what he aimed at in the way of government was quite evident, though he admitted he could not get it. If Madison, however, retailed to Jefferson all that Hamilton had said, this admission could have given Jefferson little comfort, for Hamilton had also said that "he hoped Gentlemen of different opinions would bear with him in this, and begged them to recollect the change of opinion on this subject which had taken place and was still going on. . . . This progress of the public mind led him to anticipate the time when others as well as himself would join in the praise bestowed by Mr. Neckar on the British Constitution." [6]

I see no reason for doubting the correctness of Madison's reporting of Hamilton's speech. Hamilton's son in the life he wrote of his father tried to throw doubt upon it, but the outline

[4] Madison, *Writings*, Vol. III, pp. 189 f., 191 f.
[5] *Ibid.*, p. 193.   [6] *Ibid.*, p. 190.

of notes in Hamilton's own handwriting for his speech, which the son quotes, would seem amply to support, instead of discrediting, Madison's accuracy as a reporter. Thus Hamilton jotted down, "If government in the hands of the *few*, they will tyrannize over the many. If [in] the hands of the many, they will tyrannize over the few. It ought to be in the hands of both; and they should be separated— This separation must be permanent—Representation alone will not do. Demagogues will generally prevail. And if separated, they will need a mutual check. This check is a monarch."[7]

Jefferson's auburn, sandy hair must have almost stood on end as he listened to all of this. After all America had done to get rid of monarchy, aristocracy, and privilege, after all he himself had been seeing of monarchy, at its worst, after all his dreams of a free, agricultural, self-governing people, here were talk and hope among some of the leading men of the country of establishing a European type of civilization in Jefferson's unique America.

Moreover, it was not only a question of a form of government but of how that form should be operated and moulded. Hamilton had laid down at the beginning of his speech "the great and essential principles necessary for the support of Government" as "an active and constant interest in supporting it," "the love of power," "an habitual attachment of the people," adding "force by which may be understood a *coercion of laws* or *coercion of arms*" ("a certain portion of military force is absolutely necessary in large communities"), and "influence." By the latter he said he did not mean "corruption, but a dispensation of those regular honors and emoluments, which produce an attachment to Govt." [8]

Here were all the things Jefferson feared and loathed most, —monarchy, aristocracy, privilege, a standing army to coerce

[7] J. C. Hamilton, *History of the Republic of the United States,* etc., New York, 1859, Vol. III, p. 280.
[8] Madison, *Writings,* Vol. III, pp. 184 f.

the people, and, whatever Hamilton might say, corruption as a means of governing. Hamilton's services, and they were great, should not blind us to the fact that although he worked loyally for and under the Constitution he seems never to have given up the hope that conditions would some day pave the way for the introduction of the monarchical system which he much preferred. He may or may not have been right in his preference. I myself think that in the century and a half following, the British system has shown itself the most flexible and responsive to the changing needs and conditions of its people of all forms of government but the work of a government depends not only on its form but on the people also. The Americans did not want that form of government, and for that reason if for no other it could not have worked. Hamilton saw more clearly than Jefferson the springs which move men and the motives by which they are led and act. He took a much lower view of human nature than Jefferson, and in that he was right. On the other hand, Jefferson saw more clearly than Hamilton the ideals which the Americans cherished though they might not live up to them in practice. Hamilton was cynical; Jefferson optimistic. Hamilton believed in heredity; Jefferson in environment. Hamilton believed human nature could never change; Jefferson that under right conditions it could improve. Hamilton believed America could never be governed except by the age-long European methods of corruption and personal gain; Jefferson, who had seen those methods at close range, believed that America had a unique chance in the history of the world to develop a better method. But as he listened to all Madison had to tell him, he must have pondered deeply. In the early days of his happy return he had suggested to Washington his incapacity to head the Cabinet, and his reluctance to enter the political arena and subject himself to quarrels and public criticism. His reluctance must have increased as he realized more clearly the strength of the forces let loose and the almost certain course of politics in the next few years. Nevertheless, when again pressed by Washington, he accepted the post of Secretary of State, on April 3, 1790, and the day after his eldest daughter's marriage, he set out for New York to take up his duties. Stopping in Philadelphia to call on the now fast-failing Franklin, he arrived in New York on the 21st and put up at the City Tavern, until he moved into a little house in Maiden Lane.

Of his arrival at the temporary capital Jefferson wrote long afterward that "I found a state of things which, of all I had ever contemplated I the least expected. . . . The President received me cordially, and my Colleagues and the inner circle of principal citizens, apparently, with welcome. The courtesies of dinner parties given me as a stranger newly arrived among them, placed me at once in their familiar society. But I cannot describe the wonder and mortification with which the table conversations filled me. Politics were the chief topic, and a preference of kingly, over republican, government, was evidently the favorite sentiment. An apostate I could not be; nor yet a hypocrite: and I found myself, for the most part, the only advocate on the republican side of the question, unless, among the guests, there chanced to be some member of that party from the legislative Houses." [9]

It is true that the above passage is taken from the *Anas*, which Jefferson compiled after his public life was over but while still under the influence of the passions aroused, and which are unreliable as historical evidence, even the contemporary scraps, notes, and documents having apparently been "revised" by him. However, there was probably much truth in his description of New York society. The rich families of that city had been very largely on the Tory side in the Revolution. Many of the same class had likewise been so in Boston, but the Bostonian Loyalists had for the most part emigrated

[9] *Writings*, Ford, Vol. V, pp. 159 f.

to Canada or England when the British evacuated that city, whereas the New York Tories had remained at home as the city was in the hands of the British all during the war. There, fraternizing with British officers, and cut off from the rest of their country by the "rebels," it was natural that they should become even more intensely British and "aristocratic," while Shays's rebellion and other developments had made them more than ever fearful of "the people" since the peace. It was this rich society which entertained the leading officials of the new government and which had also become the habitual society of Hamilton. He, at least, if we can believe the testimony of even his own friends, never wholly got over his desire for a monarchy. The voice of New York society was then no more than today the voice of America, and Jefferson, like other visitors before and since, overrated its importance, but he undoubtedly heard much which was deeply disturbing to one holding his opinions. Also, it must be remembered that the new government had no tradition of proved loyalty and strength behind it. Not only was the form new but it yet remained to be seen what forces might strive to capture and mould it. Moreover if Jefferson's fear of an American monarchical or "monocrat" party seems at times to rise to a mania, it must be recalled that the Federalists' fears of a "French influence" and danger seem to us now equally hysterical.

When Jefferson started at his desk, the government had been in operation for some weeks. His friend Washington was President and his closer friend John Adams was Vice-President. Adams certainly had none of Jefferson's faith in the people, and had dallied in his writings with monarchy in such a way as to lay him open to the charge of believing in it. His vanity and love of pomp, show, and high-sounding titles, even though republican, also made him appear not only absurd but possibly a little dangerous in this period of easily roused fears and suspicions. In the Cabinet, with Jefferson in the State

Department, were Hamilton in the Treasury, General Henry Knox in the War Department, and Edmund Randolph as Attorney-General. There was a Postmaster-General but the holders of that office were not to become Cabinet members until Jackson's day. Moreover, although the Attorney-General sat in the Cabinet he was of distinctly lower rank, and received lower pay, than the others. Indeed, for some years, he was not even required to be present at the capital during the sessions of Congress, and was allowed to continue in private practice, though required to give legal opinions, when requested to do so by the President and heads of departments.

In the Constitutional Convention there had been considerable discussion as to the form and function of a Cabinet but the Constitution itself contained practically no mention of it, and the departments were established by Congress during its first session in 1789. In enacting the statutes creating them there was a distinction made in that the Secretary of the Treasury alone was required to make reports and answer inquiries respecting his department when requested by either house of the legislature. All three secretaries were undoubtedly responsible to the President but Congress apparently intended to keep a closer check on the Treasury than on the other departments, probably in part from the tradition that the legislature must control the purse strings. Nothing had been said as to priority of position, and although Washington once wrote to Jefferson that he considered the State Department as the most important it was not until later that the Secretary of State became definitely the head of the Cabinet. Again, there was some vagueness as to the scope of affairs to be handled by each secretary. Hamilton had originally suggested only three departments, those of the Treasury, War, and Foreign Affairs, whereas, as we have seen, both Washington and Jefferson had laid stress on the importance of domestic affairs for the State Department. Moreover, there was the question of personality.

Knox, whose body was much weightier than his mind—he weighed nearly 300 pounds—was pompous, autocratic, military, and without good judgment. He was "the giant" of the administration but not in the usual sense, and proved a continuous "yes-man" to the physically diminutive Secretary of the Treasury, Hamilton, who loved everything connected with the army, and even insisted that his own department, and not that of War, should purchase military stores. Randolph, the Attorney-General, could be relied on by no one. He usually sided with Jefferson but was so shifty that his aid was of little worth and much uncertainty. Writing of him in 1795, Jefferson said that "he has generally given his principles to one party and his practice to the other; the oyster to one, the shell to the other. Unfortunately the shell was generally the lot of his friends . . . and the oyster of their antagonists." [10]

Thus Hamilton and Jefferson faced one another in the Cabinet. Jefferson was the senior by fourteen years. His name had rung through America on July 4, 1776, when Hamilton was a nineteen-year-old lad unknown outside New York City. Jefferson's experiences, including among them war governor of Virginia and Minister to France, had been far wider than those of his young colleague, whose most famous work, except for his defense of the new Constitution in speech and press a couple of years before, all yet lay ahead of him, Jefferson was no toady, like Knox, nor a catch-breeze, like Randolph. He had, during the previous twenty years, developed his political philosophy, and he intended to stick by it. On the other hand, Hamilton, with his consummate abilities, his egoism and intense ambition, had also his philosophy which he intended to stick by. Moreover, he evidently regarded himself as not merely head of the Cabinet, but wished to turn his office into that of a sort of prime minister. As we shall see, he even meddled seriously, and behind Jefferson's back, in foreign affairs.

[10] *Writings,* Ford, Vol. VII, p. 42.

With the knowledge we now possess, it is evident that a clash between the two men would become inevitable sooner or later. Without attempting to trace the differences further back, the American people had split into two parties over the ratification of the Constitution. We do not have to go the whole length to which Professor Beard does in his economic interpretation of the situation to recognize the real importance of the economic cleavage. As we have said, there was a conflict between the industrial and financial section of the people and the agrarian. There were also those who, thinking in political terms, feared a strong central government and preferred reserving as much power as possible to the states. There were many cleavages, but from the standpoint of Americanism the most important was that between those who trusted the sense, honesty, and capacity of the people in the last resort, and those who did not; between those who believed the people could rule and those who believed that they must be ruled. Washington, with great reluctance, had emerged from his retirement to become President because it was rightly believed that he alone could ensure the success of the new government by uniting all of the people, he alone possessing the confidence of all. He feared "faction" as he called it, and he seems to have thought that such feelings as had been aroused by the discussion over the Constitution would die down, and that government could be conducted without parties. The hope was fallacious. We can see now why it must infallibly have been so. He did not form his Cabinet on bi-partisan or non-partisan lines, as has sometimes been claimed. He put Hamilton and Jefferson into their posts because he thought they were the best men for them. He did not foresee parties or that he was bringing together into one team the leaders of opposing ideas which instead of dying out or coalescing would on the contrary become stronger and more bitter in their conflict with one another.

Five years later, he and others saw more clearly. Writing to

Timothy Pickering, a leading Federalist and reactionary in Massachusetts, Washington frankly said that he would not knowingly appoint any one to office whose opinions were adverse to those of the government; that it "would be a sort of political suicide" to do so. This, as Beard points out, shows that he recognized the existence of a considerable opposition to the policies of the government, and also that "the establishment of certain general doctrines of law does not make a government, but that the men who embody those principles in their personal views and conduct can alone make the law living and effective." [11]

That was what Jefferson, who had said he would not go to heaven if he could do so only with a party, was also to learn in the same length of time, for in the year in which Washington wrote to Pickering, Jefferson wrote to W. B. Giles that "were parties here divided merely by greediness for office, as in England, to take a part with either would be unworthy of a reasonable or moral man, but where the principle of difference is as substantial and as strongly pronounced as between the republicans and the Monocrats of our country, I hold it as honorable to take a firm and decided part, as between the parties of Honest men, and Rogues, into which every country is divided." [12]

The statesmen operating the new government all learned that if a man has strong opinions, if he thinks them important enough and cares enough for what they represent, he will fight for them. Hamilton fully realized the truth of the words just quoted from Professor Beard. He knew that the importance of a constitution lies not merely, or perhaps as much, in its words as in how it is administered. He and Jefferson had both accepted the Constitution. Neither was in opposition to the other when they first met in New York. What drove Jeffer-

[11] C. A. Beard, *Economic Origins of Jeffersonian Democracy,* New York, 1915, p. 66.
[12] *Writings,* Ford, Vol. VII, p. 43.

son into opposition, even temporarily from public life, and what brought him back eventually as the leader of a party which broke Hamilton's, was his watching Hamilton moulding the Constitution by administration into a living form opposed to all Jefferson's deepest beliefs. Indeed, it was Madison who broke first with Hamilton, and for the same reason. Madison's own words on the subject, taken down by N. P. Trist in 1834, were: "I deserted Colonel Hamilton, or rather Colonel H. deserted me; in a word, the divergence between us took place— from his wishing to *administration*, or rather to administer the Government (these were Mr. M.'s very words), into what he thought it ought to be; while, on my part, I endeavored to make it conform to the Constitution as understood by the Convention that produced and recommended it, and particularly by the State conventions that *adopted* it." [13]

Jefferson at first had apparently no suspicion of the direction in which Hamilton was to move. He probably knew, as we have mentioned, what Hamilton's views were as to what he considered the best form of government. Jefferson had accepted the Constitution as drawn and as expounded in the Federalist and by Madison personally, and had rather naïvely expected that any changes would be made by formal amendment. It was only when he, like Madison, saw it being "administered" instead of amended, and in a direction which was counter to his own deepest convictions, that he grew more and more restive and angry.

Relations, however, began pleasantly. Hamilton was charming socially, and Jefferson had already expressed his admiration for his ability and lucidity of thought. As the latest comer, Jefferson had to pick up the threads of his work after the rest of the Cabinet had got started, and also for the first few weeks he suffered from extremely severe headache. The first important question before the Cabinet after his arrival

[13] Randall, *Life of Jefferson*, Vol. III, p. 595.

was that of the assumption of the state debts. When the government had come into office, the finances of both the United States and the individual states were in confusion. Hamilton for some months had been struggling with the problem. In his tabulation he estimated the debt owed to foreigners as about $11,700,000, the domestic federal debt at about $42,000,000, and the unpaid state debts at about $25,000,000.

There was no question about the foreign debt. Every responsible American wished to see it paid in full. The chief conflict of views as to the domestic debt—aside from more or less technical points as to length of life of the bonds, rate of interest, and so on—was as to whether the holders of the old evidences of debt should receive payment at par or at various suggested prices below that. While some of the old debt was still in the hands of the original subscribers, a large part of it, at greatly depreciated prices, had passed into the hands of speculators. It was felt by many that it would be quite unjust to pay a hundred cents on the dollar to persons who had bought the debt at fifty cents or less. Hamilton wisely insisted, in the face of great opposition, that no matter who owned the certificates or what they had paid for them, the only way to establish the credit of the new nation in an unassailable position would be to honor the strict terms of its promises to pay.

Hamilton's report on the public credit, however, as presented to Congress, outlined a policy which included an even more debatable point, the assumption by the Federal Government of the debts owed by the state governments. This was considered by many as a wholly unjustifiable burden laid on the people as a whole, unnecessarily weighing down the credit of the Federal Government, and involving many injustices. Some states had large debts, some small; some had already paid part of their debts, others had not; and it was considered unfair to tax the citizens of the states which had paid in order to pay the debts of those which had not.

As to his first two contentions, Hamilton was probably wholly justified, but competent opinion varies even today as to whether the assumption measure was a wise one or not. Jefferson arrived in the midst of the dispute over its merits and while the thirty-two-year-old Secretary of the Treasury was battling against odds to save himself from defeat on it. In fact the measure was voted down once, Madison leading the fight in the House against Hamilton's plans. Jefferson at first took no side, and paid little attention to the matter, busy with other things. His experiences abroad, however, both enlightening and humiliating, had made him realize the importance of all measures to raise the public credit. All his life, both in the public and his own private affairs, he was extremely scrupulous about honoring any financial obligation. The chief opposition to the assumption measure came from the two great Middle and Southern states of Pennsylvania and Virginia, particularly the latter. The contest therefore was partially sectional. There was, moreover, another dispute, also sectional in character, beginning to make bad blood. That was as to where the national capital, temporarily established by compromise at New York, should eventually and permanently be placed. Many motives of business profit, state pride, and convenience of access entered into this thorny problem. Every one agreed that it could not be located much south of the Potomac or north of New York. The most powerful states involved were thus New York, Pennsylvania, and Virginia. The new Federal Government was as yet untried, and these two sectional problems, with the enormous heat they were generating, were genuinely alarming.

One day Hamilton met Jefferson in the street and spoke to him about the possibility of the dissolution of the Union if agreement could not be reached and asked his help, although the assumption matter was out of Jefferson's department. Thereupon Jefferson asked Hamilton to dine with him and meet some of the other leaders. This dinner party was perhaps the most important and interesting ever given in the United States. We do not know the names of the guests, but at the head of the table sat the tall figure of the Secretary of State, with his silky auburn hair, his keen gray eyes, and angular but sensitive face, doing the honors as host. There also was the alert and diminutive Secretary of the Treasury, always fascinating to both men and women, brilliant in conversation, and now intent on making one of the great plays of his career. Several "friends" occupied the other chairs around the mahogany, on which shone the soft light of candles. Jefferson's wines, as we have already pointed out, were noted even among statesmen. By the end of the evening it had been agreed that a few but sufficient votes would be altered on a test in the House, and that assumption would pass. Hamilton's power in Congress, already great, would thus become greater, and he could definitely promise that the new capital of the United States would be in Philadelphia for ten years, and after that forever on the Potomac River near Georgetown. The good-nights were said.

There is no doubt that a political bargain had been made, and that Jefferson was a party to it. The dinner was not like the one so indiscreetly forced upon him by Lafayette in Paris. He had written before it of the dangers of the situation and the need "to give as well as take," and also of the best solution probably being "a bargain" between the Eastern members of Congress and the Middle and Southern. He did not like it, with its tendency toward centralization and increased federal taxes, but preferred it to a fall in federal credit abroad and possible secession of some states.

Later on he claimed he had been duped by Hamilton in a matter which he himself did not understand. This statement cannot be taken as wholly true, though it may contain a partial truth. The assumption of the state debts had involved a somewhat hurried computation of open accounts between the Federal and State Governments in addition to the actual debts of the states in the hands of the public. Gallatin, the ablest Secretary of the Treasury after Hamilton, later estimated that the Federal Government had overpaid the states, in the assumption deal, by nearly $11,000,000, which was not actually due. But Jefferson was no mean financier himself and, for some years, had been studying the national and state debts. He should either have known the figures or have had them checked, if there was in reality such a discrepancy. Moreover, he could hardly claim that Hamilton had misrepresented the dangers of the situation. Jefferson, a rarely astute politician and with such close friends as Madison and others in Congress, had means, as Secretary of State, for forming his own independent judgment. It may be said that a "bargain" is not necessarily by any means a corrupt act. Had Jefferson merely traded a capital on the Potomac for a financial measure which he believed deeply pernicious he might well be blamed. But as he saw it at the time, there were two sectional disputes, both threatening the unity of the new and unstable country. As he wrote, "Congress met and adjourned from day to day without doing anything, the parties being too much out of temper to do business together." [14] The bargain would ensure unity again; would solve forever the dangerous dispute about the location of the capital; and would raise our credit abroad for both the national and state governments, which even today are confused with each other in Europe. It would do all this at certain costs in centralization and taxation. It is a statesman's duty to compromise a deadlock in such a way as to bring more good than evil, and Jefferson believed the bargain would do that when he made it. I do not think in this that he was deceived by Hamilton.

On the other hand, he might, with a certain justification,

[14] *Writings,* Ford, Vol. I, p. 162.

claim deception on another score. He did not as yet know Hamilton well personally. He knew that he did not approve of the Constitution in all parts, any more than Jefferson himself did, but Hamilton had declared that such as it was it should be given a fair trial and that all should work loyally under it. In handling the federal finances, Hamilton was well within his appointed province but there was nothing that enjoined him to trespass on the field of state finance. Indeed, some of those who, like Madison, understood the Constitution best, claimed that he had no constitutional authority to take money from the inhabitants of one state to pay it to those of another, which was what assumption amounted to in one aspect.

What Jefferson had not realized, and what, of course, Hamilton did not tell him, was that Hamilton had already mapped out in his own mind a series of measures which taken together would greatly alter both the working of the Constitution and the life of the nation. It may be a matter of opinion whether it was wisest and best greatly to increase the power of the Federal Government at the expense of the states, to develop the country quickly by immigration and manufactures, and largely to give over the control of government to a money class. That, however, was the object of Hamilton which Jefferson did not sense until he had worked with him for some time and seen his program and its effects develop step by step. An unbiased study of all Hamilton's papers supports this view of his policy, and lest I shall myself be considered biased, I may quote at length, on this point, one of his stanchest admirers and most laudatory biographers, the late Senator Lodge. Speaking of Hamilton's policy at this stage, Lodge wrote that it "was not merely to invigorate an existing political party or to evolve a new one, although such a result was incidental, important, and expected. Hamilton's scheme went farther, seeking to create a strong, and so far as was possible and judicious, a permanent class all over the country, without regard to existing party affiliations, but bound to the government as a government by the strongest of all ties, immediate and personal pecuniary interest. . . . The full intent of the policy was to array property on the side of the government. That once done, the experiment, Hamilton felt, would succeed, and its powers, moreover, might then be much extended. He had been unable to introduce a class influence into the Constitution by limiting the suffrage for the President and Senate with a property qualification, but by his financial policy he could bind the existing class of wealthy men, comprising at that day the aristocracy bequeathed by provincial times to the new system, and thus, if at all, assure to the property of the country the control of government." [15]

Hamilton's own papers, letters, and actions bear out the truth of his friendly biographer's statement, to the implications of which Lodge himself appears to have been quite oblivious. The implication is that Hamilton, not having been able to get the convention to agree to, or the country to accept, the kind of constitution he personally wished, deliberately set out, as Madison discovered, so to "administer" it as to foist his own ideas upon the nation. Whether those ideas were or were not better in the long run for the nation not only is an open question but is beside the present point. One is reminded of that first effort of the then "wise, rich, and good" to govern the people when Winthrop and other leaders in Massachusetts Bay deceived the citizens as to the terms of the charter in order that the leaders, who feared the people, could continue to govern them, ostensibly for their own good. Of Hamilton's personal financial rectitude, though attacked occasionally in his life time, there cannot now be the slightest doubt. As far as personal gain from high office is concerned, there is not a blemish on his whole career. His political morality was not so high, and on one noted occasion, as we shall see later, even

[15] H. C. Lodge, *Alexander Hamilton,* Boston, 1882, pp. 91 f.

New York politicians had to protest against his suggested methods of attaining his end. Of his political honesty in a high sense there is no doubt. He was indeed personally ambitious but he also believed, as members of a ruling class usually do, that his own ideas were those which were best for the nation, and if he was sometimes Jesuitical in attempting to force them on the people, he was no more so than the pious leaders of the Puritan commonwealth.

Hamilton's financial policy had only just begun to disclose itself but some of its desired effects began to appear at once. Ninety per cent of the population was agricultural. The small farmers, who constituted the bulk of those in the North and a large part of those in the South, rarely saw ready money in any amount and had no financial interests. In the South, the large and wealthy planters had usually been in debt to their London agents against the next year's crop, and the vexatious question of these pre-war debts had been raised again after peace. The genuine "money men" were comparatively few and mostly in the larger centers along the seaboard from Philadelphia northward—the merchants, shipping men, incipient manufacturers, and so on. The funding scheme, with the attendant rapid rise in the price of government securities, had immediately attached these groups to Hamilton, and their whole influence was thrown to him.

Not only had these comparatively rich men become much richer by his measure but "new rich" also arose. After the Continental currency had ceased to be worth anything, the old government had issued small promises to pay, when possible, known as "scrip," and this was scattered as widely as government war purchases had been made. This was included in Hamilton's plan to pay in full. Among the more knowing, the scrip had been rising in price from the time Hamilton's plan was first suggested, but many, especially in the agricultural sections, were ignorant of the possibilities. Jefferson thus described what happened, in the main without exaggeration. "Couriers and relay horses by land, and swift sailing pilot boats by sea, were flying in all directions. Active partners and agents were associated and employed in every state, town, and country neighborhood, and this paper was bought up at 5/— [shillings] and even as low as 2/— in the pound, before the holder knew that Congress had already provided for its redemption at par. Immense sums were thus filched from the poor and ignorant, and fortunes accumulated by those who had themselves been poor enough before. Men thus enriched by the dexterity of a leader, would follow of course a chief who was leading them to fortune, and become the zealous instruments of all his enterprises." [16]

America had started its first wild financial debauch. A close relation had also begun between government and finance. If the financial power supported its leader, its leader would also have to support it, and that power had received a great increase in wealth and political influence. The Federalist Party, rapidly becoming more commercial and northern, hailed its young chief, while the agricultural interests and the South began to lick their sore paws. Nine citizens out of ten might be farmers and ninety-nine out of a hundred might be outside the ranks of the self-styled "rich, wise, and good." It had been well to establish the credit of the new government, but the small men and farmers cared less about that than about the sort of government they were going to get and what they would have to say about it. They had feared the new Constitution in any case. They had fought to win liberty, and now the most powerful man in the new government, except Washington, preferred a monarchy; would accept a plutocracy as second-best temporarily; and believed that the people must be ruled by property owners. Jefferson must have cursed the dinner he had given.

[16] *Writings,* Ford, Vol. I, p. 161.

CHAPTER X

THE FIGHT WITH HAMILTON

THERE was, however, to be another dinner at Jefferson's house some weeks after the first. Washington had gone south in April, and had asked the Cabinet to discuss among themselves any important question, and if desired, to ask John Adams to attend, though the Vice-President was not expected to be present at Cabinet meetings. A problem came up, and as a convenient meeting place for all to discuss it, Jefferson asked the Cabinet members and Adams to dine with him. After the meal was over, and business disposed of, Jefferson wrote ("for the truth of which I attest the God who made me," he added), that the conversation got round to the British constitution. "On which Mr. Adams observed, 'purge that constitution of it's corruption, and give to it's popular branch equality of representation, and it would be the most perfect constitution ever devised by the wit of man.' Hamilton paused and said, 'purge it of it's corruption, and give to it's popular branch equality of representation, & it would become an *impracticable* government: as it stands at present . . . it is the most perfect government which ever existed." [1]

Although written long after Jefferson had become greatly embittered against Hamilton, I see no reason to doubt the essential truth of this reported conversation. Adams always admired the British constitution, though he had the sense to know it could not be introduced in America. Hamilton never made much secret of his belief in monarchy and his wish that some time circumstances might allow of its establishment. Aside from other evidence, his friend, Gouverneur Morris, at-

[1] *Writings,* Ford, Vol. I, pp. 165 f.

227

tested to this on several occasions after Hamilton's death, as we shall note later. As to the use of political corruption it fits in with Hamilton's extremely realistic view of the art of government. Whatever the truth may be, Jefferson became firmly convinced that Hamilton "was not only a monarchist, but for a monarchy bottomed on corruption." As he watched the head of the Treasury rise in power, and the Federalist Party, of which Hamilton became political leader and manager, entrench itself among the business interests, Jefferson came to regard him as an extremely dangerous man whose policies would ruin the American dream Jefferson had dreamed.

On account of both the funding operation and the assumption of the state debts, the Federal Government required a large increase in income, and Hamilton's next step was to secure the passage through Congress, against bitter opposition, of an excise tax on spirits. There had always been strong antagonism in the colonies to such a form of taxation, and this feeling was in a few years to flare up into an armed revolt in Pennsylvania, which, like Shays's rebellion, was to be much misrepresented and over-emphasized in importance and implications by those anxious to discredit the people and to increase the power of the central government. However, the states had rid themselves of over $21,000,000 in debts by turning them over to the Federal Government for payment, and the money had to be found. A "government," as distinct from the citizens, obviously never has any money of its own, and whatever grants it may make or expenses it may incur have inevitably to be followed sooner or later by the tax-gatherer reaching his hands into the pockets of the citizen.

The next step taken by Hamilton was one of the most far-reaching in the entire history of the country and one which has influenced the whole course of our constitutional development. The originality and ability of Hamilton in elaborating his various financial measures have often been much over-rated

by his admirers. He never concealed the fact that he wished
to make the American system in all respects—political, economic, and social—as much like the British as possible. His
funding plan was not original but mainly followed lines already
laid down by William Pitt, and in estimating the peculiarly
American conditions Hamilton made several bad errors, as to
interest rates, rapidity of extinction, and so on.

The most original feat of Hamilton was his realization of
the fact that not only the national finances but the whole form
and spirit of the government and fundamental law could be altered by a succession of fiscal measures. Having been disappointed in securing the form of government he wished in the
convention, and knowing that public opinion would not uphold
any direct and open change, he was astute enough to realize
that he could secure his end indirectly, and that if he could re-
produce the British financial policy and institutions they would
go far toward bringing about a deflection of the political constitution in the direction of the British one. If the President
could be turned into an "elective monarch," as Hamilton called
it; if Hamilton himself could become, not a co-equal member
of the Cabinet as mere head of a department, but a sort of
Prime Minister with his hand felt in all departments; and if
a moneyed aristocracy could be built up as a controlling class
to play the part of the governing families in England, then
the way might be paved for much else, besides the rise of that
strong central government which he believed in quite as honestly as Jefferson disbelieved in it.

As one of the main pillars of the structure he was planning,
he considered essential a central bank on the lines of the Bank
of England. The more that finance could be centralized in the
government, the more powerful the government would become,
and the greater the attachment of the moneyed interests to it.
Moreover, there were as yet only three banks in the country,
those in Boston, New York, and Philadelphia, though a fourth

was about to start in Baltimore. Hamilton was in favor of a rapid development of the nation, particularly of what we may call the "business" interest to counterbalance what he thought the undue proportion of agriculture.

Hamilton's economic ideas were vague and often incorrect. As the late Professor William G. Sumner pointed out in his biography of him, "he was under the dominion of the most vicious fallacies with regard to money and banking, and his idea of a bank did not go beyond some of the most vulgar misconceptions about it. Banks do not increase capital in the slightest degree. They make nothing; they are a part of the industrial organization, and their utility, which can hardly be overestimated, consists in heightening the circulating movement in a way which makes a certain amount of capital very much more effective." [2]   Hamilton's idea that the government should contribute its share to the capital of the bank in the form of promissory notes was essentially unsound, and was the same as that held by countless local individuals who were later to wreck their communities in successive waves of "wild-cat banking" in the West. He was right, however, in the belief that the creation of a new reservoir of *credit* would stimulate business—and, incidentally, speculation.

As in the case of the assumption of state debts, there was, nevertheless, no imperative necessity on the part of the new government for embarking on the undertaking. Additional banking facilities, provided by branches of the parent bank, might be convenient to the people, but these could be provided by private enterprise. Making borrowing more easy might hasten the growth of manufactures, the demand for foreign labor, and so enlarge the population more rapidly. It might do a number of things which some people might consider desirable, but there was no such national need for the bank as there had been for funding the federal debt; and the cry im-

2 Sumner, *Hamilton*, p. 167.

mediately went up in Congress that Hamilton was enlarging the circle of the privileged few by those who should become interested in the new institution.

The constitutionality of the scheme was also seriously open to doubt, the fight against it being led in the House by Madison, and after it had finally passed both houses of Congress, Washington called upon the Attorney-General and Jefferson for their opinions as to that point. Jefferson prepared a clear and concise statement which owing to the enormous importance of this discussion in our later history we shall have to note somewhat at length.

Opposing the measure, he asserted that the Tenth Amendment to the Constitution distinctly stated that all "powers not delegated to the United States by the Constitution, nor prohibited by it to the States, are reserved to the States respectively, or to the people." He denied that anywhere in the Constitution was there delegated to the Federal Government the right to create a bank. It could not be understood as included in any of the specific delegations, such as the power to lay taxes, to borrow money, to regulate commerce, etc. Nor could the two more general clauses be construed so as to include it. The first of these permitted Congress to collect taxes, etc., in order "to pay the debts and provide for the common defence and general welfare of the United States." Jefferson pointed out that "it is an established rule of construction where a phrase will bear either of two meanings, to give it that which will allow some meaning to the other parts of the instrument, and not that which would render all the others useless." [3]

Obviously, though Jefferson did not go into detail, Congress had the power to do many things, such as pay officials, maintain post roads, etc., which would cost money. It had the right to levy taxes not only for the debt service but all these other purposes, for the "general welfare," but, he said, the clause

[3] *Writings*, Ford, Vol. V, p. 286.

could not be twisted to mean that they could do anything at all which they might consider would be for the general welfare. If that were true the power given them would be so broad as to make the other clauses in the Constitution of no meaning whatever. Why so carefully write clauses stating specifically what Congress could or could not do if in one general clause it was to be permitted to do anything which it might think, or claim to think, was for the "general welfare"? Moreover, he added, "it is known that the very power now proposed *as a means* was rejected *as an end* by the convention which formed the Constitution. A proposition was made to them to authorize Congress to open canals, and an amendatory one to empower them to incorporate [companies]. But the whole was rejected, and one of the reasons for rejection urged in debate was, that then they would have a power to erect a bank, which would render the great cities, where there were prejudices and jealousies on the subject, adverse to the reception of the Constitution." [4]

The second general clause, he went on, is to "make all laws necessary and proper for carrying into execution the enumerated powers." A bank is certainly not *necessary*. It *might* be more *convenient* than private or state banks which would serve the same purposes but "can it be thought that the Constitution intended that for a shade or two of *convenience*, more or less, Congress should be authorised to break down the most ancient and fundamental laws of the several States; such as those against Mortmain, the laws of Alienage, the rules of descent, the acts of distribution, the laws of escheat and forfeiture, the laws of monopoly?" [5] At the end he suggested, however, that if the President's mind was not fairly certain that the bill was unconstitutional, "if the pro and con hang so even as to balance his judgment," then he might sign the bill out of respect to the wisdom of the legislature.

[4] *Ibid.*, p. 287.   [5] *Ibid.*, p. 289.

Washington turned Jefferson's opinion over to Hamilton for comment, stating that the Attorney-General also considered the act unconstitutional. Therefore he asked Hamilton for his opinion. Hamilton, with his usual diffuseness, commented on Jefferson's six pages or so with forty-six of his own. He began by saying that he had an especial interest in the matter because the measure had been his own, but that his "chief solicitude arises from a firm persuasion, that principles of construction like those espoused by the Secretary of State and the Attorney-General would be fatal to the just and indispensable authority of the United States." [6] He then proceeded to develop his theory of *implied* powers which would belong to any government for the purpose of carrying into execution *express* powers. He argued that the word *necessary* often meant "no more than *needful, requisite, incidental, useful* or *conducive* to.*" He rejected the interpretation of *absolutely* or *indispensably.* "The degree in which a measure is necessary can never be a *test* of the legal right to adopt it; that must be a matter of opinion." [7] He continued that "the moment the literal meaning" of the wording of the Constitution "is departed from, there is a chance of error and abuse. And yet an adherence to the letter of its powers would at once arrest the motions of government." He denied that Congress was limited to any purpose whatever in the raising of money, declaring that the only limitation upon it was that it could not apply money raised by taxation to "any purpose merely or purely local."

He also, in the course of his lengthy argument, into which it is impossible to enter in all its details, said that a strange fallacy had got abroad that "an incorporation seems to have been regarded as some *great independent substantive thing; as a political end of peculiar magnitude and moment.*" [8]

Knox, of course, as usual echoed Hamilton's opinion, though his own on such a subject could carry little weight. The Cab-

[6] *Works,* Lodge, Vol. III, p. 180.   [7] *Ibid.,* p. 189.   [8] *Ibid.,* p. 185.

inet, to which the President had appealed, was thus equally divided. There is a difference of opinion as to whether Hamilton convinced Washington as against Jefferson or not. Professor Channing, for example, wrote that he had, whereas Professor Bassett wrote that he had not, but that the President decided in favor of the bank on the principle that where there was an equal division in the Cabinet he would support the head of that department to which the business more particularly belonged. In any case, he signed the bill, which became law on February 25, 1791.

The subscription books for the bank stock were opened on July 4, and the whole taken up in two hours, many investors being disappointed at getting none. Another great fillip had been given to speculation, and five days later Madison wrote from New York that the "shares have risen as much in the Market here as in Philadelphia. It seems admitted on all hands now that the plan of the institution gives a moral certainty of gain to the Subscribers with scarce a physical possibility of loss. . . . It pretty clearly appears also in what proportions the public debt lies in the Country. What sort of hands hold it, and by whom the people of the U. S. are to be governed. Of all the shameful circumstances of this business, it is among the greatest to see the members of the Legislature who were most active in pushing this job openly grasping at its emoluments. Schuyler is to be put at the Head of the Directors, if the weight of the N. Y. subscribers can effect it. Nothing new is talked of here. In fact stock-jobbing drowns every other subject. The Coffee-House is in eternal buzz with the gamblers." [9] Prosperity, which seems always to occur between the first and second post-war deflations, had arrived in any case, and the capitalists of the new-born nation were behaving much as their descendants did in 1929. Colonel William Duer, at their head in New York, was speculating in every direction and

[9] Madison, *Writings*, Vol. VI, p. 55, note.

giving famous dinners at which fifteen different sorts of wine were served. By March, 1792, he was in jail for debt, and America was having its first colossal financial headache.

However, the speculation, which had been much increased by Hamilton's fiscal measures, was merely incidental to them. As far as the Federal Government was concerned, he had established its credit at home and abroad within a year after he had taken over the disordered finances, and that by itself was a great achievement. As to the fundamental disagreement between him and Jefferson regarding the theory of government and the interpretation of the Constitution, there is more to be said. This had been brought into the open by their disagreement over the bank. Jefferson, in his written opinion to Washington, had been courteous, and it is thought by some, even weakly conciliatory in his final paragraph, but Hamilton then realized that Jefferson must be downed if his own plans were to succeed. Jefferson, for his part, had no longer a shadow of doubt as to where Hamilton was heading. Hamilton's interpretation of the Constitution, with his theory of implied powers, and his definition of "necessary," had torn that document, as understood by Jefferson, Madison, and others, to shreds. If the theory were to be accepted universally there seemed no limit to what, in time, the central government might do. Hamilton now had the powerful party of wealth solidly behind him, whereas the opposition was scattered and without organization.

It is one of the anomalies of the development of American politics that Hamilton's theory *was* to stand but that citizens were to give lip-service, with revolts about once a generation against Hamiltonianism, to Jefferson's doctrines of the rights of man. It has been as though the early colonists talked the language of Hooker while they worked all the time for Winthrop.

Neither Hamilton nor Jefferson could foresee the future.

No one could in an age when practically none of the modern scientific discoveries had been made, when there was almost no application of steam, no machinery to speak of, no railroads, no electricity, and when man was still living with few more facilities for rapid development than he had had in the days of the Roman Empire. Neither could foresee the growth of the American nation from the Atlantic to the Pacific, the fantastic increase in population, the almost annihilation of time and space, the multiplication of inventions which in their effects have profoundly altered the bases of society, and the stability of social, economic, and political ideas and beliefs.

It is a mistake to think of the philosophies of Jefferson and Hamilton in the light of present-day conditions, and equally unfair to each of them. The extraordinary change which was to come over the entire world in the next century was a sealed book to them and to all men. As the world had gone before, so it appeared likely to continue to do. Manufacture in the modern sense scarcely existed at all, and gave no visible signs of what was in store. The horse, the sailing vessel, or a man's own two feet were the only means of locomotion and transport. The United States extended only to the Mississippi River, west of which lay the power of Spain, but even so it appeared as though it would take centuries to fill up the land between the river and the Atlantic seaboard. Population in America was increasing far more rapidly than in Europe, but that of the world-at-large seemed more or less stationary. Between the sixth century and 1800 that of Europe had never reached beyond 180,000,000. The measure of the forces about to be let loose on the world is indicated by the fact that in a little more than one century, between 1800 and 1914 it was about to leap from that figure to 460,000,000.

Mingled with those forces, the ideas of Hamilton and Jefferson were to be of enormous influence, forces in themselves, though neither man foresaw a world much different from that in which he lived. We have to think of them as contending with each other within the narrow limits of the eighteenth century present and the then probable future. Ignorant of the forces about to be loosed, it appeared to both men as though America had a choice of remaining almost wholly agricultural or of becoming industrialized, as the word was then understood, in any proportion she might choose. We now realize that in the nineteenth century there was to be no choice, but if Jefferson's dream of an America made up of farmers, with government kept as simple and local as possible, and with the control resting upon an agricultural yeomanry, seems naïve, Hamilton's vision of the future was almost equally limited. His highly centralized government was, indeed, to be more essential to the needs of the nation than Jefferson's ideal, but Hamilton himself did not foresee the huge concentration of wealth and the evils which his own economic system did so much to bring into being. He did not see the vested interests which it was to create, interests which would attempt to govern the people not for the sake of stability and justice, as he claimed would be the case, but for the selfish satisfaction of their own insensate greed. Had he been able to see the future he might have realized that it was not so absurd a fallacy to believe that a corporation might be, as he had laughed at others for calling it, a "great independent substantive thing."

Hamilton was ambitious and loved power, yet he was as great a patriot as was Jefferson. That he honestly believed his system was best for the country there can be no doubt. In itself, the strong government he did so much to create was to prove necessary for the kind of world into which America was all unconsciously to develop. But connected with his creation of it, his economic ideas—such as rapid industrialization, the fostering of immigration as much as possible to provide a supply of cheap labor, the tariffs and other privileges given to certain classes or groups, above all his reliance upon the wealthy as the main support of government, and the alliance between government and the privileged classes as a fundamental theorem in his political economy—were all to be of profound importance in the insidious growth of that political immorality and lack of virtue in the individual citizen which have eaten into our national character like cancers. Much of the depravity and greed of our economic and political life is Hamilton's legacy to the nation. We are very far from believing today that over-industrialization, a huge population drawn from all countries, vast cities with their proletariats, tariffs, and a government based on wealth and in alliance with it, make up a sound nation, as many were a generation ago.

Hamilton and his whole Federalist Party were essentially, as even his admirer, Professor Channing, wrote, "reactionary and aristocratic from start to finish, and became more reactionary and aristocratic with each successive year." [10] If the whole nine volumes of Hamilton's *Works* reveal scarcely an item indicating any interest in educating or otherwise improving the lot and self-respect of the ordinary man but on the other hand a desire to herd into the country as fast as possible a mass of cheap labor from anywhere, it is because, apart from the narrow range of his intellect outside of government and finance, he had no faith in the ordinary man's ever being able to become as good a citizen as himself. Jefferson's ideas of government have become inadequate for a twentieth-century America but *his* contribution to the nation was his spirit of liberalism. It is not so much the precise form of our government or the precise extent of states' rights versus the federal state which counts, as it is the spirit of our laws and of their enforcement. We have had in our history far fewer liberal leaders of ability than we have had reactionary ones. Liberalism has for the most part dwelt in the aspirations of the ordinary man, but the primary fount from which both he and his leaders have ever

[10] E. Channing, *Hist. of the U. S.*, New York, 1917, Vol. IV, p. 164.

drawn their inspiration has been the words of Jefferson. Without Hamilton the new nation might have disintegrated. Without Jefferson it would have lost its soul and that faith which has made it different from others.

In addition to the other measures already mentioned, Hamilton sent a report to Congress on the establishment of a mint, which met with little opposition. This was followed in the session of 1791–92 by his celebrated Report on Manufactures, which, although not adopted at the time, advocated a tariff for the development of infant industries, and was intended to be the capstone of his whole system, and has been an arsenal of arguments for the protectionists ever since.

Meanwhile, in accordance with the assumption deal, the government had moved to Philadelphia, for a decade, much to the disgust of many of its members. A larger city than New York, numbering about 60,000, it was less convenient, and in spite of Mrs. Bingham and her rich circle, less gay and interesting. In addition, the canny Philadelphians charged extortionate rates for anything which the unfortunate officials and Congressmen needed. After speaking of some social visits, Mrs. John Adams sighed that "when all is done, it will not be Broadway. If New York wanted any revenge for the removal, the citizens might be glutted if they would come here, where every article has become almost double in price. . . . One would suppose that the people thought Mexico was before them, and that Congress were the possessors." [11] Jefferson secured lodgings at 274 High (now Market) Street.

He had never made any secret of his growing mistrust of the Federalists' interpretation of the Constitution, but he was now unwittingly to be involved in a public controversy which he had not intended and which he regretted. In England, Burke had been declaiming against the French Revolution, and Thomas Paine, whose book *Common Sense* had had such a

[11] *Letters of Mrs. Adams,* Boston, 1840, Vol. II, p. 209.

great influence on the American Revolution, answered Burke in another volume entitled *The Rights of Man*. Madison had secured a copy, which he intended to have reprinted in Philadelphia, and loaned it to Jefferson to read, requesting its return. Jefferson read and duly returned it with a note in which he said: "I am extremely pleased to find it will be reprinted here, and that something is at length to be publicly said against the political heresies which have sprung up amongst us."

Owing to Jefferson's well-known opinions, the heresies referred to could be only the opinions of the Federalists, and as luck would have it, John Adams, Vice-President and one of Jefferson's best friends, had just been running a series of articles in *The Gazette of the United States*. Jefferson had had no intention whatever that his private note to Madison should be made public but the printer got hold of it and thought it would help the sale of the book, which, when published, carried the comment of the Secretary of State on a fly-leaf. Then began a rather tragic comedy of errors. Unknown to John Adams, his son, John Quincy, wrote a series of letters, under the pseudonym of "Publicola," attacking both Paine and Jefferson. The letters accorded so well in style and thought with the writing of the elder Adams that Jefferson and others believed him the author, just as Adams believed that Jefferson had intentionally attacked him in the note prefaced to Paine's book. Jefferson wrote to Adams telling him the facts. Adams accepted the explanation and also denied that he had had anything to do with "Publicola." Meanwhile, however, others had entered the fight on both sides, and a first-class newspaper controversy had been started, and the issues had been brought into the open.

The Gazette of the United States, edited by John Fenno, a protégé of Hamilton, was the Federalist organ. The opposition party, if it may as yet be so-called, including Jefferson,

Madison, Monroe, and others, began to realize the need of some newspaper which would present their side of the case, and, although the negotiations are somewhat obscure, it was apparently Madison who arranged with Philip Freneau, "the poet of the American Revolution," to start *The National Gazette* in Philadelphia. Jefferson had given him a small post with a salary of only $250 a year as foreign-language clerk in the extremely modest organization of the State Department. As Freneau understood only French he had to pay out of his salary the cost of translations into other languages, and there is nothing to indicate that Jefferson gave him the office to help found the paper, though Jefferson naturally was interested in having a journal founded on the Republican side. As Freneau's net emolument must have been well under the $250-a-year salary, it is ridiculous to think that the men who did help found the paper would have boggled at so small a sum among them.

Hamilton seems to have turned definitely against Jefferson after the latter had given his adverse opinion as to the constitutionality of the bank. When an opposition newspaper was started, Hamilton lost control of himself, and in the course of some months he wrote—under various pseudonyms—a series of outrageous attacks upon his colleague in the Cabinet, claiming among other things that Jefferson had opposed the adoption of the Constitution; that he had wished to repudiate the public debt; and that he had set up a paper to slander the government. Whatever names Hamilton signed, the authorship of the articles was well known, and the public was treated to the spectacle of the Secretary of the Treasury bitterly slandering the Secretary of State in public print. Jefferson himself never wrote a word for the papers, any more than Washington did, although undoubtedly Freneau got information from him. Hamilton's most ardent admirers cannot defend his action and even Lodge condemns him for lowering "his high office into the dust of a political newspaper brawl," admitting that he lost his temper.

Hamilton also accused Jefferson of moral "turpitude," of attempting to defraud, and as a sample of his language we may quote from one of his characterizations of his colleague: "How long it is since that gentleman's real character may have been divined, or whether this is only the first time that the secret has been disclosed, I am not sufficiently acquainted with the history of his political life to determine; but there is always a 'first time' when characters studious of artful disguises are unveiled; when the visor of stoicism is plucked from the brow of the epicurean; when the plain garb of Quaker simplicity is stripped from the concealed voluptuary." [12] The last phrase, as indecent as untrue, was an unfortunate one for Hamilton to use, as, within a year, he himself was to have to make public confession of his having been carrying on in Philadelphia an adulterous intrigue with a low and uneducated woman, a Mrs. Reynolds, to whose husband he had paid blackmail for the privilege.

Jefferson, who made it a lifelong practice not to reply to newspaper attacks, maintained silence, although Freneau's paper continued to attack Hamilton's policies. By the late summer of 1792 the scandal of the Cabinet quarrel had become so great as to distress and alarm Washington, who on August 23 wrote to both Jefferson and Hamilton suggesting the danger of "tearing the machine asunder" if more liberal allowance could not be made by each for the different opinions of the other.

In a long reply, Jefferson stated his views of Hamilton's policies, and spoke of his interference with Jefferson's own office. He said, however, that as far as he was concerned he would enter into no public controversy until his retirement from office, for which he longed. The bitterness of his feeling

12 Hamilton, *Works,* Vol. VI, p. 354.

was shown, nevertheless, by his statement that when he should once more be a private citizen he might find it necessary to enter the lists against Hamilton, as "I will not suffer my retirement to be clouded by the slanders of a man whose history, from the moment at which history can stoop to notice him, is a tissue of machinations against the liberty of the country which has not only received and given him bread, but heaped it's honors on his head." [13] Hamilton, in his reply, declined to stop his attacks "for the present," and stated that the future would approve of what he had done, but added that if the President "shall hereafter form a plan to reunite" the Cabinet on some "steady principle of co-operation" he would then no longer endanger a feud. [14] This young man of thirty-five, who so misjudged the verdict of posterity as to his course of action, thus declined to accede to the request of the President unless all matters should be arranged as he wished.

On the way from Monticello to Philadelphia in October, Jefferson stopped to see Washington at Mount Vernon. In the spring the Secretary had had a long talk with the President regarding his fears as to the effects upon the future of the country of Hamilton's policies, and he now had another opportunity of discussing the same subject. Washington was undecided as to whether or not he would run for President again the following year. Jefferson urged him to do so on the ground that he alone could save the nation. Washington countered by urging in turn that Jefferson should remain in office also. The President praised Hamilton's ability in having raised the public credit but suggested that Jefferson's presence would be useful in keeping things from "going too far." He rightly thought there was no danger of a monarchy, and considered that both secretaries were useful where they were. Jefferson remained until December of the following year, but the feud with Hamilton was not healed and merely deepened. Each man genuinely

[13] *Writings,* Ford, Vol. VI, p. 109.   [14] Hamilton, *Works,* Vol. VI, p. 387.

believed the other to be intellectually dishonest and a danger
to the country. There could be no harmony under those conditions, as each man, in fact, *was* honest. Washington, however, continued to take the advice of each, favoring each, as a
rule, in his own department. It is often said that the President usually took the advice of Hamilton, but actually, in foreign affairs, he rather more usually took that of Jefferson.

We must now turn for a brief glance at those affairs, the
first episode in which is of interest as showing how much more
Hamilton interfered than even Jefferson realized; and also
because of the way Jefferson handled the question of debts
which happens to have an extraordinary applicability to international affairs today.

The various infractions of the Treaty of 1783 by both Great
Britain and the United States had finally caused the sending
of an informal agent from London, followed by the arrival of
an accredited Minister, George Hammond. Hammond, like
his predecessor, at once got into confidential relations with
Hamilton. Neither nation had lived up to the terms of the
Treaty, and among other points of difference, Great Britain
had never given up her possession of some of the western trading posts. It was also claimed by the United States that in
contravention of the terms of the treaty the British had carried off American slaves. On the other hand Great Britain
claimed that the United States had not lived up to the clause
which provided that creditors on both sides "shall meet with no
lawful impediment to the recovery of the full value in sterling
money" of all bona fide debts previously incurred. The United
States had agreed to this but it had not, as a distinguished
British author has written, "agreed to help British citizens
to recover what was due them." A person, for example, may
agree not to place any impediment in the way of a man's getting home, but that is quite different from agreeing to *help*
him to get home.

We need not go into all the details of Jefferson's answer to the complaints of the British Minister. It is a document of nearly seventy pages, and has been called one of the most memorable which ever came from Jefferson's pen. He took a firm stand on all the questions involved, and, not knowing that Hamilton had been leading the British envoy to expect a much weaker reply, Jefferson asked Hamilton to read it over before sending. Hamilton returned it with various suggestions, among others that Jefferson should "extenuate" instead of "vindicating" the American position as to the debts. The document then went to Washington, who reversed Hamilton and upheld Jefferson. It next went to Mr. Hammond, who having been led into wholly false expectations by Hamilton was stunned by what he called the "extraordinary performance" of Jefferson, and immediately ran to Hamilton for explanations. The real "extraordinary performance" then became that of the Secretary of the Treasury, who, as a member of the Cabinet, lamented to a British Minister the "intemperate violence" of the American Secretary of State, adding that Jefferson's letter was far from representing the real opinion of the country. Hamilton falsely added that Washington had not seen it, and had relied upon Jefferson's sending a document which would meet the views of other members of the Cabinet.[15]

The bewildered Minister regarded this utterly indefensible action of Hamilton as a "mark of confidence," and then bethought himself of having another talk with the Secretary of State. Jefferson, however, insisted upon the text of the letter as agreed upon by himself and Washington, and left the British diplomat more bewildered than ever. No great harm was done, as the British Government was too busy with the dangerous relations with France even to consider the documents in the American case when they arrived in London. Hamil-

[15] Citations by S. F. Bemis, *Jay's Treaty*, New York, 1923, p. 106.

ton's belief that he was to be a sort of Prime Minister made him a nuisance in poking into other departments, but even a Prime Minister does not discredit and throw over his Foreign Secretary when talking with the Minister of another power. Except as an example of Hamilton's egoism, his frequent lack of judgment, and his intense hatred of Jefferson, the incident is almost incredible.

But we may here take leave of the feud, the importance of which in our general history has perhaps been often overrated. It did, however, probably hasten the formation into a powerful party of the Democrats or Republicans, as they were then called indiscriminately as opposed to the Federalists. Not only had deep fears and bitter hatreds been aroused in the leaders, but these became shared by their followers. The chief political effect of Hamilton's attacks on Jefferson was probably greatly to increase Jefferson's following and to make him a martyr-leader, always a powerful rôle in American politics.

Jefferson, in his letter to Hammond, after exploring the debt question in various directions, had passed to some general reflections. "To the necessities for some delay in the payment of debts," he wrote, "may be added the British commercial regulations lessening our means of payment, by prohibiting us from carrying in our own bottoms our own produce to their dominions in our neighborhood, and excluding valuable branches of it from their home markets by prohibitory duties. The means of paiment constitute one of the motives to purchase at the time of purchasing. If these means are taken away by the creditor himself, he ought not in conscience to complain of a mere retardation of his debt, which is the effect of his own act, & the least injurious to those it is capable of producing." [16]

He then spoke of the interruption to commerce by the war,

[16] *Writings*, Ford, Vol. VI, p. 38. This is the first draft as submitted to Washington and Hamilton.

the draining of specie and the issue of paper money. "What were the consequences?" he continued. "The stock of hard money which we possessed in an ample degree, at the beginning of the war, soon flowed into Europe for supplies of arms, ammunition and other necessaries, which we were not in the habit of manufacturing for ourselves. The produce of our soil, attempted to be carried in our own bottoms to Europe fell two-thirds of it into the hands of our enemies, who were masters of the sea, the other third illy sufficed to procure the necessary implements of war, so that no returns of money supplied the place of that which had gone off. We were reduced then to the resource of a paper medium, & that completed the exile of the hard money, so that, in the latter stages of the war, we were for years together without seeing a single coin of the precious metals in circulation. It was closed with a stipulation that we should pay a large mass of debt in such coin. If the whole soil of the U. S. had been offered for sale for ready coin, it would not have raised as much as would have satisfied this stipulation. The thing then was impossible; & reason & authority declare ['If the obstacle be real, time must be given, for no one is bound to an impossibility']. Vattel, 1, 4, 51. We should with confidence have referred the case to the arbiter proposed by another Jurist, who lays it down that a party ['is not obliged to pay more than he can, and the decision how much he can pay may be left by the other sovereign to the award of an honest arbitrator']." [17]

Passing to the question of interest as distinguished from principal, Jefferson argued at length, with citations of authorities, that "there is no instrument or title to debt so formal & sacred, as to give a right to interest on it under all possible circumstances." Quoting one of the authorities with approval he asserted that "where *by a general & national calam-*

---

[17] The quotations in brackets are in French and Latin in Jefferson's draft, and are here translated.

ity, nothing is made out of lands which are assigned for payment of interest, it ought not to run on *during the time of such calamity.*" "This," he added, "is exactly the case in question. Can a more *general national calamity* be conceived than that universal devastation . . . during the war? . . . The creditor says indeed he has laid out his money, he has therefore lost the use of it. The debtor replies that if the creditor has lost, he has not gained it: that this may be a question between two parties both of whom have lost." [18]

Jefferson was speaking of debts contracted between private parties before the declaration of war and innocent of it, but particularly in the first two passages quoted, the rule then laid down by our Department of State, when the shoe of debt was pinching our foot and not Europe's, might well be considered to have some application today. Jefferson plainly affirmed that if by the raising of tariffs and other trade barriers, a creditor interfered with the trade which the debtor had theretofore carried on, the creditor cannot then insist upon the previous terms of payment.

Jefferson was conducting the entire business of the State Department with a staff of four clerks and a messenger, at a total cost in salaries of $2300 for the five! Ample business, therefore weighed on his own shoulders. In 1790, when war was threatening between Great Britain and Spain, he at once seized the opportunity to press through various channels abroad for an increase of our privileges or rights to the navigation of the Mississippi, the lower stretch of which, including its mouth, was in the possession of Spain. Of all distinguished Easterners of his time, Jefferson was most consistently and deeply interested in the West and its problems and development, not as a business man or speculator but as an American and a statesman. The New England Federalists in particular, and most of the conservative classes elsewhere, feared

[18] *Ibid.,* p. 59.

the growth of the West (though willing to make money out of it), on account of its radicalism and also because they foresaw a lessening of their own political power as a result of the rise of new states across the mountains. Jefferson, with his belief in the common man, with his liberalism and willingness to experiment, had no such fears. As we have seen, he had advocated, when governor of Virginia, the expedition of Clark which won the Northwest for us. He had drawn up the Ordinance for the government of the new territory. Later, under him as President, the purchase of the vast Louisiana purchase was to be made, and the explorations conducted by Lewis and Clark. What he planned now is chiefly interesting as foreshadowing what was to come. There was considerable canniness in his proposals. These were briefly that we could not go to war with Spain but that if she were involved in war with England, she would not wish to add to her enemies, and that, in a word, we wanted the cession of a port at the mouth of the great river, and that if the interests of the Westerners were not considered it might be impossible to hold them in check. We had, indeed, the right of navigation of the Mississippi, but, employing a breadth of interpretation almost equal to that of Hamilton, Jefferson wrote to William Carmichael, then the U. S. Chargé d'Affaires in Spain, saying that "it may be asked, what need of negotiation, if the navigation is to be ceded at all events? You know that the navigation cannot be practised without a port, where the sea and river vessels may meet and exchange loads. . . . The right to use a thing, comprehends the means necessary to its use, and without which it would be useless." [19]

That Jefferson's determination to control the mouth of the Mississippi was no sudden inspiration in 1803 is shown by his concluding instructions to Carmichael in 1790. These were to the effect that although our wishes must be "pressed softly,"

[19] *Writings*, Ford, Vol. V., p. 217.

and that "patience and persuasion" must be used carefully until "some other circumstance turn up," he was determined in the end to obtain the object "at every risk." Gouverneur Morris, who was an intimate friend of Hamilton, and was appointed Minister to France in 1792, was instructed to warn England, if war should come, against attempting any increase of territory in America.

The progress of the revolution in France naturally greatly interested Jefferson, but throughout it, even when the utterly unsuitable Genêt arrived as Minister from the new republic to succeed Ternant, there is nothing to indicate that Jefferson took any stand which was not thoroughly American, though his sympathies were with the people struggling for an increase in liberty. When forced by the rapidity of events to take a stand as to governmental changes in France, he laid down the rule to Morris, which we have followed in the main ever since, that the United States would recognize any government "formed by the will of the nation substantially declared." [20]

Before Ternant's recall, the problem of our debt to France had been complicated by the heavy depreciation in the French paper money, the so-called *assignats*, which we could have bought up and tendered in payment. Looking forward again to conditions today we may quote from a letter written to the French Minister by Jefferson and slightly revised by Hamilton, which said that "I am authorized to assure you that the government of the United States have no idea of paying their debt in a depreciated medium, and that in the final liquidation of the payments which shall have been made due regard will be had to the equitable allowance for the circumstance of depreciation." [21] When we consider the fiscal policies of the Roosevelt administration, notably its long insistence that the little Republic of Panama should receive its annual payments

[20] *Ibid.*, Vol. VI, p. 131.   [21] *Ibid.*, Vol. V, p. 384.

agreed to by us for the use of the Canal Zone in fifty-nine instead of hundred-cent dollars, it is evident that the financial morality of the nation was higher in 1791 than in 1934–36.

During the concluding months of Jefferson's term of office, as they were to prove, the question of France became the leading one in the United States. News of the execution of Louis XVI arrived in the middle of March, 1793. A few weeks later came word of the outbreak of war between Great Britain and France, which at once raised the problem of our treaty with the latter country. Washington accepted Jefferson's view that the treaty was temporarily suspended instead of voided, but went rather further with Hamilton in his view of the extent of neutrality desirable than Jefferson would have wished. The proclamation of neutrality, in which the word "neutrality" itself was not used, was issued on the very day on which the unspeakable Genêt landed at Charleston, South Carolina, to undertake his duties as Minister.

Jefferson felt that the cause of republican France, as it then stood, was the cause of liberty throughout the world, and he was not frightened by the spilling of blood, although he later condemned the excesses of the subsequent period of the revolution. Hamilton and the Federalists generally favored England, as they naturally would with their theory of order at any price, whereas the Republicans or Democrats favored the French. Genêt's gross abuse of his privileges as Minister and his complete lack of judgment did almost as much as the massacres by the Jacobins to arouse the fear of France on the part of the Federalists, and for the next twenty years the course of American politics was to be influenced more by the repercussions of the European wars than by domestic questions.

Jefferson, in spite of his sympathies with France, maintained both the strict neutrality policy as laid down by the President, and the dignity of the nation in the face of the *opera bouffe* antics of Genêt. There was no diminution, however, of the feud between the Secretaries of State and Treasury. The latter was maintaining close relations with the British Minister while the former was trying to restrain the French one, and in May Jefferson wrote to Monroe that "H[amilton] is panic-struck if we refuse our breach to every kick which Gr. Brit. may chuse to give it. He is for proclaiming at once the most abject principles, such as would invite & merit habitual insults. And indeed every inch of ground must be fought in our councils to desperation in order to hold up the face of even a sneaking neutrality, for our votes are generally 2½ against 1½. Some propositions have come from him which would astonish Mr. Pitt himself with their boldness. If we preserve even a sneaking neutrality, we shall be indebted for it to the President, & not to his counsellors." [22]

The letter to Monroe was enclosed in one to Madison, for his perusal before forwarding, and to Madison Jefferson wrote that he was expecting by the next boat from England a model of a threshing mill "which with two horses got out eight bushels of wheat an hour." His heart had long been turning to Monticello and the quiet delights of plantation and family life. To the same friend, who had written to dissuade him from retiring, he had replied that it was true that all citizens owed a "tour of duty" to the public but no one owed his entire existence. He added that he had now been in public service for twenty-four years, for more than half of which he had wholly given up his own private life and affairs, so that further service might reasonably be allowed to depend upon his own feelings. "There has been a time," he continued, "when these were very different from what they are now: when perhaps the esteem of the world was of higher value in my eye than everything in it. But age, experience & reflection, preserving to that only it's due value, have set a higher on tranquillity.

[22] *Ibid.,* Vol. VI, p. 239.

The motion of my blood no longer keeps time with the tumult of the world. It leads me to seek for happiness in the lap of and love of my family, in the society of my neighbors & my books, in the wholesome occupations of my farm & my affairs, in an interest or affection in every bud that opens, in every breath that blows around me, in an entire freedom of rest or motion, of thought or incognitancy, owing account to myself alone of my hours & actions." In public life, he added, he was giving up everything he loved for everything he hated, while his private concerns were "abandoned to chaos & derangement." [23]

On the last day of the year, after the elections had assured the nation another four years of sound management under the presidency of Washington, and also a majority of Republicans in Congress, he handed in his resignation, regretfully accepted by the President. Jefferson's last act was to administer a stinging rebuke to Genêt, so strong that even the rather pro-British cabinet felt called upon to soften it before sending it. By January 16, 1794, the ex-Secretary was back on his Virginia hill-top fervently hoping that he was through with public life, and its quarrels and burdens forever. A year later Hamilton also resigned and returned to his law practice in New York to repair his broken fortunes. Each of the secretaries had served his country for $3500 a year, and each according to his light had given of his best. Washington's second Cabinet after appointments had been almost hawked about, only to be declined, was to contain no man of the grade of either.

23 *Writings,* Ford, Vol. VI, pp. 291 f.

CHAPTER XI

INTERLUDE

JEFFERSON was delighted to be once more at home. There he had his two daughters, his son-in-law, young Thomas Mann Randolph, and the weary statesman could devote himself at once to the rehabilitation of his affairs. These, for many years, had been almost wholly in the hands of an over- seer, never a very satisfactory way of administering them in Virginia. Reaching Monticello on January 16, 1794, he wrote his first letter to any one in Philadelphia three weeks later in answer to one from Edmund Randolph, who had succeeded him as Secretary of State, and whose note, Jefferson said, was the first he had had from the capital. There can be no doubt that he had decided to retire for good, and that he was happy in the decision. In his letter to Randolph he asserted that he intended to estrange himself from everything political.

During that year his correspondence markedly shrank. Writing to John Adams in April to thank him for a book re- ceived, he said, "Instead of writing 10. or 12. letters a day, which I have been in the habit of doing as a thing of course, I put off answering my letters now, farmer-like, till a rainy day, & then find it sometimes postponed by other necessary occupations." [1] His files bear out this assertion. His hostility to Hamilton continued, but otherwise there is no bitterness in his correspondence, and his letter to Adams was signed, as usual, "your affectionate & humble servant."

In contrast with the intrigues, gossip, and slander of the capital he found to his amazement that the people at large

[1] *Writings,* Ford, Vol. VI, p. 505.

were troubling themselves not at all about politics or international affairs. Reporting his going into Charlottesville from his hilltop on a court day, he wrote to Madison that "I could not have supposed, when at Philadelphia, that so little of what was passing there could be known even at Kentucky, as is the case here. Judging from this of the rest of the Union, it is evident to me that the people are not in a condition either to approve or disapprove of their government, nor consequently influence it." [2]

In his rare letters, he occasionally expressed an opinion on political affairs, but almost immediately turned again to the discussion of farm matters. Writing to Tench Coxe, May 1, he spoke of the danger of our being drawn into the European wars, especially by England, but as usual he wished for peace when possible. As an interesting foreshadowing of his later embargo policy, he said that he loved "Mr. Clarke's proposition of cutting off all communication with the nation which has conducted itself so atrociously. This, you will say, may bring on war. If it does we will meet it like men; but it may not bring on war, & then the experiment will have been a happy one." [3] A fortnight later he wrote to Washington, mostly about his farming operations, saying that after inspecting his lands he found that "a 10. years' abandonment of them to the unprincipled ravages of overseers, has brought them on a degree of degradation far beyond what I had expected." He spoke of a dung he had read about, "one pint of which should manure an acre," but the only mention of politics in this letter from the recent Secretary of State to the President, was, after referring to the slowness of recovery he must expect in his land, that "Time, patience, & perseverance must be the remedy; and the maxim of your letter, 'slow & sure,' is not less a good one in agriculture than in politics. I sincerely wish it may extricate us from the event of a war,

[2] *Ibid.*, Vol. VI, p. 499.   [3] *Ibid.*, Vol. VI, p. 508.

if this can be done by saving our faith and our rights. My opinion of the British government is, that nothing will force them to do justice but the loud voice of their people, & that this can never be excited but by distressing their commerce." [4]

Meanwhile, Washington had sent John Jay to England to negotiate a treaty which was to settle many of the points in dispute between the two nations. Jay was not a strong man and it would have been difficult to secure recognition of our rights from the British in any case, but Hamilton now once again betrayed an American negotiator as he had Jefferson. The Secretary of the Treasury was in the height of his career and was practically running the State Department as well as his own, as Randolph, who had been appointed in Jefferson's place, offered less resistance to encroachments than had his predecessor. The strongest weapon Jay had in his not very strong arsenal for negotiation was the possibility that the United States might join against England with Sweden and Denmark in an Armed Neutrality. He was to find, however, that this had been taken from him by Hamilton, who, without letting Jay into the secret, had informed the British Minister that such a move would be against American policy. The Minister, Hammond, naturally informed the British Government that they had nothing to fear on that score, with the result that they felt more or less free to dictate such terms as they chose. Hamilton and the Federalists had wanted peace at any price with England on account of her trade, but when, in the following year the terms of the ignominious treaty Jay had had to make became known, a howl of rage went up from the American people, and even Washington's popularity suffered from his having signed it. We did secure a necessary peace and certain advantages, but might have secured more had Hamilton kept his hands off, instead of committing what practically amounted to treachery both to the United States

[4] *Ibid.*, Vol. VI, p. 510.

and Jay. The leading authority on the treaty, indeed, says that it should in truth be called "Hamilton's Treaty," and that either the praise or blame for it belongs to him.[5]

For a year or so, Jefferson's health had given him much anxiety, and he continued to deny that he would ever again have anything to do with public life. In September, 1794, in reply to a suggestion from Washington that he should go to Philadelphia to lend a hand in affairs of the moment, he replied to Randolph, who had passed on the suggestion to him, that he was in torment from rheumatism, and that "no circumstances, my dear Sir, will ever more tempt me to engage in anything public. I thought myself perfectly fixed in this determination when I left Philadelphia, but every day & hour since has added to it's inflexibility." [6]

This note constantly recurs, and at the end of 1794 he urged Madison to run for the presidency. When Madison in turn urged Jefferson to return to public life, the latter answered at length and definitely. "The question is forever closed," he said, adding that the only interest he had politically was to keep every vote possible for the candidate of the Republican cause. After which he discussed the qualities of clover. When Monroe wrote him on public affairs, he replied in part that Monroe should try to "enrich our country with. 1. the Alpine strawberry. 2. The skylark. 3. The *red* legged partridge. I despair too much of the nightingale to add that!"

Nevertheless, he broke out at times, usually against Hamilton and his policies. In the autumn of 1794 the so-called "Whiskey Rebellion" started in western Pennsylvania. Hamilton had increased the national debt by about $5,000,000. Taxes had to be found, and the excise was making trouble among the trans-mountaineers. Too distant from markets to transport their farm produce profitably, they converted their corn and rye into liquid shape. Lack of transportation had

[5] Bemis, *Jay's Treaty, op. cit.,* p. 271.   [6] *Writings,* Ford, Vol. VI, p. 512.

first interfered with their farming profits. Then came the excise which seemed planned to add another differential in favor of the East and against the West. There were also the usual objections, among a frontier and liberty-loving people, to the inquisitorial methods of the tax gatherers. Among a rather sparse population, there was some violence and a good deal of talk. Desirous, apparently, of showing the strength of the Federal Government, Hamilton induced Washington to call out 15,000 militia from four states to over-awe the Westerners. The President and the Secretary of the Treasury even accompanied the troops part way. As in the case of Shays's Rebellion, as much as possible was made of the danger to ordered society and of the vicious character of the Americans who had refused to pay what they considered an unjust tax. It was well to show that the new government had power and could maintain order. This was perhaps as good an opportunity as was likely soon to offer, but, even so, an army of 15,000 men, who could find nobody to fight with, was a rather overdone demonstration.

Washington, who was to die in five years, and was beginning to feel the strain of his long services, was coming more and more under the influence of Hamilton, without the counter-weight of Jefferson, or of any other man of strength and contrary views, in the Cabinet. That the President should believe in a strong government was proper. That a man of his experience and judgment, however, who had fought the British Empire with most of the time a handful of troops and who had never had an army of much over 20,000 men at its maximum strength, should have considered it necessary to raise a body of 15,000 to put down what, at its worst, can be described only as sporadic rioting among his own fellow-countrymen, could seem to be explained only by the insistence of Hamilton. Hamilton's influence must also be considered as behind another mistake which the President made. The Treasury head had shaken the mailed fist in the face of the rural population, but the mechanics, artisans, and others of the "lower orders" in the towns and cities had been organizing themselves into societies for the discussion of politics, and were opposed to the Federalist policies. The increase in the excesses of the French Revolution, and the rise of the Jacobin Clubs in France were creating a panic among the conservatives and reactionaries in America. Like Shays's Rebellion and the Whiskey Rebellion, the French could be used to send shivers through society, and incidentally to stop the progress of the political organization of the Republicans. Hamilton saw his chance, and Washington's annual message to Congress, at the end of 1794, contained a scathing denunciation of the Democratic Societies as dangerous to the public welfare.

Jefferson, in spite of his denial of taking any interest in national affairs, was no silent witness to what was going on. On December 17, he wrote to W. B. Giles that "the attempt to restrain the liberty of our citizens meeting together, interchanging sentiments on what subjects they please, & stating their sentiments in the public papers, has come upon us a full century earlier than I expected." Continuing, he said, "the tide against our constitution is unquestionably strong, but it will turn. Every thing tells me so, and every day verifies the prediction. Hold on then like a good & faithful seaman till our brother-sailors can rouse from their intoxication & right the vessel.—Make friends with the trans-Alleganians. They are gone if you do not." [7]

Writing about a fortnight later to Madison he said, "the denunciation of the democratic societies is one of the extraordinary acts of boldness of which we have seen so many from the faction of the monocrats. It is wonderful indeed, that the President should have permitted himself to be the organ of such an attack on the freedom of discussion, the freedom of

[7] *Writings,* Ford, Vol. VI, pp. 515 f.

writing, printing & publishing." [8]   Jefferson then proceeded
to ask why there should be such a different attitude shown toward the Democratic clubs, "whose avowed object is the nour-
ishment of the republican principles of our constitution, and
the society of the Cincinnati . . . carving out for itself hereditary distinctions, lowering over our Constitution eternally,
meeting together in all parts of the Union, periodically, with
closed doors, accumulating a capital in their separate treasury, corresponding secretly & regularly, & of which society
the very persons denouncing the democrats are themselves the
fathers, founders & high officers."

Jefferson was evidently still keenly interested in politics,
although there is no reason whatever to consider him as an
astute silent plotter biding his time to return to the arena.
Hamilton's insistence that the Democrats were a mere "faction" and not a party with definite and worthy principles
made Jefferson furious, and although he always to the end
desired to remain on good terms personally with Washington,
he had begun to realize that the President was, as we would
say today, swinging too far to the right and becoming reactionary, as most of the older Revolutionary heroes and all the
leaders of the Federalist Party had already done or were doing. Jefferson realized the weakness of the Democrats due to
lack of organization as against the entrenched cohorts of the
Federalists, and consequently felt that Washington's attack,
with all the influence it would exert, due to his hold on the
love and respect of the nation, was an unfair blow below the
belt for the Democrats, who had as good a right to their opinions and constitutional interpretations as had the Federalists,
who occupied all the offices of government and for whose economic welfare its policies seemed specially designed. Nevertheless, this does not mean that Jefferson was plotting to have
himself elected President. As we have noted, his friendships

[8] *Ibid.*, Vol. VI, p. 516.

were notably long and strong, and even after the break with Adams, which he deeply regretted, he was always anxious for a genuine reconciliation, and happy when it came. He was extremely fond of his younger friend Madison, and it was at the end of the letter just quoted that he urged him to run for President. After living for years with Jefferson's writings, it is impossible to believe that in making such a suggestion to one of the men he loved most he could have been insincere. That he was, by "writing around," giving just the right touch here and there, building up the strength of a Democratic Party was true, but that he would have preferred some one else to be its standard-bearer is also, I think, equally true. In Congress, the power of the Democrats was much increased in 1795 by the appearance there of Albert Gallatin, a man of great ability, and in financial matters the equal, if not the superior, of Hamilton. The intellectual, retiring and shy Madison at once turned over the leadership of the opposition to him. Gallatin, however, was of foreign birth and not so widely known, so that in the course of the next year it became evident that Jefferson was, in the eyes of the country, the true national leader of the party. He then yielded to the circumstances of the case.

When the terms of Jay's Treaty, which the Federalists had tried to keep secret, were revealed to the people by publication in *The Aurora*, a Democratic paper, Jefferson again exploded with wrath in some of his letters. Hamilton had resigned from the Cabinet, January 31, 1795, but the treaty had been his work, and he still continued highly influential with Washington. In fact, for most of the few years of life left to him before the fatal duel with Burr ended it, Hamilton continued to think of himself as the one man who could save the country. Whether Washington or Adams was President, Hamilton endeavored at least to guide if not to control and dictate policies.

In a letter to Madison in May, 1796, Jefferson indicated

that he believed the treaty had grossly sacrificed the "interest, the honor & faith of our nation." He did not, as often asserted, directly curse Washington, but in a passage evidently directed at him, he wrote of "the incomprehensible acquiescence of the only honest man who had assented to it. I wish that his honesty and his political errors may not furnish a second occation to exclaim, 'curse on his virtues, they've undone his country.' " [9]

Meanwhile, in the House, Gallatin was attacking Hamilton's financing, and Jefferson wrote to Madison that "I do not at all wonder at the condition in which the finances of the U. S. are found. Ham's object from the beginning, was to throw them into forms which should be utterly undecypherable. I ever said he did not understand their conditions himself, nor was able to give a clear view of the excess of our debts beyond our credits, nor whether we were diminishing or increasing the debt. . . . The accounts of the U S ought to be, and may be made as simple as those of a common farmer, and capable of being understood by common farmers." [10]

In respect to this even Professor Chinard states that "the master financier and expert was beyond Jefferson's comprehension" and "even far ahead of his own time," [11] but I think this as unfair as was Jefferson's statement that Hamilton himself did not understand his figures. Hamilton undoubtedly did, but he was adding to the debt at just about the amount Jefferson surmised, that is a million dollars a year, and this fact, owing to the form of the accounts, was not generally realized. In handling the debt questions while in France, Jefferson had shown that he had a head for finance, and his statement that a national budget should be so clear that a farmer could understand it is quite true. The British budgets today, with all the complexity of modern government expenditures and income, infinitely beyond that of Hamilton's day, are in

[9] *Ibid.,* Vol. VII, p. 69.   [10] *Ibid.,* Vol. II, p. 61.   [11] Chinard, *Life,* p. 311.

their abbreviated form so simple and clear that they can be read in a few minutes, and be understood by any person with any mind at all. When that of 1935 was announced I happened to be living in London, and my housekeeper, not a woman of unusual mind, was eagerly awaiting its publication and at once read it when it appeared in the evening paper. If, therefore, Hamilton's budgets were not understood by a man of Jefferson's intelligence and experience, nor by members of Congress, it could not have been due to any inherent impossibility of stating the simple finances of the infant government clearly, had it been so desired.

About this same time, in 1796, occurred an incident which gave Jefferson endless annoyance. We have already mentioned that strange and wandering planet, the Italian Philip Mazzei, who for some years experimented in horticulture in the neighborhood of Charlottesville. During his stay in America he had come to know many of the leading men in Virginia, such as Jefferson, Madison, Henry, and others, and indeed had been the officially appointed envoy of that state to the Grand Duke of Tuscany when Virginia was endeavoring to borrow money from that ruler in 1779. After Mazzei's permanent return to Europe in 1785 he had written a four-volume work on the United States, which was considered the most accurate which had appeared up to then. He also continued to correspond with his Virginia friends and remained deeply interested in the country of his adoption.

On April 24, 1796, Jefferson wrote a long letter to Mazzei, then in Italy, and whose Virginian business affairs he was looking after. Jefferson's fears of the Federalists, with their desire for English institutions and their truckling to English policies, had been stirred afresh by the news of the Jay Treaty. Just when he was angered by this, Jefferson wrote, in the course of the letter to Mazzei, that "the aspect of our politics has wonderfully changed since you left us. In place of that noble love of liberty, & republican government which carried us thro' the war, an Anglican monarchical, & aristocratical party has sprung up, whose avowed object is to draw over us the substance, as they have already done the forms, of the British government. . . . Against us are the Executive, the judiciary, two out of three branches of the legislature, all the officers of the government, all timid men who prefer the calm of despotism to the boisterous sea of liberty, British merchants & Americans trading on British capital, speculators & holders in the banks & public funds, a contrivance invented for the purposes of corruption, & for assimilating us in all things to the rotten as well as the sound parts of the British model. It would give you a fever were I to name to you the apostates who have gone over to these heresies, men who were Samsons in the field & Solomons in the council, but who have had their heads shorn by the harlot England." [12]

This was a good rough analysis of the elements making up the Federalist party. Jefferson, of course, exaggerated the danger of monarchism just as Hamilton exaggerated the dangers of Shays's and the Whiskey Rebellions, and as both he and Washington exaggerated the dangers of the Democratic Clubs and of French influence. The letter, however, with its wide sweep took up not only Hamilton but Washington, John Adams and all the Federalists in its net. But Adams, with his fussy love of pomp and show had suggested that Washington's title should be "His Majesty, the President," and had not Washington himself just signed Jay's Treaty, which Jefferson considered an abject submission to England? In private talk and letters, Jefferson often indulged in exaggeration and over-emphasis, an American trait, and the basis of the contrast between American and British humor. It is not suggested that Jefferson was trying to be humorous in this letter. He was quite in earnest, but he was giving loose rein to his tendency to exag-

12 *Writings*, Ford, Vol. VII, pp. 75 f.

geration in private correspondence. His friends understood
how to take him, and he knew it. Unfortunately this particular one had the bad judgment, not to call it bad faith, to publish this private letter in an Italian translation in an Italian
newspaper, without getting Jefferson's permission, which
would certainly never have been given. Having got into print,
the letter was next translated into French, and then from
French into English, appearing in London papers. From
thence it came back to America and there it was published in
its, by that time, considerably garbled form. Jefferson knew
nothing of the far journeyings and publicity which had been
attending his intimate and confidential outpourings until a
year later the bomb burst, to his intense mortification and
annoyance, and to the natural injury of his relations with
Washington and Adams. Jefferson's political enemies made
the most of their opportunity, and the letter became one of
the most celebrated three or four in the history of American
political warfare.

Meanwhile, however, the campaign of 1796 was fought,
and it was not until after Washington had retired, Adams
had become President, and Jefferson Vice-President during
the next year, that the Mazzei letter flamed its way across the
American journalistic sky. The campaign had been an odd
contest. Washington, wisely, had definitely declined to be considered again, which left the Federalist field open to all run-
ners. Hamilton was the ablest man in the party, as Jefferson
had recognized at the time of the fight over Jay's Treaty when
he begged Madison to try to answer Hamilton's articles in
the papers as the only man capable of meeting him. On the
other hand, Hamilton could never have been elected. His over-
bearing, domineering manner, his openly expressed dislike and
distrust of those outside his narrow circle of "the rich, the
wise and the good" (in the Federalist sense), his pro-British
attitude, his defense of Jay's Treaty, and other factors had,

some fairly and others unfairly, made it impossible for him to expect high office at the hands of the people-at-large or even of the Electoral College. Moreover, now that Washington had withdrawn, party feelings no longer had any dyke to restrain them and were running wild. Jay's Treaty had been so intensely hated by the people as to have brought out one of the most notable and universal expressions of pure emotion in our history. As Jefferson remarked to Monroe, the Federalist Party was in truth "treaty foundered."

Two leading men, Jefferson and Adams, had consistently stood for American rights against the British. Adams greatly admired the British form of the government, but disliked the British people and mistrusted the British Government's policies. A wave of anti-British sentiment had swept over the nation, which strengthened the position of both Adams and Jefferson. Moreover, each had been among the best-known and most distinguished leaders in the Revolution. Adams had also served two terms as Vice-President under Washington, and for all these reasons seemed the logical Federalist candidate in spite of his well-known foibles and faults. On the other hand, Jefferson was the best-known and most-distinguished champion of the republican point of view in the, as yet, more or less incoherent and unorganized mass of Americanism.

As the summer advanced, it became more and more evident that under the absurd method of electing the President and Vice-President these two would receive the largest two votes in the Electoral College, the one receiving the highest vote becoming, of course, President and the other, Vice-President. There were then no nominating conventions and practically nothing of the modern party and campaign machinery as we know it today. Throughout the summer, Jefferson made no move in his own favor, and, indeed, scarcely touched on politics in a single private letter. He was busy rebuilding a portion of his house destroyed by fire, entertaining the Duke de

La Rochefoucauld-Liancourt and other visitors, looking after his farming work, and apparently never more remote from politics.

If, however, Jefferson had done nothing to further his election he had quite as obviously done nothing to remove his name from public discussion and so had given a tacit consent to his candidacy. On December 19, 1796, Madison wrote to him to that effect, and stated that as the returns then coming in indicated, Adams would receive the highest number of votes. He urged Jefferson to accept without hesitation the Vice-Presidency. Madison had, earlier in the campaign, declined to be a candidate himself. He urged acceptance on Jefferson not only as a matter of duty but because his presence near Adams "may have a valuable effect on his councils particularly in relation to our external system," and added that "he is said to speak of you now in friendly terms and will no doubt be soothed by your acceptance of a place subordinate to him." [13]

Although Jefferson had feared Adams's monarchical views, he practically never wavered in his belief that he was entirely honest though at times misguided, in his ideas. Jefferson at once replied, in what there is no reason to consider anything but sincere terms, that the first wish of his heart was that Madison himself should have run, and having declined to do so, that any one but himself, Jefferson, should have been chosen, and that he would much prefer the second place or none to the first. We may note, lest Jefferson's remarks seem hypocritical to a generation used to seeing intense struggle to attain public office, that the high offices of state in those days carried neither the glamour nor power which they do today, and most men were genuinely anxious to avoid them. When Jefferson had resigned as Secretary of State, Washington had had to apply to no less than six men before he could find one

[13] Madison, *Writings,* Vol. VI, p. 301.

who would accept the vacant post. John Jay resigned as Chief Justice of the Supreme Court to become a state governor, and there was difficulty in finding a successor. Federal salaries, considering the obligations, were small even for that time, and the hardships and expense of communication and personal travel not only cut an official off from his own home to an extent that can now scarcely be realized, but also entailed severe physical strain on all but the young and sturdy. The lurching, pitching stage coach on unspeakably bad roads, when there were any at all, or horseback travel, along trails with fording of streams or dangerous crossing of rivers on small flat-boats, the bad inns or none, all placed formidable obstacles in the way of accepting office. Comfortably settled in his loved home, Jefferson may well have dreaded a return to that public life which entailed much work, abuse, and discomfort, with financial loss rather than gain, and with, what he always dreaded most, the subjecting of one's self to the slanders and accusations of political opponents.

Besides Adams and Jefferson, the two candidates likely to poll most votes were Aaron Burr, of New York, and Thomas Pinckney of South Carolina, who, had our modern system of elections then been in use, would have been run as Vice-Presidents respectively on the Republican and Federalist tickets. Adams was disliked by Hamilton, who still considered himself the leader of his party, and Hamilton brought his influence to bear so that the electoral votes should be shifted to Pinckney. Although he obviously could have no part in this Federalist intrigue, Jefferson realized that the vote between himself and Adams might be very close and even a tie.

Considering the last possibility he continued in his letter to Madison, just quoted from, saying that "I have no expectation that the Eastern states will suffer themselves to be so much outwitted, as to be made the tools for bringing in P. instead of A. I presume they will throw away their second vote. In this case, it begins to appear possible, that there may be an equal division where I had supposed the republican vote would have been considerably minor. It seems also possible that the Representatives [in Congress] may be divided. This is a difficulty from which the constitution has provided no issue. It is both my duty & inclination, therefore, to relieve the embarrassment, should it happen; and in that case, I pray you and authorize you fully, to solicit on my behalf that Mr. Adams may be preferred. He has always been my senior, from the commencement of my public life, and the expression of the public will being equal, this circumstance ought to give him the preference. And when so many motives will be operating to induce some of the members to change their vote, the addition of my wish may have some effect to preponderate the scale." He added that in his mind public affairs were never so gloomy since 1783, and "let those come to the helm who think they can steer clear of the difficulties. I have no confidence in myself for the undertaking."[14]

Ten days later, writing to his friend Edward Rutledge, he voiced the same feeling, saying he would not have refused the Presidency had he been elected but "I protest before my god that I shall, from the bottom of my heart, rejoice at escaping. I know well that no man will ever bring out of that office the reputation which carries him into it." [15] In the next twelve years both he and Adams were to have seared into them the truth of that statement.

The election, fortunately, was not a tie, but it was almost as close, Adams receiving 71 votes and Jefferson 68, whereas Pinckney followed with 59 and Burr with 30. Even the lowest figure showed Burr's influence in the new Republican Party. The votes thus resulted in the election of a Federalist President and a Republican Vice-President.

The latter's letter, insisting on the election of Adams in

14 *Writings,* Ford, Vol. VII, pp. 91 f.   15 *Ibid.,* p. 93.

case of a tied vote, had been as manly as it was sincere, and it is a pity that Adams could not have seen it. Jefferson did indeed write a letter to him but sent it to Madison, leaving it to his discretion as to whether or not it should be delivered to Adams. The unfortunate matter of the introductory note to Paine's pamphlet which has already been mentioned, and the assiduity of those who always wish to foment trouble, had cast a shadow over the friendship between the two men. Moreover, although Jefferson had said no word against Adams during the campaign, indeed, scarcely a word as to anything, there was the possibility that the fact that they were opposing each other as candidates, might make for bad feeling on the part of Adams, who with all his ability and magnificent qualities, was vain, touchy, and, as Vice-President for eight years, had considered himself as the obvious "heir apparent." Finally, the closeness of the vote would be taken very hard by him. In his letter, Jefferson had congratulated Adams, and commiserated with him over the difficulties of the situation into which he was to be plunged, had wished him all success, and had said honestly that he was glad the responsibilities had not fallen upon himself. He had closed with the hope that Adams might cover himself "with glory, and happiness to yourself and advantage to us," as "the sincere wish of one who tho' in the course of our own voyage thro' life, various little incidents have happened or been contrived to separate us, retains still for you the solid esteem of the moments when we were working for our independence, and sentiments of respect & affectionate attachment." [16]

Unfortunately and, perhaps, unwisely, Madison deemed it best not to forward the letter, believing, as may have been possible, that the touchy Adams would misunderstand it and that it might do harm rather than good. Adams had reached the Presidency in an extremely disgruntled frame of mind.

[16] *Ibid.*, Vol. VII, pp. 95 ff.

He was enraged with Hamilton, whom he never forgave, for the trick by which the leader of the party had tried to beat him for office, and had succeeded so far as to reduce his vote, and as Adams thought, his consequent prestige in the nation. Possibly Madison was right in thinking it too difficult a moment for a delicate friendly gesture, but the eventual complete reconciliation between the two men in their old age, after even worse had happened between them, and the delight which each thereafter took in the renewed friendship, makes me believe that the shy Madison may have, on this occasion, been too shy and timorous.

When Jefferson arrived in Philadelphia to take the oath of office and attend the inauguration of the new President, the latter was in a better frame of mind. He had, at least, become President. In spite of Hamilton, the country had made him that, and he seems to have been considering a rather vague policy of reconciling the two parties as far as possible. As to friendly relations with Jefferson, he appears to have been as willing, if not perhaps as anxious, to cultivate them as Jefferson himself. At their first meeting he was cordial, and even made the rather fantastic offer of sending Jefferson to France as a special envoy to adjust the difficulties between the two nations. That being impossible because of Jefferson's office, he suggested Jefferson's friend Madison, who was one of the leaders of the Republicans.

Adams was never a party man and for a brief instant he may have thought that he could carry out Washington's first intention of representing the country and not a party. Even Washington had failed in that, however, and since 1789 party organization and feeling had become far more powerful forces to be reckoned with. In a few days, Adams was to feel their strength. The Cabinet, the second-rate one which he had inherited from Washington's second term, had unwisely been retained by him. When Madison's name was suggested to them as an envoy, they threatened to resign in a body if that Republican were chosen. There was one more meeting with Jefferson, at which the matter was not mentioned, and at that point personal relations of any intimacy stopped for almost a generation. The Federalist Cabinet had made it evident that a Federalist President and a Republican second in office could not be allowed to work together. Jefferson was in the administration but not of it. He was an unwanted intruder, an accident of the then electoral system.

CHAPTER XII

THE VICE–PRESIDENCY

THE office of Vice-President has always been an anomalous one in our system of government. As that official may succeed to the Presidency at any moment, he is supposed to be a man who has the necessary qualifications, such as ability, experience, and strength of character, for the office to which he may be called. Of the thirty-two Presidents, six, in fact, have advanced by accident from the Vice-Presidency. Yet Vice-Presidents, as such, are singularly out of the main current of political life. Except in the case of a tie vote in the Senate, they are supposed to preside over that body with impartiality, and are debarred from expressing their views on the floor. Washington tried to bring Adams when Vice-President into the Cabinet discussions at times, but it did not work, and the plan of joining the Vice-President to the Cabinet was not attempted again until Harding endeavored to bring in Coolidge, when once more it did not work. Adams, when President, as we noted in the last chapter, suggested that Vice-President Jefferson go on a special mission to France, but that also could not be done. Except for these sporadic efforts, the Vice-President has been relegated to the presiding chair of the Senate, and has become a singularly lonely political figure. In Jefferson's case this loneliness and semi-futility or political sterilization was more marked than in any other case, as he belonged to a party bitterly hated by those in power in the rest of the administration. Naturally left out of their councils and even largely ostracized by Philadelphia

273

society, which was pro-administration and Federalist, he had ample time in his own house or in the rooms of the American Philosophical Society to ponder and brood over the direction American affairs were taking.

In order more clearly to understand his reaction to what he saw, or believed he saw, going on about him, we may briefly recapitulate some of his ideas and points of view. The American Revolution a dozen years earlier, and now the French Revolution in progress, seemed to presage at last a movement on the part of peoples toward liberty. In practical politics, Jefferson was not nearly as pro-French and anti-British as he has often been considered. Indeed, he was willing "to marry the British fleet and nation" if France should turn against us and try to re-establish an empire on the soil of North America. What he did feel very strongly was that in the European struggle then going on, England was on the side of despotism and France on that of liberty, Napoleon, to whom he was to be greatly opposed, not having yet assumed power.

In the United States he felt that liberty and the results of our Revolution had not yet been by any means firmly consolidated and secured. If the French people could win and maintain freedom against their former oppressors, that fact would do much to strengthen the liberty party in America. There would be less danger either of its being threatened by foreign influence or attacks, or by the increasingly reactionary Federalist Party at home, should a powerful European nation successfully follow the same course that we had. Aside from a sentimental attachment to France, and preferences for French wines, culture, and society, as compared with English (none of which he allowed to interfere with his international policy for America), the point of view just explained was his sole reason for sympathy with France in her struggle against England.

His own theory of government and personal liberty had

been clearly expressed. Each measure he had proposed from the beginning had not been an isolated one in itself, springing from a passing emotion or necessity, but had been undertaken so as to fit in with and forward his general plan and hope. That being the case, he naturally looked not only to the statements of the leaders of the Federalists as to their aims but also to their measures as indicating the steps they were taking to consolidate their idea of government.

That the Federalists were becoming more and more reactionary is admitted by their best friends among historians. That they did not trust the people and that they wished to keep the control of government in the hands of the upper classes, was openly admitted by themselves at the time. They also asserted that a people which could not govern itself would have to be governed. As to all these points Jefferson was right in considering the Federalists as the deadly foes of his own dream for America. On the other hand, he much overrated the danger of any immediate monarchist plot, laying too much stress on the expressed abstract preference of certain Federalists for a monarchy. Washington took a much saner view of the situation. Nevertheless, Jefferson was not wrong in believing that some of the most influential Federalists, with Hamilton at their head, would have welcomed an eventual change in conditions which would bring about an alteration in the form of government such as would make it either a monarchy or some sort of centralized state ruled from the top, and with no dangerous idea of self-government by all ranks.

Jefferson himself did not believe that there was a large party with those views or that the people would then allow themselves to be deprived of the fruits of the Revolution, but he did believe that there were powerful and insidious plotters and that in time the people might be misled, mis-educated or in other ways be made unfit to maintain their government and rights. Jefferson fully recognized Hamilton's great ability, and feared both that and his influence. Nor can we dismiss his fears as those of an enemy who wholly mis-read Hamilton's opinions and hopes. One of Hamilton's intimate friends, according to his grandson, was Gouverneur Morris. We have already mentioned Morris's statement as to Hamilton's inveterate hatred of republican government, and may add further statements by him as to Hamilton's views.

"One marked trait of the General's character," Morris wrote, "was the pertinacious adherence to opinions he had once formed. . . . He never failed on every occasion to advocate the excellence of, and avow his attachment to, monarchical government. By this course he not only cut himself off from all chance of rising into office, but singularly promoted the views of his opponents."

Again Morris wrote a few months after Hamilton's death, that "our poor friend Hamilton bestrode his hobby to the great annoyance of his friends, and not without injury to himself. . . . He well knew that his favorite form was inadmissible, unless as a result of civil war; and I suspect that his belief in that which he called an approaching crisis arose from a conviction that the kind of government most suitable in his opinion, to this extensive country, could be established in no other way." Morris added that "when a general abuse of the right of election shall have robbed our government of respect, and its imbecility have involved it in difficulties, the people will feel what your friend once said, that they want something to protect them against themselves. And then, excess being their predominant quality, it may be a patriotic duty to prevent them from going too far the other way." [1]

Apart from ample other testimony as to Hamilton's views, this given in writing on two different occasions by one of his personal and political intimates should be reasonably con-

[1] Letters from Morris, Fe. 5, 1811, and Dec. 28, 1804, cited by Randall, *op. cit.*, Vol. I, pp. 580 f.

vincing. One of Hamilton's engaging qualities was his frank out-spokenness. If he despised the people he at least never flattered them, and made no secret of his views among his friends. If Morris thus understood Hamilton's ideas and hopes, Jefferson cannot be blamed, to say the very least, for considering him as a danger to government by the people. Jefferson had as decided views as to government as had Hamilton, but from their very nature Jefferson's could not be forced on the people but only willingly *accepted* by them, whereas the essence of Hamilton's were that monarchy must be *forced* on them sooner or later, when opportunity offered, whether the people themselves wanted self-government or a dictator.

In reading Morris's analysis of Hamilton's mind, we are looking forward to the twentieth century and our final chapter, but Jefferson, from his lonely presiding chair in the Senate in 1797, was watching contemporary events unroll in a way that gave him deep mistrust. He had seen the funding of the debt, the assumption of the state debts, the building up of a money power to influence and strengthen government, the throwing of the weight of that government to the side of business as against agriculture, the suggestion of favors in the way of protective tariffs, the beginning of the "pork barrel," the strong preference for monarchical England against revolutionary France, the raising of 15,000 troops to make, as he thought, a sort of civil war out of a bit of rioting. Now he was to see a good deal more.

This is not a narrative history of the United States, and we cannot go into the details of the Adams administration which have been written over and over again. We are interested only in some outstanding events as they influenced Jefferson, the people, and the campaign of 1800.

Adams's first mistake was, as we have noted, to retain Washington's Cabinet. Bowers puts it too strongly perhaps when he says that the three men, Timothy Pickering, Oliver Wolcott, and James McHenry, "exceeded mediocrity only in the field of treachery and mendacity," but they were all second-rate as statesmen, and were all traitors to Adams, betraying Cabinet secrets to Hamilton, who expected to rule the nation from New York, while the Cabinet took their opinions and orders from him. The President in truth had no Cabinet, though he did not realize it. All he had was a triple telephone line, if we may use an anachronism for a metaphor, to Hamilton's law office.

Adams was far from being a Republican but he also was far from being a party Federalist. Hamilton hoped to hold him by his three grappling irons to strict Federalist doctrine and policies. One of these policies was close friendship, at almost any cost, with England, and opposition to France. Another policy was, on the slightest opportunity which might be offered, to create a considerable army.

Foreign affairs were extremely difficult even for Adams, who wished to avoid war with either party and to maintain a strict neutrality, as both European nations were bullying us to their hearts' content. As far as open insult was concerned there was little to choose between them, and we could have fairly gone to war with either France or England or both. But to declare war at once on two first-class powers already at war against each other was a little too much like Kilkenny cats. To make a choice between insults was not only a nice problem but there was the second one that to attack either nation separately would be to go against the strong sympathies of one or another part of the American people. Foreign affairs had been injected heavily into the Presidential campaign, and feeling was running high.

Great Britain was less dangerous to us as a possibly expanded neighbor in America or the West Indies than France would be, and her trade was also far more important to us than that with the French. On the other hand, England had kicked, cuffed, and insulted us ever since the peace of 1783, and we were supposed to be the friend of France "for services rendered" in the Revolution. France, however, was also running amok, and had refused to receive Pinckney when sent as Minister to succeed Monroe, and was angry at the Jay Treaty, claiming also that we had violated our treaties with her. Jefferson, who had characteristically employed some weeks after taking office in compiling a Manual of Parliamentary Practice to guide him as presiding officer of the Senate—long to remain the standard for our legislative bodies—was for complete neutrality with the rest of the world. He wished commerce with all and peace with all. The difficulty was to prove, as it has been throughout our history, how to do peaceful business with a man who, when you walk upstairs to sell him goods, kicks you down again. It has been only since the World War that Americans have come to have an inkling of the futility of such an ideal.

In spite, however, of fresh insults from France, we were not yet ready for war, and, with the approval of his Cabinet, Adams sent a commission of three, Pinckney, Marshall, and Gerry, to Paris to try to adjust matters, at the same time recommending to Congress the increase of our defenses both on sea and land. Just at this time, the bomb of the Mazzei letter exploded, making relations worse between Jefferson and Adams, and intensifying bitterness between the two political parties. Although it had been a personal and private communication, Jefferson could not deny having written it, in somewhat different form, and wisely kept silent while the storm blew itself out.

Foreign affairs, however, seemed to be improving. French victories against England made it seem possible that the latter nation might prove more tractable, and much was hoped from our conciliatory mission to France. At Monticello, during the summer of 1797, Jefferson, in spite of the very bad business conditions and general bankruptcies, was preparing to re-roof his house and make other improvements, and was thinking again in terms of America. Writing to St. George Tucker the end of August, he returned to the problem of slavery and was hoping for emancipation. "The sooner we put some plan underway," he wrote, "the greater hope there is that it may be permitted to proceed peaceably to it's ultimate effect. But if something is not done, & soon done, we shall be the murderers of our own children." [2]

Three days later he wrote to Colonel Arthur Campbell that "a party has risen up among us, or rather has come among us, which is endeavoring to separate us from all friendly connection with France, to unite our destinies with those of Great Britain, & to assimilate our government to theirs. . . . Hitherto, their influence has been irresistible, and they have raised up an Executive power which is too strong for the legislature. But I flatter myself they have passed their zenith. The people, while these things were doing, were lulled into rest and security from a cause which no longer exists. [The fact that Washington was at the helm.] No prepossession now will shut their ears to truth. They begin to see to what port their leaders were steering during their slumbers, and there is yet time to haul in, if we can avoid a war with France. All can be done peaceably, by the people confiding their choice of Representatives & Senators to persons attached to republican government & the principles of 1776, not office-hunters, but farmers whose interests are entirely agricultural. Such men are the true representatives of the great American interest, and are alone to be relied upon for expressing the proper American sentiments. We owe gratitude to France, justice to England, good will to all, and subservience to none. All this must be brought about by the people, using their elective rights with prudence & self-possession, and not suffering themselves to be duped by treacherous emissaries. It was by the sober sense of our citizens that we were safely and steadily conducted

2 *Writings*, Ford, Vol. VII, p. 168.

from monarchy to republicanism, and it is by the same agency alone we can be kept from falling back." [3]

Here we already sniff from afar the campaign of 1800, for which there was to be an amount of ammunition provided which even Jefferson could not yet realize.

Congress assembled in Philadelphia in November, but little was done while the members were waiting to hear the result of the French mission. The first clap of thunder came on the 19th of March, 1798, when the President informed Congress that there was no expectation that the mission could accomplish anything compatible "with the safety, honor, or essential interest of the nation." Shortly after he sent to them the famous "X. Y. Z." letters in which the shameful story of the refusal by Talleyrand to treat with the Americans unless they paid him heavy bribes was made known to the world, the names of Talleyrand's go-betweens being indicated by the last three letters of the alphabet and retained by the President in secret.

At once the country went wild. Feeling against France rose to a frantic pitch, and the peace party was as downcast as the Federalists were jubilant. The blow was a heavy one but Jefferson kept his head. War meant for him the danger of entangling us again with Europe; victory for the feared Federalists; victory for the Northeast against the South, as party lines had become largely sectional; and meant also armies and debts and all that might strengthen the Federalists in what he considered their designs to change the form of government. For the next few months America was in turmoil, and, as we shall see, even that strong individualist, John Adams, lost his balance amidst the popular clamor, and the demands of frightened or designing Federalists. Jefferson, almost alone, rose to the full heights of statesmanship. On June 1 he wrote a letter to John Taylor which deserves to be quoted at length. Taylor had raised the question of possible secession from New

[3] *Ibid.*, pp. 169 ff.

England, and Jefferson calmly reviewed the situation. He was to a considerable extent a states' rights man, but he was also one of the strongest Union men of his time, and almost invariably condemned any talk of breaking up the union of the states.

"It is true," he wrote, "that we are completely under the saddle of Massachusetts and Connecticut, and that they ride us very hard, cruelly insulting our feelings, as well as exhausting our strength and subsistence. Their natural friends, the three other eastern States, join them from a sort of family pride, and they have the art to divide certain other parts of the Union, so as to make use of them to govern the whole. . . . But our present situation is not a natural one. The republicans, through every part of the Union, say, that it was the irresistible influence and popularity of General Washington played off by the cunning hand of Hamilton, which turned the government over to anti-republican hands, or turned the republicans chosen by the people into anti-republicans. He delivered it over to his successor in this state, and very untoward events since, improved with great artifice, have produced on the public mind the impressions we see. . . . Time alone would bring round an order of things more correspondent to the sentiments of our constituents. But are there no events impending, which will do it within a few months? The crisis with England, the public and authentic avowal of sentiments hostile to the leading principles of our Constitution, the prospect of a war, in which we shall stand alone, land tax, stamp tax, increase of public debt, &c. Be this as it may, in every free and deliberating society, there must, from the nature of man, be opposite parties, and violent dissensions and discords; and one of these, for the most part, must prevail over the other for a longer or shorter time. . . . But if on a temporary superiority of the one party, the other is to resort to a scission of the Union, no federal government can ever exist. If to rid ourselves of the present rule of Massachusetts and Connecticut, we break the Union, will the evil stop there? Suppose the New England States alone cut off, will our nature be changed? Are we not men still to the south of that, and with all the passions of men? Immediately, we shall see a Pennsylvania and Virginia party arise in the residuary confederacy, and the public mind will be distracted with the same party spirit. What a game too will the one party have in their hands, by eternally threatening the other that unless they do so and so, they will join their northern neighbors. . . . Seeing, therefore, that an association of men who will not quarrel with one another is a thing which never yet existed . . . seeing that we must have somebody to quarrel with, I had rather keep our New England associates for that purpose, than to see our bickerings transferred to others. They are circumscribed within such narrow limits, and their population so full, that their numbers will ever be the minority, and they are marked, like the Jews, with such a perversity of character, as to constitute from that circumstance, the natural division of our parties. . . . Who can say what would be the evils of scission, and when and where they would end? Better keep together as we are, haul off from Europe as soon as we can, and from all attachments to any part of it; and if they can show their power just sufficiently to hoop us together, it will be the happiest situation in which we can exist. If the game sometimes runs against us at home, we must have patience til luck turns, and then we shall have an opportunity of winning back the *principles* we have lost. For this is a game where principles are the stake." [4]

Several points are notable in this letter. Jefferson saw clearly that the diappearance of Washington from the stage had opened the way to parties, and that parties are necessary for carrying on a popular government. Also that by the na-

[4] *Writings,* Ford, Vol. VII, pp. 263 ff.

ture of things one party must always be defeated, but that no violence should ensue but merely a patient waiting and struggling for a return to power. His exposition of the evils of secession, quoted only in part, which would in time continue the unravelling process of the Union until each state might remain solitary and sovereign, was masterly and statesmanlike, and far above any analysis of the situation produced by the New England Federalists who were to preach secession for the next seventeen years, plotting for it at intervals. We may note here that both he and they indulged in practically no legal arguments. The interests of the parties, small and temporary or large and lasting, formed the basis of argument, and Jefferson looked to the latter, the larger and more abiding interests. That had been the basis of argument in the pre-Revolutionary case against England before the necessity of rationalizing that argument was felt, and a discussion of the British constitution followed, to break down in turn and to be followed by a stark appeal to the rights of man. It was the same with the secession struggle, which culminated in the Civil War. That also began with a discussion of *interests* and had in time to be rationalized by each side into fine-spun interpretations of constitutional enigmas. That Jefferson, with his personal animosity against Hamilton, his general mistrust of New England, and his hatred of all he believed the Federalists were doing to ruin his own hopes for America, should prefer to bide his time and meanwhile to maintain the Union at all risks, shows how thoroughly he had become an American and ceased to be a mere Virginian.

There was another point, of which we have spoken before and shall again, in which he had become truly American, thinking in continental and not state terms. That was his constant fostering care for the West, his desire to increase its extent and to bind it to the East. So far from fearing its sapping influence on entrenched privilege, political or economic, in the seaboard sections, he welcomed from it the democratic breezes which he foresaw would for long continue to freshen and invigorate the whole of American life. What he did not realize, in spite of the stress he laid upon the effect of taxation upon political views, was the extent to which economic interests would make themselves felt in the political parties and doctrines of the future. But that point will be discussed later.

Meanwhile, there was ample happening to make him distrust more than ever the tendency of the times toward government *of* instead of *by* the people. Congress denounced the old treaties with France as void, and authorized the expenditure of more than a million dollars for forts, arms, and ammunition; increased the navy; and authorized the raising of an army of 10,000 men. Adams appointed Washington as commander-in-chief, but as the former President was getting old and was not expected to take the field in person, interest and intrigue centered on the question of who should be second in command.

Hamilton was wild to obtain the post. Adams did not wish to appoint him, and the ensuing struggle is a rather dirty episode. Hamilton's political cohorts brought every pressure to bear upon Adams, who felt he had already submitted more than enough to Hamiltonian dictation, in addition to the fact that Hamilton's military experience in the field had been short and slight, though brilliant in the very subordinate positions he had held. When it looked as though Adams would prove incorrigibly stubborn on the point, McHenry, the Secretary of War and Hamilton's chief spy in the Cabinet, hurried to Mount Vernon to enlist the aid of Washington, and returned with word that Washington declined to serve as commander unless Hamilton were made second. Then Adams yielded to what he was told was the imperative wish of George Washington. Extracts from two letters will indicate

the character of the intrigue. Washington, whom Mc-
Henry had so misrepresented to Adams, wrote to General
Knox, who had declined to serve under Hamilton as the
latter was much younger and had always been junior in
grade. In his letter Washington apologized for his advocating Hamilton by saying that he had been "inundated with
letters which said that Colonel Hamilton was designated second in command (and first if I should decline an appointment) by the federal characters of Congress, whence alone
anything like a public sentiment relative thereto could be de-
duced." [5] The leading man in the country had thus been misled by a miserable conspiracy. The matter thus arranged by
deceiving both Washington and the President, Hamilton next,
with extraordinary ingratitude toward his agent, wrote to
Washington saying that he must do violence to friendship by
informing him that "my friend McHenry is wholly insufficient for his place with the additional misfortune of not having the least suspicion of the fact." [6] We need not go further
into this sordid episode, but few transactions, supported by
documentary evidence, could be more damning to a public
man with a high reputation for character to maintain. There
are several such in the course of Hamilton's public career
which are impossible to explain away, for in most respects his
high reputation was deserved. We can only take refuge in
Mark Twain's remark that "there is a great deal of human
nature in man."

Adams, who had been embittered by having been made, as
he had said, "a three vote president" was made more so by
having his powers as Commander-in-Chief of the armed forces,
which was his office under the Constitution, shorn from him
apparently by the ex-President and his young favorite, though
he did not know the whole intrigue. Jefferson knew even less,

[5] B. C. Steiner, *Life and Correspondence of James McHenry,* Cleveland,
1907, p. 322.
[6] *Ibid.,* p. 319.

but what he saw was that Hamilton, who as Secretary of the Treasury had urged the raising of 15,000 men to move against Pennsylvania contrary to the wish of the governor of the state, was now trying to force himself into practically first place at the head of the army in the expected war against France. Hamilton had gone as far as he could in "administering" the Constitution into the form he desired, when in the Cabinet which he had insisted upon dominating. He was still trying to dominate the government while in private life. His views, as has been shown, were not concealed but well known. He was now trying to force himself to the active command in the army ahead of his seniors who were preferred by the President. As Hamilton considered that a war was the only opportunity of still further transforming the nature of our government, Jefferson cannot be accused of being over-suspicious, though his inferences may have been unjust, if he regarded Hamilton's intriguing to make himself head of an army as a matter of very serious concern.

Jefferson had a few weeks earlier presided over the Senate when Congress passed, July 6, 1798, the famous Alien Bill, and on the 14th the Sedition Law, which seemed by skilful use of war hysteria to have swept away those liberties which he considered as the very foundation of civilized government.

The Alien Act gave the President the power to deport any alien from the country who he might decide was dangerous to the peace and safety of the nation. The Sedition Act, in almost the exact phrasing of the similar law passed during the World War, made any person liable to punishment or fine who should write or speak against the President or members of Congress with the "intent to defame" or to "bring them into contempt or disrepute." The breadth of definition of the new crime, and the irresponsible powers given to the Executive, threw the rights of free speech and press on the scrap-heap, and how dangerous war is to fundamental rights and how war hysteria unbalances the minds of almost all is illustrated by the defense of the measures by the late Professor Channing in that volume of his *History of the United States* which happened to be written in the passion of war in 1917.

President Adams, in fact, took no action under the Alien Act, although a good many, particularly French, did hastily leave the country; and there were comparatively few prosecutions under the Sedition Act, practically all directed against Jeffersonian newspaper editors and others, who criticized the policy of the Federalists. The small use made of the Acts showed how little real need there had been for this assault on personal liberties. We were not even at war, though war was threatening. The legislation was a profound mistake, indicating again the dangers inherent in the Federalist view that the people must be governed, and governed by Federalist leaders, according to their views at any cost to liberty and to the individual citizen. It is a danger inherent in the Winthrop-Cotton traditional theory of colonial Massachusetts whatever form a particular government may take at any given time.

After the adjournment of Congress, Jefferson spent the summer as usual at Monticello. He believed with his whole soul in the necessity of freedom of speech and press, and in education of all sorts, including newspaper discussion, if the people were to govern themselves. He was no pacifist, but he dreaded the effects of war on liberty. Now the Federalists had muzzled the people, authorized an army, and put at its virtual head a man who openly longed for monarchy, and who despised the people. Even Jefferson's own private letters were in danger of being opened and read by government officials, and he wrote that summer with great discretion except when his communications were to be delivered by trusted messengers. The situation was full of danger. Hamilton might not be dreaming of the rôle of Napoleon, but also he might. We have to try to sense the fears and passions of the moment in order to be able to realize both them and the intellectual conclusions they helped to form.

That Hamilton was planning for a much more centralized and consolidated government than he had yet achieved is shown by his own letter to Jonathan Dayton, speaker of the House of Representatives. In this he suggested that it would be wise to insinuate that those who opposed the government's measure intended to add force to their objections; and that while the Federalists had control of the government they should surround it "with more ramparts." Among these there should be an augmented permanent army even if there should be peace with France; increased taxation of a million or so; an enlargement of the legal powers of the Federal Government; the cutting up of the larger states into more numerous small ones, perhaps of 100,000 population each, so as to make state power more innocuous; and further laws, to be sharply enforced, against "incendiary and seditious practices." [7]

Meanwhile, Jefferson, with Madison, was cogitating over some of the points in the Constitution left uncertain. He had taken action, although his share in it was not known at the time, which had brought forth Hamilton's letter to Dayton. Jefferson had rightly claimed that neither the states nor individuals had surrendered all sovereign powers to the Federal Government. Hamilton recognized this fact in his desire practically to abolish the states by reducing them to small and impotent administrative units, though he acknowledged it could not be done at the time. But Jefferson, taking his thesis as correct, had further to decide what could be done in case the Federal Government exceeded its powers under the Constitution. Both it and the states, as well as individuals, had certain sovereign powers. In case of a conflict between them, the Constitution was silent as to who or what should decide between them, a problem never finally settled, if settled then, except

[7] Hamilton, *Works*, vol. VIII, pp. 517 ff. Letter undated but internal evidence places it in 1799.

by the Civil War. In *The Federalist,* Hamilton had suggested the Supreme Court of the United States, but the Constitution did not say so. Considering the Constitution as a compact, Jefferson decided that, as in other compacts when there was no common judge, each party had an equal right to "judge for itself as well of infractions as of the mode of redress," and that if the Federal Government went beyond its powers, as he claimed it had in the Alien and Sedition laws, then the individual states could declare such Acts void. His views embodied in the form of a set of Resolves were introduced and passed by the Kentucky legislature, and a similar set, milder in form, drawn by Madison, were passed by that of Virginia. Thus Jefferson, though a Unionist, tried to combine the incompatibles of Union and of state nullification.

The Resolves were sent to the other states for comment, and though condemned by all except Georgia and the Carolinas, which sent no answer, the replies brought out an interesting conflict of opinion. Four states suggested that the Supreme Court decide such questions in dispute. Pennsylvania wished Congress to do so in part and the Supreme Court in part. The remaining states, although pointing out the dangers of the state legislatures sitting in judgment, offered no solution of their own. That the legislators of the various states should take such divergent positions on the problem shows both how obscure it had been left in the Constitution, and that it was a fair matter of dispute and of individual opinion. Jefferson did not appear to realize that nullification might unravel the fabric of Union as swiftly as secession itself. His plan was impractical if the Union were to survive, but, on the other hand, it seemed equally impractical to hand over the sole custody of rights reserved as against the Federal Government to one branch of that government itself, which was appointed by another branch and confirmed by the third. The prospect opened was of destroying the reserved rights of states and the people, of making the Federal Government the judge of its own powers, and thus destroying the Constitution so carefully worked out to limit those powers. As Hamilton rightly pointed out, the central government could greatly enlarge its power by both "salutary patronage" and an extension of the numbers and functions of the federal courts. This was precisely what Jefferson saw and feared, and explains his later hostility to federal courts and judges.

The strength of the opposition to Federalist doctrine, however, was growing, not unobserved by Hamilton, who wrote that the opposition had acquired "more system" and was becoming bolder. Hamilton's party, however, was soon to attempt suicide, Hamilton himself at last stabbing it to death.

Adams, genuinely wishing to avoid war with both France and England, had been chafing more and more under the control exerted by the Federalist inner circle. Moreover, he had received word from our Minister to the Netherlands, Vans Murray, that Talleyrand had at last assured him that he would receive a representative from the United States with all the respect which Adams had demanded. Gerry had recently returned with the same information. Adams then consulted his Cabinet as to whether to declare war officially on France—an unofficial war with some hostilities had already been in progress—or to say in his message that a Minister would be sent on proper assurances received. The Cabinet was wholly against any new mission.

Adams by this time had become aware of the treachery of the Cabinet—except that of Wolcott—and of the part Hamilton was playing. On February 18, 1799, the President nominated Vans Murray as Minister to France without informing the Cabinet of his intention. Hamilton and the Cabinet were furious. The appointment was altered to a commission of three and every impediment was placed for months by the Federalists in the way of their embarking. Adams then took matters into his own hands again and ordered their departure for November 1. In a stormy interview the wrathy old New England statesman told McHenry plainly what he thought of him, and the Secretary resigned at once. Pickering being asked to do the same, and declining, was curtly dismissed. Wolcott, as great a traitor as the others, was not suspected, and remained. Hamilton's plans had crashed. He had lost control of the Executive; there was to be no war with France; no army for him to head. Adams had saved the country much besides a war, and had broken with his party, by whom he was considered a traitor. The way for a Republican victory had been marvellously opened far wider than Jefferson had dreamed a year or two before could have been possible.

The campaign of 1800 was one of peculiar bitterness even in American political history. The leading Federalists had done all they could not to have Adams renominated by the Congressional caucus which then performed the duty now carried out by the nominating conventions, but the President finally secured the bitter fruit. Hamilton was so insanely infuriated that he did much to hurt his reputation as a man of honor. He wrote on May 14, 1800, to Pickering, Adams's treacherous Secretary of State, suggesting that he should send copies of all documents which might reflect on either Jefferson or Adams. On the 8th, Hamilton wrote another extraordinary letter to Governor John Jay of New York suggesting that he call the legislature together at once so as to change the method of choosing Presidential electors in such a way as would ensure a Federalist victory, no time to be lost. He said that one part of the Republican Party wished to overthrow the government, and the other wanted to bring on a French revolution. Anything must be done to keep "an atheist in religion, and a fanatic in politics" from reaching the Presidency. He was aware of the impropriety of what he was urging but declared that "if one party will call to its aid all the resources which vice can give, and if the other (however pressing the emergency) confines itself within all the ordinary forms of delicacy and decorum," then popular governments must be overturned.[8] This to the man whom Hamilton had sent to England to negotiate a treaty, stealing his weapons from him before he left! The letter is one of the most interesting examples of the immoral lengths to which a man can go who believes that he and his ideas can alone save society, and that "the people" who are too stupid or immoral to govern themselves must be governed by the "wise and good" like himself. Governor Jay, himself a Federalist, endorsed Hamilton's letter with the scathing note "proposing a measure for party purposes which it would not become me to adopt."

Meanwhile, the party caucuses had nominated Adams and C. C. Pinckney for the Federalist candidates, and Jefferson and Aaron Burr for the Republican. Hamilton next wrote an extraordinary pamphlet, sending copies to some of the leading Federalists who at once urged him to suppress it, in which he gave his reasons at great length why he believed Adams utterly and in every way unfit to be President, and then urged his election. A copy fell into the hands of Burr, who gave it publicity. The Federalist Party had indeed been done to death or, at least, so mutilated that it never recovered.

If Hamilton with his clear mind could so lose his head, his sense of what was politically possible, and his moral balance, it can be imagined what lesser men, like many of the clergy of New England, would do in their hatred and fear of Jefferson whom they considered, on account of his Bill for Religious Liberty, to be an atheist, a French terrorist, and a plotter against society and civilization. In New England, the local village and town magnates, the doctors, lawyers and clergy, had worked together to control elections. The power of the established Congregational Church had been great. In Jeffer-

[8] Hamilton, *Works,* Vol. VIII, pp. 549 ff.

son they saw an inhuman monster who wished to take the power out of their hands and give it to the people whom they had hitherto controlled. For this governing group it seemed as though the end of all things was at hand. When Jefferson was elected, such a man as Theodore Dwight, brother of the Reverend Timothy Dwight, could pour out to his congregation that "the ties of marriage are dissolved; our wives and daughters are thrown into the stews; our children are cast into the world from the breast and forgotten. . . . Can the imagination paint anything more dreadful this side hell?" [9]

This monster, as pictured by the Federalists and the New England clergy, had taken an opportunity of stating his principles in answer to a letter from Elbridge Gerry at the beginning of 1799. We may quote at some length from what is one of the longest letters Jefferson ever wrote, and which he called the "profession of my political faith."

"I wish," he wrote, "an inviolable preservation of our present federal constitution, according to the true sense in which it was adopted by the States, that in which it was advocated by its friends . . . I am opposed to the monarchising it's features . . . thus to worm out the elective principle. I am for preserving to the States the powers not yielded by them to the Union, & to the legislature of the Union it's constitutional share in the division of powers; and I am not for transferring all the powers of the States to the general government, & all those of that government to the Executive branch. I am for a government rigorously frugal & simple, applying all the possible savings of the public revenue to the discharge of the national debt. . . . I am for relying, for internal defence, on our militia solely, till actual invasion, and for such a naval force only as may protect our coasts and harbors from such depredations as we have experienced. . . . I am for free commerce with all nations; political connection with none; & little

---

[9] Quoted by Henry Adams, *Hist. of U. S.*, New York, 1889, Vol. I, p. 225.

or no diplomatic establishment. And I am not for linking ourselves by new treaties with the quarrels of Europe; entering that field of slaughter to preserve their balance, or joining in the confederacy of kings to war against the principles of liberty. I am for freedom of religion, & against all maneuvres to bring about a legal ascendancy of one sect over another; for freedom of the press & against all violations of the constitution to silence by force & not by reason the complaints or criticisms, just or unjust, of our citizens against the conduct of their agents. And I am for encouraging the progress of science in all it's branches; and not . . . for awing the human mind by stories of raw-head & bloody bones to a distrust of its own vision . . . to believe that government, religion, morality, & every other science were in the highest perfection in ages of the darkest ignorance, and that nothing can ever be devised more perfect than what was established by our forefathers. . . . The first object of my heart is my own country. In that is embarked my family, my fortune, & my own existence. I have not one farthing of interest, nor one fibre of attachment out of it, nor a single motive of preference of any one nation to another, but in proportion as they are more or less friendly to us." [10]

The election showed seventy-three votes each for Jefferson and Burr, sixty-five for Adams and sixty-four for Pinckney. The equal number of votes for the two Republican candidates again showed the absurdity and danger of the method of choosing the President. There was no doubt at all as to the intention of electing Jefferson and not Burr to the higher office, but the tie threw the election into the House of Representatives where there was a Federalist majority. The Federalists were thus in the anomalous position of deciding which of two men put forward by their bitter enemies should be President. Ballot after ballot was taken without a decision being

[10] *Writings,* Ford, Vol. VII, pp. 327 ff.

reached. Jefferson was approached with the suggestion that he could at once have the office if he would make certain terms with the Federalists, but refused to become President with his hands tied. He wrote a rather pointed note to Burr regretting that his election to the Vice-Presidency would prevent Jefferson from using his services in the Cabinet, but Burr, who should have withdrawn from the race, there being no question but that the people had not intended him to be President, refused to do so, and it is said intrigued actively on his own behalf. Fortunately Hamilton hated Burr even more than he did Jefferson, and of the two considered the latter the less dangerous. To a large extent through Hamilton's influence it thus came about that, on the thirty-sixth ballot, there was a sufficient shuffle of votes to throw the balance to Jefferson and elect him President. The deadlock had continued to February 17, so that it was scarcely a fortnight between his final election and his inauguration on March 4.

CHAPTER XIII

THE PRESIDENCY

JEFFERSON was fifty-eight when he moved from Conrad's boarding house to the yet unfinished White House in the new "city" of Washington whither the seat of government had been transferred in 1800 from Philadelphia in accordance with the deal which he himself had put through with Hamilton ten years before. The "city" was as yet scarcely begun, and was as sprawling, uncouth, squalid, ugly, and uncomfortable as any mushroom town that ever sprang up over night on a frontier. The roads were alternately deep with dust or almost impassable for mud, and in summer the undrained marshes reeked with fever. Fortunately it was nearer Monticello than was Philadelphia, and Jefferson could spend much of his time in the invigorating air of his own hill-top home.

Re-elected in 1804, Jefferson was to pass eight unhappy years as Chief Executive, upon which he later looked back with as little pleasure as he did on his terms as governor. In listing his achievements for the inscription on his tombstone, as we have already noted, he set down only the writing of the Declaration of Independence, the Virginia Statute for Religious Freedom, and the founding of the University of Virginia. In other words, he placed above all else his achievements as a great liberal. Compared with what he had endeavored to do in freeing the human spirit, he considered of no account the political offices he had held. Few, if any, other statesmen who had held positions comparable to Governor, Minister to France, Secretary of State, Vice-President, and twice President of the United States, would have obliterated these from his record as Jefferson did. In this volume we are regarding him much as he did himself in considering his own life, that is, as a liberal mind and not as an executive or politician. We may say, though he would not, that his has been the greatest and most influential liberal mind that America has developed. We cannot ignore as completely as he did his official life and acts, because in part they help to interpret his mind and doctrines, but we can ignore much in his two terms as President which would necessarily find place in either a history of ·the period or a full biography of the man, to dwell chiefly on such matters as serve as footnotes to his philosophy.

His active feud with Hamilton was now over, and Hamilton himself was in another three years to be lying dead, shot in the famous duel with Aaron Burr, July 11, 1804, a victim to the last, some think, of his fixed idea that a crisis would arrive in the affairs of the country which would require the intervention of armed forces which he should and must lead. When that day should come, his personal courage could not be put in question. So the challenge to the duel was not declined, as it might have been, for Hamilton had shown in making public to the world his sordid affair with Mrs. Reynolds that he had the moral courage to flout opinion. A great man, with all his faults and weaknesses, he had rendered great services to the country, though his policies undoubtedly helped to bring about many of the evils of our modern America.

In the short years left to him, Hamilton devoted himself chiefly to repairing his own broken fortune, and no longer tried to control the course of government. Jefferson, nevertheless, was to be confronted with a new antagonist of the same party, in some ways even more important and determined than Hamilton himself—John Marshall. Marshall, who has already appeared in our story, was a kinsman of Jefferson, but never were two men more unlike. As a youth, Marshall had gone to war enthusiastically for liberty with all the devotion to the cause which might be expected of a boy living on the frontier. After the war, however, the ideas of the rising lawyer changed rapidly, and his views of debt and contract "developed until finally they became as flint," as his most eulogistic biographer wrote.[1]

Not a learned lawyer, but a man of very powerful mind, he loved money and as he grew older became, as Beveridge says, obsessed with "an almost religious devotion to the rights of property."[2] Unlike the other great national figures of his time he constantly refused to serve in public office because he could make more in private life, and when he accepted the mission to France under President John Adams, it was from a motive "largely mercenary,"[3] and he received $20,000 for eleven months' work, or three times his ordinary yearly income. Gradually Marshall's inordinate love of money, and reverence both for it and those who possessed it, changed the frontier boy into the leader of the Federalist Party in Virginia, a complete reactionary, and a close colleague of the most reactionary Federalists of all, the members of the Essex Junto in Massachusetts. There was never the slightest blemish on his financial honor, but in studying his mind we must, as even Beveridge allows, take the above facts into consideration. There was not a spark of liberalism in John Marshall.

Between such a kinsman and Jefferson there could not only be no sympathy but must be enmity if they clashed politically. At the time of Jefferson's election Marshall had at last yielded to Adams's entreaties and had become Secretary of State in place of Pickering, feeling perhaps that he could afford it as he had just got the $20,000 from Adams's administration. When the vote had been tied between Jefferson and Burr,

[1] A. J. Beveridge, *Life of John Marshall*, Boston, 1916, Vol. I, p. 223.
[2] *Ibid.*, Vol. IV, p. 4.
[3] Professor E. S. Corwin in article on Marshall in the *Dictionary of American Biography*, largely borne out by Beveridge.

42373

Marshall had declined to take sides, though urged by Hamilton to support Jefferson as the lesser of the two evils and as a far less dangerous man for President than Burr. It was quite obvious that the country had never intended to •elect Burr to the highest office rather than the great Democratic leader. Marshall knew that as well as any one. It was likely that if Burr should secure the office against the wishes of the nation Marshall would be retained as Secretary of State, and so be an heir-apparent to the Presidency. He also professed to believe Jefferson to be "an absolute terrorist," whether he really did so or not. Today if two candidates for President received equal votes, the House of Representatives would be justified in making its own choice between them, but in 1800, under the then as yet unchanged electoral law, it was obvious to every one that the tie vote between Jefferson and Burr, leaving it undecided which should be President and which Vice-President, was not due to an equally divided public opinion but to a mere accident caused by what was promptly recognized to be an unworkable system of elections. By refusing to use his influence to right the threatened wrong, and to follow the request of his own party leader, Marshall, in so far as he took sides, thus threw his influence negatively on the side of Burr.

President Adams, during the closing two months of his administration, made many appointments to office, the picturesquely but wrongly named "midnight appointments." Between February 1 and March 3, 1801, he sent in no less than 216 nominations to the Senate, and there can be no real defense of his action in filling posts with men inimical to his successor. Practically every office in the gift of the government was already occupied by a Federalist yet the people had called upon Jefferson, a Democrat, to direct the government for the next four years. To continue, right up to the very hour almost of leaving the Presidency, to stuff Jefferson's house with enemies was both unfair and ungenerous on the part of Adams. It was even politically indecent. Adams cared nothing about patronage as such or building up a personal following and machine. There can be only two reasons suggested for his unfair use of the appointing power. One is that he wished to show his resentment against his old friend who had defeated his own re-election to office, and the other that he genuinely feared for the safety of the nation with Jefferson at the helm.

For the bulk of the attempted 216 appointments it would seem as though the first explanation must be the correct one, especially as Adams also showed his resentment by leaving Washington the night before the inauguration, refusing to remain to welcome his successor, the only President who has ever failed in performing that courtesy. With regard to certain judicial appointments, however, the second reason may also have been influential. Popular feeling had made it seem likely that no further steps toward changing the Constitution in the Federalist direction would be likely through the legislative branch. Leading Federalists, however, had recognized that what had proved impossible in the constitutional convention and what might now prove so in Congress, might yet be achieved through the federal courts. The number of these and of judges had been increased, and it was considered important that they should be controlled by the party of the "wise and good." Having offered the Chief Justiceship of the Supreme Court to John Jay, who declined it, Adams appointed John Marshall, one of the incoming President's bitterest enemies to the position. Marshall was to take up the work of "administering" the Constitution where Hamilton laid it down, and was to be equally, if not more, instrumental in altering it.

In spite of the bitterness of the recent campaign, Jefferson in his inaugural address struck the note of reconciliation. He spoke mildly of the "animation of discussions" during the contest "which might impose on strangers unused to think freely, and to speak and write what they think." [4]   Now the fight was over, and all would range themselves under the laws and work for the common good, bearing in mind the "sacred principle that though the will of the Majority is in all cases to prevail, that will, to be rightful, must be reasonable; that the Minority possess their equal rights, which equal laws must protect."

"Every difference of opinion," he said, "is not a difference of principle," adding, in an oft-quoted and misunderstood passage, that "we have called, by different names, brethren of the same principle. We are all republicans; we are all federalists." Jefferson and his party had been accused, as we have seen, of wishing to overthrow the very foundations of society. On the other hand, he himself had combated the small group of Federalist leaders whom he believed to be plotting or hoping for the overthrow of the Republic in favor of a monarchy. What I think he intended by the passage was to show that, as he well knew, the Democrats wished to maintain government, law, and order, as well as the Federalists, and that the "Monocrats" did not represent the mass of the people. Between the two extremes of the ultra-reactionaries and the supposed, but non-existent, anarchists, all Americans believed in union and a republican form of government however much they might differ as to the powers to be given to its several organs.

A reign of terror had been freely predicted. Jefferson removed this fear in another passage. "If there be any among us who wish to dissolve this union, or to change its republican form, let them stand undisturbed, as monuments of the safety with which error of opinion may be tolerated where reason is left free to combat it." That is indeed a statement worthy of a great liberal, and one may contrast it with the Alien and Sedition laws of the preceding administration, and with the

---

[4] *Writings,* Ford, Vol. VIII, p. 2. I quote from the first draft as printed by Ford, which scarcely differed from the speech as delivered. I have, however, changed the abbreviations used by Jefferson into the words for which they stood in the manuscript.

modern governments of some of the great powers of Europe where freedom of speech and press has been completely suppressed.

"Sometimes it is said," he continued, "that Man cannot be trusted with the government of himself— Can he then be trusted with the government of others? Or have we found angels in the form of kings to govern him?—Let history answer this question." He might have added or angels in the form of dictators, efficiency experts, small governing classes, or other individuals or groups whether from the top or bottom of society.

He next listed the blessings of America, and said that to them for perfect felicity one thing more must be added: "a wise and frugal government, which shall restrain men from injuring one another, shall leave them otherwise free to regulate their own pursuits of industry and improvement, and shall not take from the mouth of labor the bread it has earned." He then enumerated the principles which ought to shape the administration of government as:

Equal and exact justice to all men, of whatever state or persuasion, religious or political.

Peace, commerce, and honest friendship with all nations, entangling alliances with none.

The support of the State governments in all their rights, as the most competent administrations for our domestic concerns, and the surest bulwarks against anti-republican tendencies.

The preservation of the General government, in it's whole constitutional vigor, as the sheet anchor of our peace at home, and safety abroad. . . .

Absolute acquiescence in the decisions of the Majority, the vital principle of republics, from which is no appeal but to force. . . .

The diffusion, and arraignment of all abuses at the bar of the public reason.

Freedom of Religion, freedom of the press, and freedom of

person under the protection of the Habeas corpus: and trial by juries, impartially selected.

He also spoke of economy in public affairs, honest payment of all debts, and encouragement of agriculture, "and of Commerce as its handmaid."

It was not so much a Presidential inaugural address as it was a platform of liberalism regardless of party. Throughout it there breathed the spirit of the liberal who places the happiness, the welfare, and the liberty of the individual citizen above all forms and policies of any particular government or party. It is as easy to analyze it critically and to shatter some of its logic as in the case of the Declaration of Independence. Americanism, however, is real even if it be not logical, and these two documents are the earliest literary sources from which Americans drew long draughts of the pure American doctrine. Americanism as a state of mind developed from all the conditions of American life—not simply from the frontier, important as that was—but from all the conditions, combined as they have been nowhere else. America has been unique in its combination of the remoteness, the richness and the vastness of the land, its varying climates, the rapidity of its development and population growth, and many other factors. From all of these emerged naturally the American spirit. To the verbal interpretation of this spirit no other statesman of his time contributed to the people as did Jefferson—not Hamilton, Washington, John Adams, Madison, nor any other until Lincoln. The Inaugural Address, even more than the Declaration, gives expression to the American mood and spirit. It gathers into itself in one great stream all the rivulets of Americanism and liberalism having their springs in the earliest days of settlement, such as the political liberalism of Hooker and the founders of Connecticut, the religious toleration of Williams in Rhode Island, the self-reliance and freedom of the frontier, and all the rest. It is not the Constitution but the Declaration of Independence, Jefferson's first inaugural and Lincoln's Gettysburg address, which voice the inarticulate soul of the millions of Americans who in spite, often, of having their feet in the mire, have looked aloft and afar to dream the dream of America.

A few days after his inauguration Jefferson wrote to John Dickinson that "the storm through which we have passed, has been tremendous indeed. The tough sides of our Argosie have been thoroughly tried. Her strength has stood the waves into which she was steered, with a view to sink her. We shall put her on the republican tack, & she will show by the beauty of her motion the skill of her builders." [5]

From the formation of the government it had been in Federalist hands, and almost all office-holders were of that party, there being only 30 Republicans in even the 228 principal posts. Naturally, and more wisely than Adams had done, Jefferson selected a new Cabinet from among men he could trust, chief among them being Madison as Secretary of State, and Gallatin as Secretary of the Treasury. He did not, however, contemplate a clean sweep of minor officials. He did not believe, he wrote to one place-seeker, in mere rotation of office, and, writing to Monroe, he declared that "deprivations of office, if made on the ground of political principles alone, would revolt our new converts." Some removals there must be, but "they must be as few as possible, done gradually, and bottomed on some malversation or inherent disqualification." [6] He believed that office should be open to all and based on fitness, but his position was, as we have just noted, peculiar. Had the government existed for a long time, with a reasonable alteration of parties in power, there would have grown up a fair balance in the public service even without any spoils system, each party having appointed officials to vacant posts

[5] *Writings*, Ford, Vol. VIII, p. 7.   [6] *Ibid.*, p. 10.

during its tenure of office. But in 1801 the opposition came into power for the first time since the government had been set in operation scarcely more than a dozen years before, and thus found practically every position in the hands of enemies. Jefferson did not change his views, but had to some extent to yield to popular and sectional pressure. Vacancies, as he wrote, "by death are few; by resignation none." In the course of his eight years there were therefore removals. To such length as he went, which cannot now be accurately determined, he may be said to have inaugurated the spoils system, but he resisted that system on principle, and it did not come to full blossom until Jackson's day.

Connected with the removals was the repeal by the Democrats of the Judiciary Act, passed in 1801 just before the Federalists went out of power. The first three articles of the Constitution had provided for a legislature, an executive and a judiciary, whether the order in which they were named and their functions defined had anything to do with their relative importance in the eyes of the framers or not. We have already noted that the instrument did not state, in case any one of the departments acted, or was supposed by any one to act, contrary to the fundamental law of the Constitution, how or by whom its acts should be passed upon and adjudged unconstitutional. In the Kentucky Resolves, Jefferson had suggested that the state legislatures should decide, at least in so far as they could nullify laws which they deemed unconstitutional as passed by Congress. It may be noted, however, that the Executive and the Judiciary might, either of them, also act beyond its constitutional powers. The jurisdiction, for example, of the federal courts was limited. Suppose some judge should insist on going outside that jurisdiction, or the Supreme Court itself should do so. Who should then decide on the constitutionality of the judicial acts of the Judiciary itself?

With reference to the theory of state legislative review of acts of Congress, nine states had disagreed with Kentucky and Virginia and none had agreed. Although this had no effect on Calhoun and the Nullifiers of his later generation, it does seem to have had on Jefferson, either because of his theory of majority rule or because of further consideration on his own part. At any rate, he changed his theory. In a passage of his Presidential Message of December 8, 1801 (deleted when the message was sent to Congress), he defended his pardon of certain citizens condemned under the Sedition Act, on the new ground that each of the separate and co-equal divisions of the government had the right and duty to determine, each for itself, the constitutionality of the acts of the other. He did not apparently realize that this could result only in administrative chaos, and was as bad as state legislative review and nullification.

Marshall had also been considering this same point for some years, and had come to the conclusion, advocated by a number of the states in their replies to the Kentucky Resolves, that the ultimate judge should be the Supreme Court. On the one hand there were three equal and co-ordinate branches of partially sovereign Federal Government, and on the other a growing number of partially sovereign states. There were thus two problems involved. First, who should decide in case of disagreement as to the constitutionality of acts performed by any one of the three departments of the Federal Government; and second, who should decide in case of disagreement between the Federal Government and any, several, or all of the states? The Constitution contained no answer, and the problem in fact was, apart from that, incapable of a perfectly legal or logical solution.

A merely practical solution, if one were possible, had to be found, and fortunately the political genius of the Anglo-Saxon race cares more for practicability than for law or logic.

On the whole, Marshall's plan to make the Supreme Court the final arbiter as to the constitutionality of laws passed by Congress, although not perfect, was probably the best solution then and better than any as yet suggested since. But there were two difficulties in the way. One was that, except by a wide interpretation of the Constitution, as to which people might differ, and which they might or might not accept, the court in arrogating to itself the right to pass on the constitutionality of the acts of the other two branches of government was itself transcending its own strictly constitutional sphere of activity. It might therefore be considered as itself acting unconstitutionally. The second difficulty, related in part to the first, was that if one branch of the government thus made itself the sole and final arbiter of what was constitutional, there would be no judge of its *own* acts, it having made itself the sole judge of them also. It would have been impossible, for political reasons, to have secured an amendment to the Constitution giving the power to the Supreme Court. In one of the most momentous personal decisions ever taken by a single individual in matters affecting the long history of an entire people, Marshall determined that when opportunity offered he would, for the Court, *assume* the power. After that, all would depend on the acquiescence or non-acquiescence by the nation at large. He then waited for a case which would be of such a nature as would give him his chance.

A certain William Marbury, otherwise totally unknown to fame, had been one of the forty-two new justices of the peace nominated by Adams on March 2, and confirmed by the Senate next day just as Adams was leaving office. The commissions of these men had been withheld by Jefferson who refused to recognize the appointments. Marbury and three others applied to the court for a writ of mandamus ordering Madison as Secretary of State to deliver their commissions to them. Thus began the celebrated case of *Marbury* vs. *Madi-*

son. In April 1802, the Judiciary Act of the Republicans abolishing certain federal courts was passed. This Act also did away with all but the February term of the Supreme Court, which thus had to take an enforced holiday until the beginning of 1803. It was not until then that Marshall had his long-awaited chance. He ruled that Marbury was entitled to remedy but that the Supreme Court under its specified powers in the Constitution did not have *original jurisdiction* in the case, although in the Judiciary Act of 1789, in clause thirteen, the Court had been authorized to issue such a writ, when called for, "to officers of the United States" in spite of the fact that it was not one of the powers given to it by the Constitution.

Herein lay Marshall's opportunity. Handing down a decision for the unanimous Court, he declared that as clause thirteen of the 1789 Act required the Court to do something that it was not permitted to under the Constitution, therefore the clause was null and void, because unconstitutional. We may note that it is true that the power which Congress had granted added another to those among the specified ones, and that if Congress could do that it might add to the powers of the Court indefinitely and so completely alter the form of government, but as there was nothing said in the Constitution about the Court's power to pass on the constitutionality of legislative acts, the grasping of that unmentioned power in a decision in which the Court was ruling that its own powers could not constitutionally be increased was an act of sublime audacity. The Court, merely by its own interpretation of a vague and obscure clause in the Constitution, had seized for itself the greatest and most important power it has possessed ever since.

If the Union was to be preserved, however, some solution of the problem, almost insoluble legally and politically, as to ultimate interpretation and preservation of the Constitution, had to be found, and in spite of obvious drawbacks, Marshall's bold solution was probably the best, as we have said. At any rate, with many grumblings from time to time, it has, with the exception of the Civil War, been quietly accepted, and is now considered as much a part of our Constitution as though it had been written into it originally in words so plain that all could see. It has also given a comparative flexibility to the Constitution, in spite of complaints, which it could not otherwise have attained.

An old nation, like England, slowly developing down the ages, "from precedent to precedent," could have an unwritten constitution. When, however, England and Scotland, as independent powers, were joined in the "United Kingdom" a written Act of Settlement had to be drawn up, to define the rights, powers, and relations of each. When the thirteen independent states formed a Union in America they were in the same position. A written constitution for the Union was as essential as in the case of England and Scotland. Such a written constitution, nevertheless, had the drawbacks that it might prove too rigid to meet the needs and conditions of a rapidly changing age, and also that it might break up the Union if no agreed-upon mode of interpreting it could be settled upon.

Jefferson, in so far as any public expression or action was concerned, acquiesced in Marshall's assumption of power, though he disbelieved in it. Indeed its legal basis has been somewhat undermined by later decisions of the Court itself as to the constitutionality of the 1789 Act and Jefferson's right to remove Marbury. Marshall's knowledge of law was not perhaps very good, but his courage and statesmanship were great. Jefferson continued to believe that there was no reason why the judiciary should set itself above the executive or the legislature, any more than that either of them should set itself above the judiciary, and that in case of dispute the final decision should in some way rest with the people. It is neither impossible or even perhaps unlikely or undesirable that in time some modification of the present method may be developed which may combine the ideas of both Jefferson and Marshall.

Hamilton had early formulated the same doctrine as that so boldly put into practice by Marshall, and the leading Federalists counted upon the federal courts to mold the Constitution in the direction which they wished. They desired to use the courts for practical political, and not merely legal, ends. Indeed, no secret was made of it. Adams's "midnight appointments" and the hurriedly passed Judiciary Act both appear to have been efforts to thwart the Jeffersonians before they came into power. Naturally all this was not lost on so good a lawyer and astute a politician as Jefferson himself. The Federal Judiciary having now declared itself superior to the Executive and the Legislature, the President decided to test possible methods of controlling the courts by impeachment of judges. The impeachments by the Republicans appear to me to have been much over-emphasized by most historians. Impeachment was no new method of getting rid of unfit or unwanted public officials, the most noted case being that of Warren Hastings in England. There had been impeachments of judges in the several states, notably Pennsylvania, but when the Pennsylvania politicians went too far, the Jeffersonian judge of the State Supreme Court took sides with his Federalist colleagues. The first successful federal impeachment of a judge was that of Pickering of New Hampshire, but the animus was obviously not political. It does not appear that Jefferson was greatly interested in the case, and certainly not from the political angle. Pickering had become insane from drink and was quite unfitted to sit on the bench. Whether or not it was fair to charge an insane man with guilt is another matter. He had to be got rid of if justice were not to be a mockery. Impeachment offered the only way out of an impossible situation.

The leading case during the Jefferson régime was that of

Samuel Chase of Maryland, an associate justice of the Supreme Court. It may or may not have been a test case to see whether Marshall himself could be got rid of. Possibly it was, though the charges would have had to be different. It may be agreed that judges should be utterly impartial and above politics. Chase had constantly used his position to make political harangues in court against the new administration, and had predicted ruin for liberty and the country if it remained in power. His impeachment before Congress was distinctly an administration policy, and it would have been far better had it not been undertaken. Its complete and ignominious failure was a blow to Jefferson's prestige, but it is not fair to claim, as Chase did, that the Republicans had made an attempt to destroy all courts as such. The courts and judges had gone into politics, and in the extremely formative stage in which the government then was it was natural that politicians should try themselves against the courts. If the Supreme Court set itself, without constitutional authority, above the Executive and the Legislature, there was no reason why they should not try their strength against the Court. All was yet in flux, and the assumed power of the Court had not then been accepted and sanctioned by over a hundred and thirty years of usage. Today we would not tolerate such an attack on the courts as the administration made. On the other hand we would not tolerate such actions as Chase indulged in as an Associate of the Supreme Court. The failure of his impeachment, however, secured, and fortunately so, a much larger degree of freedom to the judiciary.

It has been said that Hamilton, probably because of his unusual precocity and not because of a closed mind, had accumulated his whole stock of leading ideas by the time he was twenty-five. Jefferson had not developed his whole political theory quite so rapidly, but he had developed it fully long before he became President. His eight years in office yield no new ideas of importance nor any striking modifications of the old ones. So far as his intellectual history is concerned we have to do only with how he put his already formed ideas into practice when confronted with supreme power and responsibility.

One of the chief points in Jefferson's political system was his belief in the fundamental necessity for complete freedom of speech and press in any system of government which rested upon the consent, honesty, and intelligence of the people themselves. As a liberal this would have been a point for which he would have striven under any form of government but it was also one of the corner-stones of the particular form of government which he believed might be tried with success in America. He had ample opportunity to demonstrate his own loyalty to the doctrine.

Adams, in spite of magnificent qualities, was both egotistical and touchy. Jefferson was not an egoist but, as we have already heard him confess, he was extremely sensitive to criticism, especially when he believed it unjust or knew it to be wholly false. Public life had its tortures for him. Almost all our Presidents, especially those who have been marked personalities or who have been protagonists in especially emotional periods of politics, have been unmercifully assailed in the opposition press but few have been subjected to such unwarranted attacks upon their private moral character as was Jefferson. In a period when the clergy were of great influence, he had made the general body of them, of all denominations, hostile to him by his fight for religious liberty and disestablishment. Jefferson added fuel to the flame by a somewhat tactless act almost at the beginning of his administration.

Thomas Paine had rendered great service to America in the Revolution by his book, *Common Sense*. Returning to Europe, he had later written a defense of the French revolution in his *Rights of Man*, an able rejoinder to Burke's attack, as we have already noted. For this he was exiled from England and went to France. There he was after a while imprisoned, but later released by the intercession of the American Minister. While in prison he wrote *The Age of Reason,* a defense of eighteenth-century Deism. Paine was a born revolutionary but he was a Deist and not an atheist. The orthodox ministry of that day made little distinction between the two, however, and even in the twentieth century Theodore Roosevelt could speak of the man who had rendered such service to America when needed, as a "dirty little atheist." If Roosevelt could say that in our time, we can imagine the hatred of many for Paine in his own day when his political and religious ideas made him anathema to the orthodox and conservative.

Jefferson and John Adams were both profoundly religious and ethical men but neither were orthodox Christians and were perhaps nearer to the position of modern Unitarians than anything else. Jefferson believed that a man's religious beliefs were a matter between himself and God only, and no one else's business. He always declined to discuss his own views, and in Paine he saw only the man who had done much for America (in spite of an unjust attack he had later made on Washington), and who had defended the rights of man throughout his life. When Paine was allowed to leave France, Jefferson offered him passage to America on a naval vessel, and at once loosed a storm of abuse.

The next year, 1802, a pamphleteer, whom Jefferson had at times assisted, but who turned out to be thoroughly disreputable, attacked Jefferson in a publication full of the vilest slanders with regard to his private moral life, charging him also with cowardice, dishonesty, and almost everything which a dirty mind and venial pen could spew out. As the historian, Henry Adams, who was assuredly no defender of Jefferson, wrote, Jefferson had been justified in befriending Callender before his character was known, and Callender's assault on his benefactor was an attempted "act of dastardly assassination, which the whole Federalist press cheered." Since one questionable episode in his early youth, Jefferson's personal life had been without stain. In all personal relations—as friend, relation, trustee—his integrity was as great as that of Washington himself, with more warmth of personal affection and regard. As to intimate relations with the other sex, Adams also says that "Jefferson was feminine; he was more refined than many women in the delicacy of his private relations," yet "even men as shameless as Callender himself winced under attacks" of the sort Callender had now delivered.[7]

Whether it is because of Puritan repressions, or the lack of normal emotional outlets, or what-not, it has been a characteristic trait of the American public to delight in listening to and spreading slanders about the very men they elect to high office. Almost every scandalous story about Jefferson which is still whispered or believed can be traced to the lies in Callender's book. At the moment when the Federalists were going wild with joy over showing that the head of the nation was one of the basest of men, Paine arrived. He had not accepted the invitation of passage on the *Maryland*, and had delayed a year.

No one who does not understand Jefferson's true character and sensitiveness can realize what he endured as he heard slanders about him echoed unctuously or joyously throughout the country, and believed by a large part of his fellow-citizens. But the strength of his attachment to liberalism was shown by his refraining from using his power to attack the press in any quarter. Even that staunch lover of liberty, John Adams, had been goaded into doing so, stung by the attacks of journalists and political hacks. Jefferson, writhing in the White House, remained true to his belief that the education of a sovereign people required complete freedom of speech and press, and that in the end truth would be sifted and would

7 *Hist. of the U. S., op. cit.,* Vol. I, pp. 323 f.

prevail. He wrote to personal friends, who were sometimes far from wise in their defense of him, but as far as the public was concerned he remained silent, and brought no action against any one.

We have already spoken of Jefferson's great interest and belief in the West. He was neither an imperialist nor an expansionist. Our territory already stretched to the Mississippi, and in his Inaugural Address he had spoken of our country as possessing "room enough for all descendants to the 100th and 1000th. generation." No one yet foresaw the age of invention, though Jefferson himself fairly stumbled into the America of the future in two letters he wrote to Monroe, then governor of Virginia, in November, 1801.

The first was a note of introduction to be carried by "Mr Whitney at [sic] Connecticut, mechanic of the first order of ingenuity, who invented the cotton gin now so much used in the South; he is at the head of a considerable gun manufactory in Connecticut, and furnishes the U. S. with muskets undoubtedly the best they receive. He has invented molds and machines for making all the pieces of his locks so exactly equal, that take 100 locks to pieces and mingle their parts and the hundred locks may be put together as well by taking the first pieces which come to hand. . . . Leblanc in France had invented a similar process in 1788 and had extended it to the barrel, mounting & stock. I endeavored to get the U. S. to bring him over. . . . I failed and I do not know what became of him." [8]

Here was the cotton gin, which was to fasten slavery on the South, to create the "cotton kingdom," and to transfer the control of our southern section from the aristocratic planters of Virginia and South Carolina to the, for the most part, newer plutocrats and nabobs of the "Lower South." Here, also, was the germ of mass production which was eventually

[8] *Writings*, Ford, Vol. VII, p. 101.

to have such profound effect upon us and the world. It is not without its irony that Jefferson, the agrarian who wished manufactures only as "the handmaid of agriculture," had unwittingly made an effort to introduce it into America even before it spontaneously arose from Yankee inventiveness!

But if Jefferson did not see the future in these things, he did peer further into it in another letter to Monroe ten days later. The governor had asked about the possibility of planting penal colonies in the West, either within or without our then borders. Jefferson objected strenuously, and in the course of his argument wrote that "however our present interests may restrain us within our limits, it is impossible not to look forward to distant times, when our rapid multiplication will expand itself beyond those limits, & cover the whole northern, if not the southern continent, with a people speaking the same language, governed in similar forms, & by similar laws." [9]

There is nothing to indicate that Jefferson desired to be the agent in any such expansion or that he expected it to occur until "distant times." His own intense interest in the West was more immediate. His Western policy had two main objects, other, of course, than the fundamental one of keeping the West contented within the Union. These were to let nothing interfere with the free navigation of the Mississippi River as the main outlet for Western produce and so the basis of its prosperity and well-being. The other was not to allow any aggressive European nation in place of the decaying Spain to establish itself to the west of us with the probable contingency of again drawing us into the interminable European wars. His belief in the uniqueness of the American experiment was equalled by his desire to preserve that uniqueness by maintaining as nearly complete isolation from Old-World entanglements and influences as possible.

In spite of much intrigue and many annoying circum-

[9] *Ibid.*, p. 105.

stances, Spain, owing to her growing weakness, was for the moment as desirable a neighbor as we could have on the west. In the winter of 1800–1801, however, rumors came from Europe that Napoleon was bringing pressure to bear upon Spain to retrocede the former vast possessions of France in the Mississippi Valley known as "Louisiana," not, of course, the present state of that name but a territory as large as the whole of the then United States. Such rumors had gone about before, but this time Napoleon was in earnest. He wished not only to reconquer Hayti from the blacks but to straddle the two continents of Europe and America. On October 15, 1802, the long-protracted French-Spanish negotiations were consummated, and "Louisiana" was ceded after a written pledge was given that France would never alienate it. It was a worthless one, as Napoleon's word was ever worthless. At a stroke of the pen the entire American position was altered. One of the strongest powers in the world, headed by a ruthless and colossally ambitious despot, had become our neighbor and controlled the mouth of the Mississippi. When the news was out, the Federalists, who had always disliked and mistrusted the West, but who nevertheless saw an opportunity to combine with it against the Republicans, urged the Westerners to seize New Orleans by force, which would have brought on war with France. The whole position was full of danger for Jefferson.

January 11, 1803, the President appointed Monroe as special envoy to France to join our Minister there, Robert R. Livingston, to see if some determination as to the Mississippi navigation question, previously considered settled by the Treaty of 1795 with Spain, could be reached. Meanwhile, luckily for us, European affairs had not gone as Napoleon had hoped. The peace which he had made with England was of short duration. His hands were again to be tied by war in the Old World, and he could afford to waste no more troops in Hayti or to dream of an empire in America. With the agility of mind possessed by him he suddenly began to think of selling Louisiana to the United States, regardless of his pledge to Spain. It would at once relieve him of a drain on his military resources and give him much-needed cash.

Jefferson's instructions to his envoys had contemplated no such contingency. They had been to offer fifty million francs for New Orleans and the two Floridas or thirty-seven millions for New Orleans alone. If France would not sell, then they should insist upon a perpetual guarantee of the right of navigation and deposit, and, failing to secure even that, to negotiate immediately with England with a view to joining her in the war. No matter how much Jefferson might care for France, the interests of America, for him, came first as always.

Livingston, awaiting the arrival of Monroe, had been negotiating on the basis of the above instructions, with no encouragement from the French. Suddenly he was amazed to be asked point-blank what the United States would pay for the whole of Louisiana. Within a day or two, Monroe arrived, and the rest was a matter of bargaining. Without full authority to do so, the envoys finally bought Louisiana for approximately $15,000,000, giving us the whole of the Mississippi River and increasing our territory from 900,000 square miles to 1,800,000. It was, perhaps, the most stupendous bargain in history.

When the treaty confirming the sale reached America, Jefferson was in a dilemma. The purchase of New Orleans or even the Floridas might have been considered as mere rectification and settlement of boundaries and claims, but to double the size of the country and erect new states had no constitutional warrant whatever, and Jefferson had been a strict constructionist. He himself said that if such a thing could be done under the "general welfare" clause then there was no Constitution. Anything could be done. The advantage to the United States, however, was incalculably great. It was less at the time in the addition of territory, much of it unexplored and unknown, than it was in freeing the Mississippi, binding our former West to us, and in ridding ourselves for another thousand miles or so westward of European neighbors and potential enemies. When the Senate confirmed the treaty, Jefferson showed himself to be no doctrinaire by promptly signing it, though he did so with the hope that a constitutional amendment would be passed validating his act. Confronted by such a peculiar and fateful crisis for the nation, there can be no doubt that Jefferson was justified, but the amendment was never passed nor even seriously considered. As in the case of the assumption of revisionary power by the Supreme Court, the people merely acquiesced, showing how profound an effect on the Constitution an almost unanimous national opinion may have without formal amendment. It is noteworthy, however, that doubling the size of the nation during his term of office was another achievement which Jefferson did not inscribe on his tombstone.

It is sometimes affirmed that the credit for the purchase belongs far more to Livingston, or to him and Monroe combined, than to Jefferson, but this is not so. Jefferson had determined by one means or another to oust the French from New Orleans, and when, in the early stages of the negotiations, Congress had appropriated $2,000,000, the President on his own responsibility had authorized the envoys to go up to fifty million francs or even higher. Neither of them was a skilful diplomat, and when Napoleon offered them the whole of Louisiana on a platter for sixty millions it did not require any great ability, with that stroke of luck, to bring Jefferson's policy to the conclusion unexpected by all. The envoys, who were neither of them bold in character, might well have hesitated to raise $2,000,000 to $15,000,000 without communicating with the government in Washington, involving a delay of several months, and with the danger of capture at sea. Jefferson may have strained his own constitutional powers in so greatly increasing the sum appropriated in the expectation that, the object attained, Congress would stand behind him, but at least it had been he and not the envoys who took almost the entire risk.

The disposition of the citizens in the purchased territory has a distinct interest for the student of Jefferson's theory of government. According to the treaty the ceded territory was to be incorporated into the rest of the United States and the inhabitants admitted "as soon as possible" to all the rights of other American citizens. Jefferson has often been blamed for not setting up self-government promptly according, as it is claimed, to his theory. The refusal to do so, however, illustrates clearly his lasting contention that self-government is possible only under certain conditions, and that the American experiment was unique. The population in New Orleans and the rest of the newly acquired territory was almost wholly French with some Spanish, and of a type, Jefferson believed, which was not ripe for self-government. He did not consider that it would succeed there until such a time, probably soon, when sufficient Americans who were accustomed to working the machinery of self-government should have settled on the other side of the old international boundary. Had Jefferson been a doctrinaire he would have insisted upon the setting up of the forms of government he believed in as best, *when possible*, in the new territory. He would have made the same mistake that Wilson did more than a century later when he believed that Mexico or the Balkans could provide overnight the same sort of electorate as England or America if only the *forms* of self-government were established. Perhaps nothing illustrates better than this refusal to grant immediate self-government how firmly Jefferson kept his feet on the ground instead of being wafted away by theory. It was equally characteristic of his practicality and love of facts and information that almost coincident with his appointing Monroe as envoy to France he asked Congress to appropriate $2500 to finance an expedition to explore the West and its resources—the famous Lewis and Clark expedition—and took immense interest in the whole course and results of the explorations.

A matter connected with the West which absorbed public attention for a good part of 1806–1807 was the mysterious expedition of Aaron Burr. Always an intriguer, and discredited with the public by his killing of Hamilton, Burr had gone to fish in the dark and troubled waters of Spanish and American plotting across the mountains. The history of the Southwest for a decade prior to this still remains one of the mysteries of American history. Characters connected with the plots and counter-plots, schemes of disunion and also of conquest and annexation, include all types from Alexander Hamilton to General Wilkinson of the U. S. Army, the latter seemingly a traitor to both his own country and Spain while he took pay from each. The Burr episode, although it looms fairly large in the history of the period, has little importance for us in this volume. At first, Jefferson did not take Burr's movements or possible plans seriously. Then, becoming alarmed by what was reported to him, he had Burr arrested, brought to Richmond and tried on a charge of treason. John Marshall's brother-in-law, J. H. Daveiss of Kentucky, and another of his relations, former Senator Humphrey Marshall of the same state, had been chiefly instrumental in spreading abroad rumors of Burr's plot. When, however, Burr reached Richmond as a prisoner, the Chief Justice of the United States, before whom he was to be tried, actually attended a dinner given in the prisoner's honor!

There was insufficient evidence to convict Burr of the crimes charged, especially as Marshall defined treason, and the trial was mainly notable as an unseemly duel between the Chief Justice and the President, which lessened the dignity and popularity of both. On one point Jefferson, by his defiance of the

Justice, established an important precedent. Marshall insisted that Jefferson appear personally in court at the request of Burr's attorney. Jefferson properly insisted in return that the President could not be summoned to appear in court here, there, and everywhere, at any time and as many times as any attorney in any case might demand. If this were so, he would be unable to perform the duties to which the nation had elected him, and his enemies could always get rid of him by summoning him to appear in a court in Maine, Louisiana, or other remote parts, dragging him away from Washington for weeks at a time. This is so obvious that Marshall's reiterated demand can only be considered as having its motive in a wish to humiliate the President, especially as it was combined with rather insulting remarks. If the conduct of the trial throughout reflects no credit on Marshall, on the other hand, Jefferson's interference and his evident personal wish to have Burr convicted were uncalled for, unwise, and undignified. He had done his duty when he had had Burr arrested and brought to trial. After that it would have been far better had he maintained a neutral attitude and allowed justice to take its course.

Of far more interest for our purpose was Jefferson's great and unsuccessful experiment in his second term of trying to find a coercive substitute for armed warfare.

Jefferson, as we have noted, was not a pacifist. When the Bey of Tripoli repudiated his treaty with us in 1801, Jefferson at once brought him to terms by force, and in a brilliant little war, in which our small navy showed to much advantage, secured both from him and from the Sultan of Morocco better terms than those accorded to any other nation. If a fight could not be avoided, Jefferson was willing to face it, but as a liberal he realized the insane waste, suffering, and the danger to liberty involved in war. Although a nationalist in the sense that he was intensely American and wished that the United States could be as nearly self-sufficing as possible and

have as little as might be to do with others, he was never a
nationalist in the sense that he was deceived by words or conceived of the "nation" as an entity in itself. The nation for
him was the sum total of the individual citizens comprising
it. A nation as something apart and by itself was an absurdity. A nation could not be happy, except as the individual
citizens were happy. The pernicious doctrine, which has been
so unhappily developing in many countries in the past half
century, that a nation can be strong, happy, rich, powerful,
great, and free, even though its government takes away all
these attributes from its citizens, would have seemed insane
folly to him. Nation had a very real meaning for him, but it
was a meaning rooted in the lives of human beings. To erect
a noun into a super-personality, to fall down and worship it,
to sacrifice the freedom and happiness of humanity to it,
would have appeared to him as a new form of fantastic and
insane idolatry.

Thus he envisaged war in human terms. Almost from the
beginning of our government, we had been entangled as a
neutral in the everlasting quarrels of Europe. In his Fare-
well Address Washington had pointed out that Europe had a
"set of primary interests" which had almost no relation to us,
which would constantly involve her nations in controversies with
one another, "essentially foreign to our concerns." He had
pointed out that if we could remain united and peaceful, the
time was not distant—he said elsewhere twenty years—when
we could force the world to respect our neutral rights. We
were to remain out of war for almost the twenty years, thanks
to Adams and Jefferson, but European nations neither in that
period nor since have observed neutral rights, and a century
later, powerful as we had become, we were to be drawn into
the fatal maelstrom of the World War because of that fact.

Jefferson's idea was much the same as Washington's, that
we should have commercial relations with other nations but as

little political connection as possible. Neither realized how commercial relations inevitably bring political ones in their train. Had the United States then, or at any time, been entirely self-sufficient, self-consuming, so to say, and self-sustaining, so that we had no commerce with others, we might have remained untouched by European conflicts unless actually invaded, but that has always been impossible. This was, however, the ideal of Jefferson, derived perhaps from the example of his own estate which was remarkably balanced in the production and consumption of everything produced or needed. Even that was not wholly so, however, and Jefferson sold surplus crops and bought wines and books and other things in Europe.

America had, in fact, a very considerable commerce, chiefly with Great Britain, but also with the French possessions and elsewhere, and as a neutral whose rights were trampled upon we could not remain untouched by the Napoleonic wars, little as we were interested in the direct objects of the belligerents. In fact, apart from our commerce, it had been due to the war that we had been able to acquire Louisiana, which showed how closely our destiny was involved with European ambitions and conflicts.

If, on the one hand, our commerce was largest with Great Britain, on the other we had a special grievance against her in her insistence on stopping our vessels and impressing seamen from them. Except by the United States, the right of expatriation was at that time nowhere recognized, as it is only partially today by many nations. If born a citizen of France or the British Empire, emigration, even naturalization elsewhere, did not relieve the individual from military and other duties demanded from him by the land of his birth. Those nations and others thus claimed the right to seize what they considered their own citizens where found, and to impress them for duty. The matter was not important as between us and France. Few Frenchmen settled in America, and in any case, from difference in language and type, could easily be recognized. Not only, however, did many come here from various parts of the British Empire but there was so much fraud in giving them naturalization papers in America, and the difficulty of distinguishing between a native-born Englishman or Irishman in America and an immigrant, that many genuine Americans were seized by the British naval authorities.

Moreover, in the course of the war, Britain changed the rules of the game for neutrals. Naturally the war, as later the World War, gave a great impetus to our carrying trade. Much additional capital, especially in the shipping section of New England, was invested in it, for although the danger of capture was great the possible profits were also correspondingly so. In 1800, Sir William Scott, afterward Lord Stowell, judge of the British High Court of Admiralty, had decided (in the case of the *Polly*), that if an American ship took on a cargo in the French colonies, landed it in America, paid duty, and then took it on again for France, the voyage was broken and the trade legal. A large business had been done under this ruling, though the American duty was remitted on re-export. In 1805, in the case of the captured *Essex*, Scott reversed his previous ruling and declared such cargoes liable to capture by the British.

In 1806 Napoleon issued his "Berlin Decree" declaring the British Isles blockaded, and prohibiting any neutral from trading with them under penalty of having ship and cargo seized as lawful prize of war. From then on, Napoleon's decrees as issued were answered by equally impossible "Orders in Council" by Britain, until scarcely a shadow of legal right was left to neutrals if decrees and orders were valid. Both nations preyed on our commerce, each with the idea of injuring the other and also of the prize money which captures brought to officers and crews. Apparently between 1803 and 1814 the British captured 917 American vessels, and the French 558.

By 1806 the situation was becoming intolerable. Jefferson had the options of tamely submitting, of going to war, or, diplomacy having now failed, of finding some substitute for war which would restore our rights without armed hostilities. There was so little to choose between the insults of the two European powers that, to be logical, we would have had to go to war with both, as in Adams's day.

The great interest of Jefferson's attempted solution is that he chose economic pressure as his weapon (so much in favor today in some quarters as an alternative to war), and that his experiment with it is the only one which has ever been tried on a grand scale.

Americans of that day were quite familiar with the theory, for in the various Non-importation and other trade agreements between Americans before the Revolution the weapon had had, for a while at least, a fair degree of success. The extent of America's trade is indicated by the fact that for the year ending October 1, 1806, our exports (including re-exports) amounted to the then unprecedented figure of $101,-000,000 and our imports, the majority of which came from Britain, to about $15,000,000. As compared with 1774, our economic weapon thus seemed to have become powerful indeed. In the spring of 1806 Congress considered it sufficiently so to employ it by passing a Non-importation Act against British manufactures, which the President suspended temporarily in the hope that Monroe, our Minister to England, might gain concessions.

He was unable to do so, however, and in June of the following year England proceeded to a further outrage which even she had to apologize for. The American ship of war *Chesapeake* sailed from Hampton Roads, not quite ready for sea, due to delays in fitting her out. Some miles off the coast she was ordered to stop by the British ship *Leopard*, whose captain demanded the right to search her for British subjects. British commanders had stopped American merchant vessels but this was the first time they had dared to stop one belonging to the American navy. On the refusal of the American commander to allow his ship to be searched, the British opened fire on her, killing or wounding twenty of our men. In view of the unprepared condition of the *Chesapeake*, she was unable to fight and had to surrender and yield to search. Three sailors, two Americans and one British deserter, though his presence had been unknown to the commander, Barron, were taken off.

A howl of rage went up from America, and Jefferson by a word could have had war against England. He held the situation, however, in spite of being accused of pusillanimity. He issued a proclamation forbidding British war vessels to enter American waters, and prohibiting all intercourse with them. England backed down to the extent of returning the Americans seized, but refused other adjustment of difficulties. In December, 1807, Jefferson tried his own experiment, securing the passage by Congress of a Bill prohibiting the export of any produce whatever from an American port or the clearing of any American vessel for a foreign port. This Embargo Act was supplemented by two others early in the following year.

The result was interesting. Within a year the exports from New England dropped 75 per cent, those from the Middle States 78 per cent, and those from the South 85 per cent. From various causes the effect on British commerce and merchants was much less than anticipated, but the effect on America was severe. Prices of farm products declined on an average over 50 per cent. Ship building fell off by two-thirds in a year. In order to enforce the laws, the number of public officials greatly increased, as did also the interference with the private life and liberties of citizens. Clandestine shipments partly nullified the effects of the policy. Shipping merchants faced bankruptcy. New England, the center of the shipping trade, openly threatened resistance to the law by force of arms, and even secession from the Union. Ships had to patrol the coasts, and soldiers were placed on the Canadian frontier. "This embargo law is certainly the most embarrassing one we have ever had to execute," Jefferson wrote to his Secretary of the Treasury. "I did not expect a crop of so sudden & rank growth of fraud & open opposition by force could have grown up in the U. S. I am satisfied with you that if orders & decrees are not repealed, and a continuance of the embargo is preferred to war (which sentiment is universal here), Congress must legalize all *means* which may be necessary to obtain it's end." [10]

A few days earlier he had written to Meriwether Lewis that "our foreign affairs do not seem to clear up at all. Should they continue as at present, the moment will come when it will be a question for the Legislature whether war will not be preferable to a longer continuance of the embargo." [11] To John Langdon, who had declined the post of Secretary of the Navy and was then governor of New Hampshire, the President wrote, thanking him for his efforts to enforce the law, saying that "I have been highly gratified with the late general expressions of public sentiment in favor of a measure which alone could have saved us from immediate war, & give time to call home 80 millions of property, 20 or 30,000 seamen, & 2000 vessels. These are now nearly at home, & furnish a great capital, much of which will go into manufactures and seamen to man a fleet of privateers, whenever our citizens shall prefer war to a longer continuance of the embargo. Perhaps however the whale of the ocean may be tired of the solitude it has made on that element, and return to honest principles; and his brother robber on the land may see that, as to us, the grapes are sour. I think one war enough for the life of one man: and you and I have gone through one which at least may lessen our

[10] *Writings*, Ford, Vol. IX, p. 202, Aug. 11, 1808.
[11] *Ibid.*, p. 200.

impatience to embark in another. Still, if it becomes necessary we must meet it like men, old men indeed, but yet good for something." [12]

These are not the words of a theorist either as to statesmanship, economics or pacifism. Based on Revolutionary experiment, theory, and, at first the will of Congress, Jefferson had hoped to find a substitute for war in economic pressure, but he had an open mind as to its possible success. At last he had to acknowledge its failure. The pressure on the enemy was not great enough to bring results in a nation mad with war. On the other hand, the pressure on our own citizens was too great to allow of continued patriotism, morality, and obedience to law. Indeed, it threatened rebellion and a break-up of the Union. In spite of theory, it is doubtful if any more reliance could be placed on the same weapon today. Unless other exceptional conditions existed, Jefferson's experiment with economic pressure would seem to prove it less a double-edged sword than a boomerang, which would return to disrupt the nation which used it rather than hit the nation aimed at. It was not, however, a complete failure, though it created such intense feeling against Jefferson as to make the end of his second term as President almost as unhappy as that of second term as governor. March 1, 1809, he signed a Bill passed by Congress, repealing the Embargo completely, and substituting in its stead an Act merely prohibiting trade with Great Britain and France until one or the other should suspend or repeal its respective Decrees or Orders in Council. Nevertheless, the Embargo had been worth trying, though its lesson seems now to have been lost; and it did keep us out of war without loss of prestige until 1812, thus avoiding nearly six years of waste of blood and treasure. The conditions of the war held out no hope to us of gain of any sort by fighting at once the two great contestants or siding with one against the

[12] *Ibid.*, p. 201.

other when both were equally the legitimate objects of our attack.

Meanwhile, we had strengthened ourselves for the rather futile War of 1812, and in spite of the interruption to commerce by the Embargo, Jefferson had carried out his pledge of an economical government. Between 1792 and 1800 the Federalists had increased the national debt by over $8,000,000 in spite of Hamilton's supposed great abilities as Secretary of the Treasury and later financial adviser. The Jeffersonian Republicans, between 1800 and 1810, reduced it $27,500,000, or counting in the $15,000,000 paid for the Louisiana Territory, by $42,500,000. There had been no moral question involved in the European struggle. Napoleon was a tyrant who wished to subdue the world to his own will. Britain was a nation of comparative freedom, but such freedom as she had was for herself alone—we might almost say for certain classes in herself alone. As far as neutrals in the rest of the world, or her claims to the high seas, were concerned, she was as ruthless as Napoleon himself. For the rest, we received redress through diplomatic channels for the outrageous *Leopard-Chesapeake* incident, and we could have gained no more by going to war then in a fit of mass anger than we did by the course Jefferson took. Moreover, the world learned, or had a chance to do so, that economic pressure is not a substitute for war, though it might prove a useful weapon to stave off our being dragged into a conflict if it did not last too long.

CHAPTER XIV

THE END OF AN ERA

IT was with an unfeigned sense of relief that Jefferson turned at last from Washington to settle for good at Monticello. There he arrived March 17, 1809, after seeing his loved friend and trusted associate Madison inaugurated as President. For the next sixteen years, or almost till the last of Jefferson's life, the White House was to be occupied first by Madison and then by Monroe, and so Jefferson was always in close and friendly touch with the four administrations succeeding his own two. His advice was frequently asked, both as a friend and as an experienced statesman, but not as leader of the party. Jefferson made no effort, as Hamilton had, to retain that position, and his replies were always marked by distinguished tact. There was friendly exchange of opinions between the ex-President and his two successors, but no effort on his part to dictate policies, and he studiously avoided criticism of them, even when Madison allowed the city of Washington to be burned by the British.

Jefferson's days up to his death were occupied for almost every moment with his business affairs, his innumerable avocations, an immense correspondence, and constant entertaining of noted strangers, as well as friends, who came from all parts of the world to see the "sage of Monticello." Besides that estate with its 5000 acres he had acquired also "Poplar Forest," about seventy miles away, which he frequently visited although the house now there was not built until several years after he left the Presidency. On the two estates were over 200 slaves, and in addition to the purely agricultural operations there were mills to be run and all the various forms of work to be arranged and overseen which enabled this community of two hundred and odd souls to be almost self-sustaining. The planning, the dovetailing into one another of all the parts, and the superintending of this complex little hive of industry was a heavy task calling for knowledge, ability, and much hard work. All this Jefferson now largely took on his own shoulders instead of leaving it, as he perforce had had to in the past, to overseers who, to say the least, had done their work none too well. There is an old Spanish saying that "the eye of the master fattens the horse," and for twenty-five years, since Jefferson had sailed for France as Minister in 1784, his continuous public life had required him to trust largely to employees to manage his plantations. The years had also been peculiarly difficult, and Virginian agriculture from various causes, not the least having been depreciated currencies, had never recovered the position it had held before the Revolution. Lucky indeed was even the richest Virginian who did not find his lands burdened with debt.

Jefferson set himself valiantly to the task. Even in midwinter, January, 1811, he wrote that from breakfast to noon or sometimes to dinner, he was "mostly on horseback, attending to my farm or other concerns." The few hours he could pass in his study were consumed by correspondence with strangers, with little time for personal letters.

The depreciating of currencies has become such a popular form of trying to raise one's self by one's own boot-straps in our own day that we may here discuss Jefferson's sufferings from earlier experiments and his views on money and debt. The landed property which came to him with his wife was valued at $40,000 but was burdened with a debt to British merchants of $13,000. Jefferson, who had a horror of debt, either personal or public, sold land to raise the $13,000 and to clear the rest of his property of such an incumbrance.

Then came the Revolution, and it was impossible to transmit the money. The Virginia Legislature passed a resolution stating that any one owing British merchants might deposit the money in the State Treasury and be protected. As is invariably the case in war, few people realized at its beginning the length of time it might last or its devastating effects. The Revolution was no exception, and at its beginning most people did not believe, or wish, that it would result in separation from Britain.

Jefferson was anxious to get his debt paid and off his mind. He deposited the money in the Treasury. Later the Legislature rescinded the resolution, and the deposits were returned to those who had made them *but* in Treasury certificates which had depreciated so greatly that Jefferson was just able to buy an overcoat with what had been his $13,000. He again sold property to clear the debt but got paper money which again depreciated as fast as the certificates. When the war was over he wrote his British creditors that he was desirous of settling the debt. Certain laws had been passed behind which he might have taken refuge but he wrote that "what the laws of Virginia are, or may be, will in no wise influence my conduct. Substantial justice is my object." Thus he virtually paid the same debt three times. No wonder he rose in wrath whenever Hamilton or others accused him of not wishing to honor obligations.

Unlike Marshall, Jefferson had derived no financial benefit from the high public offices he had held, and few if any then did so in such positions. Even frugal John Adams, accustomed to the simplicities of a small Massachusetts farm, found it impossible to make both ends meet on official salaries. Jefferson had not been extravagant or ostentatious but as Minister, Secretary of State, Vice-President and President, the dignity of the nation required a decent scale of living and demanded a certain amount of entertaining. The two terms as

President cost him nearly $8000 above the salary. When he retired to Monticello, with his hands as clean, he said, as they were empty, he was deeply troubled about his affairs.

He was now nominally a private person, with no salary, yet he was in fact still public, and the public swarmed to Monticello to see him. People of all sorts fairly pushed their way into his house to catch a glimpse of him, as well as the distinguished visitors who came to claim his hospitality. A granddaughter wrote of Monticello during these years, and of the drain on Jefferson's time and resources caused by visitors: "they came of all nations, at all times, and paid longer or shorter visits. I have known a New England judge bring a letter of introduction to my grandfather and stay three weeks. The learned Abbé Correa, always a welcome guest, passed weeks of each year with us during the whole time of his stay in the country. We had persons from abroad, from all the States of the Union, from every part of the State—men, women and children. . . . People of wealth and fashion, men in office, professional men, military and civil, lawyers, doctors, Protestant clergymen, Catholic priests, members of Congress, foreign ministers, missionaries, Indian agents, tourists, travellers, artists, strangers, friends. Some came from affection and respect, some from curiosity, some to give or receive advice or instruction," and others from every possible motive. His daughter, Mrs. Randolph, when asked the largest number of unexpected guests she had been called upon to house overnight, answered "fifty." [1]

Any one who is known to the public falls a victim to its unthinking demands, but the position of Jefferson was peculiar. After Washington's death, he was the one American whom all other Americans and foreigners most wished to see. There was no decent inn in the neighborhood, which was also remote from

[1] Most of these details are taken from Chapter XXI, Randolph, *Domestic Life of Jefferson*.

any fair-sized town. Virginia had had no "tourist travel" and it had always been customary if a stranger of decent standing appeared in a neighborhood that he should be welcomed in some private house. But on no other house had they ever descended in such locust swarms. They literally ate Jefferson out of house and home, burdened as he was with financial difficulties due to the depressed state of farming and to the fluctuations in the currency.

Books had always been his chief delight. At his remote Poplar Forest, where he fled now and then to oversee the plantation and to escape from visitors, he had a little library which he had had made for convenience when staying in Washington. There were a hundred books or so (in the smallest obtainable editions, for ease in travel) of prose and poetry in English, French, Italian, Greek, and Latin. He always had to have books at hand.

The chief joy of his life, however, was perhaps his library at Monticello, which he had been collecting since a boy. It had cost him near $50,000, and was the finest in America. When the British wantonly burned the city of Washington in 1814, of which the English historian Green wrote that "few more shameful acts are recorded in" British history, the capitol was among the public buildings destroyed, and with it the small library gathered in it for the use of Congress. Jefferson, because of the nation's need and his own pressing ones, decided to offer his library for sale to the government. After much haggling and opposition on the part of some of the Congressmen, the government offered Jefferson $23,950, less than half of its value, even the odd $50 short of a round price being almost an insult. Jefferson accepted, and only a book-lover can realize the depth of painful emotion with which the old man had to see his loved books packed and carted off to the capitol of an ungrateful nation.

We may pass over the remainder of this painful aspect of

Jefferson's last years quickly. In 1816 he turned over the management of his affairs to his devoted grandson, Thomas Jefferson Randolph, who did all he could to save the estate, at least for Jefferson's life. A crushing blow came with the bankruptcy of an old friend, some of whose notes Jefferson had long before endorsed. The panic of 1819 swept the country. In the last year of his life he asked permission of the state legislature to sell a part of his estates by means of a lottery, a method which had occasionally been employed before and which might save the remainder to him. At first the request was refused. The necessity for it had caused Jefferson deep mortification and the refusal by the legislature was, from every aspect, a great blow to the old patriot now eighty-three years of age. However, his reply, when the news was broken to him by a friend, was dignified and showed no bitterness over the ingratitude of his own state. "I had hoped," he wrote, that "the length and character of my services might have prevented the fear in the legislature of the indulgence asked being quoted as a precedent in future cases. But I find no fault with their strict adherence to a rule generally useful, although relaxable in some cases, under their discretion, of which they are proper judges."

The legislature finally changed its vote, but it was too late. His troubles having become known to the public, the mayor of New York quickly raised $8500 by popular subscription and sent it to him. Philadelphia sent $5000, Baltimore $3000. To its shame, Virginia gave nothing. But even these sums were insufficient, and after his death, there was still $40,000 debt on the estates, which his grandson eventually paid off, but without being able to save Monticello to the family. Although Jefferson's last months were thus filled with agony over his position, he fortunately died without knowing that his beloved home, created wholly by himself, was to pass into the hands of strangers. Such was the gratitude of the strong young democracy of which he had been the leader, in which he had so firmly believed, and which he had served for over fifty years at the expense of his personal happiness and fortune.

We may now turn back to consider Jefferson's views on debts and money as contrasted with Hamilton's. In a debt-ridden world, cursed by over-expanded credits and fluctuating currencies, they may appear to many, as they are, sounder than those of the great Secretary of the Treasury.

War with England had at last come in 1812, and the financing of it caused Jefferson special concern. In the summer of 1813, writing to his son-in-law, J. W. Eppes, then again a member of Congress, Jefferson pointed out that "It is a wise rule and should be fundamental in a government disposed to cherish its credit, and at the same time to restrain the use of it within the limits of its faculties, 'never to borrow a dollar without laying a tax in the same instant for paying the interest annually, and the principal within a given term; and to consider that tax as pledged to the creditors on the public faith.' On such a pledge as this, sacredly observed, a government may always command, on a *reasonable interest*, all the lendable money of their citizens, while the necessity of an equivalent tax is a salutary warning to them, and their constituents against oppression, bankruptcy, and its inevitable consequence, revolution."

The term of the loan, he believed, should be of reasonable length, and he then developed a favorite theory that it should not be for more than a generation. "The earth belongs to the living, not to the dead. . . . Each generation has the usufruct of the earth during the period of its continuance." Suppose, he asks, one generation be "bound to acknowledge the debt, to consider the preceding generation as having had a right to eat up the whole soil of their country, in the course of a life, to alienate them from it (for it would be an alienation to creditors), and would they think themselves either le-

gally or morally bound to give up their country and emigrate
to another for subsistence? A limit to the length of time for
which debts could be contracted would also, he wrote, "be a
salutary curb on the spirit of war and indebtment, which, since
the modern theory of the perpetuation of debt, has drenched
the earth with blood, and crushed its inhabitants under burthens ever accumulating. . . . In seeking, then, for an ultimate term for the redemption of our debts, let us rally to this
principle, and provide for their payment within nineteen years
at least. Our government has not, as yet, begun to act on the
rules of loans and taxation going hand in hand. . . . I hope
yourself and your committee will render the immortal service
of introducing this practice. Not that it is expected that Congress should formally declare such a principle. They wisely
avoid deciding on abstract questions. But they may be induced to keep themselves within its limits."

Again, he wrote, "we cannot believe, or act as if we believed,
that although an individual father cannot alienate the labor
of his son, the aggregate body of fathers may alienate the
labor of all their sons, of their posterity, in the aggregate, and
oblige them to pay for all the enterprises, just or unjust,
profitable or ruinous, into which our vices, our passions, or
our personal interests may lead us." [2]

In a long and illuminating letter to Samuel Kercheval in
1816, Jefferson extended the same theory to the Constitution.
After remarking that "the true foundation of republican government is the equal right of every citizen, in his person and
property, and in their management," and that "private fortunes are destroyed by public as well as by private extravagance," he continued. "Some men look at constitutions with
sanctimonious reverence, and deem them like the ark of the
covenant, too sacred to be touched. They ascribe to the men

[2] All the quotations are from three letters from Jefferson to Eppes, June 24,
Sept. 11, and Nov. 6, 1813, in *Writings,* Ford, Vol. IX, pp. 388–419.

of the preceding age a wisdom more than human, and suppose what they did to be beyond amendment. I knew that age well; I belonged to it, and labored with it. It deserved well of its country. It was very like the present, but without the experience of the present; and forty years of experience in government is worth a century of book-reading; and this they would themselves say, were they to rise from the dead. I am certainly not an advocate for frequent and untried changes of laws and constitutions. I think moderate imperfections had better be borne with; because, when once known, we accommodate ourselves to them, and find practical means of correcting their evils. But I know also, that laws and institutions must go hand in hand with the progress of the human mind. . . . We might as well require a man to wear still the coat which fitted him when a boy, as civilized society to remain ever under the regimen of their barbarous ancestors. It is this preposterous idea which has recently deluged Europe in blood. Their monarchs, instead of wisely yielding to the gradual change of circumstances . . . have clung to old abuses, entrenched themselves behind steady habits, and obliged their subjects to seek through blood and violence rash and ruinous innovations. Each generation is as independent as the one preceding, as that was of all that had gone before. It has then, like them, a right to choose for itself the form of government it believes most promotive of its happiness; consequently, to accommodate to circumstances in which it finds itself, that received from its predecessors." [3]

Indeed he urged that the Constitution might undergo revision at stated periods so as to keep it in adjustment to changing conditions, and believed that "if this avenue be shut to the call of sufferance, it will make itself heard through that of force, and we shall go on, as other nations are doing, in the endless circle of oppression, rebellion, reformation; and op-

[3] *Writings,* Ford, Vol. X, pp. 37 ff.

pression, rebellion, reformation, again; and so on forever." It is interesting to note that on the day when I copy this passage, Sir Josiah Stamp, one of the best foreign observers of the United States, writes that "so far from the United States' Constitution being fixed, and any change or new feature treated with great jealousy as something to be undertaken only under direct pressure, change ought to be recognized as in the normal course, and it should be a feature of the Constitution that provision for amendment should arise systematically or automatically and at regular intervals. The burden of political discussion would then be, not whether such and such a matter should be dealt with by an amendment to the Constitution, but what matters are proper to insert in the regular constitutional amendment of a particular forthcoming year." [4] There would be difficulties about this, difficulties which Jefferson himself recognized, but there is no doubt that the flexibility which he urged will be more and more necessary as conditions of life alter with increasing swiftness. On the other hand, as he pointed out, changes should not be made lightly or frequently nor, above all, illegally merely by an official, a branch of government or a party in power for the moment.

Jefferson was equally concerned about the huge emissions of paper money and the extension of credit by the state banks. "It is from Great Britain," he says, "we copy the idea of giving paper in exchange for discounted bills, [but] the unlimited emission of bank paper has banished all her specie, and is now, by a depreciation acknowledged by her own statesmen, carrying her rapidly to bankruptcy, as it did France, as it did us, and will do us again, and every country permitting paper to be circulated, other than that by public authority, rigorously limited to the just measure for circulation. Private fortunes, in the present state of our circulation, are at the mercy of those self-created money lenders, and are pros-

[4] *London Times*, July 5, 1935.

trated by the floods of nominal money with which their avarice deluges us. He who lent his money to the public or to an individual, before the institution of the United States Bank, twenty years ago, when wheat was well sold at a dollar the bushel, and receives now his nominal sum when it sells at two dollars, is cheated of half his fortune; and by whom? By the banks, which, since that, have thrown into circulation ten dollars of their nominal money where was one at that time."

He then discusses the quantity theory of money, and the disadvantages of paper money as not based on metallic coin. Prices, he points out, bear a relation to the amount of money in circulation. Paper money can easily be issued by banks or the government, and as the amount rapidly rises so will prices, and so will creditors be defrauded and foreign trade hampered. Had he himself not, as he often said when he passed it, sold a farm for $13,000 to pay a debt, and then because of the effect of the paper money, received back just enough to buy an overcoat?

Even if one claimed that within a country a rise in prices due to a depreciated medium of exchange might work no harm, which is not so, yet "where a nation is in a full course of interchange of wants and supplies with all others, the proportion of its medium to its produce is no longer indifferent. To trade on equal terms, the common measure of values should be as nearly as possible on a par with that of its corresponding nations, whose medium is in a sound state. . . . Now, one of the advantages of specie as a medium is, that being of universal value, it will keep itself at a general level, flowing out from where it is too high into parts where it is lower. Whereas, if the medium be of local value only, as paper money, if too little, indeed, gold and silver will flow in to supply the deficiency; but if too much, it accumulates, banishes the gold and silver not locked up in vaults and hoards, and depreciates itself."

Anticipating by a half century the criticism by Professor

Sumner, already quoted, of Hamilton's belief that banks created "capital," Jefferson denied it, and speaking of the demand of the banks to issue $90,000,000 more of notes at the moment, he quoted Adam Smith on the demands of the Scotch bankers to the banks which were already over-extended. It is as fresh and applicable today as when it was written. "Those traders and other undertakers having got so much assistance from banks, wished to get still more. The banks, they seem to have thought, could extend their credits to whatever sum might be wanted, without incurring any other expense besides a few reams of paper. They complained of the contracted views and dastardly spirit of the directors of those banks, which did not, they said, extend credits in proportion to the extension of the trade of the country, meaning, no doubt, by the extension of that trade, the extension of their own projects beyond what they could carry on, either *with their own capital*, or with what they had credit to borrow of private people in the usual way of bond or mortgage. The banks, they seem to have thought, were in honor bound to supply the deficiency, and to provide them with all the capital they wanted to trade with. . . . It was the duty of the banks, they seemed to think, to lend for as long a time, and to as great an extent, as they might wish to borrow."

It is impossible to quote all the important passages or even note all the economic topics discussed, but Jefferson has been considered by so many to have been a rather impractical theorist that these letters are of importance in proving the extremely firm grasp he had on sound economic principles. He was over-subtle in his analysis of what constituted a "generation," but his theory that in general one generation should not bind another and that a debt when created should carry with it the means of gradual liquidation is a practical as well as sound and honest one. Much of the difficulty in which the world, and especially the United States, finds itself today is

due to Hamilton's false idea as to how real "capital" is created, and the ignoring of Jefferson's beliefs as to debt and its
liquidation. No man in his senses would loan money on a suit
of clothes, the loan not to become due for fifty years, yet in
effect that is what almost all governments and corporations, to
say nothing of individuals, have been doing. Unless the whole
world could agree, which it could not, not to borrow beyond
certain limits in war, each nation must fail in sound finance,
but that surely does not apply to peace times and to debts
created for domestic purposes. Yet railroads, public utility,
and other concerns put out bonds not due for a century or
more. One of the leading corporations has even made its debt
perpetual! Towns and cities borrow money not payable for
fifty years or more to build roads and other things that may
not last ten years. A generation, such as the extravagant one
of the 1920's, is thus led into all sorts of personal and public
heedlessness by buying or building whatever may take its
fancy, paying only the interest and leaving their children to
pay the principal, or to default on it. In time, taxes no longer
go for the orderly running of governments and the needs of
the present, or earnings for a return upon the capital invested,
but to pay the interest on the huge piles of debt created for
long periods and without due provision for redemption. If it
were not for these intolerable burdens of debt, there would be
less extravagance in flush times, taxes would be much smaller,
returns on investments safer, and a period of lessened production and consumption would lose much of its terror. Receiver-
ships or bankruptcies rarely occur in the case of governments,
municipalities, or corporations which have none or only a limited amount of outstanding debts. It has been our failure to
follow, in some reasonable degree, Jefferson's theory of financing that has led, about once each generation, to a general
bankruptcy and repudiation, with untold suffering to investors and the rest of the people. Debts have been repudiated

or forcibly reduced, and then the game has started all over again. Yet it has been reserved for the present Democratic Party in power to have advanced the theory that when a railroad or other corporation got into trouble because of too great a load of debt and fixed charges, the way to extricate it was to make it borrow more!

The Napoleonic wars had nearly wrecked the civilization of Europe. Napoleon himself was in exile, but the Bourbons were back in France, and as Jefferson surveyed the scene he knew so well, he could see no prospect of lasting European peace or of a liberalizing of ideas which might bring the outlooks of the Old and New Worlds into more harmonious and peaceful relation to one another. Of England, in the years immediately following 1815, Green wrote in words singularly applicable to today, "the pressure of the heavy taxation and of the debt, which now reached £800,000,000, was embittered by the general distress of the country. The rapid development of English industry for a time ran ahead of the world's demands; the markets home and abroad were glutted with unsaleable goods, and mills and manufactories were brought to a standstill. The scarcity caused by a series of bad harvests was intensified by the selfish legislation of the landowners in Parliament. Conscious that the prosperity of English agriculture was merely factitious, and rested on the high price of corn [meaning grain] produced by the war, they prohibited . . . the introduction of foreign corn till wheat had reached famine prices. Society, too, was disturbed by the great changes of employment consequent on a sudden return to peace after twenty years of war, and by the disbanding of the immense forces employed at sea and on land. The movement against machinery which had been put down in 1812 revived in formidable riots, and the distress of the rural poor brought about a rapid increase in crime." [5]

[5] J. R. Green, *Short History of the English People,* New York, 1896, p. 837.

Both the current situation and the prospects in Europe increased the traditional American desire to keep ourselves as remote as possible from it all. The fact that after nearly twenty years of trying to keep ourselves free of European broils we had at last been sucked in in 1812, indicated that in the case of a general war between our commercial customers we could not remain permanently isolated and neutral. The fact deepened the desire, one of the strongest and most lasting in the American, to have as little to do with the Old World as possible. By taking part in European affairs, we could do nothing to maintain peace, and would only multiply the chances of our being embroiled every time the age-long hatreds among European peoples or the ambition of a ruler or a nation brought on war. When we signed the Treaty of Ghent in December, 1815, we turned, with an immense sigh of relief, to the development of our own country. To subdue to man's use one of the greatest and richest continents in the world was a huge and congenial task. It was in a way a simple one, because so largely physical and practical. For that reason the minds of almost all, high and low, educated or untutored, could be canalized into one stream of effort, that of making America a place to live in. As we worked westward across our own lands, Europe, far across the sea to the east, became more and more remote from our thoughts and desires. The end of the second war with Great Britain marked the beginning of a more intense Americanism than ever.

The next few years saw successive revolts of the South American colonies from Spain and Portugal. Jefferson, although watching their struggles for liberty with interest and sympathy, had, unlike the later Wilson, no thought of interfering with the internal affairs of any other people, and saw, besides, the possibility of our entangling ourselves again with Europe if we took the side of the revolted provinces. His constant desire to remain aloof from Europe, unhampered in carrying on our own experiment in government, steadily increased. Throughout Monroe's second term that President was in frequent correspondence and even consultation with Jefferson as to the policy to be pursued toward both South America and Europe.

Jefferson never swerved from his belief as to the latter, and as a sample of many letters we may quote from one of June 11, 1823. After mentioning that he finds "Horace and Tacitus so much better writers than the champions of the gazettes," and can offer to the President only commonplace ideas on political questions, he repeated what he had already so often written and said. "I have ever deemed it," he wrote, "fundamental for the United States, never to take active part in the quarrels of Europe. Their political interests are entirely distinct from ours. Their mutual jealousies, their balance of power, their complicated alliances, their forms and principles of government, are all foreign to us. They are nations of eternal war. All their energies are expended in the destruction of the labor, property, and lives of their people. On our part, never had a people so favorable a chance of trying the opposite system, of peace and fraternity with mankind, and the direction of all our means and faculties to the purposes of improvement instead of destruction. With Europe we have few occasions of collision, and these, with a little prudence and forbearance, may be generally accommodated. Of the brethren of our own hemisphere, none are yet, or for an age to come will be, in a shape, condition, or disposition to war against us. And the foothold which the nations of Europe had in either America, is slipping from under them, so that we shall soon be rid of their neighborhood." [6] In the policy to be announced some months later, known ever since as the "Monroe Doctrine," Jefferson had his part, and approved of the pronouncement. Largely framed by John Quincy Adams, then Secre-

6 *Writings,* Ford, Vol. X, p. 257.

tary of State, it did in fact merely embody to a great extent the sentiments of most American statesmen from Washington down, and the feelings of all plain Americans that we wanted to keep out of Europe and have Europe keep out of the two Americas.

Two of the most engaging traits in Jefferson were the wide range of his interests, and the flexibility of his mind. As to the latter we may again note that, unlike, on the one hand, Hamilton and the other "Anglo-men" who wished to engraft the British form of government onto America, and, on the other those who believed that the American form should be suitable for all peoples, he kept reiterating to the end that a people and its institutions must fit each other, and that not only is no one form of government good everywhere but neither is it so at all times. It must alter to suit the changing needs of those for whom alone it was and is designed. In considering his mind we may also note that he held, so to say, two grades of ideas in his political theory. The distinction was much that which he made between a Bill of Rights, embodying those rights which no constitution could ever be allowed to infringe, and the more pragmatic rules which found their place in the Constitution, and which might be altered to suit conditions. Jefferson remained throughout his entire life an ardent and consistent liberal. No experience and no personal provocation however severe, ever shook for a moment his insistence upon the value and necessity of education, of freedom of press and speech, and such other general ideas as formed his liberal attitude.

Nevertheless, there was a second order of ideas on which he was quite open to conviction either by events or argument, and some of which he gradually altered. One of these was his original belief that manufacturing should be merely the handmaid to agriculture and be kept very limited. By the end of his second term as President, he had been taught by the lesson of war that we must have more manufacturng than he had desired, though he still argued for a mere equilibrium between manufacturing, commerce, and agriculture which would enable us to import such raw materials as we could not produce, export the surplus crops we could not consume, and manufacture enough for our own needs and no more. Without imperialist tinge, his was a form of modern economic nationalism.

By 1816 he had advanced somewhat further and he explained the view then held in a letter to Benjamin Austen. Alluding to Austen's remark that he was quoted as opposed to manufactures by those merchants who wished to continue importing from England, Jefferson replied: "There was a time when I might have been so quoted with more candor, but within the thirty years which have since elapsed, how are circumstances changed! We were then in peace. Our independent place among nations was acknowledged. A commerce which offered the raw material in exchange for the same material after receiving the last touch of industry, was worthy of welcome to all nations. It was expected that those especially to whom manufacturing industry was important, would cherish the friendship of such customers. . . . This was the state of things in 1785, when the 'Notes on Virginia' were first printed; when, the ocean [was] open to all nations, and their common right in it acknowledged and exercised under regulations sanctioned by the assent and usage of all. . . . But who in 1785 could foresee the rapid depravity which was to render the close of that century the disgrace of the history of man? Who could have imagined that the two most distinguished in the rank of nations . . . would have suddenly descended from that honorable eminence, and setting at defiance all those moral laws established by the Author of nature between nation and nation, as between man and man, would cover earth and sea with robberies and piracies, merely because strong enough to do it with temporal impunity; and that under this disbandment of nations from social order, we should have been despoiled of a thousand ships. . . . We have experienced what we did not then believe, that there exists both profligacy and power enough to exclude us from the field of interchange with other nations: that to be independent for the comforts of life we must fabricate them ourselves. We must now place the manufacturer by the side of the agriculturist. . . . If it shall be proposed to go beyond our own supply, the question of '85 will recur, will our *surplus* labor be then most beneficially employed in the culture of the earth, or in the fabrications of art? We have time yet for consideration, before that question will press upon us; and the maxim to be applied will depend on the circumstances which shall then exist; for in so complicated a science as political economy, no one maxim can be laid down as wise and expedient for all times and circumstances, and for their contraries." [7]

Had we and other nations been able to follow Jefferson's theory instead of Hamilton's as to manufacturing at most what was needed only for domestic consumption, "progress" (so-called until 1929) would have been slower and population would have increased less rapidly, with us as with others. On the other hand, the turning of one nation after another into a workshop to produce goods, not for consumption but for sale, with the attendant fight for areas of raw materials and markets not only brought on the World War, but left even ourselves with ten millions of unemployed. It also ended in the commercial stalemate of each nation insisting on selling and on refusing or being unable to buy. Jefferson's "equilibrium," as explained to Madison in 1809, was in reality a dream of a planned economy which would make us as independent of the rest of the world as circumstances then permitted, maintaining a healthy citizenry and comfortable standard of living, a

[7] *Writings,* Ford, Vol. X, pp. 9 ff.

dream which almost every nation is dreaming today—after the nightmare of world competition and world slaughter.

The closing years of Jefferson's life were to witness what he himself considered one of his three greatest achievements, the founding of the University of Virginia. We have constantly noted his intense interest in education, and the part he expected it to play in our experiment of a self-governing democracy. To a large extent his had been a voice in the wilderness, and practically nothing had been done since his masterly report in 1779. In 1800 he had tried to take advantage of an apparent opportunity to reorganize William and Mary College but had been balked, chiefly by the opposition of the clergy. His interest never waned, although during his eight years as President of the nation he had had no time for any such project as the establishment of an institution of higher learning, independent of any church control or influence, such as he had always intended to be the capstone of his state system of education and citizenship. In 1814 he became a trustee of the as yet unorganized "Albemarle Academy," and saw an opportunity which this time was real. On September 7 he wrote a letter to Peter Carr in which he spoke of the proposed institution as an "academy or college." He had for long hoped, he said, that the state would take up the subject of education, and provide an establishment "where every branch of science, deemed useful at this day, should be taught in its highest degree." There was at that time no one else, possibly in the entire world, who was so capable of laying the broad foundations of such an institution as was Thomas Jefferson. His breadth of mind and interests, his intellectual tolerance, his reading and knowledge were unequalled by any other then living American. John Adams came, perhaps, second, but wide as was also his incessant reading, his range of interest was narrower. His special fields were law and government, and he cared little for either the arts or the beginnings then being made of modern science. Jefferson could

match him in both the first two fields and in addition was an
American pioneer in such branches of science as ethnology,
geography, botany, paleontology, and others. He was an architect and musician. He had a small but good collection of
paintings and sculpture. In a day before the modern specialist
had arrived, "to know more and more about less and less," Jefferson had an adequate knowledge, for his time, of an amazing
number of subjects.

He had also made a special study of universities abroad on
which he had made notes. To these he now turned, and, with
his usual insistence on fitting institutions to people and not
the reverse, he continued in his letter to Carr, saying that no
one European university should be used exclusively as a model
but that it is "for us to select from their different institutions
the materials which are good for us, and, with them to erect
a structure, whose arrangement shall correspond with our own
social condition." [8] He then went on to lay out the entire
plan of organization and study. We need not enter upon the
full history of the opposition and difficulties encountered and
surmounted until "Central College," as the Academy had become, was in turn incorporated as the University of Virginia
in 1819. Although naturally he had help from the trustees
and other friends of the project, never was an institution more
the result of one man's effort in all aspects of its founding.
Jefferson not only pushed the legislative, legal, and other business matters, but arranged for faculty appointments, sending
to England to get the best professors there available; planned
the courses of study; and was the architect of the buildings,
erected around one of the most perfect campuses possessed by
any American university. He was already seventy-seven when
the university received its charter, and when he died at eighty-
three all the buildings were completed except the Rotunda
which he had designed from the Pantheon in Rome. The un-

[8] *Memorial Edition*, Vol. XIX, pp. 211 ff.

dertaking would have been an amazing feat for any man even in the prime of life. Jefferson became the first head of the institution, which had been in operation for a year before his death.

One of the pleasures of his old age, and one of the romantic incidents in our history, was the reconciliation between him and John Adams and the complete renewal of their early friendship. We have already noted Jefferson's affection and loyalty. Most of his friendships were both deep and lifelong. Adams also, in spite of his egoism, vanity, and peppery temper, was a good friend. Although touchy over little things and suspicious of the motives of others, his mind was never small. He had long felt both respect and affection for Jefferson when politics intervened to spoil the relationship.

At the beginning of his presidency, Jefferson unwittingly did an act which the Adamses, more particularly Mrs. Adams, considered one of petty persecution. Their son, John Quincy Adams, was one of the Commissioners in Bankruptcy in Massachusetts. When the law was altered in 1801 and new appointments were to be made, Jefferson appointed another in place of young Adams, without even knowing that the latter had held the post until Mrs. Adams wrote three years later, at the time of the death of Jefferson's daughter. The formal and cold note at least opened the way for explanations, and when Mrs. Adams complained of Jefferson's removal of her son, he told her, on his honor, that he had made the new appointments without enquiring as to who had held the offices before.

There was, however, no reconciliation until Doctor Rush, a mutual friend of both men, undertook to bring it about. He wrote to Jefferson in 1811 suggesting that the old friendship might be renewed, and Jefferson replied in a long letter, explaining all that had led up to the gradual separation but adding that although he would be happy to renew the friendship he feared Adams might not easily drop his suspicions. At the end of the year, however, he again wrote to Rush, saying that he had found by report of two of his friends who had been North and seen Adams, that the old man did not entertain for him the "jaundiced sentiments" of Mrs. Adams, and that he had remarked, "I always loved Jefferson, and still love him." "This," Jefferson added, "is enough for me. I only needed this knowledge to revive towards him all the affections of the most cordial moment of our lives. Changing a single word only in Dr. Franklin's character of him, I knew him to be always an honest man, often a great one, but sometimes incorrect and precipitate in his judgments; and it is known to those who have heard me speak of Mr. Adams, that I have ever done him justice myself, and defended him when assailed by others, with the single exception as to political opinions. . . . I wish, therefore, but for an apposite occasion to express to Mr. Adams my unchanged affections for him." [9]

He explained that there was awkwardness in resuming a correspondence unless occasion offered, but time would bring it. Rush at once wrote to Adams, who replied on Chistmas Day in an amusing and characteristic letter. He ran over the political differences but denied that there was any feud and asserted that "I have always loved him as a friend." [10] On New Year's Day, 1812, a week later, Adams wrote a short but friendly letter to Jefferson himself sending him some specimens of New England homespun cloth. Jefferson replied immediately—and from then until death separated them fourteen years later, the correspondence continued to the evident great delight of both. Their friendship had begun in the stirring days of the Continental Congress in 1774. They had worked together in France and England. They had been genuinely attached to one another. Perhaps the two best-read men in America, they could discuss almost any topic with one

[9] *Writings,* Ford, Vol. IX, pp. 299 ff.   [10] Adams, *Works,* Vol. X, p. 11.

another. They wrote of books, history, religion, education, immortality, government, ethics—anything which came into their heads—and the range of subjects was extraordinary. It was in many ways the most remarkable correspondence in American letters, and as one reads it, one has only to think of Hamilton as trying to take part in it fully to realize the essential limitations of his mind and interests, powerful though the former was. Many of the letters ran to three and, one, even to four thousand words. Adams once wrote six long letters to his recovered friend in seventeen days, and although because the pressure on Jefferson's time was greater than that on Adams's he wrote less frequently, his letters were usually the longer.

Adams had suggested in one letter that they ought not to die until they had explained themselves to each other, and it is impossible to run over all the subjects on which they attempted to do this. Before, however, taking leave of Jefferson's political opinions we may quote one passage in which he again shows his attitude toward democracy. "I agree with you," he wrote to Adams, "that there is a natural aristocracy among men. The grounds of this are virtue and talent. . . . There is also an artificial aristocracy, founded on wealth and birth, without either virtue or talents; for with these it would belong to the first class. The natural aristocracy I consider the most precious gift of nature, for the instruction, the trusts, and the government of society. And, indeed, it would have been inconsistent in creation to have formed man for the social state, and not to have provided virtue and wisdom enough to manage the concerns of the society. May we not even say, that that form of government is the best, which provides the most effectually for a pure selection of these natural aristoi into the offices of government? The artificial aristocracy is a mischievous ingredient in government, and provision should be made to prevent its ascendency. On the question, what is the best provision, you and I differ. . . . [I do not believe it] necessary to protect the wealthy; because enough of these will find their way into every branch of the legislation, to protect themselves. . . . I think the best remedy is exactly that provided by all our constitutions, to leave to the citizens the free election and separation of the aristoi from the pseudo-aristoi, of the wheat from the chaff. In general they will elect the really good and wise. In some instances, wealth may corrupt, and birth blind them; but not in sufficient degree to endanger society."

"With respect to aristocracy," he continued, "we should further consider, that before the establishment of the American States, nothing was known to history but the man of the old world, crowded within limits either small or overcharged, and steeped in the vices which that situation generates. A government adapted to such men would be one thing; but a very different one, that for the man of these States. Here every one may have land to labor for himself, if he chooses; or, preferring the exercise of any other industry, may exact for it such compensation as not only to provide for a comfortable subsistence, but wherewith to provide for a cessation from labor in old age. Every one, by his property, or by his satisfactory situation, is interested in the support of law and crder. And such men may safely and advantageously reserve to themselves a wholesome control over their public affairs, and a degree of freedom, which, in the hands of the *canaille* of the cities of Europe, would be instantly perverted to the demolition and destruction of everything public and private." [11]

As they grew older and friends fell off increasingly by death, the problem of religion crept more into the correspondence. It is as impossible, as it is unnecessary, to try to define in precise metaphysical terms the beliefs of either. In general they agreed. Both believed in God but not in the Trinity of

[11] *Writings,* Ford, Vol. IX, pp. 425 ff.

the Christian religion, and both detested Calvinism and the
priesthood of an established church. Jefferson, whom the
clergy and even Hamilton had denounced as an atheist, compiled in his last ten years, from the New Testament in Greek,
Latin, French, and English, what he called *The Life and
Morals of Jesus*, without accepting the dogmas of Christian-
ity. As a system of ethics and morality, however, he came to
believe the Christian superior to any other.

Replying to a remark in a letter from Adams, he wrote,
"the result of your fifty or sixty years of religious reading, in
the four words, 'Be just and good,' is that in which all our
enquiries must end; as the riddles of all the priesthoods end in
four more, 'ubi panis, ibi deus.' " [12] The problem of immortality came up with the death of Mrs. Adams in 1818. To Adams,
Jefferson wrote, "it is some comfort to us both, that the term
is not very distant, at which we are to deposit in the same
cerement, our sorrows and suffering bodies, and to ascend in
essence to an ecstatic meeting with the friends we have loved
and lost, and whom we shall still love and never lose again." [13]
To this Adams replied, "I know not how to prove, physically,
that we shall meet and know each other in a future state. . . .
My reasons for believing it, as I do most undoubtedly, are that
I cannot conceive such a being could make such a species as
the human, merely to live and die on this earth. If I did not
believe in a future state, I should believe in no God. . . . And,
if there be a future state, why should the Almighty dissolve
forever all the tender ties which unite us so delightfully in this
world, and forbid us to see each other in the next?" [14]

Slowly the two old friends failed. Adams's palsied hand
could no longer indite his letters to Jefferson, which he had
to dictate, but they continued. July 4, 1826, approached. It
was the fiftieth anniversary of the Declaration of Independence

---

[12] *Writings,* Ford, Vol. X, p. 73.   [13] *Memorial Edition,* Vol. XV, p. 174.
[14] Adams, *Works,* Vol. X, p. 363.

of which Adams and Jefferson were the last remaining signers but one. For several days Jefferson had been sinking into a stupor. About seven in the evening of the third, as his attending doctor wrote, "he awoke, and seeing me staying at his bedside, exclaimed, 'Ah! Doctor, are you still there?' in a voice, however, that was husky and indistinct. He then asked, 'Is it the Fourth?' to which I replied, 'It soon will be.' These were the last words I heard him utter. Until towards the middle of the day—the 4th—he remained in the same state, or nearly so, wholly unconscious to everything that was passing around him. His circulation was gradually, however, becoming languid; and for some time prior to dissolution the pulse at the wrist was imperceptible. About one o'clock he ceased to exist." [15]

In Quincy, the fast-failing old John Adams was sitting in his chair all that day, mumbling incoherently and evidently rapidly approaching his own end, as the sounds of the celebration of the Fourth came distantly through the windows. Suddenly and distinctly, he murmured, "Thomas Jefferson still lives," and expired. Unknown as yet Jefferson had died an hour before. When the nation learned of the extraordinary coincidence, it was received with hushed awe, as though a mysterious portent. Death had struck simultaneously at the two most shining marks in the land, and as the past symbolically went down to the grave, an era was dramatically closed.

[15] Randolph, *Domestic Life*, pp. 424 ff.

CHAPTER XV

PULSE BEATS OF DEMOCRACY

U P to the death of Jefferson, the people both in local and national governments had been ruled almost wholly by the "rich, the wise, and the good" or the intellectuals. Even Jefferson himself, in spite of leading what he called "the revolution of 1800," was distinctly an intellectual, and an aristocrat to his finger tips. His theoretical democracy was limited, although it went far beyond what most of the conservatives in his lifetime believed safe for society. He did believe, as they did not, that in America it would prove safer to rest the ultimate source of power in the people as a whole than in any single class or group. But, as we have seen, his democracy had decided limitations. First, he believed that such an experiment as he spent his life in trying to carry out could be successful only in America. Second, that it could succeed even in America only under certain conditions of economic society. Thirdly, that a pure democracy was out of the question unless it could be progressively fostered among the people by the development of the right conditions. He believed that it would have to be by economic conditions which would give the mass of the population a personal interest in maintaining law, order, and security of person and property; by the development of responsibility and character; and by the development, again, of knowledge and the power to reason and judge. Until the people thus progressed, he believed that, although they should be the fount of power, they should merely elect others to the higher offices to govern for them. Jefferson was no believer in having the people decide all questions for themselves, and turning their judges, legislators, and executives into "office boys" or "rubber stamps."

Under the right conditions, he believed that the people would progress, and perhaps become increasingly capable of exercising more and more directly their powers of government. His view is well expressed in a letter to Doctor Walter Jones in 1814. Commenting on a newspaper article which Jones had published, Jefferson wrote that there was just one sentence he would have altered. "It is near the end of the first page," he said, "where you make a statement of genuine republican maxims; saying, 'that the people ought to possess as much political power as can possibly exist with the order and security of society.' Instead of this, I would say 'that the people, being the only safe depositary of power, should exercise in person, every function which their qualifications enable them to exercise, consistently with the order and security of society; that we now find them equal to the election of those who shall be invested with their executive and legislative powers, and to act for themselves in the judiciary, as judges in questions of fact [i.e., as jurymen] that the range of their powers ought to be enlarged,' &c. This gives both reason and exemplification of the maxim you express." [1]

In fact, none of the leaders of even the republican party, in the sense in which the term was used in 1800, believed in democracy. Madison had tried to avoid its dangers by arranging under the Constitution to have the various branches of the government derive from different sources among the electorate. As he wrote, "A distinction of property results from that very protection which a free Government gives to unequal faculties of acquiring it. There will be rich and poor; creditors and debtors; a landed interest, a monied interest, a mercan-

[1] *Writings*, Ford, Vol. IX, p. 447.

tile interest, a manufacturing interest. . . . In addition to these natural distinctions, artificial ones will be created. . . . It remains then to be enquired whether a majority having any common interest, or feeling any common passion, will find sufficient motives to restrain them from oppressing the minority. . . . If two individuals are under the bias of interest or enmity against a third, the rights of the latter could never be safely referred to the majority of the three." [2] He realized that with an increase in population, the number of the poor, and those working for wages without property, would increase, and he particularly dreaded the rise of groups which would set their own selfish interests against those of others or of the community as a whole—those "pressure groups" which we have unhappily come to know so well.

But regardless of theory and justified or unjustified fears, democracy was inevitable in America. Not one but a succession of a thousand frontiers, as well as other influences, saw to that. Most of what we have called "Americanism,"—not the "Americanism" of innumerable reactionary organizations today, but the old Americanism—had its roots deep in the soil of simple communities close to earth, with few social distinctions, little money, and much hard work for every one.

The uniqueness of Jefferson was that, with a full realization of the dangers, he nevertheless aligned himself from the beginning with the major forces in American life, and never wavered. It is that which made him so much more "American" than any of the others among his contemporaries. But his democracy was no moon-calf vision. He believed that, on the whole, the entire people could be trusted to do justice better than could any one man or group or class. That made for safety of government and for orderly progress instead of revolution. But government, for Jefferson, was not a theory or an end. It was only a practical means. The end was a happy

[2] Madison, *Works,* Vol. V, p. 29.

and humane life for as many as might be. He was a liberal first and a democrat second.

We have said that democracy was inevitable in America. It has developed in many European countries largely from theory, and as an overlay of older social systems shot through and through with remnants of institutions, ways of thought, habits, instinctive reverences and obediences. Little more than three centuries ago there were practically no white men on the North American continent. The body of the American nation today of a hundred and twenty-five million people has grown from the aggregation of innumerable tiny body-building cells, little settlements here, there, and everywhere. First, they were along the Atlantic coast, spreading with amazing rapidity, by historical measure, from that coast to the Pacific. In every case the settlement, the cell, was started by a solitary individual or a small group. In the process each individual or group has been thrown upon his or their own resources at the start. Every one of them, often against mighty odds, has had to clear the land, build houses and fences, scrabble a living, make homes, discuss with, and help, each other in local problems. To expect such people under such conditions to be content to be ruled and regulated by some remote authority was impossible. Self-reliance, democracy, independence grew as crops before the first seeds of our material crops were planted in the ground.

As we noted in the introductory chapter, the question as to who should rule was raised almost coincident with the first settlements. The problem and the struggle have continued unceasingly ever since, in varying forms. An interesting point about this American struggle is that it has a rhythm, a pulsebeat. About once every generation, or on an average of every thirty years, what we may call Americanism in the sense of a desire to free one's self from the trammels of being governed or exploited (which is much the same thing) by others, has risen like a tide to high-water mark, resulting in loud protests, political upheavals, and even war depending on the severity of the crisis.

We look back on these periods as "waves of radicalism," although often the radicalism of one generation becomes the accepted conservative theory of the next. We may run through the ten periods quickly, using New England, as the most unified group of colonies, as an example before the national period. It may be noted that as the stage enlarges and conditions become more complex, the crises tend to become more acute.

The first we may consider as occurring about 1634 to 1636 which we mentioned in the first chapter. Not only were there an economic crisis and political demands for an increase of popular self-government, but it was a time of general radical ferment, resulting in the banishment from Massachusetts of Roger Williams, Ann Hutchinson, Wheelwright and others, and the settlements of Connecticut, Rhode Island, and New Hampshire. The intellectual and political life of Massachusetts had been stirred to the depths.

About twenty-five years later there was a strong reaction of the people against the magistrates, though of less importance, following the last executions of Quakers in 1659.

Again, about a quarter of a century later came the uprising against the Andros régime, and the overthrow of the government in 1689.

Roughly twenty-five to thirty years after this, political and intellectual radicalism was again rampant. John Wise was preaching the purest democracy which had yet been urged in Massachusetts. Yale, in 1714, warned its students against the new ideas in vogue, and the Assembly in Massachusetts so overrode Governor Shute for some years that he was practically forced to abdicate and flee. In this period the insistence on cheap money was one of the issues.

In the 1730's, feeling between debtors and creditors, farmers and moneyed men, rose rapidly. The "popular party" had gained control of the legislature, and currency legislation together with the "Land Bank" scheme threatened to ruin the moneyed class. There was terror on the one hand, and threats of armed rebellion on the other. Things reached such a pass that the "Land Bankers" by thousands would probably have marched on Boston had it not been that Governor Belcher was removed and Shirley appointed in his place.

A generation or so later came the Declaration of Independence, preceded by several years' discussion of the rights of man, and followed by war.

With independence we entered on our national period. In the next quarter of a century there were the local disturbances of Shays's Rebellion and the Whiskey Insurrection but on the national stage at first the conservatives, in the drafting of the Constitution, and then the reactionaries of the later Federalist period were able to dominate until Jefferson's "Revolution of 1800." The Republicans came into power in 1801, just twenty-five years after the Revolutionary Party had declared to the world that all men are created equal. Mild as the "revolution" was, we have seen the horror and dread with which it was regarded by the rich. It was, in fact, a genuine uprising of the poorer and debtor classes against the mercantile, financial and more privileged ones. The movement was formed of an incongruous alliance, which has always remained a weakness in the Democratic Party, of the farmer and the city wage earner, whose interests in reality are quite diverse from one another, and who can unite only as against other classes.

In the popular movement, however, the farmers were increasingly to dominate, and with the expansion of the country the farmers were more and more to mean "the West." Twenty-eight years after Jefferson's revolution came a far mightier one, and "the people" rose and smote as they never had before. Against, as has been claimed, "two-thirds of the news-papers, four-fifths of the preachers, practically all the manu-facturers, and seven-eighths of the banking capital," [3] Andrew Jackson of Tennessee was swept into the White House by a genuine rising of the mass, and the most scurrilous campaign America had yet witnessed. For the first time a genuine man of the people had been placed at the head of the government, and the people swarmed into all parts of it. The spoils system came to full flower. In most ways no two men could have been more unlike than Jefferson and Jackson, yet they had certain underlying concepts in common. Both believed in the people as the fount of power; both mistrusted banks and the moneyed class; both believed that government should be kept simple and at a minimum; both were States' Rights men yet each placed Union higher; both believed in strict construction of the Constitution; both dwelt far from cities and were essentially agrarian in outlook.

After the terrific overturn of the Jackson victory, it was thirty-two years before a man of the plain people, and again a Westerner, was elected President. The trend was shown in the campaign of William Henry Harrison, but although, in that rather hilarious and good-natured contest, efforts were made to induce people to believe that the Western candidate wore a coon-skin cap and lived in a log cabin, he was in reality a man of considerable wealth, living in a mansion where he loved to dispense generous hospitality.

It was in the successful nomination of Lincoln for President at Chicago in 1860, against the experienced, nationally known, cultured statesman of the East, Governor Seward of New York, that the ordinary man again won a great victory. Incidental to Lincoln's election came war, the freeing of the slaves and other results with which we are not at the moment concerned. What we are interested in in this very rapid survey is

[3] Claude G. Bowers, *Party Battles of the Jackson Period,* Boston, 1928, p. 31.

Lincoln's relation to democracy and the common man. He was the first Presidential candidate of the Republican Party of today, a party which claims to stem back to Hamilton and the Federalists, just as the present Democratic Party invokes Jefferson as its founder. That places Lincoln apparently half way down the line of Republican Party leaders between Hamilton and Hoover. This, however, misplaces Lincoln entirely. It is true that the modern Republican Party has dressed itself in Hamilton's clothes. As the conservative party it has stood for a strong central government, imperialism, the close alliance of business and government, tariffs and other privileges, and has been far more concerned, except for occasional lip-service, with the old Federalist "rich, wise, and good" than with the daily lot of the farmer or the factory hand. In Republican eyes, the mortgagee of the farm or the owner of the factory has been more important than the farmer or the factory hand, as the former and their kind have also been the more important contributors to campaign funds. As a conservative party—and government in a democracy cannot be carried on properly without both a conservative and a progressive or liberal party by whatever names they are called—the Republican Party has frequently done magnificent work. It is a complete misconception of Lincoln, however, to regard him as in the Hamiltonian tradition.

We need not consider particular policies. It is true that Hamilton was for a protective tariff, and the new Republican Party after the panic of 1857 wrote a tariff plank into its platform in 1858 and again in 1860. This was to catch votes in the East, particularly in the manufacturing and politically highly important state of Pennsylvania. Lincoln, who cared nothing about a tariff, accepted the platform, and the enormous prosperity of manufacturing during the years of war, a prosperity which would have come, tariff or no tariff, made the tariff claimants more powerful than ever and they became lastingly dominant in the party.

We are dealing in this book with more fundamental things than tariff policies. As to such fundamental matters as to who shall govern, as to privilege for the few, as to trust in the common people—Lincoln was as far from Hamilton as the two poles, and close to Jefferson. "The people—your people, Sir, is a great beast," was the after-dinner expression of Hamilton's attitude, and we have already tried to make clear his more serious opinions as to popular government. Lincoln's equally informal utterance, "God must love the common people, He has made so many of them," though somewhat humorously illogical, was not sarcastic, and expressed one of the very deepest traits in Lincoln's character and mind—his affection for and faith in those common folk from whom he, most uncommon, had sprung, and among whom he had been nurtured. In the greatest speech he ever made—the Gettysburg Address now carved in marble on his memorial—he went straight to Jefferson. "Four score and seven years ago," he began, "our fathers brought forth on this continent a new nation, conceived in liberty, and dedicated to the proposition that all men are created equal." And after the few brief, immortal words, he closed with the dedication of himself and the nation to the task of seeing that "this nation, under God, shall have a new birth of freedom; and that government of the people, by the people, for the people, shall not perish from the earth."

As against the Federalist wish for a governing class and for keeping the suffrage as narrow as might be, Lincoln came out clearly. "A majority," he wrote, "held in restraint by constitutional checks and limitations, and always changing easily with deliberate changes of popular opinions and sentiments, is the only true sovereign of a free people. Whoever rejects it does, of necessity, fly to anarchy or to despotism. Unanimity is impossible; the rule of a minority, as a permanent arrangement, is wholly inadmissible; so that, rejecting the majority principle, anarchy or despotism in some form is all that is left." [4]

The generation following the Civil War saw enormous changes. The war had made the North rich. The discovery of gold and silver mines, of petroleum wells had added a new group of great fortunes to those made during the contest by government contracts and shoddy manufacturing. The Union had been maintained, and the country had become one and indivisible from the Atlantic to the Pacific, from Mexico to Canada. Transcontinental railroads were built. Telegraph and other industries began to be consolidated from many small companies into units of national size. "Big business," largely concentrated as to control in the Northeast, began to loom as a menace to the lives and fortunes of the ordinary citizen. Western farmers felt themselves throttled by the rates charged by warehouses and railroads, as others felt themselves threatened by other forms of corporate wealth. The steady decline in the world production of gold as compared with the needs of trade for currency was such that commodity prices were declining alarmingly, and the burden of debt growing intolerable.

Thirty-five years after Lincoln entered the White House, a new leader arose, to voice the woes, fears, and demands of the common man, particularly of the West. Bryan cannot, of course, be at all compared in intellectual stature with either Jefferson or Lincoln, but if his knowledge and mind were very restricted, and the policies he pursued as remedies were wrong or inadequate, the evils against which, among the leaders of the nation, he almost alone inveighed, were very real. The

[4] Cited by W. S. Carpenter, *Development of American Political Thought,* Princeton University Press, 1930, p. 163.

Republicans might well get into a frenzy of terror but they themselves suggested no remedies for ills which were so deeply disturbing to the ordinary man.

Indeed, the platform on which Bryan ran for President, on which he almost won, and which frightened wealth as it had not been frightened since the campaigns of Jefferson and Jackson, has to a great extent, though I believe unwisely, gradually become the law of the land in the past three years. As usual, mention was made of Jefferson, and special stress was laid upon the rights of "freedom of speech, freedom of the press, freedom of conscience, the preservation of personal rights, the equality of all citizens before the law, and the faithful observance of constitutional limitations." What so terrified capital was the statement that the party was opposed to monometalism and demanded that gold and silver should both be used at the ratio of sixteen to one; insistence that government bonds should not be paid in gold; criticism of the Supreme Court for having declared an income tax unconstitutional; the demand that the powers of the interstate commerce commission be enlarged; the denouncing of the profligate waste of the money wrung from the people by oppressive taxation, and of the "arbitrary interference by federal authorities in local affairs as a violation of the Constitution." [5] Just thirty years later, we may indeed rub our eyes as we read!

There had been no campaign like it since that of Jackson. Recalling how the people then rose and won in spite of the whole power of wealth against them, we may quote the account given by Mrs. Lodge, wife of the Old Guard Republican Senator, to Sir Cecil Spring-Rice. With infinite relief after the result was known, she wrote, "The great fight is won and a fight conducted by trained and experienced and organized

[5] Platform in E. Stanwood's *History of the Presidency*, Boston, 1898, pp. 542 ff.

forces, with both hands full of money, with the full power of
the press—and of prestige—on the one side; on the other, a
disorganized mob at first, out of which burst into sight, hearing and force—one man, but such a man! Alone, penniless,
without backing, without money, with scarce a paper, without
speakers, that man fought such a fight that even those in the
East can call him a Crusader, an inspired fanatic, a prophet!
It has been marvellous. . . . We acknowledge to $7,000,000
campaign fund against his $300,000. We had during the last
week of the campaign 18,000 speakers on the stump. He alone
spoke for his party. . . . It is over now but the vote is
7,000,000 to 6,500,000." [6]

This was the tenth of what we may call the generation-long
pulse beats of the American popular movement, and this time
the people did not win. Something had gone wrong with
the rhythm of American life. No one can tell precisely what
it was. Perhaps, for one thing, it was the seven-million-dollar
campaign fund against three hundred thousand. Perhaps another reason was the fact that the frontier had been officially
declared closed six years before, and the vast open spaces
where careers and empires could be carved out were no more.
Another cause may have been that the old alliance between
farmer and city worker had been too hard pushed. Farmers
were offered renewals of mortgages for five years on easy
terms if they would vote for McKinley; factory workers were
told there would be no jobs if Bryan were elected and they
need not return. The farmer had his farm, and could stand
firm, but for the city worker the threat of no money for food
or rent after election if too many of them voted for Bryan was
a more serious matter. The steady shift in occupation, which
means habits of life, may also have counted. In 1800, 90 per
cent of the population had been engaged in agriculture. By

[6] *Letters and Friendships of Sir Cecil Spring-Rice*, ed. Stephen Gwynn, London, 1929, Vol. II, p. 197.

1890 only 35½ per cent were engaged in agriculture, lumbering and fisheries combined, whereas all the rest were engaged in business, or professional, domestic, and personal services. Jefferson's vision of an America formed of small independent landowners had been eaten away, census by census.

At any rate, whatever the causes were, at its tenth pulse beat the rhythm of American life had broken, and that life has been confused ever since. In considering Jefferson's theory of generations, the first obvious thought that strikes one is that there is in reality no such thing as "a generation." If a generation be considered as of about thirty years, we are most certainly not all born in one year to die thirty years later. During those years there are alive and active persons of all ages, from the infant to the nonagenarian. Naturally in the thirty years or so between the pulse beats of popular uprisings there have been all sorts of cross currents at work. Nevertheless, both in economics and politics there was, until 1896, a certain regularity of prosperity and conservatism changing into depression and radicalism. This was probably due in part to the crowd spirit, mass psychology or whatever one may choose to call it. In the wild days of 1925–29 it was not merely the young, adventurous and inexperienced who were carried away by the "New Era" ideas of speculating, of expanding our living scales, and of piling up debt. Many of the old and conservative were also, and more and more as the general madness grew. In this example, if developed further than I here have space for, we may find an explanation for the generation pulse beat even if there is no such thing physically as a distinct and universal generation at any one time. The regularity of the economic crises with attendant radicalism of thought is due largely to psychological and not to economic causes.

Had the forces of unrest come to control power at the appointed period in 1896 instead of being defeated, the regular cycle would probably have followed the normal course for the next thirty years or so. The pendulum would have swung through its usual wide arc. Instead of that, it hovered uncertainly over a more circumscribed one. We had as President for two terms, Theodore Roosevelt, who was neither radical nor conservative, and who never knew, any more than any one else did, precisely what he really was. He had something of both Hamilton and Jefferson in him, though he detested the latter, and wrote to Lodge that although Bryan was "a shallow demagogue" he did not believe that "he is a bit worse than Thomas Jefferson." [7] Roosevelt, however, went in some ways much further than Jefferson would have even in his own day, and so probably still further than Jefferson might have done in the twentieth century, as, for example, in placing the power of direct legislation and judicial decisions on law as well as on fact in the hands of the people. It is impossible to conceive of Jefferson advocating popular recall of judges in a city population. Social-minded to a large extent, Roosevelt was also as autocratic as Jackson, who, although elected by the somewhat misguided enthusiasm of the people, insisted on doing things as he personally wished. Roosevelt's "Big Stick," wielded in the Panama Canal matter and many others, was, to say the least, no symbol of liberalism.

When, after Taft's one term, Roosevelt's ego burst both himself and the Republican Party, and ensured the election of Wilson as a Democrat, the new President came in with a mandate only from a minority of the electorate, and not in answer to an overwhelming resentment on the part of the majority of the people. It was no "revolution" which brought the former college president in as President of the United States, about midway of the "generation." A well-meaning, social-minded idealist, Wilson was a sort of closet liberalist

[7] Selections from Correspondence of Theodore Roosevelt and Henry Cabot Lodge, New York, 1925, Vol. II, p. 224.

philosopher who had had no direct contact with the masses and who did not understand the psychology of peoples. Unlike Jefferson, he was doctrinaire, and believed that the American type of government would bring happiness, instead of often confusion, to any people regardless of their training and capacity.

Normally we should have elected Bryan in 1896, then had a bout of radicalism and reform, gradually grown prosperous and conservative, and next, as abuses began to be too glaring and affect too many people, have approached the position by around 1926 or so where another upheaval, house-cleaning, and loud demand for further freedom from trammels of all sorts, and for greater self-government, would have caused an overturn. Instead of that, the strong purge due in 1896 not having had effect, our bowels were, so to say, merely kept queasy by Roosevelt and Wilson. We then settled down to the twelve years of political, social, and spiritual constipation under Harding, Coolidge, and Hoover. We were as a nation neither normally healthy nor genuinely happy, though we believed ourselves to be so from the auto-intoxication of fantastically rising prices and seeming increase of personal and national wealth and incomes.

When, after the three futile and unhappy years following the crash of 1929, Hoover was overwhelmingly cast out of office, and Franklin D. Roosevelt was returned in his stead, the eleventh pulse beat, somewhat overdue, was entirely different from any of the previous ten, and perhaps was not a genuine one. The tenth had failed, but the eleventh had scarcely started. The frantic desire of the American people in the election of 1932 was not for reform, not for greater self-government, not for the redress of abuses, but to show their resentment at having lost their money, and to install some one, almost any one, who might stand a better chance of getting it back for them than did Hoover. The huge majority which the second

Roosevelt piled up on a conservative platform, and under which Hoover crumpled, was no echo of a cry for liberty or reform. It was a yell for cash and jobs. The real pulse beat may or may not come, out of due time, in 1936.

CHAPTER XVI

JEFFERSON TODAY

WE began our story with a struggle over the nature of government in America almost precisely a century and a half before the adoption of the Constitution. We have now reached a point almost precisely a century and a half after. What is the situation in this present period of ours, and what is its relation to the problem of who shall govern, to the liberalism of Jefferson and to those personal liberties which he believed alone made life worth living? Must the people, after all, be governed instead of governing? Is Jefferson, to whom both the Democratic Party and its candidate harked back in their pledges of the last Presidential campaign of 1932, to be abandoned, and are we to replace him, as many claim is the necessity of the hour, by a Hamilton? To pose these questions properly we must perhaps devote a somewhat disproportionate space to the happenings of the past three years.

Since Jefferson's day there has been great advance toward a complete democracy, at least in the political machinery. Madison's plan, for example, of drawing different departments of government from different parts of the electorate, has failed. The President has come to be elected directly by the people as have members of the Senate. The suffrage has been widely extended, not only by taking in new classes of men but by taking in women as well. Congress has largely ceased to be a *representative* and genuinely debating body, and Con-

gressmen under pressure have largely come to use their delegated powers to carry into effect merely the expressed will of
their constituents, or of a noisy and influential minority of
them.

In the election of 1932 approximately 22,500,000 votes
were cast for President Roosevelt, 16,000,000 for Hoover, and
only 730,000 for the Socialist candidate, Norman Thomas.
The depression had already lasted for two years. The shock
of the colossal crash coming after the dream of lasting and
ever-increasing prosperity which had been dreamed by all
classes, had had a profound effect on the psychology of the
American people. Losses had been enormous, and more widely
distributed than ever before owing partly to the nation-wide
participation in the stock-market orgy. Unemployment was
heavy, and resentment was deep against both fate and the political and business leaders. In many other countries revolution was rife.

The election, in which a larger number of voters partici-
pated than ever before, had therefore a peculiar interest.
Strangely enough there was extraordinarily little radicalism
in evidence. It is true that the vote of the Socialist Party was
largely increased from 1928, a year of widespread prosperity,
but even so it was far below the numbers polled by it in 1920
—920,000—or even those of 1912. Moreover many who were
not genuinely Socialist voted the ticket because they wished
to show their disgust with the recent record of the Republicans without voting, on the contrary, for Roosevelt. The
16,000,000 who voted for Hoover were assuredly anything
but radical.

In considering the election, perhaps the most critical test
our great democracy had been called upon to face since that
of the election of 1864, we now come to the 22,500,000 citizens
who voted for Roosevelt. What was it they wanted as against
the less than a quarter of a million Socialists, so-called, and

the 16,000,000 Hoover conservatives? There were probably many, a great many, who, in the extraordinarily despondent mood of the nation, felt that a change, any change, was essential to restore morale. But to judge the motives of the great majority of those who voted for the Democratic Party, we must examine the platform put forth by that party and the campaign speeches of its candidate.

The platform was chiefly remarkable for two things, its insistence upon a conservative handling of the economic situation, and the quite unusually strong statements pledging the carrying into execution of the policies outlined.

It began, naturally, with an attack on the policies which had been pursued by the Republicans. It then, with admirable simplicity, named those policies which the Democrats advocated and those which they condemned. As to the former, it stated that "we advocate an immediate and drastic reduction of governmental expenditures by abolishing useless commissions and offices, consolidating departments and bureaus and eliminating extravagance, to accomplish a saving of not less than 25 per cent in the cost of Federal government." Also, "maintenance of the national credit by a Federal budget, annually balanced on the basis of accurate executive estimates within revenues." "A sound currency to be preserved at all hazards," and the calling of an international monetary conference. "A competitive tariff for revenue, with a fact-finding tariff commission free from executive interference." There was a plank on unemployment relief. Unemployment and old-age insurance was advocated but the platform stated that such insurance should be under *state* and not federal laws. Farmers were promised the "enactment of every constitutional measure" that would enable them to receive prices above the cost of production.

"Strict and impartial enforcement of the anti-trust laws" was promised for the better protection of labor and the small man; and also the development, in the public interest, of water power then owned by the nation. The investing public was to be better protected. Holding companies interested in interstate commerce were to be *regulated* (not abolished), as were also rates of utility companies operating across state lines. The various stock exchanges were likewise to be regulated, and there was a conservative plank as to banks.

Among the things condemned were "the improper and excessive use of money in political activities"; "paid lobbies"; "the open and covert resistance of administrative officials to every effort made by Congressional committees to curtail the extravagant expenditures of the government and to revoke improvident subsidies granted to favored interests"; and "the extravagance of the Farm Board, its disastrous action which made the government a speculator in farm products, and the unsound policy of restricting agricultural production to the demands of the domestic markets."

In the most solemn manner this platform was declared to be "a *covenant* with the people" to be faithfully kept. "The people," it said, "are entitled to know in plain words the terms of the *contract* to which they are asked to subscribe." [1]

In his speeches Roosevelt, as candidate, laid heavy stress on the financial aspects of the situation. "I accuse the present [Hoover] administration," he said, "of being the greatest spending administration in peace times in all our history—one which has piled bureau on bureau, commission on commission, and has failed to anticipate the dire needs or reduced earning power of the people." Again, "I know something of taxes. For three long years I have been going up and down this country preaching that Government—Federal and state and local—costs too much. I shall not stop that preaching. . . . I propose to you, my friends, and through you, that

[1] Quotations are from the platform as published in *The New York Times*. July 1, 1932.

Government of all kinds, big and little, be made solvent and that the example be set by the President of the United States and his Cabinet." "This," he said again, "I pledge you, and nothing I have said in the campaign transcends in importance this covenant with the taxpayers of this country."

He did say that if men and women were starving, he regarded it as the duty of the government to raise money for them by taxation, but he added, "let us have the courage to stop borrowing to meet continued deficits. Stop the deficits and let us also have the courage to reverse the policies of the Republican leaders and insist on a sound currency." "Here at least [unsound currency] is one field in which all business— big business and little business and family business and the individual's business—is at the mercy of our big Government in Washington." "If, like a spendthrift, it throws discretion to the winds, is willing to make no sacrifice at all in spending, extends its taxing to the limit of the people's power to pay and continues to pile up deficits, it is on the road to bankruptcy."

Speaking of the Republican deficits, he said, "the truth is that our banks are financing these stupendous deficits, and that the burden is absorbing their resources. All this is highly undesirable and wholly unnecessary. It arises from one cause only, and that is the unbalanced budget. . . . Now, ever since the days of Thomas Jefferson, that has been the exact reverse of the Democratic concept—which is to permit Washington to take from the states nothing more than is necessary to keep abreast of the march of our changing economic situation. In the latter philosophy I shall approach the problem of carrying out the plain precept of our party, which is to reduce the cost of the current Federal Government by 24 per cent. Of course, that means the complete realignment of the unprecedented bureaucracy that has assembled in Washington in the last four years [1928–1932]."

Elsewhere he said, "It is my pledge and promise that this

dangerous kind of financing shall be stopped and that rigid governmental economy shall be forced by a stern and unremitting administration policy of living within our income."

As to the relations between government and business, he said, "I have warned the country against unwise governmental interference with business; I have pointed out that the policies of the present leadership of the Republican Party in the last few years have constituted dangerous back-seat driving."

He vehemently denied Hoover's assertion that at one time the government had been nearly forced off gold, because, Roosevelt said, had that been so, having recently sold governmental bonds, if the government "failed so to advise the banks and private investors who purchased nearly $4,000,000,000 of these Federal securities [redeemable in gold], they were guilty of amazing dishonesty; they were cheating the investment public; and could not even appropriate to themselves the solace of future oblivion, because their names would have been remembered in terms of anathema for a century to come." The Republicans, he also said, "claim that the Democratic position with regard to money has not been made sufficiently clear. The President [Hoover] is seeing visions of rubber dollars. This is only a part of his campaign of fear. I am not going to characterize these statements. I merely present the facts. The Democratic platform specifically declares, 'We advocate a sound currency to be preserved at all hazards.' That is plain English." [2]

The major part of both the party platform and the speeches of the candidate could be considered sound Jeffersonian doctrine. Both party and candidate pledged themselves with unusual solemnity to sound money, to a reduction in the functions of government, to a reduction in the number of Federal employees, to a decrease in taxation, to economy, to balanced

[2] Quotations are from those conveniently assembled by G. H. Lorimer, editor of *The Saturday Evening Post* in the issue of December 22, 1934.

budgets, to many of the things for which Jefferson had always stood; and the President for the first few months after his inauguration did a magnificent piece of work. Entering office at the precise moment of the banking crisis he handled it with a skill and cool courage which won him the admiration and confidence of the entire nation. The short, crisp messages which he sent to Congress in quick succession but ordered sequence indicated that within the promises of his party he had in mind a well-defined policy.

Then came the change, almost as sudden as it yet remains inexplicable. He broke some of his most solemn and important pledges to those who had elected him, and smashed the covenant which his great party had also made on its honor with the people. As this book is not a contemporary political tract we need not enter upon details known to all men, but we may point to a few of the broken pledges.

Instead of balancing the budget, the huge deficits have been piled up of approximately $3,068,000,000 for 1933, of $3,965,000,000 for 1934, and $3,575,000,000 for 1935, with no balancing in prospect. Instead of reducing the number of bureaus and commissions, he has multiplied them as never before, and instead of maintaining a "sound currency," no one knows yet what the currency may be. The gold content of the dollar has been reduced to approximately fifty-nine cents, and the President has secured authority to reduce it to fifty. Owing to the failure to balance the budget, inflation and paper money are well within bounds of possibility. Instead of relieving banks of their burden of financing government, the government has loaded them up with Federal obligations as never before. Instead of paying government obligations in gold after issuing them with a gold clause, the government has repudiated this obligation and denied the citizen access in future to the Courts for possible redress.

Although the platform had condemned the Farm Board for

making the government a "speculator in farm products," the government by July, 1935, had thrown the Liverpool cotton markets into confusion by having engineered what a world-known financial journal called "the greatest cotton corner in history." Although the platform had condemned the resistance of previous administrative officials to Congressional efforts to save money, the present administration has demanded, and received, powers and presidential control over the spending of such vast sums as have never been granted to any President before, even in war. With the election coming the next year, Roosevelt secured for himself a fairly free hand with the spending of $4,880,000,000, a sum probably never before at the disposal of a single individual in the history of the world. Instead of continuing to condemn the "dangerous back-seat driving" of business from Washington, Roosevelt attempted, hurriedly and without well-considered plans, through the NRA and other bureaus, to regulate the business structure of the nation to an extent never tried elsewhere except perhaps in Italy and Russia under dictatorships. So vast indeed have been the changes which the President has sought to introduce that there is some foundation for calling the whole group of policies the Roosevelt Revolution, as some of his admirers term it.

We may note several points. For one, speaking as a historian, I cannot recall any other President and party which in our American past have gone so far in the solemnity of the pledges given the voters that they would jointly carry out the specific policies to which they had each pledged themselves. Nor, even when promises have been more lightly given, do I recall any other such repudiation of them. That repudiation has not been the result of overwhelming circumstance but has largely resulted from the endeavor to make over the whole pattern of our social and economic life in accordance with a new design which happens to meet with the personal approbation of a President. The question at once arises, how can self-government continue if a people cannot put trust in the most solemn pledges of the party and candidates for whom the majority may vote? If we cannot do so, then the system of party government must crumble, and we have nothing to take its place, except dictatorship or revolutionary chaos.

Another point is the relation of the Executive branch of the government to the Legislative and Judicial. For nearly three years the Executive was able to make himself almost independent of the other two, a situation never contemplated in the Constitution. Until there were signs of revolt in the early summer of 1935, his personal popularity with the country reduced Congress to the abject position of a rubber stamp. It voted him practically all moneys and all powers asked, whether constitutional or not. Under the NRA he was even given power to legislate by himself. It is incredible how the lawyers in Congress could ever have conceived that the power they gave him was constitutional. One of the oldest and simplest maxims of the law is that a delegate cannot delegate to some one else the power delegated to himself. As the Supreme Court declared, when at last it had a chance to pass upon the basis of the NRA in the Schechter Poultry case on May 27, 1935, the Constitution provided that "all legislative powers herein granted shall be vested in a Congress of the United States, which shall consist of a Senate and a House of Representatives," and that they, as delegates of the people for that purpose, could not delegate legislative power to the President.

The legislature, however, had already practically abdicated in favor of the Executive. But the Supreme Court was still there. It may be true or not, as has been openly asserted in public print without, so far as I know, denial being made, that a prominent legal member of the "Brain Trust" suggested to the President that although the legislation might be unconstitutional, nevertheless, if a case could be kept out of the Su-

preme Court for two years the new system of regulating industry would have become so intertwined with the economic
system of the nation as to prevent the possibility of an adverse
decision by the Court. At any rate there are indications that
cases were kept out of the Court as long as possible. In the
case of the Guffey Coal Control Bill, its constitutionality was
evidently almost more than doubtful. In the leading editorial
of July 8, 1935, *The New York Times*, without, so far as I
know, contradiction, stated that it "seems to be true, that the
Attorney General of the United States flatly gave his opinion
to Mr. Roosevelt that the bill is unconstitutional. It is known
that good lawyers in both houses of Congress hold the same
view." Nevertheless, as reported in the press, the President,
in a letter to the chairman of the Ways and Means Committee
of the House, urged that the House should "not permit doubts
as to the constitutionality, however reasonable, to block the
suggested legislation," and that although "no one is in a position to give an assurance that the promised Act will with-
stand the constitutional test" nevertheless "the situation is so
urgent and the benefits of the legislation so evident that all
doubts should be resolved in favor of the Bill." The Act, when
passed, did not even stop the threatened coal strike.

On this theory Congress could not only itself take part in
governing unconstitutionally, but, if supine enough, could as
in the NRA legislation, delegate unconstitutional powers to a
President. As they are unconstitutional even when given to a
President, they could just as well be given to any one else.
Under the right conditions of public unrest it might take, according to this mode of operating government, not two years,
but only two weeks to transform the character of our government altogether. Parliamentary government in England,
much like civilization itself, continues because parties and governments "play the game" according to rules. When individuals, governments, or peoples throw over the rules of the

game, confusion and violence ensue. There are legitimate ways of formally amending our Constitution, or altering it by other means, and when the people are really decided on an issue, the Constitution can even be amended within a year or two, as was recently shown in the repeal of Prohibition. But if the Executive or Congress, instead of the people, is to decide what is or is not desirable in the Constitution, and act or legislate according to his own ideas—when either ceases, in a word, to play the game according to the rules—then constitutional government by the people might soon become a mockery. We would thus arrive at what Lincoln predicted, either anarchy or despotism.

It is quite obvious that in the twentieth century our own government, or any government, cannot confine itself to the comparatively simple tasks of the eighteenth century. Jefferson himself strongly advocated constant adjustment to new conditions. But such changes may come in three spheres, in that of the extent of government, in that of the form of government, and in that of fundamental rights and liberties.

The rapid increase in the extent of government has its own dangers. It is estimated that the number of Federal officeholders will have increased by around 200,000 before Mr. Roosevelt comes up for re-election. In a democracy not only does a large bureaucracy become dangerous for free elections, but it tends to perpetuate and extend itself, and to become a class apart. It tends also, as is now seen in France, to render the governmental financial situation precarious by refusing to submit to either increased taxes or reduced salaries. When a sufficient part of the population gets on government payrolls, this makes a dangerously rigid structure of both governmental income and expenses. Even now, if the estimates quoted above are correct, in a little over two years the workers for government in America have risen from 3 per cent to 16 per cent of the whole. Yet we are as yet, apparently, only at the beginning of the regulation of the economic life of the country, or of the government's direct participation in it as principal or partner, as measured by the desires of those now in charge. Even before the Supreme Court decision declared the NRA unconstitutional, that legislation had largely broken down because it went such a long way in the attempted regulation of business without going still farther.

But to pass to the changes in the form of government. Many of those theorists who are so fond of making blueprints of how government could regulate all business so as to bring about balance between supply and demand, production and consumption, do away with crises and bring a comfortable scale of living to all regardless of individual ability or energy, seem not to realize that even an unsuccessful attempt to do this involves fundamental changes in government organization and theory. In spite of the vast multiplication of those bureaus and commissions which the President and his party so thoroughly condemned and promised to reduce, only a beginning has been made in attacking the problem of national planning if it is to accomplish the objectives so glibly talked about. Yet already, on the theory of a "Crisis" and the consequent necessity of centralized control for rapid action, we have seen the attempted changes made, such as the practical abdication of Congress; the handing over of legislative and large financial powers to one man, the President; the various attempts to nullify the power of review by the Supreme Court; the erection of mere rulings by bureau heads into laws of the land; the claimed necessity of abolishing a large area of states' rights.

An extension of national planning, not as government ownership of this or that, or as soil reclamation and other experiments on a limited scale and now constitutional, but a planning on some greater NRA scale of all industry, will inevitably require even greater concentration of power in the hands of one man or a small group. As any large business man can tell, business is frequently and unexpectedly in a "crisis." Any great corporation has to be run by a few and not by a democracy. Wherever the totalitarian state has been tried, it has been found essential, even apart from personal ambitions, to centralize control, and to do away with popular government. To run all business from Washington in a country so vast and so complex as ours—to tell a woman in the Adirondacks whether or not she can buy a pig, a farmer in Kansas how many bushels of corn he can raise, a manufacturer whether he can add to his factory or must reduce his output, and so on *ad infinitum*—would require, even if possible, a form of government not only incompatible with the Constitution but antipathetic to American temperament and involving control in a thousand ways over our individual lives. It is unfair and misleading to paint for the American people only a rosy picture of the happier possible results of such a system and not to tell them also of the unpleasant by-products which are certain.

The United States Government would become the greatest business corporation in the world, infinitely larger than any of ours today, because trying to control and co-ordinate them all besides all the small private businesses and farms of the land. In the summer of 1935 the President seemed to be attacking "bigness" in business and fortunes. As to the former most business men will agree with Justice Brandeis of the Supreme Court who wrote in 1913 that "in every business concern there must be a size-limit of greatest efficiency. What this limit is will differ in different businesses and under varying conditions in the same business. But whatever the business or organization there is a point where it would become too large for efficient and economic management, just as there is a point where it would be too small to be an efficient instrument. . . . Organization can never supply the combined judgment, initiative, enterprise and authority which must come from the chief executive officers." [3] But if this is true of a single corporation, how much more would it be true of a government which attempted to run practically *all* corporations and *all* the business affairs of the entire American people! Even if a personnel of super-human wisdom could be found to run it all, that personnel would have, more and more, to abolish government by the people. Long-term policies would have to be pursued, and the business would be so complex that, aside from the natural desire of a bureaucracy not to be disturbed but to consider, as John Cotton declared in early Massachusetts, that a public office is a life estate, it would be impossible to allow so trained and delicate a machine to be overturned at short and regular intervals by popular elections. Nor could policies be liable to be interfered with at any moment by an adverse vote in Congress.

Other results would also follow. Even if complete economic catastrophe could be averted, which is very far indeed from being assured, the national income instead of being increased would dwindle. Various factors would contribute to this. In almost all cases in America, government operation has proved less efficient than private. There is less incentive for efficiency, because there is always the taxing power to fall back on for deficits, accounts are not checked by outside auditors, and figures can always be juggled, as is reported in the cases of the Post Office and the TVA, to disguise the true returns.

Moreover, any one enterprise becomes so lost in the maze of the total operations of government that the taxpayers, unlike stockholders, cannot tell anything about its finances. In addition, the initiative of the individual, still ostensibly left in private business, lessens when he becomes wrapt round in a mass of government regulations which take the place of his own judgment; when he cannot take independent action; when the government may prevent him from making profits which he

[3] Louis D. Brandeis, *The Curse of Bigness*, New York, 1934, p. 116.

sees he otherwise might, or even when it helps to pay his deficits. It has been said that one reason why the railroads and utilities in many cases have been run less efficiently than the great industrial corporations is that business leaders of the first rank, men who may, like even politicians, make mistakes but who have energy, ambition and vision, do not, to a great extent, now care to devote their lives to those fields because they are too circumscribed by regulations of all sorts to give executives the opportunity for legitimate development.

But there is more than this. Under any form of totalitarian state personal liberty is bound to be lost. Such a state obviously cannot be run without practically universal obedience to its orders. Even if the delicately adjusted plans for harmonizing production, consumption, and distribution on a national scale contrived by a central bureau could be made to work at all, they certainly could not be made to do so if, apart from interference by Congress or state legislatures, any considerable body of citizens refused to do as they were told. Every state of this nature, or approaching it, has found this out. Public opinion must be unified in support of it and its policies, either by persuasion or force. Hence come both propaganda and control of the press, the radio, public meetings, and then entire loss of freedom of speech. Even in the experiment as tried by us so far, never has any government before carried on such propaganda as this one has. Besides the small army of press agents, appointed, it has been said, to a great extent contrary to law, there has also been the remarkable control of the radio.

Control of the press follows automatically for obvious reasons in the wake of the totalitarian state. The situation in Italy, Germany, and Russia is well known. Doctor Goebbels' instructions to the German press early this year well express how much public discussion is allowed. "Our state," he said, "is a leader state. The necessity and utility of every decree

are thoroughly examined before it is approved by the Cabinet.
. . . Consequently press comments pro and con projected legislation tending to arouse interested groups are useless to the
public welfare, since they have no result except the excitation
of the citizenry." The newspaper editor, he added, must be
the "best propagandist" for the government, "alert for whatever task of propaganda the hour may demand of his paper." [4]

So far has the belief in the control of the press gone in our
day that in an interesting map accompanying an article by
Walter Duranty, who claims to have had more experience
with censorship abroad than any other correspondent, the only
countries shown as still possessing a completely free press are
Norway, Sweden, Denmark, Holland, and Great Britain. Censorship varies from partial and covert, but actual, to complete.

If the millions comprising a great nation today are to submit willingly and universally to government by an individual
or group, not only must they sooner or later be played upon
by propaganda, and prevented from hearing any point of
view other than that of those governing them, but freedom of
speech must also be suppressed, which means not only the
actual loss of that freedom but also the dangers of spies, *agents
provocateurs*, and false accusations brought by personal enemies. Other methods of unifying sentiment come into play.
Mass emotion for the leader and his policy has to be stirred
by ever more and more violent methods. Education is altered
with this end in view. Books which do not fit in with the leader's ideas are banned. Free discussion and the search for truth,
regardless of where it may lead, cannot be allowed. Differences of all sorts, forming groups, whether of religious belief,
political belief or intellectual belief, begin to appear more and
more inimical to continued control by a government which is
imposed on a people and not created by them. These differences, with greater or less degree of ruthlessness, are then

[4] Quoted in *New York Herald Tribune*, March 22, 1935.

ironed out. When confidence or loyalty begin to wane, then
the last throw is a war against the foreigner, as in the case of
Italy's attack on Abyssinia. But we need not follow the classic
course of events in such cases further.

I am not so absurd as to say that we have reached beyond
the point of approach toward a totalitarian state today or
that Roosevelt is aiming at dictatorship. I do not believe the
latter. But I do say that the policies which he has been pursuing, both economically and constitutionally, lead in that
direction, and such an end seems to be desired by many of
those to whom he listens. Peoples do not usually willingly and
knowingly in advance organize the totalitarian state or a dictatorship for themselves. These come about when economic
and political conditions have become so disorganized or chaotic as to give an individual or a minority group their chance
to seize power, and when for many the accepting of what they
think is a temporary loss of what is presumed to be only a
portion of their personal liberties is preferable to the position
in which they find themselves at the time. Thus far we have
gone only part way on the road, made classic by example after
example, which leads toward loss of liberty, as it does toward
inflation, ruin, and economic chaos. Roosevelt, in his campaign speeches, predicted that precisely such courses as he
has pursued—unbalanced budgets, increased expenses, and so
on—would lead to bankruptcy and financial collapse. Should
his prediction come true, even though he himself would have
been the agent in producing his predicted results, the way
would then be open.

We may pull up in time. The nation may decide that too
much control, as contrasted with regulation, of business, means
of necessity, when carried beyond a certain point, the domi-
nance of a small central power over all. We may realize that
trying to abolish as far as possible the parts hitherto played
in our government by the Supreme Court and Congress, and

concentrating power in the hands of the Executive and heads of bureaus, leads in the same direction.

It may be that it is too late, that the change in the nature of our population and of their occupations, so different from what Jefferson counted upon, has made his belief in the people as the source of power no longer valid. It may be that the changes in our form of government, such as the direct election of President and Senators, the supineness of Congress, the development of pressure groups, may have made government by the people impossible. I do, however, believe that those personal liberties which Jefferson considered as fundamental in any genuinely civilized and humane life, are still fundamental and worth every effort to save. I do not mean that we should sit supinely by and insist that nothing be done in a new age to cope with the relations between government and industry. Almost precisely as our forefathers, in the governmental crisis of 1787, had to cope with the then inadequacy of our government for the problems with which it was confronted, so the generation of young men, and women, now coming on, is confronted with a new crisis, a crisis which will have to be resolved peaceably by intelligence and good will or violently in revolution. What I do mean is that in the process of that resolution we must be careful not to let slip all the advance made in personal liberties in the past five hundred years, carrying us back not merely to 1787, but to the depth of the Dark Ages.

It has been said often in the past year or two, sometimes by distinguished men, that we need a Hamilton in our crisis. I think this is false. If it means that we need him for the disorganized public finance, federal, state, and municipal, the answer is that there are plenty of men today who know what is wrong. Roosevelt himself knows it, or did before election. He pointed it all out in convincing speeches, and gave his word of honor he would remedy it if elected. He did not. Hamilton had no original ideas in finance, and followed the work of the English Pitt. The English today have made the greatest recovery of any nation because they have followed the time-honored methods of economy, balancing budgets, restoring confidence, reducing taxation—precisely what Roosevelt promised us he would do, and did not.

If it means that we need a Hamilton in government and politics, I would say that what we need is not his piling up of government debt and greater extension of government interest in banks and industry. As we have pointed out, it has been in considerable measure due to the original Hamiltonian policies of attaching special groups and classes to government by helping them to feed at the public troughs (tariff and others), of building up financial, commercial, and manufacturing business as fast as possible, of inviting immigrants of all sorts to help the rapid development of the country, that we have got into the moral, political, and economic mess we are in today.

Jefferson looked forward to a slow agricultural development of the nation whose lands, if kept for the descendants of the American stock of his day, he believed would afford homes and modest comfort for a thousand generations. It is not too much to say that the growing ruin now overtaking areas of imperial size in our country is due in no small measure to the theories and practices of the Hamiltonian school of thinkers and politicians. Alliance between government and business, which so easily became corrupt, the enormous increase in population largely due to fostered, as well as permitted, immigration, the belief that support of government must come from private fortunes largely dependent on government, the "get-rich-quick" complex which these and other factors developed, have been responsible for the wholesale destruction of our forests and the devastation of plains and prairies, for the plight of the farmer today, and perhaps of the nation in another two generations.

Again, if those who proclaim that we need another Hamil-

ton at present, mean that we need him to enforce his fundamental maxim that the people cannot govern themselves, cannot be trusted, and must be governed, then it is too late for
that. Every attempt to reduce the power of the people has
failed in America from the days of Winthrop and Cotton
down to the present. For better or worse, we live in the House
of Democracy. We may be forced out of it by a dictatorship,
unwittingly lured out of it by false promises of economic
Utopia, or abandon it in despair, but we will not give up our
tenancy simply to go back along the road again to Hamilton's
House of King, Lords, and Commons or anything like it. The
road, whether it lead to wilderness, prison, or a "more abundant life," lies ahead into the unknown and not backward to
the already tried and discarded.

What we need is not a Hamilton but a Jefferson, to per-
suade the masses, as Hamilton could never do, that the "more
abundant life," if thought of only in terms of economics and
state planning, will be ashes in our mouths if we cannot at the
same time retain those personal liberties of action, speech,
press, thought, and religion which alone make life worthy. Free,
for the most part, as the air we breathe because our ancestors
won these liberties, we may not appreciate how essential they
are to the happiness and dignity of human life until they are
forced from us as the air is when we are clutched by the throat
and strangled, as the spiritual and intellectual lives of the
European totalitarian states are being strangled today. These
liberties are our birthright, bequeathed from the struggles of
our forefathers, and if we sell them for a mess of pottage, we
should know what we are doing in advance. As General Smuts
well said, "even more than political principles and constitutions
are [now] at stake. [It is] the vision of freedom, of the libera-
tion of the human spirit from its primeval bondage." And
again, "Dictatorship can only be tolerated as a temporary

expedient, and can never be a permanent substitute for free self-government. Without it, peace, contentment, and happiness, even manhood itself, are not possible." [5]

We need not try to consider in detail what Jefferson would do if President today. It is as impossible as it is useless to attempt it. We do know, however, that he believed in a strict construction of the Constitution but for frequent changes to meet changing needs, provided the changes were made by orderly amendment and were carefully considered. He was for states' rights, but for union first. He was for placing power in the hands of the people and feared individual or group usurpation. He was for as little government as might fit the needs of the time, and for as much decentralization as possible. He feared unnecessary government expense, and the growth of a vast body of government officials. He was opposed to any alliance between government (with its powers and gifts) and business, with its greedy needs. He was for maintaining government credit by sound currency and balanced budgets. He was against repudiation of obligations. He was opposed to incurring debt, public or private, whenever possible not to do so. He was against the veterans' organization of his time and other groups which might bring pressure to bear on the government. He was for the farming interest as against building up the manufacturing. He was opposed to rapid immigration, and changing the nature of the American stock.

Some of these and other points of view which he held as an American of more than a century ago, which we have already discussed, he might or might not alter today. That is unimportant. What is important was his consistent and never-changing devotion to liberal ideals, to freedom of speech, thought, action, press, and religion. Any form of the modern totalitarian state would have been a prison house for him in

[5] J. C. Smuts, *Freedom,* London, 1934, pp. 34, 32.

which, no matter if he possessed millions or what is falsely held out as economic liberty and economic security, he would have felt his soul stifling and his nature degraded.

As Smuts says again, "In many if not most European countries the standard of human freedom has already fallen far below that of the nineteenth century. Perhaps I do not exaggerate when I say that of what we call liberty in its full human meaning—freedom of thought, speech, action, self-expression—there is today less in Europe than there has been during the last two thousand years." [6] The exiled professors, authors, musicians, others, and even racial groups from what only a generation ago were among the enlightened nations of the Old World bear ample testimony to the truth of this statement. Spending much time the past few years working in England, I have felt, as one European country after another has shut its citizens off from the free political and intellectual life of the modern world, and the dark shadow has crept nearer and nearer, much as a Roman of the falling Empire must have felt as he watched the drawing in around Rome itself of the barbarian hordes who knew not civilization.

As I type these words I read in the morning paper that Doctor Gurtner, the German Minister of Justice, has just announced that hereafter judges will not be bound by existing laws in order to inflict punishment for "crimes" but that they will be enabled to sentence persons for doing what in their judicial opinion is wrong from the "uniform national view." One's mind at once goes back to the comment by Hooker quoted from his letter to Winthrop in the first chapter of this book, that "in the matter which is referred to the judge the sentence should lie in his breast, or be left to his discretion, according to which he should go, I am afraid it is a course which wants both safety and warrant. I ever looked at it as a way which leads directly to tyranny, and so to confusion," and that "I

[6] *Ibid.,* p. 30.

should choose neither to live nor leave my posterity under such a government." Shall we, the posterity of his generation and the heirs of their struggles, be more willing than he to "live under such a government"?

In all our planning for national control, in such changes as we may make in our Constitution and government, in all we do, however necessary it may be to meet the changes of an altered world and age, let us not forget the liberalism and the devotion to fundamental human freedoms and liberty of Jefferson. Difficult as it may be to reach a more efficient, a smoother running or more ethical economic and social order by central control even by destroying liberty, it will be infinitely more difficult both to reach it and to preserve liberty. But that is the challenge, for without liberty the American people more than any other except the English, will find themselves fed and clothed, perhaps (and perhaps not), but spiritually in chains which will bite into their flesh and sear their souls.

Of all the great and widely extended nations of the world, America and the British Empire are the only ones which yet enjoy comparative complete freedom for the individual citizen as Jefferson understood it. If as a result of economic debacle or from other causes, we should go out into the wilderness of lost rights, then indeed, slightly to misquote Lincoln's words, "government of the people, by the people, for the people, shall perish from the earth." Our long line of American Liberals, from Williams and Hooker, down through the illustrious Jefferson to later ones of recent days, who have striven for a "more abundant" life spiritually for mankind on this continent shall all have so striven in vain.

FINIS

INDEX

42373

9/23/97

DATE DUE

JAN 26 '73	APR 2 4 '84		
E H	APR 2 5 1984		
JUL 5 '73	MAY 15 84		
E H	MAY 1 1 1984		
JAN 6 '75			
E M			
JUL 1 2 '77			
JUL 8 '77			
NOV 1 '77			
NOV 1 '77			
MAR 1 4 '78			
MAR 15 78			
OCT 2 0 '81			
OCT 2 0 1981			
NOV 10 '81			
NOV 4 1981			
FEB 1 '83			
JAN 2 5 1985			
GAYLORD			PRINTED IN U.S.A